Sustainable Development Goals Series

The **Sustainable Development Goals Series** is Springer Nature's inaugural cross-imprint book series that addresses and supports the United Nations' seventeen Sustainable Development Goals. The series fosters comprehensive research focused on these global targets and endeavours to address some of society's greatest grand challenges. The SDGs are inherently multidisciplinary, and they bring people working across different fields together and working towards a common goal. In this spirit, the Sustainable Development Goals series is the first at Springer Nature to publish books under both the Springer and Palgrave Macmillan imprints, bringing the strengths of our imprints together.

The Sustainable Development Goals Series is organized into eighteen subseries: one subseries based around each of the seventeen respective Sustainable Development Goals, and an eighteenth subseries, "Connecting the Goals", which serves as a home for volumes addressing multiple goals or studying the SDGs as a whole. Each subseries is guided by an expert Subseries Advisor with years or decades of experience studying and addressing core components of their respective Goal.

The SDG Series has a remit as broad as the SDGs themselves, and contributions are welcome from scientists, academics, policymakers, and researchers working in fields related to any of the seventeen goals. If you are interested in contributing a monograph or curated volume to the series, please contact the Publishers: Zachary Romano [Springer; zachary.romano@springer.com] and Rachael Ballard [Palgrave Macmillan; rachael.ballard@palgrave.com].

Shoko Yamada
Editor

Mitigating the "Skills Gaps"

A Realist-Constructivism Analysis of Work Competencies in the Global South

Springer

Editor
Shoko Yamada
Graduate School of International Development
Nagoya University
Nagoya, Japan

Graduate School of Asian and African Area Studies
Kyoto University
Kyoto, Japan

ISSN 2523-3084 ISSN 2523-3092 (electronic)
Sustainable Development Goals Series
ISBN 978-981-95-7967-9 ISBN 978-981-95-7968-6 (eBook)
https://doi.org/10.1007/978-981-95-7968-6

This work was supported by Tokai National Higher Education and Research System.

This Springer imprint is published by the registered company Springer Nature Singapore Pte Ltd.
The registered company address is: 152 Beach Road, #21-01/04 Gateway East, Singapore 189721, Singapore

Introduction

Skills and Knowledge in Today's World

What makes people competent at work? This question is becoming complicated with the emergence of new technologies and the hastened pace of global economic exchanges. Based on the observations of colleagues or our own experience, most of us would be able to say that theoretical knowledge about one's occupation is not enough to fulfill the tasks. Suppose you are a staff member of the accounting office of a company. Before applying your accounting expertise, you have to be able to read the necessary information from receipts, invoices, and other documents, classify them by the types of expenses and offices or persons who submitted them, and check if they are justifiable charges to the company. If you need to clarify something, you must find the appropriate people and talk to them. Also, in today's offices, the ability to handle computer-based programs (including typing skills) is a precondition. In this example, you would see that good performance in work requires us to combine different types of abilities, such as counting and classification (cognitive abilities), communication (noncognitive abilities), handling computer-based programs (technical abilities), and judging what to do, with whom to talk, and in what order (metacognitive abilities).

The coronavirus pandemic and artificial intelligence (AI hereafter) development have also affected workplace demands on abilities. During the pandemic, to avoid infection, we had to work together virtually, without physical contact and in-person communication. Various tools utilizing technologies were introduced rapidly, which changed our mode of communication and the ways we collaborate, divide tasks, and evaluate each other's performance. As the work process becomes less visible to co-workers and supervisors, remote work has made performance evaluation more output-based than before, which used to value contribution in the process more, intangible as it may have been. Such a tendency toward output-based evaluation persists even after the pandemic, affecting workers' behavior and priorities.

Generative AI is said to take over a large part of white-collar jobs. When ChatGPT, the groundbreaking generative AI program, first came out at the end of 2022, there was much talk of a technological singularity in 2045, when AI will surpass the level of the human brain. The pace at which AI will catch up with humans will accelerate rapidly because of the exponential curve of improvements in the accuracy of its machine learning. A long-lasting public myth that white-collar jobs, accessible only after years of general education, reward people with higher income and social status is fading. Meanwhile, skilled artisans, such as plumbers, carpenters, and electricians, are in short supply and in high demand, even at high prices. Some readers must have heard the media reporting the emergence of "blue-collar billionaires" in an astonished but ironic tone.

In an age when a large part of routine work that requires cognitive information processing can be done by AI and humans' work performance is evaluated by outcomes, what kind of abilities do we need to be productive and succeed at work? The social transformations discussed above pose fundamental challenges to conventional ways of thinking about skills and knowledge. In the last couple of decades, amid a changing environment, terms such as "employable skills," "core competencies," or "21st-century skills" have proliferated in policy and organizational discourse, calling for reconceptualizing socially functional human abilities. Yet, their meanings remain ambiguous. While education and training systems are expected to respond to changing labor market needs, they operate within institutional and curricular structures that evolve far more slowly than workplaces themselves. As a result, complaints about skills mismatches persist, even as investments in education and training expand.

Against this backdrop, understanding work-related competencies in their genuine sense requires more than compiling general, abstract lists of "desirable skills" or proposing reforms to school curricula while sitting at a desk. It requires a deeper reconsideration of how competencies are formed, recognized, and valued, and how they relate to the social, institutional, and economic environments in which work takes place.

Our Position

Recognizing the lack of analytical clarity despite the centrality of skills in development discourse, our series of surveys was conducted to provide accurate evidence on work-related competencies, categorizing them into various types of skills and examining their mutual relationships. The language of "skills gaps" has been ubiquitous worldwide, indicating a mismatch between the skills demanded by the labor market and those developed, particularly in school. This book focuses on countries in the Global South, where policymakers advocate increased investment in and reform of education and training, viewing them as the basis for economic takeoff. "Skills gaps" are also identified by employers as constraining productivity, and international development agencies frame them as a key obstacle to decent employment and inclusive growth. Yet when pressed to specify what exactly is lacking, where mismatches occur, and how they are produced, explanations often remain vague or inconsistent.

One reason for this impasse lies in the widespread reliance on proxies and abstractions. Formal educational credentials continue to serve as stand-ins for human abilities, despite broad acknowledgment that schooling captures only a narrow portion of what workers actually do at work. At the same time, newer frameworks emphasizing noncognitive or transversal skills frequently produce decontextualized lists that travel easily across reports but poorly reflect the realities of specific workplaces. Empirical research mirrors this divide: large-scale quantitative studies privilege comparability but strip away context, while qualitative case studies offer rich insight yet struggle to inform broader policy debates.

I have observed these tensions through field-based research and sustained dialogue with actors involved in skills formation and use—government officials, educators, employers, and workers—particularly in African industrial contexts. While the realities of the workplace require workers to have complex problem-solving abilities, the means to assess, evaluate, or discuss them are not established. Workers routinely demonstrate judgment, coordination, and adaptive behavior that remain invisible in conventional metrics of skills.

These experiences led to a central concern that motivates this book: how can we develop an approach to understanding work-related competencies that takes context seriously without abandoning the possibility of comparison, synthesis, and policy relevance? Rather than proposing yet another typology of skills or a prescriptive model of reform, this volume seeks to rethink the conceptual and methodological foundations on which discussions of competencies are built.

The core argument advanced in this book is that work-related competencies are socially constructed yet structurally conditioned. They are not fixed attributes that individuals acquire once through education and carry unchanged across contexts, nor are they reducible to formal qualifications, isolated skills, or personality traits. Instead, competencies emerge through ongoing interaction between individuals and their environments—workplaces, institutional arrangements, market conditions, and social norms—while being shaped by material and regulatory structures that constrain and enable action.

To capture this dual character, the book advances a theoretical framework termed Realist-Constructivism. This approach brings together constructivist insights, which emphasize the contextual, relational, and subjective formation of knowledge and skills, with critical realist attention to underlying mechanisms and structures that exert causal influence beyond individual perception. Realist-constructivism allows competencies to be examined as outcomes of situated practice while remaining analytically connected to broader sectoral, national, and global dynamics.

From this perspective, competence is best understood through performance in context: how individuals mobilize cognitive, technical, noncognitive, and metacognitive resources to respond to concrete demands. While what counts as competent performance varies across settings, this variation is patterned rather than arbitrary. It reflects the interaction of micro-level workplace relations, meso-level institutional and organizational arrangements and culture, and macro-level economic and structural forces. Understanding competencies therefore requires analytical tools capable of tracing connections across these layers without collapsing them into a single explanatory logic.

The book further argues that prevailing approaches to skills measurement are ill-equipped to address this challenge. Reliance on educational credentials or narrow cognitive tests obscures important dimensions of work-related ability, while purely contextual descriptions limit cumulative learning across cases. In response, this volume introduces a set of empirical instruments designed to assess diverse dimensions of competencies in a manner that is both context-sensitive and cross-sectionally comparable. These assessments are complemented by an intervention grounded in social learning and behavioral modeling, illustrating how theoretical insights into competency formation can inform practical efforts to address identified gaps.

Taken together, the book challenges linear models of education-to-work transition and calls for a reorientation of how skills development is analyzed and supported. By grounding analysis in the lived realities of work while remaining attentive to structural conditions, it offers an alternative pathway for understanding—and engaging with—human competencies in a rapidly changing world.

The Structure of this Book

This volume is composed of eight chapters. The first chapter will lay the theoretical foundations of Realist-Constructivism, followed by Chaps. 2 and 3, which explain how our theoretical model is operationalized through specific methodologies and strategies for adapting to the skills assessment of workers in the garment industries in Ethiopia, Ghana, South Africa, and Pakistan.

From Chap. 4 on, based on empirical evidence, we will demonstrate how realist-constructivism will enable us to understand micro realities, linked seamlessly to macro systems, using the detailed data gathered through our package of instruments.

Aside from its theoretical and methodological contributions, this volume provides insights for policymakers and practitioners seeking ideas to reform their human resources development policies and practices. While our analysis highlights the unique situations of competency development in respective workplaces, our methodology allows us to distinguish general and context-specific findings. Thus, some general patterns can also be found in other micro-ecologies of the Global South.

In the following, I will provide short summaries of the respective chapters.

Chapter 1 establishes the theoretical foundation of the volume. After clarifying key concepts related to skills and competencies, it reviews literature across multiple disciplines to show that, although knowledge and skills are embodied in individuals, their acquisition is fundamentally collective and their value socially constructed. Work-related abilities are thus shaped through the interaction of individual subjectivity, social relations, workplace cultures, and broader economic and structural conditions. To analyze this complexity, the chapter introduces Realist-Constructivism as the guiding framework. While constructivist approaches capture contextual diversity, they lack analytical synthesis; Realist-Constructivism, by contrast, enables abductive reasoning that links micro-level practices with macro-level structures. It provides a conceptual and methodological lens that can be applied to various social studies. In this volume, I demonstrate its potential by examining how competencies are formed, recognized, and valued, particularly in the context of skills gaps in the Global South.

In *Chap. 2*, I will detail the environment in which the competencies of workers are shaped. Based on the conceptual model provided in this chapter, factors that affect the ways the epistemology and ontology of reality are shaped will be explained as generative mechanisms. First, regarding the econo-productive mechanism, the chapter will provide an overview of the macroeconomic trade dynamics, international development aid, employment, and determinants of skills demand. Then it will shift the focus to the structural-regulatory mechanism, which includes policies and regulations related to labor, employment, and the education system—particularly TVET. Workers' competencies are shaped by the micro-ecologies of their workplaces, which are constantly influenced by these generative mechanisms. To analyze competencies through a Realist-Constructivist lens, it is essential to examine these mechanisms at multiple levels: micro, national, industrial, and global. In this chapter, as a foundation for further discussion based on empirical evidence, I will review the generative mechanisms affecting workforce competency development, focusing on the Global South and, specifically, the four countries involved in this study.

Chapter 3 will introduce the methodology we developed to evaluate and cultivate youths' work-related competencies, which operationalize the theoretical framework of Realist-Constructivism. First, the chapter will introduce the module designed to assess workers' competencies and to uncover the true nature of the "skills gaps" between stakeholders on both the demand and supply sides of the labor market. Drawing on the Realist-Constructivism framework, this module explores the epistemology and ontology of workers' competencies. It does so by combining questionnaires for employers, workers, and educators—gathering their perceptions on detailed skill sets—with tests designed to measure workers' actual abilities. This approach allows for a bottom-up analysis of the diverse realities within the micro-ecologies of these four countries while ensuring comparability across cases. Unlike many academic works that remain at the philosophical level, our team's approach makes the concept of abductive reasoning into a set of practical steps.

The chapter also explains a unique program we developed to train noncognitive abilities using board games. Regardless of the widely recognized importance, there has been a lack of effective methods for training workers in noncognitive abilities, which cannot be acquired by memorization but depend highly on behavioral applications. Based on the psychological theory of behavioral modeling, we created a training program that includes two board games, enabling participants to reflect on their behavior in simulated scenarios.

Chapter 4 demonstrates how context-relevant Realist-Constructivist analysis of varieties of skills can be conducted without compromising the generalizability of its findings. The comparison is made not only between countries but also at the level of firms to better grasp in detail the factors determining the relationship between competencies and wages. As an empirical study, it aims to present factors that are common and peculiar to specific national or micro-ecologies. The chapter tries to achieve this goal by closely examining the variables of socio-emotional skills and personality traits while also paying attention to those of school education, cognitive and practical skills, and the socio-economic backgrounds of workers. In addition to the micro-ecologies of the workplaces, the chapter will also discuss the learning ecologies of TVET institutions by comparing the perceptions of TVET teachers and students.

Chapter 5 provides an up-close examination of the country-level ecology of competency formation in the garment production industry in Ethiopia. In the other three case countries, we could not acquire as complex data as in this country to examine stakeholders' positionalities and perceptions in clear contrasts. Therefore, the multifaceted analyses of the nexus of actors and generative mechanisms showcased in this chapter will demonstrate, if fully operationalized as in Ethiopia, how Realist-Constructivism enables us to reach abductive reasoning to grasp the national ecology of workforce competency development.

While the authors have published papers on "skills gaps" based on comparisons between different sets of stakeholders in Ethiopia, we have not synthesized them into a coherent analysis of the national ecology. This chapter will combine the discussions and findings from the past works of the team to provide a comprehensive understanding of a national ecology.

Unlike other analytical chapters that highlight the nature of competencies in specific micro-ecologies, *Chap. 6*, using cross-national data from Pakistan and Ghana, untangles how generative mechanisms, particularly those concerning economic and sociocultural aspects, shape female workers' skill formation across different micro-ecologies. This chapter examines variations in skills and characteristics between formal and informal workers in the two countries. The results from the logistic regression models showed significant demographic and skill divergences between Ghanaian informal and formal workers in most domains, whereas these differences were not observed among Pakistani workers. The heterogeneity observed in Ghana is attributed to the intersection of greater market opportunities for microentrepreneurship in the garment sector and less restrictive gender norms in society, compared to those in Pakistan. Instead, the variation in skill formation among Pakistani female workers is rather associated with conditions within the micro-ecology.

Chapter 7 examines the effects of the training program developed based on our competency assessment findings. Socio-emotional noncognitive abilities—consistently shown in our surveys to influence workers' productivity—are the focus of this intervention. To train these abilities effectively, our team created a board-game-based program grounded in behavior modeling theory, enabling trainees to learn through observation, simulation, and engaging game activities.

The chapter analyzes the program's efficacy using data from 501 workers in Ethiopian garment-sector small and medium enterprises, applying a quasi-experimental design with pre- and post-intervention questionnaires. The training, centered on two board games and guided reflection, significantly improved participants' work-related noncognitive abilities, and the analysis further identifies factors associated with workers' levels of abilities. To address the potential interests of training practitioners and policymakers in adopting the technique, the chapter outlines the steps to develop game-based training (GBT) for noncognitive abilities.

Chapter 8 will conclude the volume by synthesizing the discussion made in earlier chapters. While it re-emphasizes the academic values of Realist-Constructivist competency assessment and training, in this chapter, the author will allocate more space for discussing policy implications and empirical meanings of the proposed type of study.

Today, we face an unprecedentedly interconnected and fast-changing world in which individuals must judge what they need to know to be effective at work. It requires constant upskilling and lifelong learning for all workers. At the same time, it causes significant challenges to the institutionalist approach to training and education based on pre-set curricula and systems.

The last chapter of this volume calls for reconsidering competency development based on the close analysis of the micro-ecologies of workplace and learning sites, while reconciling the analysis of broader generative mechanisms abductively. It also argues that academic theories and methods should be updated according to the changes in the realities on the ground.

Graduate School of International Development
Nagoya University, Nagoya, Japan

Graduate School of Asian and African Area Studies
Kyoto University, Kyoto, Japan
syamada@nagoya-u.jp

Shoko Yamada

Acknowledgments

I remember the morning I decided to return to graduate school to pursue not only a PhD, but also, hopefully, an academic career. I was staying at a hotel at the top of the hill in a small town in Guinea, West Africa. I was a young member of a consulting team working on the feasibility study for a large-scale school construction project funded by an international development agency. Day after day, we visited planned construction sites and held meetings with community members to hear about the current situation regarding education and community development, as well as their desire for having a school. People at various sites unanimously appealed to us for the need for schools. It was in the late 1990s, and the global aid community had agreed to accelerate school construction in societies where access to primary education hadn't been universalized. Back then, northern countries and their development agencies devoted a large amount of resources to programs that fulfilled basic human needs, including education, in the developing world through infrastructure building and technical cooperation. It was the golden age of international development cooperation, during which Western humanitarianism prevailed, to which policymakers and the masses, not only in aid-providing societies but also those receiving aid, bought in.

As a young consultant, I lacked the knowledge and experience to critically examine the complex system of development cooperation and its normative and financial underpinnings. However, after conducting a series of community gatherings in Guinea, a sense of discomfort emerged in my mind. "School is not a magic bullet to 'educate' and 'develop.' Haven't these people educated their children and youths when they didn't have access to schools? There should have been socially embedded ideas and methods of education and learning, even without an institutionalized format." As a practitioner, I didn't know how to find the answers to these questions that were stuck in my mind. Finally, that morning, still in bed, hearing the noises and voices of local people preparing breakfast and washing themselves, I decided to become a scholar.

Therefore, from the very beginning of my academic career, I have been a seeker of the meaning of knowledge and learning. I have always been skeptical about statements of school omnipotence. Today, given the massive influence of artificial intelligence and information technology, it must have become much easier to find people who share my sentiment in seeking means to overcome institutionalist assumptions about schools and education, and to consider human learning as a seamless, lifelong process. I am pleased to be able to publish this volume, after nearly a decade of data accumulation, in this historical period when the potential of human abilities is being reconsidered anew.

For years, I have conducted research related to vocational education and learning at work, encompassing national skills development policy analysis, questionnaire surveys with students and teachers in TVET institutions, as well as ethnographies of apprentices in informal auto-repair workshops. During those research projects, I had various opportunities to meet policymakers, government officials, staff from international development agencies, teachers, students, and their parents. Countless times, I heard complaints about "skills gaps" from different mouths. As a field researcher, I wanted to do more than just unilaterally gather information from local people to publish findings in academic circles. Thus, as a way to explore the possibility of my contribution to the societies about which I do research, I started the Skills and Knowledge for Youths—SKY—project to untangle the nature of perceived "skills gaps."

I would like to first acknowledge the significant contributions of the researchers involved in the SKY project as staff members. Dr. Christian S. Otchia, one of the co-authors of Chap. 5 and now an associate professor of the Graduate School of International Development, Nagoya University, was the first full-time researcher for the SKY project, who joined the team soon after being awarded his PhD. Dr. Yuki Shimazu, now an associate professor at Aichi Shukutoku University, was an assistant professor at the GSID-NU, where the SKY project is based, and was one of the founding members of the project. Dr. Kyoko Taniguchi was a scholar funded by the Japan Society for Promotion of Science, affiliated with the GSID-NU, when the SKY project was launched. These founding members devoted a significant amount of time to developing the prototypes of the assessment module and conducting field tests.

Dr. Natsuki Kondo worked on the SKY project for four years, energetically expanding the horizon of our operation to Ghana. I wish her success in her recent appointment as an Associate Professor at Meijyo University. Mr. Yujiro Yamazaki also worked on the project since his time as a PhD. student and later as a full-time staff member. Several PhD students were involved in the project as research assistants: Dr. Emmanuel Estrellado, now Designated Assistant Professor of the SKY project; Dr. Pimmada Charoensilp, now a Researcher at Chulalongkorn University, Thailand; Mr. Mark Camiling; Mr. Hun Seyhakunthy; and Mr. Tripathi Yashasvi Kumar. Particularly, Dr. Estrellado and Dr. Charoensilp co-authored several reports, policy briefs, and a journal article with me. They are also authors of Chaps. 6 and 7 in this volume. I should also mention the name of Mr. Takahiro Hayakawa, who joined the team in 2023 as the coordinator. Based on his extensive experience as a businessperson, he sensed the unspoken management needs of the team and filled the gaps here and there. Without him, I would have been overwhelmed by the managerial responsibilities for which I was not trained.

The SKY project expanded its activities from skills assessment to noncognitive skills training in 2021. The design and operationalization of board-game-based training would not have been possible without the fresh ideas and insights of young members who are passionate about games. Recently, we received invitations to demonstrate and implement our training programs in a few countries. I hope the SKY project's new chapter as the training provider will reward the young members with excitement and wider acknowledgment.

Our operation was also supported by competent in-country staff, without whom we could not have achieved what we intended. In Ethiopia, Mr. Fekadu Nigussie Deresse, now the Director of Labour Market Analytics, Ethiopia Investment Commission, has always been our pillar, both mentally and practically, as the node of networking and the tireless, enthusiastic, yet pragmatic executor for the team. He is one of the co-authors of Chap. 5.

In Ghana, Dr. Philip Kofi Aniah, now a senior lecturer at the University of Development Studies, supported Dr. Kondo closely and successfully led the data collection in the country. Unfortunately, due to the COVID-19 pandemic, the dissemination workshop we had planned to hold in Accra did not take place, but we hope to continue the partnership.

We would like to express our gratitude to the staff members of the License Division at Kumon Institute of Education Co., Ltd., a leading Japanese educational company, with whom we conducted a skills assessment and experiment to evaluate the impact of the Kumon method of mathematics education on working adults in garment factories in South Africa. It was a wonderful partnership with Mr. Kentaro Miyoshi, Ms. Mariko Suzuki, and Mr. Shunji Ise, and we hope our paths will cross again in the near future. In South Africa, our operation was strongly backed by the research assistant hired by Kumon, Ms. Nomvuyo Molefe.

Our operation in Pakistan was realized by the invitation of the staff members of the Japan International Cooperation Agency. We are grateful to Ms. Keiko Yokoi and Ms. Sara Watanabe of the Human Development Division for being in charge of making legal, financial, and administrative arrangements between two bureaucratic (slow and complicated) organizations—a national university, on the one hand, and a national development cooperation agency, on the other—and enabling the collaborative exercise to happen. We owe a great debt to Mr. Shinichiro Nakahara, then in-house technical advisor to the Punjab Technical Education & Vocational Training Authority, and Ms. Maria Gulraize Khan, a locally hired expert, for sharing their insights based on their expertise and experience. They also carefully followed up on communications with stakeholders and collected questionnaire responses and test results.

In addition to those directly involved in our research practices, we are indebted to numerous individuals and organizations that have expressed interest and provided us with support and opportunities. H.E. Lemma

Teshome, then State Minister for Technical and Vocational Education and Training in the Ministry of Education, always expressed interest in our findings. With his encouragement and auspices, we were able to co-organize the participatory workshop with the Ministry of Education and the Textile Industry Development Institute in August 2017. We are also grateful to the past presidents, managers, and staff of the Kaizen Excellence Center of Ethiopia, which was the counterpart to our Japan International Cooperation Agency-funded project to develop and field-test the game-based training. Their positive feedback and deep engagement in GBT propelled us forward, making us believe in the unique value of our approach.

The financial support we received from various organizations was the fuel that powered our engine. I was awarded multiple scientific research funding (KAKEN) from the Japan Society for Promotion of Science (JSPS): Grant-in-Aid for Scientific Research (B) for the period between 2015 and 2017; International Collaborative Research Acceleration Fund (B) for 2018–2022; Grant-in-Aid for Scientific Research (A) for 2021–2025; and International Collaborative Research Acceleration Fund (B) for 2024–2029. The United Nations University provided us with funding for three years, from 2017 to 2019. Japan International Cooperation Agency (JICA) concluded a grassroots cooperation contract with us for the period of 2021–2023. JICA also contracted with us to conduct a training needs assessment in Punjab, Pakistan, between 2023 and 2024. The collaboration with the Kumon Institute of Education Co., mentioned above, was enabled by funds provided by the Ministry of Education, Culture, Sports, Science and Technology (MEXT) of Japan, under the Edu-Port Japan program.

While I started the project with some core ideas and strategies, theorizing it and accumulating evidence took time. By receiving comments from academics, policymakers, and the general public, the ideas gradually took shape. In this sense, I would like to express my gratitude to the scholars with whom we published and who reviewed our manuscripts. In 2021, I co-edited a volume titled "Industrial Skills Development in the Developing World" in Japanese with Prof. Izumi Ohno, now Professor Emeritus of the National Graduate Institute for Policy Studies. Back then, the SKY project alone was not ready to organize a volume on its own. Collaboration with Prof. Ohno's team enabled us to consider the theme of human resources development from a broader perspective. In 2023, I co-edited with Prof. Simon McGrath at the University of Glasgow the special issue titled "Skills for Development Revisited" for the International Journal of Educational Development. This partnership enabled us to reach a wider audience and network with scholars, particularly those in Europe, with whom we had not previously worked.

Last, but not least, I would like to express my gratitude to my colleague in GSID-NU, Associate Professor Dr. Francis Peddie. While I devoted my best efforts to theorizing Realist-Constructivism, based on our empirical surveys and an extensive review of literature from diverse disciplines, I was unsure if my non-native English texts could convey the ideas in the way I intended. Frank kindly volunteered to read the first couple of theoretical chapters with academic and English native eyes and guaranteed that the messages were clear and convincing. Frank, your endorsement gave me the boost I needed to finish this challenging endeavor.

Now, this book is in the capable hands of Ms. Juno Kawakami, Acquisition Editor at Springer Japan. I trust her timely support based on the understanding of the authors' conditions. I am grateful for her accompaniment throughout this process.

Shoko Yamada
December 2025

Contents

About the Editor and Contributors

About the Editor

Shoko Yamada Graduate School of International Development, Nagoya University, Nagoya, Japan

Graduate School of Asian and African Area Studies, Kyoto University, Kyoto, Japan

As a professor of education and development, Professor Yamada has conducted extensive research on educational policymaking and implementation in the Global South, with a particular focus on Africa. One of her consistent research focuses is the formation and social and personal values of skills and knowledge among youths. Since the mid-2010s, she has been leading the Skills and Knowledge for Youths (SKY) research project, which assesses the skills of industrial workers using the evaluation tools developed uniquely by the project. She has also analyzed the discourse around global agendas, such as SDGs and MDGs, and how national governments and stakeholders in education and skills development adopt them. Her recent books include "Special Issue: Skills for Development Revisited" (edited with Simon McGrath, International Journal of Educational Development, Vol. 102, 2023), "Knowledge, School, and Social Structure in Africa" (edited with Akira Takada and Shose Kessi, Langaa Publishing, 2021), and "Post-Education-for-All and Sustainable Development Paradigm: Structural Changes with Diversifying Actors and Norms" (Emerald, 2016).

Contributors

Pimmada Charoensilp Center of Excellence on Migration and Development, Institute of Asian Studies, Chulalongkorn University, Bangkok, Thailand

Emmanuel Estrellado Graduate School of International Development, Nagoya University, Nagoya, Japan

Fekadu Nigussie Deresse Ethiopia Investment Commission, Addis Ababa, Ethiopia

Christian S. Otchia Graduate School of International Development, Nagoya University, Nagoya, Japan

Abbreviations

2PL	Two-Parameter Logistic
AfDB	African Development Bank
AGAM	Association of Ghana Apparel Manufacturers
AGOA	African Growth and Opportunity Act
AI	Artificial Intelligence
AIP	Anticipatory Interactive Planning
AME	Average Marginal Effects
ANC	African National Congress
ANOVA	Analysis of Variance
BA	Bachelor of Arts
BADEA	Arab Bank for Economic Development in Africa
BMT	Behavior Modeling Training
BRICS	Brazil, Russia, India, and China
BSc	Bachelor of Science
CAD	Computer-Aided Design
CBT	Competency-Based Training
CME	Coordinated Market Economies
COC	Certificate of Competency
COTVET	Council for TVET
COVID	Coronavirus Disease 2019
CTCP	Clothing and Textiles Competitiveness Programme
DID	Difference-in-Differences
DV	Dependent Variable
DVD/CD	Digital Versatile Disc/Compact Disc
EOS	Ethiopian Occupation Standards
ESDP VI	Education Sector Development Program IV
ETH	Ethiopia
ETW	Education Training Work
ETWC	Education-to-work continuum
FA	Faculty of Arts
FDI	Foreign Direct Investment
FP&M SETA	Fibre Processing and Manufacturing Sector Education and Training Authority
FSc	Faculty of Science
GBT	Game-Based Training
GDP	Gross Domestic Product
GHA	Ghana

GIZ	Deutsche Gesellschaft für Internationale Zusammenarbeit
GPT	Generative Pre-trained Transformer
GRM	Graded Response Model
GVC	Global Value Chain
H&M	H&M Hennes & Mauritz AB
HR	Human Resource
IFC	International Finance Cooperation
ILO	International Labour Organization
ILOSTAT	ILO Department of Statistics
IMF	International Monetary Fund
IRT	Item Response Theory
IsDB	Islamic Development Bank
ISSRA	Institute for Strategic Studies, Research, and Analysis
JHS	Junior High School
JICA	Japan International Cooperation Agency
LME	Liberal Market Economies
MA	Master of Arts
MANOVA	Multivariate Analyses of Variance
MAR	Missing at Random
MDG	Millennium Development Goals
MNC	Multinational Corporations
MSc	Master of Science
NAVTTC	National Vocational and Technical Training Commission
NDB	New Development Bank
NEET	Not in Education, Employment, or Training
NQF	National Qualifications Framework
NSS	National Skills Strategy
NVQF	National Vocational Qualification Framework
OECD	Organisation for Economic Cooperation and Development
OHS	Occupational Health and Safety
OJT	On-the-Job Training
OLS	Ordinary Least Squares
PAK	Pakistan
PCA	Principal Component Analysis
PhD	Doctor of Philosophy
PIAAC	Programme for the International Assessment of Adult Competencies
PISA	Programme for International Student Assessment
PKR	Pakistani Rupee
POMP	Percentage of Maximum Possible
PPP	Public–Private Partnerships
PVH	PVH Corp., formerly known as the Phillips-Van Heusen Corporation
SD	Standard Deviation
SDG	Sustainable Development Goals
SDT	Self-Determination Theory
SETA	Sector Education Training Authorities
SHS	Senior High School

SKY	Skills and Knowledge for Youths
SME	Small and Medium Enterprises
SMEDA	Small and Medium Enterprises Development Authority
STEP	Skill Towards Employment and Productivity
TCP	The Children's Place
TDAP	Trade Development Authority of Pakistan
TV	Television
TVET	Technical and Vocational Education and Training
UNDP	United Nations Development Programme
UNESCO	United Nations Educational, Scientific and Cultural Organization
UNICEF	United Nations Children's Fund
UNIWA	Union of Informal Workers Associations
UNP	United Nations Population
USAID	United States Agency for International Development
USD	United States Dollar
VET Africa	Vocational Education and Training for Africa
WRNA	Work-Related Noncognitive Abilities
WWII	World War II
ZAF	South Africa
ZPD	Zone of Proximal Development

A Theoretical Model for Work-Related Competencies

1

Shoko Yamada

Abstract

This chapter lays the theoretical foundation of the volume by addressing the contested role of schools in producing employable skills amid rapidly shifting demands. It begins by defining competencies and skills. Then, based on a review of literature from different disciplines, it highlights that while knowledge and skills are embodied in individuals, acquisition occurs through collective processes and their value is socially constructed. Abilities at work are thus shaped by the nexus of learners' subjectivity, social relations, workplace cultures, and the global economic and structural conditions. To analyze such complexity, the author proposes Realist-Constructivism as the guiding framework. Pure constructivism captures diverse cases but lacks synthesis, while Realist-Constructivism enables abductive reasoning that bridges macro-level deduction and micro-level interaction. Combining the benefits of inductive and deductive approaches, Realist-Constructivism investigates the sociocultural, structural-regulatory, and econo-productive mechanisms that influence how competencies are formed and valued. This chapter, therefore, establishes a conceptual and methodological lens for exploring skills gaps in the Global South within broader contexts of change.

Keywords

Taxonomies of human abilities · Psychology of learning · Schooling myth · Networked learning · Industrial skills development · Abductive reasoning

1.1 Conceptualizing the Competencies

Understanding what it means to be "competent" at work is far from straightforward. Across academic disciplines and policy arenas, terms such as skills, knowledge, abilities, capacities, and competencies are often used interchangeably, obscuring the fact that the very people who use them are unclear about what they mean. This conceptual ambiguity is not merely semantic; it has significant consequences for how learning is organized, how work performance is evaluated, and how interventions aimed at developing human abilities are designed and justified.

In much of the existing literature, competencies are treated either as individual attributes that can be accumulated through education and training, or

S. Yamada (✉)
Graduate School of International Development, Nagoya University, Nagoya, Japan

Graduate School of Asian and African Area Studies, Kyoto University, Kyoto, Japan
e-mail: syamada@nagoya-u.jp

S. Yamada (ed.), *Mitigating the "Skills Gaps"*, Sustainable Development Goals Series,
https://doi.org/10.1007/978-981-95-7968-6_1

as standardized bundles of skills whose value is assumed to be transferable across contexts. Such approaches tend to abstract competencies from the social, institutional, and economic environments in which they are formed and exercised. As a result, they struggle to explain why individuals with similar educational backgrounds perform differently at work, or why skills deemed valuable in one setting fail to translate into productivity in another.

This chapter begins by noting the increasing misfit of the institutionalist imagination of the school-to-work transition in today's dynamic world, which assumes that learning and working are two distinct domains of human action and that the former precedes the latter in our lives. As the premise transcending the volume, I will explain how work-related competencies cannot be understood in isolation from the contexts in which they are enacted. Competence is not simply a stock of knowledge or a set of technical proficiencies, but a relational and situational capacity to mobilize cognitive, technical, and noncognitive resources in response to concrete demands. What counts as competent performance is therefore shaped by workplace cultures, organizational norms, power relations, regulatory frameworks, and broader economic conditions, as well as by individuals' subjective interpretations of these environments.

To analyze such complexity, it is necessary to move beyond disciplinary silos and single-paradigm explanations. Education studies offer rich insights into learning processes but often underplay labor-market dynamics. Economics provides tools to examine the contribution of human abilities to labor market outcomes (such as salaries and promotions), but because of econometric demands for common quantitative indicators across large populations, it relies heavily on proxy indicators, such as years of schooling or major, that may not accurately reflect human abilities. Psychology illuminates the mental states and personality traits that underlie individual behavior and motivation. It is useful to understand the intrinsic determinants of individuals' learning and career development, but it does not help us much in understanding the extrinsic factors, such as social, cultural, and economic conditions surrounding that individual. Sociology foregrounds structure and power but may leave the agencies of individuals underspecified. This chapter seeks to integrate these perspectives by developing a conceptual framework that captures both the socially constructed nature of competencies and the real structural conditions that shape their formation and valuation.

The purpose of this chapter is therefore twofold. First, it clarifies key concepts and reviews competing approaches to understanding skills and competencies, highlighting their assumptions and limitations. Second, it introduces Realist-Constructivism as an analytical stance that allows competencies to be examined as emergent outcomes of interaction between individuals and their multi-layered social ecologies. By establishing this framework, the chapter provides the theoretical grounding for the empirical analyses and methodological strategies developed in the remainder of the volume.

Even though we carefully classified them, it is still difficult to use the terms related to human abilities in a distinctive manner. In this volume, we use the term 'ability' in the most general sense, with no intention of relating our statements to taxonomies. Also, as I will explain shortly, "competency" and "capability" are higher-order categories in the taxonomy of human abilities. Therefore, these are the likely words we use when the statement does not directly relate to specific cognitive, technical, or noncognitive capacities for an individual to perform tasks, which would be referred to as "skills" and "knowledge".

1.1.1 The Schooling Myth

We used to live with a rather simple idea that education happens in school and before employment. Of course, accumulating experience and acquiring new knowledge and skills after graduation are important for leading a meaningful adult life. Regardless, such post-school learnings were likely to be treated as extra to the formal schooling during childhood and adolescence rather than essential parts of human capacity development.

The trust in pre-employment schooling has been so prevalent that young people and their families try to prolong their schooling period to high school, undergraduate, or even post-graduate levels. Also, employers often use the level of educational certificates held by job seekers as the criteria for selection (Card, 2001). Moreover, with few exceptions, new employees' starting salaries are based on educational credentials. Such popular beliefs and practices align closely with national policies on human resources development, particularly in societies where formal education is not widely accessible, such as in the Global South. These governments nearly unanimously claim the necessity of longer years of education for cultivating a highly skilled workforce and justify their large public spending on education (e.g., Department of Higher Education and Training, 2020; Galán-Muros & Roser-Chinchilla, 2024; Government of United Arab Emirates, 2017). Further, the academic research tradition of estimating human beings' abilities as a form of capital to enhance industrial productivity frequently uses years of schooling as the proxy indicator of human abilities (Oxley et al., 2008). (More discussion on the measurement of human capital analysis will be made in Sect. 1.4 of this chapter.)

In sum, there has been a deep-rooted faith in schools as the mechanism to grant credentials of individual values in the labor market, both in ordinary people's lives and in policy-related and academic discourses. Such faith tends to lead to the uncritical assumption that the credentials represent human abilities accurately and comprehensively. However, today's dynamic realities of workplaces and the surrounding economic and social environment cause increasing complaints about the mismatch of knowledge taught in school to that needed in the real world. The school curriculum is designed to transmit subject-based knowledge according to the logic and sequence selected by subject experts. Since it teaches the same content to diverse students whose experiences and ways of applying learned knowledge to future work and life vary, the school curriculum is meant to be general. Therefore, criticism of the irrelevance of school education to specific industrial needs may not fit its purpose (United Nations Educational, 2012, pp. 81–85). Also, even if the government and policymakers attempt to reform the curriculum and education system, the pace of change in a formal structure cannot catch up with the fast-evolving needs of industries and societies (Asadullah, 2019, pp. 1–10).

Further, here lies a more fundamental question than administrative and operational ones regarding the reform of the education system to match the market demands for knowledge. It is the difference in ideas about the nature of knowledge and its formation between people in the education and economic sectors. When there are different orientations in understanding the concept of knowledge and learning, it often becomes difficult to grasp why there are always misunderstandings, despite the use of the same words such as "knowledge," "skills," "competencies," or "skills development." As I will discuss more with evidence from our surveys in Ethiopia in Chap. 5, teachers and administrators in the education system are driven by the shared belief that there are pre-set packages of knowledge that learners must master, whose rationality is justified by the experts in the authoritative position. According to them, however diverse the realities to which the learners have to apply the knowledge after leaving school, the value of learning basics is perennial. Meanwhile, people in the economic sector react more directly to market dynamism and look for individuals with specific abilities to complete the tasks in front of them and the programs to train such abilities quickly and in a focused manner. The former attitude can be said to be based on authoritarian epistemology (Feldman, 1995), while the latter has a high affinity with empiricist and constructivist epistemology (Alston, 1998; Olssen, 1995). I will return to this point later in the chapter.

1.1.2 Limitations of the "Education-to-Work Transition" Discourse

Promoters of the idea of an "Education-to-work continuum (ETWC)" consider that the fields of education (E), training (T), and work (W) are independent sectors that need to be connected well so that people move from education to training and to work—"the linear trajectory" smoothly (Faul et al., 2023; United Nations Children's Fund, 2019). The assumption is that the discontinuities or the malfunction of respective sectors will cause problems such as unemployment or mismatches between the specialization for which the learners were trained and the field in which they are employed. It is said that the underprivileged population—e.g., in terms of households' socio-economic background, gender, or ethnicity—will experience more disadvantages from the ETW disconnection than others. In order to mitigate such discontinuities, various measures are proposed and implemented, such as allocating more time for practical than theoretical education in school (Eichhorst et al., 2015; Zimmermann et al., 2013), increasing internships through closer school-industry partnerships (Pillay et al., 2013), strengthening career guidance at educational institutions (Asare et al., 2023); recognition of prior learning (Castle & Attwood, 2001), among others.

Such proposals to enhance ETWC are based on the hypothesis that an individual progresses on a straight and linear path from basic education to professional training and on to work—hopefully to decent work, and that each step takes place in a sphere exclusively dedicated to E, T, or W. Such a conceptual framework would work when the society is less fluid, and most of the activities and the organizations in which these activities happen are formal and registered. To put it differently, for the ETW continuum to be planned based on the labor-demand projection and managed accordingly, the public authority—the government—should handle all stages of E, T, and W. For that matter, learning must almost always happen in formal schools, and the government must have the latest statistics on the student population by age, gender, field of specialization, and the level of certificates to be granted after completing the designated course. Similarly, most of the employers of school graduates should be formal companies registered and pay taxes to the government. If a large part of people learn skills through informal apprenticeships and find jobs in unregistered workshops in the informal economic sector, the basis of the ETWC hypothesis will collapse. In addition, this model does not take into account the fact that work-education trajectories among the youths in the Global South are generally complex. People go back and forth between education and work while accumulating both work experience and formal education through the spiral process of career development (Otchia & Yamada, 2019; Yamada, 2021).

In the Global South and most societies worldwide, lifelong learning is becoming a well-accepted idea of how individuals should keep updating their knowledge and skills to meet the changing demand and climb the career ladder. Nowadays, the formation of knowledge and skills is increasingly a matter of individuals' subjective choice, in close relation to their plan and strategy for their life and career. Unlike the ETWC hypothesis, E and T do not always precede W, and people do not proceed with these stages linearly and straightforwardly.

This "discontinuity" among E, T, and W seems to be based on the institutionalist's naïve hope that human activities should be regulated under function-based institutions. Such a hypothesis does not apply to the field of education in the first place, as it is human nature to learn from experience and interactions with or without formal school. The misfit of this hypothesis grows further with the advancement of the knowledge economy. Today, the media often reports the urgent need for upskilling adult workers to keep up with the industries' skills demands, and various educational service providers advertise programs for adult learners on skills for improved performance in work, such as computer programming, foreign language, and management. Some of these programs are offered by traditional educational institutions like universities, which lead to degrees and diplomas. However, learners do not always choose such degree-bound long-term programs as the most desirable options, compared to short-term crash courses, which train people on specific techniques immediately applicable to the work.

If the absolute goal of this kind of discussion is to find the means to match the skills needed with interventions to equip workers with them, it would be more productive to free ourselves from the institutionalist framework of the ETW continuum. Meanwhile, the removal of the institutionalist mindset will bring to the forefront the challenge of benchmarking the level of individuals' abilities, taking into account the fluidity and context-specificity of the skills demand. Benchmarking a person's abilities against others requires a standardized measure that pins down their relative positions. For example, a company manager may want to know the strengths and weaknesses of their workers in contrast to those of other companies in the same industry. They may even want to compare their people to workers in other countries. However, given the changing demands for skills and knowledge, applying a standardized measure will likely sacrifice the adaptivity of the assessment and the relevance of findings to the context. Alternatively, a study that only pays attention to the local dynamics of demands and supplies of the workforce's abilities would end up being merely a detailed description of a specific situation. It is possible to duplicate such case studies with different populations in different workplaces, but these would be parallel cases without a common thread based on which one can contrast the characteristics of individuals and workplaces across the board. As I will explain in detail in Chap. 3, our team developed a unique approach to assessing workers' abilities in a standardized manner but cross-sectionally.

So far, I have only in passing discussed the different types of abilities humans have to handle to solve real-life problems. The example of the person working in the accounting office of a company I presented at the beginning shows that cognitive abilities (theoretical knowledge, literacy, numeracy, and other "brain work") are only the tip of the iceberg of human capacities. There is a large domain of noncognitive abilities, including interpersonal, socio-emotional skills, and various behaviors at work. Also, technical and practical skills are necessary to conduct tasks using tools and machines. Moreover, of course, individuals have to be able to think about how to combine those skills to solve problems in front of them, which is metacognitive ability. In the next section, let us review recent scholarly discussions about these abilities.

1.2 Human Skills and Abilities

Regardless of what they are called—21st-century skills, core competencies, or employable skills—scholars and policymakers have a broad consensus that a nonconventional framework is necessary to conceptualize individuals' abilities to keep up with unpredictable and fluid situations. Meanwhile, those promoters of the new types of abilities do not provide any concrete idea of what they are. According to the online Glossary of Education Reform, "*21st-century Skills*" refer to a broad set of knowledge, skills, work habits, and character traits that are believed—by educators, school reformers, college professors, employers, and others—to be critically important to success in today's world (Great Schools Partnership, 2016, see also Binkley et al., 2012; Le Deist & Winterton, 2005; OECD, 2005; Scott, 2015). In fact, this phrase does not specify anything except that the contents of 21st-century skills depend on what stakeholders *believe* to be important. Another buzzword of the age, *Core Competencies*, is a similarly context-bound idea of individuals' abilities, but from the private sector's perspective, aiming to enhance their comparative advantages in the competitive market (Prahalad & Hamel, 1990). A web search will provide various classifications and examples of "core competencies" as quick references for business operators. In their lists, you would find various capacities such as communicating well, taking on leadership, being accurate in work, being patient, etc. Still, they are just abstract categories whose substances in real workplaces are left to be defined by people on the ground. Now, let us turn to another popular term, *employable skills*. This term describes the types of abilities that employers would appreciate and that job seekers should know. The idea is that by having a clearer idea of the skills demanded in the labor market and developing or upgrading one's skills accordingly, an individual would have a better chance of employment or a salary rise (Brewer, 2013). Here again, the domains of abilities said to be desirable include not only technical skills and cognitive knowledge but also attitude, behavior, and personality.

After all, these fashionable terms converge on the same undefined field that today's workers need to have a set of knowledge, skills, attitudes, and personality traits to perform well in the constantly evolving world; but what it actually means cannot be discussed universally, as it depends on the perceptions of people in the context. The common objective of discussing these abilities is to find means to enable many people to acquire abilities to solve problems in their lives and work. Then, wherever individuals acquire such abilities, so far as the results are positive, it should not be a matter of debate. It relates to the disillusionment of school education, as discussed above. However much we try to improve programs in high schools and universities, it would be unrealistic to expect all stakeholders in education and labor markets—educators, employers, and workers—to have the same idea about meaningful education. In such a context, even though formal education would remain an important means of developing some fundamental (mostly cognitive) abilities as a general preparation for the members of the society, other means, such as an apprenticeship, on-the-job training, evening learning centers, or educational apps, are equally important paths to create people with problem-solving capacities in diverse industries and positions.

Later, I will discuss the implications of emerging theories about knowledge on methods and approaches for grasping and improving the workforce's abilities. Respective theories lead to different approaches to education and training, either deductive or inductive. They also influence the ideas and methods of measuring individuals' abilities at work. However, before touching on these issues, it would be useful to consider concepts related to the theme of this volume, namely, competency, capacity, ability, knowledge, and skill.

1.2.1 Taxonomies of Human Abilities

It is challenging to develop a coherent framework to address issues of human abilities, as there is considerable overlap in the related terminologies. People often use these terms as if they are interchangeable. In fact, in most cases, it isn't easy to classify people's observed abilities to any of them exclusively. In reality, specific *skills* to operate a machine would be inseparable from the *competency* to achieve the goal of producing the product.

As I summarized in Fig. 1.1, scholars place *competency* at the top of the hierarchy of human abilities, which is the broad concept of an individual's capacity that cuts across specific domains of knowledge or skills. Both competency and *capability* are bundles of particular *skills, knowledge*, and behavior of applying them to the tasks at hand. Taxonomies often treat behavior as a part of skills in the sense that skills are observed only when acted on by the person who holds them.

The difference between competency and capability is that the former is the concept that describes the ability to achieve the intended outcomes by applying knowledge and skills, while the latter is not bound by the outcomes. Put differently, competency is the overall ability to solve problems. Meanwhile, capability is the set of skills and knowledge required in the context. For example, if you are in the factory production line, you must know how to use the machine, read the specifications of clients' orders, or control the speed of sewing. Such a combination of skills and knowledge is a capability. At the same time, having this capability does not guarantee that you demonstrate the competency to produce products with optimal speed and minimum defects (Hase & Davis, 1999; Stephenson, 1994; Westerhuis, 2011). Skills and knowledge are acquired through education, training, or experience. They are building blocks of higher-order abilities and indispensable for competencies to flourish. Knowledge tends to refer to a collection of facts, information, and theories, while a skill tends to be explained as the ability to apply knowledge to conduct a task (Radovan, 2017). Again, pursuing accuracy in distinguishing knowledge and skill would not be productive, although we should not be indifferent to the ideas behind classifications. Knowledge and its application are along a seamless continuum of human abilities. In fact, as I will review soon, many sub-categories of skills, including cogni-

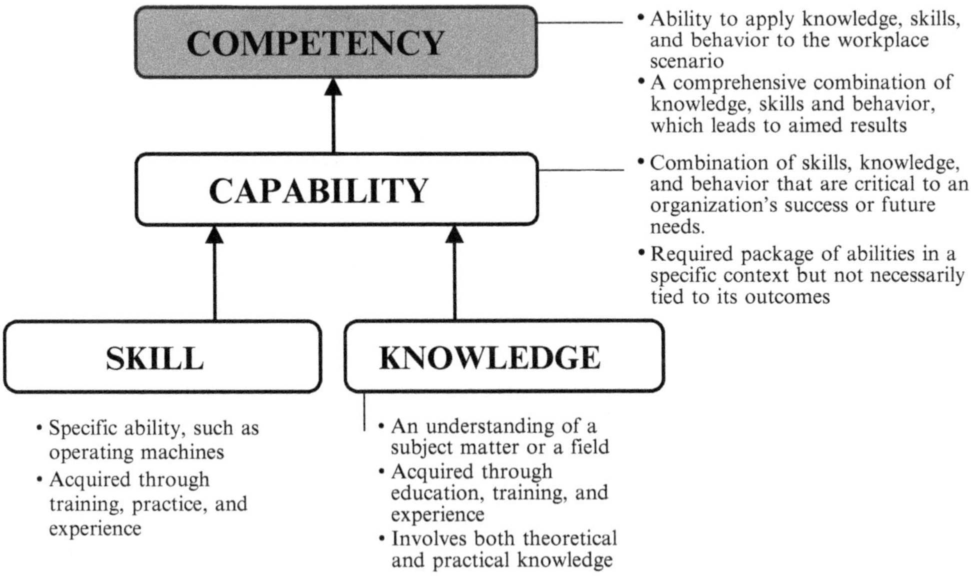

Fig. 1.1 Relationships among concepts on human abilities (developed by the author based on Hase & Davis, 1999; Stephenson, 1994; and Westerhuis, 2011)

tive ones, are proposed by different entities, greatly overlapping with knowledge of facts and theories.

In this volume, we use the term *ability* in a most general sense when there is no intention of relating our statements to the taxonomies.

1.2.2 Cognitive, Metacognitive, Noncognitive, and Technical Skills

Nowadays, there is a broad-based consensus among international development practitioners and policymakers that skills development is a key to economic advancement. Various reports and policy briefs of development agencies highlight the role of noncognitive skills in enhancing cognitive capacities and productivity at work (for example, UNESCO, 2013; World Bank, 2020; World Economic Forum, 2023).

Scholars also propose renewed approaches to understanding skills, particularly from the fields of psychology, economics, and education. For example, based on econometrics, Bowles et al. (2001) argue that cognitive skills explain only 20% of education's effects on labor market outcomes, such as employment and wage increase, and noncognitive skills are the significant explanator of the remaining 80% (see also Heckman et al., 2006). Psychology focuses on the personal quality that makes an individual perform certain tasks. Anderson and Krathwohl (2001) adapted the classic taxonomy of cognition by Bloom et al. (1956) to fit the demands for skills in the twenty-first century, which places significance on abilities to critically evaluate acquired knowledge and create new ideas, not merely processing and applying them. There are efforts to incorporate perspectives from multiple disciplines in explaining and assessing skills in the contemporary context (Green, 2011; Kautz et al., 2014). For example, some economic studies, including the World Bank's Skill Towards Employment and Productivity (STEP) survey, adopted a psychological scale called the "Big Five[1]" to measure noncognitive skills.

[1] The Big Five personality traits represent a taxonomy developed in the 1980s according to psychological theory, namely, extraversion, agreeableness, openness to experience, conscientiousness, and neuroticism. There are several established measures of the Big Five, which comprise questionnaire items to be responded to by individual participants.

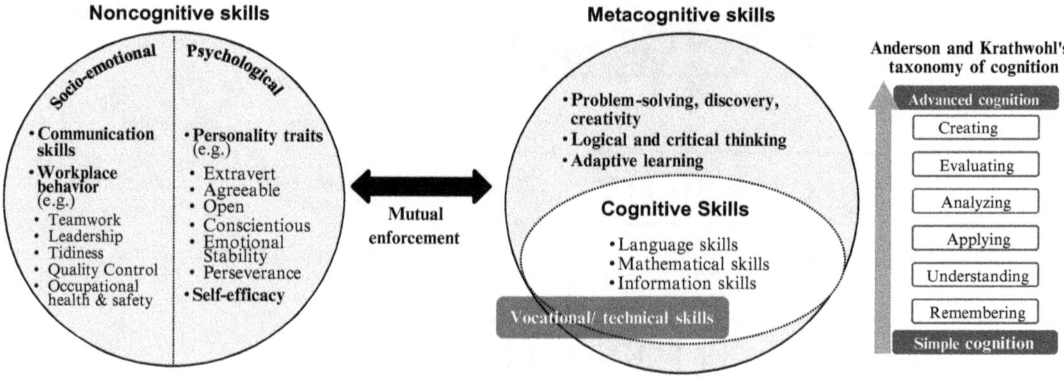

Fig. 1.2 Taxonomy of skills (developed by the author based on Anderson and Krathwohl (2001) and other literature cited in this section)

Similar to the cases with competencies and capabilities, scholars propose various typologies of skills. Even when they use common terms like cognitive or noncognitive, the meanings they attach to them are not exactly the same. For example, some scholars treat noncognitive and socio-emotional skills separately, while many consider them to overlap significantly. Economists tend to equate noncognitive skills with personality traits (Brunello & Schlotter, 2011; Lee & Ohtake, 2012), while educationists consider learners' sense of self-efficacy or grit to be the key noncognitive abilities that contribute to higher learning outcomes (Rosen et al., 2010; Tepper & Yourstone, 2018).

After reviewing literature from different scholarly and practical positions, in Fig. 1.2, I have summarized the working definitions of skills to be used in this volume. *Cognitive skills* involve the intellectual processes of collecting, remembering, understanding, and applying information. Knowledge derived from textbooks, manuals, or class lectures closely relates to this category of skills. At the same time, humans do not acquire knowledge exclusively from texts. They also learn through sensorimotor and experience. That's why *technical and vocational skills*, which are basically operative, have been grouped here.

Technical and vocational skills to operate machines and tools and complete tasks hands-on are crucial in understanding the abilities of industrial human resources. Although they may appear different, office-based operative skills, such as those to use a computer and information technology, are also a part of technical and vocational skills. Recently, the importance of the practical application of knowledge and skills has been highlighted, as knowing things without utility is considered unsatisfactory. Accordingly, as I will discuss in Chap. 2, in the field of technical and vocational education and training (TVET), nowadays, it is a popular measure taken by the Ministry of Education and TVET institutions around the world to prioritize practical learning over theoretical, by increasing lesson hours in the school workshops and internships at the private companies. Among such promoters of enhanced practicality of education, the operative aspect of technical and vocational skills is far more emphasized than that of cognitive knowledge. Given such orientation seen in the TVET-related policy discourse, I consider that it doesn't fit the reality of industrial skills development to treat technical and vocational skills as a sub-category of cognitive skills, putting aside any academic theories on the psychological process of human cognition. Therefore, in Fig. 1.2, I plot the technical and vocational skills that overlap with cognitive and metacognitive skills but are independent.

Metacognitive skills consist of thinking, making judgments, and applying knowledge to contexts by synthesizing different skills encompassing cognitive, technical, and noncognitive ones. Problem-solving, which is said to be the key element of core competencies in the twenty-first century, requires metacognition to apply cognitive skills to the context. I have adopted the taxonomy of cognition by Anderson and Krathwohl to indicate the gradation of the depth of cognition between cognitive and metacognitive skills. Varied aspects of human learning are arranged hierarchically, proceeding from the simplest functions to those that are more complex. At the bottom of the hierarchy lies the ability to "remember" learned facts and basic concepts, followed by "understanding" and "applying" them in new situations different from the original ones. Gradually, the brain process becomes complex and enters the domain of metacognition. In fact, the boundary between cognition and metacognition is not clear and depends on the context and the individual.

For effective problem-solving at work, metacognition should accompany accurate analysis of the environment and task requirements, which is inseparable from *noncognitive skills*. Noncognitive skills are defined as the individual's behavior, attitude, or patterns of thought that take shape through social interactions. As the concept of noncognitive skills describes each individual's tendency in thinking and acting, it has both social and psychological aspects (Borghans et al., 2008). On one hand, it represents the ability to grasp what the supervisor or the customer wants and to plan the work to meet such expectations. It would also involve a favorable relationship and collaboration with colleagues. On the other hand, there are no fixed ways to react to the environment and the surrounding people. For example, an extrovert's behavior in the workplace may differ significantly from that of a reserved, quiet co-worker. However, this fact does not negate the possibility that they will become excellent co-workers. The former aspect of noncognitive skills is considered *socio-emotional*, while the latter is the domain of *personality traits*.

Among policymakers and practitioners, we often experience that the terms *soft skills* or *interpersonal skills* are better understood and appreciated, with the meaning that roughly equates to socio-emotional aspects of noncognitive skills. This fact also makes us manipulate the terminology according to the audience, which sometimes causes the risk of blurring the conceptual boundaries of our research. It is understandable that policymakers of governments aspiring to achieve economic growth or people closely involved in daily productive activities of companies express great interest in socioemotional aspects of workforces' noncognitive skills because they consider such workplace attitudes to be directly related to productivity. Meanwhile, as explained above, economists and psychologists focus greatly on personality traits when they talk of noncognitive skills. It has been an inherent challenge of our research project, particularly when we try to present our ideas to different types of audiences, not to be drawn by their assumptions about familiar vocabulary, but to hold our core ideas consistent.

Our research is designed to grasp cognitive, noncognitive (both socio-emotional and personality sides), and technical/vocational skills separately and in mutual relationships. Since the participants are workers with less than 3 years of experience in the production line of garment factories, the cognitive tests are set at a difficulty level equivalent to Grade 7 in school. Regardless, our tests were not copies of those to evaluate the mastery of the school curricular contents. We developed test items to reflect workplace requirements of cognitive abilities and problem-solving. Therefore, our module allows us to assess literacy and numeracy demanded at work and the ability to combine information from multiple sources and make a rational judgment. Even though the vocabulary and techniques tested are not complicated, to a certain extent, the tests measure both the cognitive and metacognitive abilities of participants. Also, as stated above, we treat technical and vocational skills as a stand-alone category and conduct practical tests to measure such skills separately from written tests to assess theoretical knowledge about the vocation in which the participants work.

1.3 Social and Contextual Development of Skills and Knowledge

Nonaka and Takeuchi (1995) stated that the knowledge needed to do a job smoothly is developed through experience and judgments made in the situation, and disseminated through human relationships, regardless of the type of workplace, the tasks, or the rank of the concerned person. They referred to the knack, instinct, and know-how acquired through experience as *tacit knowledge*, in contrast to *explicit knowledge* that can be documented in notes and manuals. Tacit knowledge is difficult to express or extract, and thus, it is also difficult to transfer to others. At the same time, as Polanyi (1966) indicates, it is crucial to understand how tasks can be achieved successfully even when the paths to get there are not explained explicitly.

Imagine an auto mechanic in a small repair workshop in a developing country who does not have a computer to detect car parts causing a malfunction. What the customers bring to him is a broken car. Where does the problem lie? It may be in the engine, battery, ignition, cell motor, or anything. Instead of checking all parts of the car, a skilled mechanic would intuitively judge what to do and solve problems quickly. By asking why he chose that way, you may get some kind of explanation. However, the most important elements that led to the decisions are often not verbalized. Such is the tacit knowledge.

This example may give the impression that tacit knowledge is a matter in a society that has limited access to technologies or in traditional sectors where expertise is shaped only through observations of the seniors' work and years of experience. However, the model of knowledge creation proposed by Nonaka and Takeuchi is based on the analysis of global automobile companies. In fact, even in offices where information is extensively documented and transferred as such, a large part of problem-solving at work still depends on tacit knowledge.

The concept of tacit knowledge, which is embodied by a person, shaped and shared through interactions with others both inside and outside of the organization, has a lot of commonalities with that of noncognitive skills discussed today. Noncognitive skills are increasingly recognized for their contribution to success at work. In an unpredictable, fast-changing environment, individuals must respond to skill demands based on their judgment made through interaction with others and the environment. Of course, noncognitive skills alone would not constitute the complete package of effective skills. Basic cognitive and technical abilities would also be preconditions. Still, we can safely claim that today's formation of knowledge and skills is highly relational and contextual. Even when we know the goal (e.g., repairing a car), there are myriad paths to get there, albeit unknown.

1.3.1 Accumulative Versus Networked Learning

Until recently, most people would have agreed that knowledge must be acquired systematically. School lessons are structured in such a way that students gradually build knowledge from introductory to more advanced and abstract levels. When learning mathematics, students do not start with differential and integral calculus; they begin with arithmetic, algebra, and geometry before moving to more complicated content. Even when students don't understand the practical utility of the lessons, teachers advise diligence because of the assumed future needs of the knowledge. It is not only about abstract cognition and theoretical learning. The same applies to technical and vocational skills. Regardless of the cry for increasing the practical relevance of their education, TVET institutions still follow the conventional curriculum to accumulate knowledge from basic to advanced.

Such an approach to learning is in line with an epistemology—philosophy of knowledge—called *authoritarianism*. In the genealogy of epistemologies, cognition has been considered a mental process that consists of three elements: (1) a fact in front of an individual, (2) an individual who recognizes the fact and judges its presence to be true or false, and (3) reliable reasoning as the basis of such a conclusion. Authoritarian epistemology considers that the reasoning behind judging the trustworthiness of the facts comes from a transcendental authority, away from the subjectivity of the person (Ellis, 2015). The promoters of accumulative learning tend to look for justification of the value of their knowledge from curricular experts or the Ministry of Education because they are the authorities who package the contents to learn according to the logic of school subjects and academic disciplines. Depending on where to look for justification of the trustworthiness of knowledge, epistemologies branch out. In contrast to authoritarianism, rationalists generally look for scientific evidence as a criterion for the truth (Woolhouse, 1988). Meanwhile, empiricists maintain that rational reasoning will come from the experience a person has accumulated (Cottingham, 1988).

For example, in my country, Japan, there is a belief that "when the catfish makes a fuss, earthquakes happen." Since it is an earthquake-prone country, this belief is supported by repeated observations of catfish behavior in different places and historical moments, and came to be regarded as a somewhat relevant sign to predict the disaster. Also, there have been serious efforts to scientifically prove the causal relationship between catfish hyperactivity and earthquakes. After all, there is no concrete scientific evidence, although quake observation and research institutions still keep catfish. If you are a rationalist, you will shun this belief for not being scientific. Empiricists would consider it reliable because the belief is based on countless observations across generations. Authoritarians would see what the government or experts say and trust their judgment.

It is the human subject who judges the correctness of cognition and what constitutes knowledge. At the bottom of such judgment is reasoning. Depending on where a person looks for the source of reasoning, the meaning of knowledge and its trustworthiness differ. In a nutshell, variations and controversies among classic Western epistemologies stem from this point.

Earlier, I stated that the relevance of the *accumulative learning* of authority-selected knowledge was rarely questioned. In other words, there has been a broad-based consensus about the universal value of such authoritative knowledge. The judgment of its value is externally made, but not by the learner himself/herself. However, in today's dynamic society, it is becoming less certain if such objective reasonings are always applicable. At the same time, we face the challenge of where we should look for reasoning to support our epistemology.

Technology has made it easy for us to access information. We can get ideas and information from multiple sources and combine them to serve our own purposes. Unlike accumulative learning, online exploration makes it easy for us to access ideas from different disciplines on the same issue. For example, by typing the keyword "U.S. presidential election," you will immediately get recommendations of websites from the algorithm, which stretches from election procedure and portraits of the candidates to the potential impact of election results on stock prices and the economy. In this process, you will not experience any barriers between political science, economics, and sociology. You can construct your own package of knowledge driven by your curiosity, stimulated by the daily news and environment. I call it *networked learning*.

You may say that applying knowledge and skills in the workplace differs from a web search. However, there is one significant commonality across different modes of knowledge formation today. There is a growing demand for self-guided packaging of knowledge gained from different sources to respond to the need to solve problems in the face of evolving reality. While networked learning may appear more unrestrained and convenient, the metacognitive requirement is heavier for judging whether the constructed package of knowledge is justifiable.

The visual images of two approaches to knowledge acquisition—accumulative versus networked learning—are presented in Fig. 1.3. Their difference is that the former builds with blocks of knowledge based on an established structure until an answer can be found at the top of the structure, whereas the latter is a free exploration driven by the learner's curiosity and

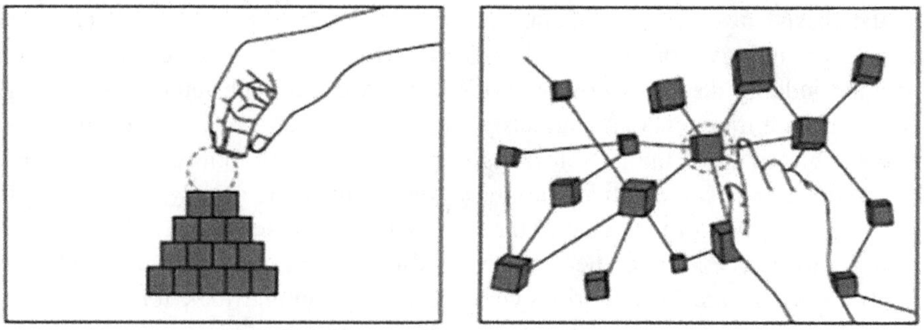

Fig. 1.3 Images of accumulative and networked learning (reproduced from Yamada, 2019, p. 9)

demand from the environment to which s/he applies knowledge. The advantage of accumulative learning is that the logical structure is provided by authorities and shared widely. This approach would be effective for mastering a specific subject systematically. At the same time, when that structure of knowledge is divorced from reality and loses relevance to the dynamic social situation or learners' interests, learned knowledge may become like a collection of specimens or encyclopedias on a shelf: nice to have but rarely used.

The latter approach, free exploration, is not constrained by any established knowledge structure. As long as pieces of information are collected and connected according to a consistent interest and logic, they can constitute a unique package of knowledge that may break through the traditional, familiar authoritarian epistemology. I would say that networked learning is based on *constructivism*. According to this epistemology, knowledge is not passively received but is actively built up by the cognizing subject.

According to this epistemology, the function of cognition is adaptive and serves the subject's organization of the experiential world, not the discovery of an objective ontological reality (Ernst von Glaserfeld, 1996).

Our research presented in this volume is motivated by the goal of grasping the knowledge of workers based on constructivism. The snapshot assessment of workers' skills makes us understand *what* they know but does not allow us to know *how* they learned. Therefore, it is not possible to retrospectively determine whether the learning was more accumulative or networked. Meanwhile, it is our strong conviction that the skills and knowledge demanded in the workplace are diverse and influenced by various factors such as characteristics of the industry, social norms, company size, management style, and so on. While intra-firm conditions and employers' attitudes directly affect workers' skills formation, external factors such as market trends and customer expectations are also significant determinants of skill demands. Workers sense such demands from multiple directions and respond to them by trying to fit well into the organizational culture and be rewarded for such efforts. In this sense, the developed skills/knowledge pack—composed of various cognitive, noncognitive, and metacognitive skills—is the product of interaction between the environment and the individual, which is precisely a constructivist process of formulating abilities.

1.3.2 Social Construction of Knowledge

Given the increasing importance of subjective reasoning and emerging modes of knowledge formation through networked learning, it would also be important to consider the collective process of learning. In general, classic Western epistemologies share the proposition that cognition is an individual mental process. Against that, many scholars have expressed their concerns about overlooking the possibility of collective knowledge constructions. They think such an individualized conception of learning conceals the true nature of knowledge. As the social psychologist Gergen claimed, excessive emphasis on the education of individuals makes the dependence of knowledge on relationships invisible (2009, pp. 259–303). Luhman expressed concern from a sociological perspective that, despite significant changes in the relationships among humans, education, and society, there have not been substantial reflections of those changes in pedagogy (2004, p. 12). Pentland, a philosopher of information, explained that collective learning happens as ideas flow among people. While the pace of exchanging ideas may differ depending on social contexts and dynamics, it is through such interactions that common knowledge takes shape (2014, p. 37). Understanding how scholars have theorized the cognitive and social implications of such intersubjective processes requires closer attention to collective learning.

Scholars point out that social learning often happens without explicit sharing. Levinson, an interactional sociolinguist, argued that to learn from and resonate with others, individuals anticipate and interpret others' perspectives, infer the intentions behind their actions, and adjust their own behavior in ways that correspond to those perceived intentions. He viewed intersubjective collaboration—possible even without language—as a fundamental aspect of human nature (1995, pp. 253–255). Therefore, the behaviors of individuals who share the same conditions tend to converge on similar points. Goody used the term anticipatory interactive planning (AIP) for the partly innate and partly socially developed human capacity to anticipate others' actions, calculate the short- and long-term costs and gains, and be attentive to signals about the consequences of one's own behavior (1995, p. 1). The higher the AIP capacity, the better the communicative capacities at the logical and cognitive levels too. Scholars who highlight the importance of behavior modeling and collective intelligence consider knowledge formation to be about resonance and sympathy based on shared values and an attitude of learning from others.

Some may consider it a form of socialization when novice members of a community, exposed to its traditions and habits, gradually become full-fledged participants who embody the transmitted traditions (Lave & Wenger, 1991). However, while there is a dimension of socialization in AIP, it is less about joining the existing community and more about constructing a common understanding by sensing the interests and behavior of others. As this process is based on interactions, the content of community traditions is not fixed but changes according to the dynamics among participants and the environment. While a broad cultural framework is conditioning the interaction, its contents are not permanently inscribed.

Through this review of scholarly works from various disciplines, including sociology, linguistics, psychology, anthropology, and philosophy, it becomes clear that there is a growing acceptance of the view of knowledge as collectively constructed through interactions. Of course, individuals embody knowledge. However, the process of building it is highly collective. The types of knowledge and abilities individuals develop are determined by their personalities, evaluation of their own potential, and reaction to the shared values and environment. Such a perspective about the social construction of knowledge echoes Nonaka and Takeuchi's description of *tacit knowledge*, which is embodied and shared among people working together without explicit verbalization. Notably, scholars who discuss the presence of collective intelligence unanimously call for attention to the nonlogical, sensory abilities of human beings to resonate with others. The very fact that scholars from different research interests and disciplinary backgrounds converge on a similar discussion about interactive learning indicates that today's dramatically changing realities require new approaches to analyzing knowledge formation.

1.4 Measuring Socially Embedded Human Abilities

Now, let me turn to the methodologies to grasp human abilities. Abilities are neither visible nor countable. Moreover, we are now talking about the organic totality of varieties of skills embodied by an individual. The visible outcome of exercising such abilities is whether the person can solve the problem. However, the "problem" in this case is not as straightforward as solving a mathematics problem in the classroom. Unlike in mathematics, where questions are presented with unquestionable clarity, in real life, identifying the problem itself is a significant part of the abilities. Also, a math question in school has only one correct answer, so you must find the right path to reach it. In the workplace, both the solutions and the paths are diverse, and the person has to strategize and select what s/he considers to be the best, based on the observation of the situation and their skills and knowledge.

In sum, assessing the abilities in today's workplace is like chasing after moving targets. Still, abandoning the effort to address this issue would lead to policies to close the skills gap without knowing the exact nature of the gap between what the industries expect workers to do and what the workers can actually do. It would also lead to the misuse of indicators that do not capture realities as proxies for human abilities.

"A means to measure working adults' abilities with reasonable accuracy and comprehensiveness has to be proposed. Further, data and the analysis from such measurement should serve as evidence for policymaking and business to make more relevant policies and plans for human resources development." This conviction took shape in my mind through repeated discussions with government officials, TVET teachers, staff of international development agencies, and local business owners in several developing countries, particularly in Africa. They frequently use the word "skills gap" to indicate the ineffective match between education and employment. Stakeholders blame each other for the lack of quality service and cooperation. However, when asked what they meant by the phrase "skills gap," their explanations tended to be ambiguous and lacked specificity. It is rather a natural consequence that the policies were not effective because there was no clear understanding or evidence of expected types of abilities, and policies are made based on impressions from their ad-hoc, unsystematic observations and institutionalist assumptions about the role and function of the education system.

In an earlier section of this chapter, I said that the institutionalist framework to segregate pre-employment education and the world of work, which assumes a linear transition from the former to the latter, does not match the contemporary situation. Regardless, it is difficult for both policymakers and academics to trespass the boundaries between the education and economic sectors because they are administered by different ministries and studied in different academic fields. This fact also leads to a lack of data linking people's education and training before employment with their required and actual abilities at work now. The Ministry of Education assesses students' learning outcomes from curriculum-based school education, which primarily focuses on the cognitive aspect. Once students graduate, the Ministry of Education or schools do not track their abilities based on their experience and continuous learning. Meanwhile, the Ministry of Labor does not specialize in measuring the workforce's abilities. To bridge these two worlds of education and work and to contribute to the improved accuracy of skills development plans, we need cross-sectional data, a methodology to yield such data, and a new multi-disciplinary theory. The search for a broad theoretical framework and methodology linked to it is one of the drives that makes me propose realist-constructivism in Sect. 1.6 of this chapter.

1.4.1 Human Capital Theory on Economic Outcomes

It would be useful to review *human capital theory* and its related analytical methods, as they examine the relationship between human abilities and the performance of individuals who possess these abilities in the labor market. This research tradition of estimating human beings' abilities as a form of capital to enhance industrial productivity has evolved since the 1960s (Becker, 1964; Schultz, 1961).

In economic terms, capital indicates assets and inputs used to produce goods and services. Before Schultz and Becker, neoclassical economists considered only physical capital and natural resources as inputs to the economic production process. Physical capital represents facilities, equipment, infrastructure, and other artificial materials needed to produce products and services. Factories, highways, or airports are typical examples of physical capital for economic development that respective companies and national governments invest in. Increased physical capital is expected to contribute to higher production and economic returns. That's why, even though the infrastructure building involves significant expenses, such costs are considered worthwhile investments for future return. Meanwhile, labor (workforce) was considered a cost because employers paid wages to them. What was groundbreaking in the proposal of the human capital theory then, which is nowadays taken for granted, is that the workforce's abilities are also an important form of capital for economic gains for individuals and society. Abilities in this context are defined as not only the skills and knowledge, but also health, nutrition, and other conditions for workers to be effective at work.

Justification of investment in workers' capacity development, which the human capital theory has provided, has been used by governments of countries around the world in allocating budgets, staff, and other resources to education. It also opened the way to estimate the impact of human abilities on economic growth quantitatively.

While myriad econometric approaches have been proposed, the basic idea shared among them is (1) to set the dependent variable to represent economic outcomes such as wages of individuals or GDP[2] of the country; (2) to include indicators to represent human abilities among other explanatory variables such as physical capital, resources, and workplace conditions; and (3) regress (1) against (2) and estimate the relative contribution of respective explanatory variables to increase economic outcomes.

While it is not the objective to provide methodological details of human capital research, what I would like to draw the attention of the readers to is that the econometric analysis requires quantitative indicators of human abilities. As I stated earlier, there is no conclusive data about human abilities, as they transcend the domains of different ministries and academic disciplines. Regardless, policymakers appreciate and trust quantitative evidence more than qualitative evidence. This inclination toward quantitative data is becoming more prevalent because of the increased popularity of data science and the promotion of evidence-based decision-making. Therefore, it is important to confirm if the indicators used in econometric modeling as the proxies of human abilities represent them properly. If not, we should consider how we can develop more relevant indicators.

Mincer's (1974) classic human capital analysis model treated years of schooling as a proxy for one's abilities brought about by education, whereas all other work-specific contributors to skills improvement were treated as unmeasured "experience." Critics point to some significant limitations of Mincer's model. First, earnings do not demonstrate linear augmentation by increased years of schooling (Woessmann, 2003). Second, critics suspect that the schooling years effect is likely to be caused by the diploma effect—that is, employers presume an applicant's level of proficiency based on the degree held, which causes selection bias (Allen & van der Velden, 2001; Card, 2001). Finally, many scholars argue that external factors such as location, overall quality of the education system, and labor mobility affect the relative importance of schooling years to explain earnings (Hanushek & Kimko, 2000). Nevertheless, school attendance has been used widely in the absence of indicators that represent human capital abilities more precisely (Oxley et al., 2008).

Another cause of such reliance on educational credential data is the shared orientation among analysts toward modeling the human capital contribution on labor market outcomes in a generalizable manner. In contrast, attention to individual skills would require a more micro approach that

[2]GDP (Gross domestic product) is the total monetary or market value of all the finished goods and services produced within a country's borders in a specific time period.

accounts for the diverse composition of skills according to the work context. Grasping the nuanced pictures of the situations where the skills are demanded and used often contradicts the demand for extracting generalized lessons that can be applied to other situations. The latter is based on the analytical paradigm called *positivism*, which deductively summarizes the diverse realities into some patterns according to the hypothesized combination of factors and variables. The former is *constructivism*, which attempts to construct the understanding of realities through interpreting the subjective perspectives of the people in the context. While positivism converges many cases to a limited number of models, in constructivism, the more cases studied, the more difficult it is to synthesize, as the details of the realities make researchers pay more attention to the differences than the similarities across cases. When there is a strong call for concise proposals to be straightforwardly adopted as policy measures, positivism tends to appeal to practitioners more than interpretivism, which provides details but is hesitant to summarize them based on objective judgment.

In sum, data on diverse skills are needed if policymakers and practitioners are serious about improving the relevance of their education and training programs in today's world. At the same time, if the detailed case studies end up being a bunch of inconclusive parallel cases, they would not be amenable to such research needs. Therefore, the search for the indicators of skills that are context-relevant and, at the same time, comparable cross-sectionally is needed. The quest is not only for specific skills indicators that are better suited for the twenty-first-century demands. It is also closely related to the need to bridge the two research paradigms—positivism and interpretivism—to bring the research closer to the demands of society.

1.4.2 Measuring Diverse Skills

We know that school-related indicators differ from measures of abilities, but finding the means to measure such abilities is challenging. In the long history of standardized measurement of learning achievement, most tests have focused exclusively on measuring the cognitive dimension of knowledge, such as reading written materials, grasping concepts, and memorizing. However, in recent years, there have been calls for measuring noncognitive and metacognitive abilities, which are also crucial (Bowles et al., 2001; Heckman & Rubinstein, 2001). Further, in the case of TVET, students should acquire functional work-related skills (Fastre et al., 2014).

The Programme for International Student Assessment (PISA), conducted by the Organisation for Economic Cooperation and Development (OECD), is the leading case of multi-country tests of problem-solving skills. It is targeted at assessing the abilities of 15-year-old students in the areas of science, mathematics, reading, and finance. It is unconventional in the sense that tests are designed to assess the application of learned knowledge rather than the recitation of memorized knowledge. Still, it does not serve our objective of understanding the abilities of working adults. Also, some observers have expressed concerns that Western assessment tools may not be valid in other countries due to cultural and contextual differences in assessment techniques and the overarching constructs. In response to such concerns, PISA for students in developing countries was designed and started in 2014 (PISA for Development: PISA-D). So far, eight countries have participated in the school-based implementation of PISA-D: Bhutan, Cambodia, Ecuador, Guatemala, Honduras, Paraguay, Senegal, and Zambia.

Regarding working adults, despite impediments, scholars have explored the means to examine the effects of workers' abilities on labor market outcomes. Most of them look at the results of cognitive tests conducted after employment, in addition to the level of certificates of school education (Allen et al., 2013; Desjardins & Rubenson, 2011; Green & McIntosh, 2007; Pellizzari & Fichen, 2017). Such academic efforts to assess the effects of skills were made possible partly because of the creation of large datasets that include numerous samples of adult workers. The

OECD's Programme for the International Assessment of Adult Competencies (PIAAC) is the largest among datasets of this kind. Since most large-scale international assessments are for students, the PIAAC's contribution to assessing the cognitive capacities of working adults—literacy and numeracy—is significant. Still, it focuses solely on the cognitive aspect of problem-solving and does not cover noncognitive and practical job-related skills.

Turning to the assessment of noncognitive skills, we find most of the existing studies are based on self-reported assessment, although recent studies have tried to use indicators that would suggest certain behavioral tendencies, such as criminal record, employment in a leadership position (Kuhn & Weinberger, 2005), or length of retention in one job (Kristof, 1996) to represent behavioral orientations of sample populations (Kyllonen, 2013). J. J. Heckman and Rubinstein (2001) compared wages and unemployment among youth with different secondary education certificates, assuming common behavioral traits among respective certificate holders. There have also been efforts to use records of psychologists' interviews based on common criteria to capture attitudinal patterns and relate them to a sample's labor market outcomes (Lindqvist & Vestman, 2011). A large part of the body of literature on the impact of noncognitive skills on labor market outcomes uses proxies of such skills but does not capture them in real work contexts.

Another trend in economic studies to measure the effect of noncognitive skills on labor market outcomes is to use the "Big Five" scale of personality traits adopted from social psychology (Cubel et al., 2016; Gensowski, 2018). The World Bank's STEP survey, conducted in 17 low- and middle-income countries between 2012 and 2017, adopted the Big Five scale to grasp the personality traits of working adults.

In sum, important efforts have been made to measure adults' cognitive abilities and personality traits or find proxies of socio-emotional skills. However, grasping adults' problem-solving abilities in their totality, as presented in Fig. 1.2 of this chapter, is yet to be achieved.

1.5 Psychology of Learning and Career Development

So far, I have reviewed academic discussions on the compositions and nature of human abilities and the importance of a person's interactions with other people and environments in developing their unique sets of abilities. I also pointed out the challenges of measuring such intangible abilities in a visible and comparable way while maintaining the connectedness to the context in which the person applies the abilities to perform the tasks.

Something as important as the social aspect of formulating abilities has yet to be discussed, which is psychology. Unlike in school, where the contents and procedures of learning are preset, adults' learning is driven by their evaluation of needs, aptitude, and motivations. In an effort to upgrade their abilities and succeed in their careers, people strategize the contents and mode of learning according to opportunities available, desirable, and feasible for them.

Also, as mentioned earlier, noncognitive skills are composed of socio-emotional and psychological (personality) aspects. Similar to other scholars, we also adopted the Big Five personality scale in our assessment to untangle how personality affects valued workplace behavior. Since we take the position that behaviors are adjusted in response to the culture and expectations in particular contexts, the influence of personality is also relative. Regardless, it would be worth visiting scholarly discussions about the relationship between personality and work.

Furthermore, when designing educational programs for working adults, it is essential to consider the psychology of the learners. As we extensively introduce in Chap. 7, based on assessments of various skills of workers multiple times with different populations, we developed a unique training program to improve noncognitive skills for people working on the factory floor of the garment industry. Each time we conducted the skills assessment and reported the findings, we received inquiries from companies, industry associations, and government offices about the support we would provide for mitigating the identified skills gaps. To respond to such calls, we explored the best way to contribute and decided that noncognitive skills training would be our unique contribution based on our academic background and expertise. The reasons for this decision are two-fold: one is that many existing entities, such as formal schools, industry-specific training bodies, and in-house training at companies, offer training in cognitive and hands-on technical skills. Instead of duplicating similar programs, it is more productive for us to link companies and workers with those entities so that the diagnosed skills needs are matched with suitable training. Another reason is that noncognitive skills training is the domain where our advantage as an academic team specialized in knowledge and learning can be exploited. We recognized the limitations of conventional lecture-based approaches to noncognitive skills training, which often require participants to memorize or discuss abstract concepts in a meeting room detached from their work environment. Therefore, we designed our unique training program using board games that simulate the real work situation as closely as possible. While we will explain the details of our training program in later chapters, in this section, I share its theoretical foundations, which are predominantly psychological, namely social learning and behavioral modeling.

1.5.1 Theories on Motivation and Career Choice

Regarding the factors influencing individuals' career decisions, sociologists and economists tend to highlight the antecedents that condition individuals' attainment of social status—that is, they try to find patterns in the relationships between career choices and social, economic, and educational factors (Croll, 2008; Hossler & Vesper, 1999; Pascarella et al., 1991).

In contrast to those that focus on extrinsic conditions for people's career options, there are theories that examine the relationship between subjective experience and career choice. Social learning theorists hold that an individual learns from interactions with the environment and other people and that the experiences and knowledge acquired in this way will become the basis for the individual's subjective career decisions (Bandura, 1986; Holland, 1997). While there are factors that individuals cannot control, such as the economic conditions or industrial structure of society, people shape some trust in themselves and their own capacities to produce designated levels of performance, which Bandura (1986) referred to as a sense of "self-efficacy." According to Super (1980), satisfaction in work and life depends on the degree to which people find positions in which their abilities, interests, values, personality traits, and self-esteem can be expressed. Also, when they feel the possibility of getting such fulfilling opportunities, people become more willing to learn new knowledge and develop their careers. Lent et al. proposed the social cognitive framework of career development, comprising three mutually related domains, whereby an individual initially forms and elaborates career-relevant interests; secondly, selects career options; and thirdly, pursues one of these options with perseverance and continued performance (1994, pp. 79–80).

Maslow (1954) also stated that there are five stages of human needs,[3] and that once the basic and instinctive needs for survival are met, people desire to be accepted and respected by society, and finally, they continually try to grow toward self-realization and actualization. Maslow's theory is often cited in the business administration literature, where it suggests that workers must be given incentives and recognition that will satisfy their needs for recognition and self-fulfillment. Earlier, I mentioned that an important element in developing problem-solving abilities in the workplace is workers recognizing their role in society through interaction between their subjective experience and the environment. Workers who understand their role begin to feel that they have the capacity to actualize the self-image they

[3] The hierarchy of needs starts with basic physiological needs and deepens according to the following order: safety, love and belonging, esteem, and self-actualization.

aspire to and believe that if they lack competence, it can be acquired through learning.

With significant exceptions (Aryeetey et al., 2013; Langevang & Gough, 2012; Osuji, 1976), there are few studies on career decision-making and workplace self-fulfillment of mid to low-skilled workers in developing countries, particularly in sub-Saharan Africa. Moreover, applying the models developed in Europe and North America without modification would be problematic. Given such a lack of academic attention, it is significant to shed light on the social and psychological determinants of career decisions and satisfaction among these populations.

1.5.2 Personality Traits and Job Performance

Many psychologists have studied personality traits and their contribution to job performance. They try to identify which personality traits are strong predictors of success at work. For example, Barrick et al. (2001) demonstrate that, among the Big Five personality traits, the combination of higher *conscientiousness* and lower *neuroticism* is found to be associated with higher job performance across most types of jobs. Meanwhile, there are studies that contrast the effects of personality on job performance by type of job or position at work (Kerr et al., 2017; Zhao & Seibert, 2006). As a background in which these studies flourished, we cannot forget the business demands to use such analysis as tools to manage organizations, train staff for different types of responsibilities, and select employees.

Still, the relationship between personality traits and performance is often not direct but mediated by habits, skills, and knowledge (Motowildo et al., 1997). Campbell et al. (1993) argue that job performance results from the combination of factual knowledge, procedural knowledge, and motivation. While there is a drive to present some general patterns in trait-performance relationships, some scholars point out the importance of contextual factors. Motowidlo et al. suggested the strong linkage of personality traits with performance requirements in the context, which appears as attitudes such as enthusiastic persistence, volunteering for extra work, or helping others (see also Barrick et al., 1998; Hough et al., 1998; Tett & Burnett, 2003).

To rephrase it in our terms in this volume, personality traits affect how cognitive and technical skills are used to perform a task. At the same time, such general patterns of personality-skills relationship cannot fully explain people's attitudes at work because such attitudes are shaped by their interactions with the situation. This latter part of the personality-skills relationship can be considered the equivalent of the socio-emotional dimension of noncognitive skills. The perspective I have demonstrated from multiple disciplinary angles that abilities are socially constructed is supported here again by the person-situation interactionism of job performance in applied psychology.

1.5.3 Applying Behavioral Modeling Training

Based on social constructionism, some specialists in education and training propose that noncognitive skills are better learned contextually in a specific manner, as it encourages trainees to make sense of abstract concepts in actual situations (Kechagias, 2011). Learning based on particular contexts allows learners to gain the ability of "how to perform" instead of knowing only the 'what.' For example, when deductive training delivers the concept of 'time management skills' to trainees, they merely conceptually learn that it helps individuals organize, prioritize, and plan things well. They do not know precisely how, when, or to whom to perform such good organizing behavior at the workplace.

Along with such consideration, Behavior Modeling Training (BMT) emphasizes that humans learn by observing others' behaviors. The BMT approach is grounded in Bandura's (1977) social learning theory. A well-known experiment by Bandura et al. (1961), the Bobo Doll experiment, found that after having a group of children watch a video of an adult assaulting an inflatable doll, the children performed the same assaulting actions on the doll when left to play with it without guidance. This experiment concludes that observing social models influences individuals' behavioral changes.

The social learning theory focuses not only on observational learning but also on the modeling process. Observed behaviors are not effectively learned unless the observation goes through the following steps of the modeling process: (1) Attention, (2) Retention, (3) Reproduction, and (4) Motivation (Bandura, 1977). These steps are coined as the BMT approach, in which trainees learn by observing a model or models' behavior, remembering them, performing the observed behavior, and motivating themselves to apply the behavior in real-life situations (see also Decker & Nathan, 1985).

The BMT approach enhances declarative knowledge (knowledge of "what") and procedural knowledge (knowledge of "how," sometimes referred to as skill reproduction). Therefore, the BMT is presently applied for psychological and interpersonal skill training interventions across various disciplines, such as leadership training (Waldman et al., 2013), parental skills training (Gelatt et al., 2010; Law et al., 2018; Webster-Stratton, 1982), and cross-cultural skills training (Harrison, 1992).

As I will explain in detail in Chap. 3, our non-cognitive skills training is based on this idea of behavioral modeling. It aims to capture changes at behavioral levels, which do not happen without fundamental internalization of the reasons and values of such behaviors. It is a logical extension of our commitment to social constructivism in grasping and describing the abilities in their totality without being divorced from the context in which knowledge is acquired and used.

1.6 Bridging Constructivism and Realism

1.6.1 The Ecology of Work and Learning

Until now, I have discussed that the questions about abilities at work lie on the nexus of people's subjectivity, their social relationships, the culture of workplaces and societies they belong to, and the global trend of the knowledge economy today. Values and contents of abilities are not universal but defined and developed at the intersection between the expectations from multiple ends and the psychology of the individuals who use their abilities at work. Therefore, problem-solving abilities are behaviors that appear as a result of a mental process, which is to select relevant knowledge and skills from the repository in one's mind and body, package them, and apply them to the situation requiring a solution. The focus of evaluating abilities is not on the contents of skills and knowledge but on their application. The paths to the solution must be multiple, but they are often not verbalized, but tacit and difficult to transfer. Because of this limited transferability of problem-solving abilities, we consider behavioral modeling as a breakthrough in training such abilities, shifting the attention from tangible sets of transferable skills and knowledge to shaping behavior by letting participants judge the reason and process of applying them.

I haven't touched on policies and systems of education and training of the industrial workforce much. Considering that the formation of work-related abilities occurs in the network of institutions and actors with different perspectives and roles, the government and TVET are important institutional actors. They set a system framework, regulate with policies and rules, decide the contents of the curriculum, and allocate financial, physical, and human resources for teaching to happen. I will discuss issues of policies and structure extensively in Chap. 2. One of the reasons for setting a separate chapter for them is to avoid the impression of this volume as a case study of policy application. "Skills Development" is a fashion in the policy world, particularly in the Global South. There are trends in system design, policy measures, and arrangements for skills development. As this volume is written with the hope of contributing not only to the theoretical and methodological discussion among scholars but also to practitioners, it is indispensable to touch on them. At the same time, policies and systems are not the main background; they are among many factors that determine the nature of the discourse and practices among the actors involved. Also, in this volume, I try to avoid the vocabulary of "skills development" as much as possible, because it would give a strong flavor of policy studies to this volume. We desire our discussion not to be contained by the pre-set framework of policy-oriented discourse and by the imagination that people attach to this vocabulary. Also, according to the taxonomies presented earlier in this chapter, *skill* is a subclass that constitutes higher-order abilities such as *competency* and *capability*. Therefore, mixing the words at the different levels of the conceptual hierarchy would blur the focus of our discussion. Thus, much research related to the TVET system and skills development policies will be reviewed in Chap. 2, but not here.

Similar to us, some scholars criticize the institutionalist approach to the formation of work-related competencies and promote holistic analysis of the ecosystem (Aldinucci et al., 2023; Maurer et al., 2023; McGrath, 2023; Powell & McGrath, 2019; Ramsarup et al., 2022). Such an effort to grasp the particularity of the context leads scholars to shift attention from the national level to the regional level. There are many studies of this kind from South Africa, which is among the countries that adopted the now-popular "competency-based training" model from Australia and Germany as early as the 1990s (Allais & Wedekind, 2020; Wedekind et al., 2021). Also, some studies focus on specific social groups. For example, Standing (2002) highlights the gendered nature of work and learning, while others suggest that the mutual enforcement of poverty and gender enhances inequality in developing work-related competencies (DeJaeghere, 2017; Wignall et al., 2023; Yamada et al., 2024). Dagar (2023) shed light on the skills-related experience of refugees in India, while Lynch et al. (2023) explored the cases of disabled youth in Bhutan.

Many studies have been conducted on competency development for specific industries, including ourselves (Kraak, 2009; McGrath, 2015; Wedekind & Mutereko, 2016; Yamada et al., 2018; Yamada & Otchia, 2022). Because of the difficulties of systematic data collection, there have been fewer studies on competency development in the informal economic sector than in the formal sector. However, there have been works describing the unique characteristics of competency development through traditional apprenticeship and work in the informal sector (de Neve, 2005; Sonnenberg, 2012; Yamada, 2021).

As these studies suggest, the more contextualized the analysis of competency formation becomes, the more diverse the pictures become. Therefore, while it is important to accumulate more cases for deeper understanding, it is also important to develop methods to approach these diverse situations in a comparable manner without losing sight of contextual dynamism. What is needed here is to establish a standard tool to be applied to understand diverse cases without imposing pre-set models. This is the philosophy behind the modules and programs we developed and implemented, including both the competency assessment and noncognitive skills training.

1.6.2 Realist-Constructivism in Understanding Work-Related Competencies

So far, I have explained that abilities are developed constructively. Constructivism here indicates that learning occurs at the interface between the social demand for knowledge and the learner's internal motivation. It is a social construction in the sense that knowledge is meaningful only when it is put to use; but in order for it to be used, that knowledge must be understood, appreciated, and demanded by society. At the same time, it is a matter of individual decisions about where to extend curiosity and pick up materials to learn. Therefore, as Dewey (1897) has stated, learning is both *sociological and psychological*. According to constructivism, there is no pre-set universally valued knowledge, but the judgment about rationality and relevance of the knowledge is *constructed* through social interaction. Another aspect of constructivism is that respective learners *construct* their unique packages of knowledge despite being conditioned by society's norms, values, and necessities.

Here, I must introduce Realism as a philosophical position that, unlike constructivist approaches, holds that reality exists independently of human perception, interpretation, or social agreement. From a realist standpoint, social phenomena such as institutions, labor markets, or skill demands are not merely products of discourse among subjective actors, but have real existence and causal effects, even without psychological involvement or cognitions of actors. In the social sciences, this position has often been associated with the positivist research paradigm, which assumes that social reality can be observed, measured, and explained through regularities analogous to those in the natural sciences (Hempel, 1970; Popper, 2002). While constructivism is particularly effective in revealing how skills, competencies, and knowledge are interpreted and valued differently across settings, without an ontological anchor, it risks relativism and lacks explanatory leverage beyond localized descriptions. Realist approaches respond to this concern by reasserting the existence of underlying structures and causal relations.

Here, I am using the words constructivism and realism without being strictly bound by any discipline. What I call constructivism here may be understood as empiricism in epistemology (Alston, 1998; Olssen, 1995), interpretivism in research paradigms (Schwandt, 1998), phenomenology in philosophical methodology (Husserl, 1973), and social constructivism in psychology (Vygotsky, 1978) or the sociology of knowledge (Detel, 2001). Likewise, realism is not a unitary concept: across philosophy and the social sciences it encompasses diverse positions, including naïve realism, scientific realism, and social realism, all of which share the ontological claim that a reality exists independently of human perception or belief, while differing in their assumptions about observability, causality, and the status of scientific knowledge (Bunge, 1998; Putnam, 1981). While a full engagement with these diverse traditions would require more extensive philosophical elaboration, such an undertaking lies beyond the scope of this volume. Instead, to be sincere to the objective of representing the realities derived from detailed empirical analyses based on fieldwork, I am going to use Realist-Constructivism, a theoretical framework that bridges "constructivism" and "realism", the common denominators of contrasting positionalities across these different academic disciplines.

While the term realist constructivism has been used in international relations theory, most notably by Barkin (2010), to reconcile realist attention to power with constructivist analyses of norms and identity at the level of states, the usage in this volume differs in both scope and purpose. Rather than addressing interstate behavior, this study employs realist-constructivism to bridge epistemological and ontological concerns in the analysis of individuals' experiences and the competencies developed from them. It does so by combining constructivist insights into learning, meaning, and subjectivity with a realist commitment to the existence of social, institutional, and economic mechanisms that shape the formation and valuation of human capabilities across contexts.

The small circles named "micro-ecology" in the conceptual model of Fig. 1.4 represent the above idea of constructivism. Individual workers develop their competencies influenced by the expectations and attitudes of superiors and colleagues, as well as customers or other people external to but related to the workplace. Since this volume is about competency formation, in the later chapters, trainers and educators, both in-house and from formal institutions such as TVET, are touched on as a part of the micro-ecology of competency development.

Earlier, I stated that gathering many cases in parallel will lead to relativism without synthesis. In Fig. 1.4, multiple "micro-ecologies" are mapped, which are composed of interpersonal relationships with socio-physical spaces where individuals develop and apply their competencies. Each micro-ecology has its own unique culture, values, and business needs. Therefore, describing the characteristics of workers' competencies in each micro-ecology is meaningful for an in-depth understanding of the process and context of competency formation. At the same

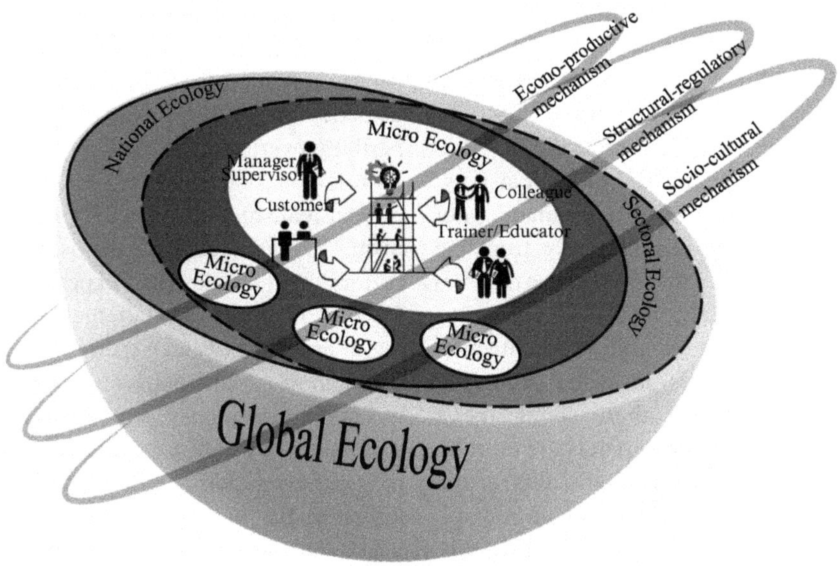

Fig. 1.4 Conceptual model of the realist-constructivism of competency

time, that doesn't give us a broader picture of the factors contributing to competency formation beyond the specificities in the micro-ecology. Some of the determinants of competencies can be found commonly across micro-ecologies. However, if the researcher does not have any comparative lenses, it would be difficult to distinguish commonalities from specificities. Also, one micro-ecology may demonstrate commonalities with other micro-ecologies in multiple different ways. As I indicate in Fig. 1.4, micro-ecologies may share their industrial characteristics with others in the same industry across national borders ("sectoral ecology"). Meanwhile, those operating in the same country may share the same national characteristics regardless of industry differences ("national ecology"). Still, all these micro-ecologies are part of the global society and are influenced by the spread of the knowledge economy and recent discourse about new competencies, albeit to different degrees ("global ecology"). As such, the micro-ecologies and individual workers who develop and apply competencies are under multi-layered, multi-faceted ecologies.

To grasp the nature of individual competencies, extreme constructivism without abductive reasoning is unsatisfactory. Close constructivist observation of micro-ecology should incorporate factors that transcend specific geographic locations and industries. By doing so, it will make a unique contribution not only as an academic inquiry about human learning and abilities but also as an empirical investigation to provide evidence-based suggestions for policies and practices. At the same time, it is not an option to rely on the top-down approach of positivism or the assumption of institutionalism that learning happens in regulated institutions along standardized procedures.

There has been academic discussion that the abductive inference to synthesize interpretive and positivist perspectives is necessary (Lombrozo, 2012; Ramsarup et al., 2022; Walton, 2004). At the philosophical level, the existence of abductive reasoning as a human cognitive process and its importance have been pointed out for a long time. However, it has been difficult to establish a methodology to conduct it consciously as a part of the research procedure to get a detailed picture of ontological realities while bridging two scientific paradigms.

Bhaskar (1975) proposed Critical Realism, a philosophical position that opposes positivism, which pursues a narrowly scientific universal set of rules on social realities while, at the same time, avoiding falling back to epistemological relativism alone (see also, Archer, 1995). He argues that the real exists independent of how we perceive it. It means that the ontological presence does not disappear even if a person does not recognize it or perceive it differently from the real. Since cognition is a mental process that differs by person and social group, there are multiple ways to judge what the real is. Meanwhile, ontological existence does not differ according to perceptions. Therefore, there should be a rational judgment to decide which is the morally and epistemically rational understanding of the real. The trinity of ontological realism, epistemological relativism, and judgmental rationality characterizes Bhaskar's critical realism (Bhaskar, 1998; Bhaskar et al., 2018), and judgmental rationalism cannot be reached without abductive inference.

In the sense that he proposes to bridge between positivism and interpretivism, or between extremely objective ontology and subjective epistemology, his fundamental concern is similar to that of other philosophers who argued for abductive inference. Also, as was the case with other philosophical proposals, although it attracted many scholars from different academic fields at the theoretical level, Bhasker's critical realism has not been applied much as a methodology for research practices (for example, Dobson, 2001; Khazem, 2018). Regardless, it is a significant contribution of critical realism, which has not been found in other philosophical works, that it presents practical criteria and guidelines for adopting it in empirical research.

Bhaskar et al. (2018, p. 35) propose what they call the "laminations of scale," which spread concentrically from the sub-individual to the macro level in order to structurally understand the influence exerted by social actors and systems on the phenomena the researchers are interested in investigating. In Fig. 1.4, I adopted this idea of layered influences by conceptualizing "national ecology," "industrial ecology," and "global ecology" as the outer circles surrounding the micro-ecologies that directly involve individuals developing competencies. At the same time, unlike Baskar et al., who set these levels as concentric and incrementally extended outwardly, I consider that national and industrial ecologies partially overlap.

Another conceptual tool I have adopted from critical realism is the idea of "generative mechanism." The generative mechanism is the nexus of factors that make us experience the real. Observable events are only the tip of the iceberg, but a large part of our experiences are driven by invisible values and behaviors, both at the collective and individual levels, conditioned by culture, social dynamics, the psychology of involved people, and even their hereditary biological characteristics. By untangling these largely hidden generative mechanisms, we can better understand the causes and backgrounds of phenomena. While Bhaskar et al. (1998, p. 109) propose three mutually enforcing mechanisms, namely, socio-cultural, psychological, and biological, I have modified and included socio-cultural, structural-regulatory, and econo-productive mechanisms in Fig. 1.4. The socio-cultural mechanism involves socio-cultural values and categories such as gender, age, class, cultural norms, habitation, and family, among others. The structural-regulatory mechanism is composed of policies and regulations related to labor, employment, and competency development. The education system, particularly TVET, would be part of this mechanism. The econo-productive mechanism relates to commercial practices, the business environment, and the labor market. It would include market conditions or measures for business promotion.

In this volume, when we present the analyses of the outcomes of competency assessments and training, these three generative mechanisms will be examined for each micro, national, industrial, and global ecology, so that clear pictures of the ontological reality backed by the diverse epistemologies of stakeholders will be presented coherently based on rational judgment.

Working adults' competencies can only be grasped by the realism approach because they are meaningful in the context in which they are used. For this reason, it is necessary to understand the industrial structure, the workplace situation, and the policy background.

As shown in this chapter, how people perceive competencies, find their potential in them, and try to improve them are determined by their relationships with the environment. It is the constructivist approach to understanding competencies at the intersection between psychology and sociology. Meanwhile, mere constructivism is not enough to understand the micro-ecology of competency formation in its totality, which is embedded in the nexus of generative mechanisms that tacitly but significantly affect the judgment of individuals. Investigation of the socio-cultural, structural-regulatory, and econo-productive mechanisms at micro to global levels will help our abductive inference of the working adults' competencies in the four countries we surveyed, three in Africa and one in South Asia. We call it the *Realist-Constructivism theory* on competencies.

As mentioned earlier, there are not many cases where the theoretical framework of abduction is translated to the level of methodology and used in fieldwork. In the following chapters, this volume will try to demonstrate how a module of competency assessment can grasp the diverse composition of skills and knowledge in a comparable but contextually responsive way. It also presents how the data collected in such a manner can serve the abductive inference of the ecology of competencies at multiple levels.

1.7 Synthesis

This chapter has developed a conceptual and epistemological foundation for analyzing work-related competencies in contexts characterized by rapid economic change, institutional diversity, and shifting modes of learning. By reviewing debates across education, economics, psychology, sociology, and philosophy of knowledge, it has argued that competencies are neither reducible to formal educational credentials nor fully explicable through isolated individual attributes. Instead, they are formed through socially embedded and context-specific processes, shaped by interactions among individual subjectivity, workplace relations, institutional arrangements, and broader economic conditions. The realist-constructivist framework proposed here offers a way to hold these dimensions together analytically, allowing close attention to micro-level practices while situating them within wider structural and regulatory ecologies. This framework provides the conceptual basis for the empirical and methodological analyses that follow, through which the book examines how competencies are formed, valued, and potentially transformed in diverse work environments of the Global South.

References

Aldinucci, A., Valiente, O., Hurrell, S., Zancajo, A., 2021. Understanding aspirations: why do secondary TVET students aim so high in Chile? Journal of Vocational Education and Training.

Allais, S., & Wedekind, V. (2020). Targets, TVET and transformation. In A. Wulff (Ed.), *Grading Goal 4* (pp. 322–338). Brill.

Allen, J., M. Levels, and R. van der Velden. (2013). "Skill Mismatch and Skill Use in Developed Countries: Evidence from the PIAAC Study." ROA Research Memoranda No. 017. Maastricht, Netherlands: Research Centre for Education and the Labour Market.

Allen, J., & van der Velden, R. (2001). Educational mismatches versus skills mismatches: Effects on wages, job satisfaction, and on-the-job search. *Oxford Economic Papers, 53*(3), 434–452.

Alston, W. P. (1998). *Empiricism.* Routledge Encyclopedia of Philosophy, Taylor and Francis. https://doi.org/10.4324/9780415249126-P014-1

Anderson, L. W., & Krathwohl, D. R. (Eds.). (2000). *A taxonomy for learning, teaching, and assessing: A revision of Bloom's taxonomy of educational objects.* Allyn & Bacon.

Aryeetey, E.-D., Doh, D., & Andoh, P. (2013). Choosing an apprenticeship: skills preferences amongst the youth. *International Development Planning Review, 35*(2), 135–153. https://doi.org/10.3828/idpr.2013.10

Asare, Samuel, Pauline Essah, Francis A. Gatsi, William Ohene Annoh, Richard Cliff Ekumah, A. Ampah, & Jennifer N. Udeh. (2023). "The Role of Career Services in Tertiary Students' Transition to Employment: Voices from Africa." Michael Carton and Christine Hoffman (eds). The Education-Training-Work Continuums: Pathways to Socio-Professional Inclusion for Youth and Adults, NORRAG Special Issue 08. pp. 80–84.

Asian Productivity Organization. (2019). *Education Reform for the Future of Work: The Shift to a Knowledge Society.* Author.

Bandura, A. (1997). Social Learning Theory. In *Social learning theory Prentice Hall: Englewood Cliffs* (Vol. 1). Prentice Hall.

Bandura, A. (1986). *Social Foundations of Thought and Action: A Social Cognitive Theory*. Prentice-Hall.

Bandura, A., Ross, D., & Ross, S. A. (1961). Transmission of aggression through imitation of aggressive models. *The Journal of Abnormal and Social Psychology, 63*(3), 575–582.

Barrick, M. R., Mount, M. K., & Judge, T. A. (2001). Personality and performance at the beginning of the new millennium: What do we know and where do we go next? *International Journal of Selection and Assessment, 9*, 9–30.

Barrick, M. R., Stewart, G. L., Neubert, M., & Mount, M. K. (1998). Relating member ability and personality to work team processes and team effectiveness. *Journal of Applied Psychology, 83*, 377–391.

Bhaskar, R. (1975). *A Realist Theory of Science*. Verso.

Bhaskar, R. (1998). Philosophy and scientific realism. In M. Archer, R. Bhaskar, A. Coollier, T. Lawson, & A. Norrie (Eds.), *Critical realism*. Essential readings.

Bhaskar, R., & Danermark, B. (2018). *and Leigh Price*. Interdisciplinarity and Wellbeing.

Becker, G. S. (1964). *Human capital: A Theoretical and Empirical Analysis with Special References to Education*. University of Chicago Press.

Binkley, M., Erstad, O., Herman, J., Raizen, S., Ripley, M., Miller-Ricci, M., & Rumble, M. (2012). Defining twenty-first-century skills. In P. Griffin, B. McGaw, & E. Care (Eds.), *Assessment and teaching of 21st century skills* (pp. 17–66). Springer-Verlag.

Bloom, B. S., Engelhart, M. D., Furst, E. J., Hill, W. H., & Krathwohl, D. R. (1956). Taxonomy of Educational Objectives: The Classification of Educational Goals. In *Handbook I: Cognitive Domain*. David McKay Company.

Borghans, L., Duckworth, A. L., Heckman, J. J., & Ter Weel, B. (2008). The economics and psychology of personality traits. *Journal of Human Resources, 43*(4), 972–1059.

Bowles, S., Gintis, H., & Osborne, M. (2001). Incentive-Enhancing Preferences: Personality, Behavior, and Earnings. *American Economic Review, 91*(2), 155–158.

Brunello, Giorgio, and Martin Schlotter. 2011. Non Cognitive Skills and Personality Traits: Labour Market Relevance and their Development in Education & Training Systems, IZA Discussion Paper No. 5743. Bonn: Institute for the Study of Labor

Campbell, J. P., McCloy, R. A., Oppler, S. H., & Sager, C. E. (1993). A theory of performance. In N. Schmitt & W. C. Borman (Eds.), *Personnel selection in organizations* (pp. 35–70). Jossey-Bass.

Card, D. (2001). Estimating the Returns to Schooling: Progress on Some Persistent Econometric Problems. *Econometrica, 69*(5), 1127–1160.

Castle, J., & Attwood, G. (2001). Recognition of Prior Learning (RPL) for access or credit? Problematic issues in a university adult education department in South Africa. *Studies in the Education of Adults, 33*(1), 60–72.

Cottingham, J. (1988). *The Rationalists (A History of Western Philosophy: 4)*. Oxford University Press.

Croll, P. (2008). Occupational Choice, Socio-economic Status and Educational Attainment: A Study of the Occupational Choices and Destinations of Young People in the British Household Panel Survey. *Research Papers in Education, 23*(3), 243–268.

Cubel, M., Nuevo-Chique, A., Sanchez-Pages, S., & Vidal-Fernandez, M. (2016). Do Personality Traits Affect Productivity? *Evidence from the Laboratory. Economic Journal, 126*(592), 654–681.

Dagar, P., Rethinking skills development and entrepreneurship for refugees: The case of five refugee communities in India, International Journal of Educational Development, Volume 101, 102834.

Decker, P. J., & Nathan, B. R. (1985). *Behavior modeling training: Principles and applications*. Greenwood.

De Jaeghere, J. (2017). *Educating Entrepreneurial Citizens*. Routledge.

Department Of Higher Education and Training, Government of South Africa (2020). Revised Strategic Plan 2020–2025 chrome-extension://efaidnbmnnnibpcajpcglclefindmkaj/https://www.dhet.gov.za/SiteAssets/Planing%2CPolicy%20and%20Strategy/DHET%20Revised%202020-2025%20Strat%20Plan%20.pdf. Accessed on October 15, 2024.

Desjardins, R., and K. Rubenson. (2011). "An Analysis of Skills Mismatch Using Direct Measures of Skills." OECD Education Working Paper No. 63. OECD.

Detel, W. (2001). Social Constructivism. *International Encyclopedia of the Social & Behavioral Sciences, 2001*, 14264–14267.

Dewey, J. (1897). My Pedagogic Creed. *School Journal, 54*(3), 77–80.

Dobson, P. (2001). The philosophy of critical realism - An opportunity for information systems research. *Information Systems Frontiers, 3*, 199–210.

Dobson, P. & P. Love. 2004. Realist and postmodernist.

Eichhorst, W., Rodríguez-Planas, N., Schmidl, R., & Zimmermann, K. F. (2015). A roadmap to vocational education and training in industrialized countries. *Industrial and Labor Relations Review, 68*(2), 314–337.

von Glaserfeld, E. (1996). *Radical Constructivism: A Way of Knowing and Learning*. Routledge.

Ellis, E. (2015). Kant's political thought. *Oxford Bibliographies..* https://www.oxfordbibliographies.com/view/document/obo-9780199756223/obo-9780199756223-0138.xml

Fastre, G. M. J., van der Klink, M. R., Amsing-Smit, P., & van Merrienboer, J. J. G. (2014). Assessment criteria for competency-based education: A study in nursing education. *Instructional Science, 42*, 971–994.

Faul, Moira V., Chanwoong Baek, and Sangheon Lee (2023). "Foreword." Michael Carton and Christine Hoffman (eds). The Education-Training-Work Continuums: Pathways to Socio-Professional Inclusion for Youth and Adults, NORRAG Special Issue 08. pp. 3–5.

Feldman, R. (1995). "Authoritarian Epistemology." Philosophical Topics, vol. 23, no. 1, pp. 147–69. JSTOR.

Galán-Muros, V.; Roser-Chinchilla, J. (2024) Relevant indicators in higher education plans: from reporting to forecasting. *UNESCO IESALC Policy Brief Series*, number 3.

Gelatt, V. A., Adler-Baeder, F., & Seeley, J. R. (2010). An interactive web-based program for stepfamilies: Development and evaluation of efficacy. *Family Relations, 59*(5), 572–586.

Gensowski, M. (2018). Personality, IQ, and Lifetime Earnings. *Labour Economics, 51*, 170–183.

Gergen, K. J. (2009). *Relational Being: Beyond Self and Community*. Oxford University Press.

Glossary of Education Reform. (2016). "21st Century Skills." https://www.edglossary.org/21st-century-skills/. Accessed on August 21, 2024.

Goody, E. N. (1995). In E. N. Goody (Ed.), *'Introduction: some implications of a social origin of intelligence' in Social Intelligence and Interaction: Expressions and Implications of the Social Bias in Human Intelligence* (pp. 1–34). Cambridge University Press.

Government of United Arab Emirates. 2017. National Strategy for Higher Education 2030. https://u.ae/en/about-the-uae/strategies-initiatives-and-awards/strategies-plans-and-visions/human-resources-development-and-education/national-strategy-for-higher-education-2030. Accessed on October 15, 2024.

Green, F. (2011). What is skill? An inter-disciplinary synthesis. Centre for Learning and Life Changes in Knowledge Economies and Societies.

Green, F., & McIntosh, S. (2009). Is There a Genuine Under-Utilization of Skills Amongst the Over-Qualified? *Applied Economics, 39*(4), 427–439.

Hanushek, E. A., & Kimko, D. D. (2000). Schooling, Labor-Force Quality and the Growth of Nations. *American Economic Review, 90*(5), 1184–1208.

Harrison, J. K. (1992). Individual and combined effects of behavior modeling and the cultural assimilator in cross-cultural management training. *Journal of Applied Psychology, 77*(6), 952–962. https://doi.org/10.1037/0021-9010.77.6.952

Hase, S., & Lester Davis. (1999). From competence to capability: the implications for human resource development and management. Paper presented to Millennial challenges in management, education, cybertechnology, and leadership: Association of International Management, 17th Annual Conference, San Diego, p. 6–8 August.

Heckman, J. J., Stixrud, J., & Urzua, S. (2006). The effects of cognitive and noncognitive abilities on labor market outcomes and social behavior, Working Paper No. 12006. National Bureau of Economic Research.

Heckman, J. J., & Rubinstein, Y. (2001). The Importance of Noncognitive Skills: Lessons from the GED Testing Program. *American Economic Review, 91*(2), 145–149.

Holland, J. L. (1997). *Making Vocational Choices: A Theory of Careers* (3rd ed.). Psychological Assessment Resources.

Hossler, D., Schmit, J., & Vesper, N. (1999). *Going to College: How Social, Economic, and Educational Factors Influence the Decisions Students Make*. Johns Hopkins University Press.

Hough, L. M., Ones, D. S., & Viswesvaran, C. (1998). April. Personality correlates of managerial performance constructs. In *Paper presented at the 13th Annual Conference of the Society for Industrial Organizational Psychology*.

Husserl, Edmund. 1997. Die Idee der Phänomenologie (Gensho gaku no rinen), Tokyo: Sakuhin Sha, first published 1973.

International Labour Organization. (2013). *Enhancing youth employability: What? Why? and How? Guide to core work skills*. ILO.

Kautz, Tim, James J. Heckman, Ron Diris, Baster Weel, and Lex Borghans. 2014. Fostering and Measuring Skills: Improving Cognitive and Noncognitive Skills to *Promote Lifetime Success*. OECD Education Working Papers No. 110. OECD.

Kechagias, K. (2011). Teaching Soft Skills. In K. Kechagias (Ed.), *Teaching and Assessing Soft Skills* (1st ed., pp. 53–76). 1st and 3rd Gymnasium 56760 Neapolis. http://research.education.nmsu.edu/files/2014/01/396_MASS-wp4-final-report-part-1.pdf

Kerr S. P., Kerr W. R., Xu T. (2017). *Personality traits of entrepreneurs: A review of recent literature*. Working Paper 18–047. Harvard Business School.

Khazem, D. (2018). Critical realist approaches to global learning: A focus on education for sustainability. *International Journal of Development Education and Global Learning, 10*(2), 125–134.

Kraak, A. (Ed.). (2009). *Sectors and Skills*. HSRC Press.

Kristof, A. L. (1996). Person-organization fit: An integrative review of its conceptualizations, measurement, and implications. *Personnel Psychology, 49*(1), 1–49.

Kuhn, P., & Weinberger, C. (2005). Leadership skills and wages. *Journal of Labor Economics, 23*(3), 395–436.

Kyllonen, P. C. (2013). Soft skills for the workplace. *Change*, 16–23.

Langevang, T., & Gough, K. V. (2012). Diverging pathways: Young female employment and entrepreneurship in sub-Saharan Africa. *The Geographical Journal, 178*(3), 242–252.

Lave, J., & Wenger, E. (1991). *Situated Learning: Legitimate Peripheral Participation*. Cambridge University Press.

Law, G. C., Neihart, M., & Dutt, A. (2018). The use of behavior modeling training in a mobile app parent training program to improve functional communication of young children with autism spectrum disorder. *Autism, 22*(4), 424–439.

Le Deist, F. O. D., & Winterton, J. (2005). What is competence? *Human Resource Development International, 8*(1), 27–46.

Lee, S., & Ohtake, F. (2012). The Effect of Personality Traits and Behavioral Characteristics on Schooling, Earnings and Career Promotion. *Journal of Behavioral Economics and Finance, 5*, 231–238.

Lent, R. W., Brown, S. D., & Hackett, G. (1994). Toward a unifying social cognitive theory of career and academic interest, choice, and performance. *Journal of Vocational Behavior, 45*, 79–122.

Levinson, S. C. (1995). In E. N. Goody (Ed.), *'Interactional biases in human thinking' in Social Intelligence and Interaction: Expressions and Implications of the Social Bias in Human Intelligence* (pp. 221–260). Cambridge University Press.

Lindqvist, E., & Vestman, R. (2011). The labor market returns to cognitive and noncognitive ability: Evidence from the Swedish Enlistment. *American Economic Journal: Applied Economics, 3*(1), 101–128.

Lombrozo, T. (2012). Explanation and Abductive Inference. In K. J. Holyoak & R. G. Morrison (Eds.), *The Oxfordd Handbook of Thinking and Reasoning* (pp. 260–292). Oxford Universit Press.

Luhman, N. (2004). Das Erziehungssystem der Gesellschaft (Kyoiku no Shakai Sistemu), Tokyo: Tokyo Daigaku Shuppankai, first published 2002.

Lynch, P., Schuelka, M., Johnstone, C., Brown, R., Tshewang, S., Assessing and supporting the transition of young persons with disabilities into meaningful work opportunities in Bhutan, *International Journal of Educational Development*, vol. 101, 102820.

Maslow, A. (1954) 1997. *Motivation and Personality.* 3rd ed. Pearson.

Maurer, M., Haolader, F., & Shimu, S. (2023). VET for all: assessing the case of Bangladesh. *International Journal of Educational Development, 101*, 102819.

McGrath, S., 2015. Understanding interactive capabilities for skills development in sectoral systems of innovation. LMIP Report No. 7, Human Sciences Research Council, Pretoria.

Mincer, J. (1974). *Schooling, Experience, and Earnings.* NBER Press.

Motowidlo, S. J., Borman, W. C., & Schmit, M. J. (1997). A theory of individual differences in task and contextual performance. *Human Performance, 10*, 71–83.

Nonaka, I., & Takeuchi, H. (1995). *The Knowledge-Creating Company: How Japanese Companies Create the Dynamics of Innovation.* Oxford University Press.

OECD (2005). Definition and Selection of Competencies (DeSeCo). OECD.

Olssen, M. (1995). The epistemology of constructivism. *Contemporary Issues in Education, 13*(2), 82–94.

Otchia, C., & Yamada, S. (2019). Reconciling Heterogeneous Results on Returns to Skills in Ghana and Kenya. *Journal of Education and Work, 32*(5), 484–499.

Osuji, O. N. (1976). Patterns of occupational choice and aspiration in conditions of economic and technological underdevelopment. *Journal of Vocational Behavior, 8*(2), 133–144.

Oxley, L., Le, T., & Gibson, J. (2008). Measuring Human Capital: Alternative Methods and International Evidence. *Korean Economic Review, 24*(2), 283–344.

Pascarella, E. T., & Terenzini, P. T. (1991). *How College Affects Students: Findings and Insights from Twenty Years of Research* (Vol. I). Jossey-Bass.

Pellizzari, M., & Fichen, A. (2017). A New Measure of Skill Mismatch: Theory and Evidence from PIAAC. *IZA Journal of Labor Economics, 6*(1), 1–30.

Pentland, A. (2014). *Social Physics: How Social Networks Can Make Us Smarter*. Penguin.

Pillay, H. K., J. Watters, S. Hay, W. Hoff. (2013). Partnerships to promote the school to work transitions: evidence from the field. Presented in the *JVET 10th International Conference*, 2013-07-05-2013-07-07.

Polanyi, M. (1966) 1983. *The Tacit Dimension.* Reprint, Gloucester, MA: Peter Smith.

Powell, L., & McGrath, S. (2019). *Skills for Human Development.* Routledge.

Prahalad, C.K. and Gary Hamel. 1990. "The Core Competence of the Corporation," *Harvard Business Review*, May-June 1990, pp. 1–15.

Radovan, M. 2017."Knowledge and skills: A critical view," 40th International Convention on Information and Communication Technology, Electronics, and Microelectronics (MIPRO), Opatija, , pp. 630–634

Ramsarup, P., Lotz-Sisitka, H., & McGrath, S. (2022). A laminated, emergentist view of skills ecosystems. *Journal of Critical Realism, 21*(5), 571–588.

Rosen, J. A., Glennie, E. J., Dalton, B. W., Lennon, J. M., & Bozick, R. N. (2010). *Noncognitive Skills in the Classroom: New Perspectives on Educational Research.* RTI International.

Schultz, T. W. (1961). Investment in Human Capital. *American Economic Review, 51*(1), 1–17.

Schwandt, T. A. (1998). Constructivist, Interpretivist Approaches to Human Inquiry. In N. K. Denzin & Y. S. Lincoln (Eds.), *The landscape of qualitative research: theories and issues.* Thousand Oaks.

Scott, C. L. (2015). The future of learning: What kind of learning for the 21st century? (Education Research and Foresight Working Paper 14). United Nations Educational, Scientific and Cultural Organization.

Sonnenberg, K. (2012). Traditional Apprenticeship in Ghana and Senegal: Skills Development for Youth for the Informal Sector. *Journal of International Cooperation in Education, 15*(2), 93–105.

Standing, G. (2002). *Beyond the New Paternalism.* Verso.

Stephenson, J. (1994). Capability and Competence: Are they the same and does it matter? *capability, 1*(1), 3–4.

Super, D. E. 1990. "A Life-Span, Life Space Approach to Career Development." In *Career Choice and Development*, edited by D. Brown, L. Brooks, and Associates, 197–261. 2nd ed. : Jossey-Bass.

Tepper, R. J., & Yourstone, S. A. (2018). Beyond ACT & GPA: self-efficacy as a noncognitive predictor of academic success. *International Journal of Accounting & Information Management, 26*(1), 171–186.

Tett, R. P., & Burnett, D. D. (2003). A Personality Trait-Based Interactionist Model of Job Performance. *Journal of Applied Psychology, 88*(3), 500–517.

United Nations Children's Fund. (2019). *Transitions from School to Work.* UNICEF.

United Nations Educational, Scientific and Cultural Organization (UNESCO). 2013. *EFA global monitor-*

ing report 2012: Youth and skills—Putting education to work. Author.

VET Africa 4.0 Collective, 2023. *Transitioning Vocational Education and Training*. Bristol University Press, .

Vygotsky, L. S. (1978). *Mind in society: The development of higher psychological processes*. Harvard University Press.

Waldman, D. A., Galvin, B. M., & Walumbwa, F. O. (2013). The development of motivation to lead and leader role identity. *Journal of Leadership and Organizational Studies, 20*(2), 156–168.

Walton, D. N. (2004). *Abductive Reasoning*. University of Alabama Press.

Webster-Stratton, C. (1982). The long-term effects of a videotape modeling parent-training program: Comparison of immediate and 1-year follow-up results. *Behavior Therapy, 13*(5), 702–714.

Wedekind, V., Mutereko, S., 2016. *Employability and curriculum responsiveness in post-school education and training*. LMIP Report No. 22, Human Sciences Research Council, Pretoria.

Wedekind, V., Russon, J.-A., Ramsarup, P., Monk, D., Metelerkamp, L., & McGrath, S. (2021). Conceptualising regional skills ecosystems. *International Journal of Training and Development, 25*(4), 347–362.

Westerhuis, A. (2011). The meaning of competence. In M. Brockmann, L. Clarke, & C. Winch (Eds.), *Knowledge, skills and competence in the European labour market*. Taylor and Francis.

Wignall, R., Piquard, B., & Joel, M. (2023). Up-skilling women or de-skilling patriarchy? *International Journal of Educational Development, 102*, 102850.

Woolhouse, R. S. (1988). *The Empiricists (A History of Western Philosophy: 5)*. Oxford University Press.

World Bank. (2020). *World Development Report 2019: The Changing Nature of Work*. World Bank.

World Economic Forum. 2023. Future of Jobs Report 2023: Insight Report. Author.

Wossmann, L. (2003). Specifying human capital. *Journal of Economic Surveys, 17*(3), 239–270.

Yamada, Shoko. 2019. A theory of knowledge - The act of "knowing" in the era of the information cloud. Toshindo. (published in Japanese).

Yamada, S. (2021). Traditional Apprenticeship as an Educational and Life Experience: Life Stories of Young Auto Repair Apprentices in Kumasi, Ghana. In Y. Ofosu-Kusi & M. Matsuda (Eds.), *The Challenge of African Potentials: Conviviality, Informality and Futurity*. Langaa Publishing.

Yamada, Shoko, Pimmada Charoensilp, Emmanuel Estrellado, Yuki Shimazu. 2024. Employable Capacity Development for Women Project in Punjab: Summary Report of the Training Needs Assessment. Submitted to Japan International Cooperation Agency. Skills and Knowledge for Youth Project, Nagoya University.. https://skills-for-development.com/wp/wp-content/uploads/2024/07/TNA-final-Report-2023-Mailing-version-compressed.pdf

Yamada, Shoko, and Christian Otchia. 2021. "Differential Effects of Schooling and Cognitive and Noncognitive Skills on Labor Market Outcomes: The Case of the Garment Industry in Ethiopia." *International Journal of Training and Development* (forthcoming).

Yamada, S., Otchia, C., & Taniguchi, K. (2018). Explaining Differing Perceptions of Employees' Skill Needs: The Case of Garment Workers in Ethiopia. *International Journal of Training and Development, 21*(4), 51–68.

Zhao, H., & Seibert, S. E. (2006). The big five personality dimensions and entrepreneurial status: A meta-analytical review. *Journal of Applied Psychology., 91*, 259–271.

Zimmermann, K., Biavaschi, C., Eichhorst, W., Giulietti, C., Kendzia, M. J., Muravyev, A., Pieters, J., Rodrìguez-Planas, N., & Schmidl, R. (2013). Youth unemployment and vocational training. *Foundations and Trends in Microeconomics, 9*(1–2), 1–157.

2 Conditions of Competency Development in the Global South

Shoko Yamada

Abstract

Before providing empirical cases, within the Realist-Constructivist framework presented in Chap. 1, this chapter discusses econo-productive and structural-regulatory mechanisms that condition the formation of workforce competencies in the Global South. It reviews macroeconomic dynamics such as global trade, value chains, and foreign investment, showing how they affect labor productivity, job creation, and skill valuation. Issues such as reliance on raw material exports, vulnerability to external shocks, and the "race to the bottom" in low-wage economies highlight persistent challenges. The chapter also explores labor market mismatches, decent work, and the balance between generic and firm-specific skills. On the structural-regulatory side, the chapter traces the evolution of technical and vocational education and training (TVET) and the global shift toward competency-based training (CBT), analyzing tensions between distributive and coordinative welfare models. At the end, the chapter provides an observation of econo-productive and structural-regulatory conditions specific to Ethiopia, Ghana, South Africa, and Pakistan, illustrating how global trends, national policies, and firm-level ecologies interact to shape competencies, revealing both commonalities and context-specific differences.

Keywords

Macroeconomic trade dynamics · Varieties of labor market · Skills development policies · Decent work · Global policy trends · Economic environment for skills formation

2.1 Introduction

In the previous chapter, I presented our conceptual model of Realist-Constructivism in analyzing the competencies formation of working adults (see Fig. 1.4). In it, as the enmeshed factors that condition humans to recognize their experience as real, I proposed three generative mechanisms: socio-cultural, structural-regulatory, and econo-productive mechanisms. Adapting the analytical tools of Bhaskar's critical realism, I defined the socio-cultural mechanism to be composed of socio-cultural norms and categories, such as gender, age, class, cultural norms, habitation, or family, among others. The structural-regulatory mechanism is made

S. Yamada (✉)
Graduate School of International Development, Nagoya University, Nagoya, Japan

Graduate School of Asian and African Area Studies, Kyoto University, Kyoto, Japan
e-mail: syamada@nagoya-u.jp

S. Yamada (ed.), *Mitigating the "Skills Gaps"*, Sustainable Development Goals Series,
https://doi.org/10.1007/978-981-95-7968-6_2

of policies and regulations related to labor, employment, and competency development. The education system, particularly TVET, is part of this mechanism. The econo-productive mechanism involves commercial practices and the business environment, including market conditions and measures for business promotion.

Individual workers' competencies are shaped and experienced in the micro-ecology of workplaces, which is under constant influence from these generative mechanisms. Therefore, it is necessary to examine these mechanisms at each micro, national, industrial, and global level when we consider the competencies in a Realist-Constructivist manner. As a precondition for further discussion, which will be based on empirical evidence, in this chapter, I will review the generative mechanisms surrounding workforce competency development in the Global South in general and particularly in the four countries where the study was conducted. Out of three mechanisms, I will highlight econo-productive and structural-regulatory mechanisms here, cascading the focus from the macro to the national and industrial levels. The discussion about the socio-cultural mechanism will be held for the later chapters, because social and cultural influences appear differently according to the dynamics of the specific micro-ecology, even in the seemingly same cultural group, and making general statements would induce cultural determinism. Thus, we discuss the effects of the socio-cultural mechanism only when we can provide empirical evidence.

2.2 Econo-productive Mechanism of Workforce Development

2.2.1 Macroeconomic Trade Dynamics in the Global South

The Global South encompasses diverse countries, primarily in Africa, Latin America, the Caribbean, and parts of Asia. Despite diversities, these nations have common historical backgrounds of economic marginalization within the global trading system, often relegated to roles that reinforce dependency on more developed economies. However, in recent years, the Global South has begun to assert its influence in macroeconomic dynamics, and some of them have caught up with industrialized nations in the Global North. It's been a while since the BRICS[1] facilitated investment and trade within the Global South directly without being mediated by the states and private firms originating from the North. The New Development Bank (NDB), commonly known as the BRICS Bank, provides low-interest loans for infrastructure development and other projects in developing countries (New Development Bank, 2024). Arab states are also providing development assistance to Africa and Asia through the Islamic Development Bank (IsDB), the Arab Bank for Economic Development in Africa (BADEA), and other institutions (BADEA 2024; IsDB, 2024). Altogether, these initiatives to strengthen ties among economies of the Global South have contributed to making them not only economic alliances but also geopolitical blocs. Emerging markets have outperformed developed economies since the turn of the century, and even after the stagnation caused by the COVID-19[2] pandemic, their pace of growth continues to be high. According to the projection by the Economist Intelligence Unit (2022), average annual growth in non-OECD[3] economies during the 2022–2026 period will be 3.9%, compared to the OECD member states of 1.8%.

Despite such a positive outlook and changing gravities of geopolitics and the global economy, many countries in the Global South are still struggling with challenges that have plagued

[1]The name BRICS originally came from the initials of Brazil, Russia, India, and China, which hosted the first BRICS Summit in 2009, but the BRICS Summit was later joined by South Africa in 2010 and Egypt, Ethiopia, Iran, and the United Arab Emirates in 2024.

[2]Coronavirus disease 2019.

[3]OECD—The Organisation for Economic Co-operation and Development is an intergovernmental organization that has been known as the "developed countries' club," mostly from Western Europe and North America, with some significant exceptions like Japan. Recently, its membership expanded to 38, including countries with lower economic standards on different continents. Still, it exhibits the characteristics of conventional developed economies.

them for a long time regarding international trade. First, they tend to rely on exports of raw materials, such as minerals and agricultural products, with no or limited value added. Lack of diversity in the export materials and limited processing make them vulnerable to external shocks such as fluctuations in demand and commodity prices (Eum & Lee, 2022; Mania & Rieber, 2019). The limitation of value-added production is greatly attributed to the limited abilities of human capital. Without a workforce with enough technical skills to process raw materials, the country cannot aim to export technology-dependent products that are competitive in the global market. That's why many governments aspiring for fast economic growth raise human resources development as a pillar of their national development plans (for example, Human Resource Development Council of South Africa, 2022; Uganda National Planning Authority, 2020). Since this volume is about the abilities of workforces, I will come back to this point and discuss it in more detail. Before that, let me touch on other factors that characterize the econo-productive mechanism of the workforce's competency development in the Global South.

As I introduced in the previous chapter, even before human capital started to attract the attention of economists and policymakers in the 1960s, physical capital was considered a significant precondition for economic growth, requiring investment. That remains the case today. In many developing countries, poor infrastructure, including inadequate transportation networks, unreliable energy supplies, and limited access to technology, is said to hamper competitiveness in the global market. While most governments recognize the importance of such physical capital, developing economies tend not to have the capacity to invest in costly infrastructure-building projects. Therefore, they have relied on loans from development finance institutions such as the World Bank, the International Monetary Fund (IMF), and regional development banks. However, as many countries were unable to keep up with interest payments even on loans at lower interest rates than those offered by private banks, since the 1980s, agencies that provided development loans repeatedly announced debt relief. In return for such relief measures, indebted country governments were required to adopt reform plans prescribed to improve economic regulations and governance (Elbadawi, 1999; Freytag & Pehnelt, 2009). In the 2000s, emerging economies also started to offer development aid for less developed economies. As mentioned above, their funding agencies, such as NDB and IsDB, provide alternative channels to conventional Western donors for less developed countries to acquire funds for developing physical capital. Such diversification of foreign assistance on which the less developed countries rely contributed to changing the power relations between these countries and Western developed countries (McCormick, 2008; Woods, 2008).

As such, the role of the national government in constructing economic infrastructure, acquiring financial resources for it, and regulating the domestic market is crucial. At the same time, the main drivers for the macroeconomic performance of the catch-up economies are trade relations with overseas companies. Today, private firms extend production networks across multiple countries, with each country specializing in specific stages of the production process based on its competitive advantages. From research, development, and product design to assembling, marketing, and distribution, stages of production are linked through the Global Value Chain (GVC). For countries trying to take off economically, attracting foreign direct investments (FDIs) from such global firms and being part of the GVC is an important step (Coe et al., 2008; Dicken et al., 2001). However, more often than not, political instability, weak governance, and corruption are pervasive in these countries, deterring investment, disrupting trade, and undermining economic development efforts (Mengistu & Adhikary, 2011). Therefore, even though the FDI is the trade activities of private firms, stability and peace, just governance of the state, and regulation and structure that encourage investments are indispensable.

Many developing countries are facing double-bound restrictions. On the one hand, low economic status hinders the states from allocating resources to formulate human and physical capital. On the other hand, political instability and lack of governance, which are, in fact, causally related to the low economic standard of the public, often result in distancing foreign firms that might have otherwise established their production bases in the country. Meanwhile, there are voices that foreign investing firms, attracted by cheap labor, tend to treat workers as a part of global value chains, prioritizing corporate profits and not paying attention to the quality of employment and human rights of workers. In other words, FDI-driven economic growth alone may leave behind the welfare for which the government has to perform its tasks (Appelbaum, 2005; Barrientos et al., 2011).

As the explanation in this section indicates, macroeconomic trade dynamics, which may appear unrelated to daily realities in the workplace, directly and indirectly impact the status and conditions of employment on the ground. As a result, the econo-productive mechanism influences what a worker considers important abilities and actively seeks to strengthen them: whether the company is part of a global value chain or a small or medium-sized enterprise that only makes products for the domestic market, or whether the country in which the company is located prioritizes the concerned industry in attracting FDIs and proactively offering support. These are critical extrinsic determinants of how a person's abilities are valuated, both by him/herself and others.

2.2.2 Labor Productivity and Competencies: Social and Individual Development Needs

Based on the understanding of the influence of the macroeconomy on individuals' aspirations and work, let us look more closely into the relationships among economic growth, labor productivity, and employment. Figure 2.1 compares the annual economic growth rate and the evolution of labor productivity in different regions of the world. The bar graphs show the GDP[4] per person employed for 2005, 2015, and 2023, and the line graphs show the annual economic growth rate for the same periods. The GDP per person employed is often used as the proxy indicator of labor productivity, representing the economic value of production by individual workers in an economy. On the other hand, economic growth rates provide the ratio of GDP growth from the past year, regardless of the size of the economy. As discussed earlier, the growth centers of the world that demonstrate high economic growth rates are concentrated in South and East Asia and Africa, even though the economic growth rates fluctuate, particularly in Africa. A clear trend is that those regions with higher growth rates are also characterized by lower labor productivity than some regions that do not grow fast, such as Europe and Central Asia, and North America.

In sum, despite the speed of catch-up, fast-growing economies in Asia and Africa do not necessarily have the workforce to generate much economic value added. Here are two possible causes. One is the case of resource-rich countries, which earn foreign capital by exporting unprocessed raw materials. In this case, as I discussed in the previous section, the economies of these countries are vulnerable to external conditions, such as international commodity prices, which are beyond their control. Also, growth dependent on unprocessed material exports does not create many jobs domestically, while the wealth from exports is monopolized among a small number of people with mining concessions. Such narrowly based growth is not only fragile but also causes economic inequality within the country, which in turn tends to generate social discontent and political instability. Therefore, to distribute the benefit of economic growth, the creation of jobs is key (Kpognon et al., 2022). At the same time, jobs that provide workers with stable incomes do not occur automatically. Only when the basis for value-added manufacturing is created in the country will employment expand.

Another possible cause of the low labor productivity in fast-growing economies is the *race to*

[4]Gross domestic product.

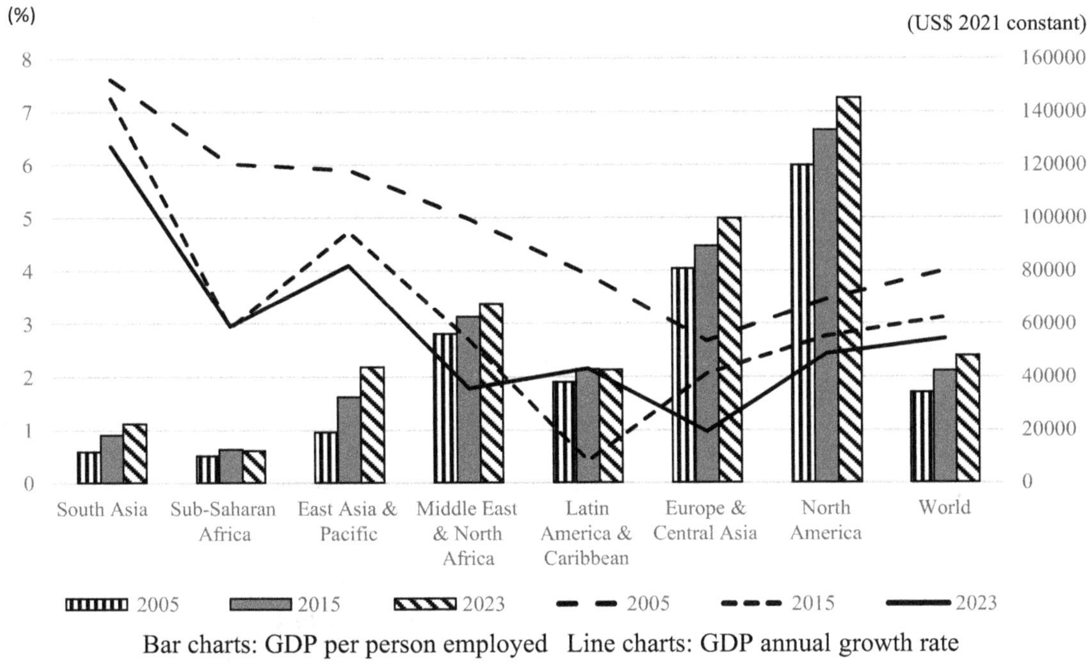

Fig. 2.1 Economic growth and labor productivity growth by region (produced by the author based on World Bank, 2024)

the bottom (Olney, 2013). I mentioned earlier that developing countries try to attract FDIs as a step to economic take-off and become a part of the global value chains. A trap of such a strategy is that foreign firms may end up exploiting cheap labor without localizing higher-order production processes and contributing to upgrading the workforce capacities on site. Still, governments often hesitate to raise the minimum wage for fear of losing foreign investors to other developing countries whose labor is cheaper. In this case, the national economy may grow in the short term, but cannot escape the vicious cycle of low wages and low value-added production. It also means that the welfare of the workforce does not improve. Meanwhile, some surveys suggest that foreign investing firms also try to secure competent workers as a key to their business success, although the degree and form of devolving the power and responsibility are always context-bound and challenging (Farndale et al., 2010; Scullion & Starkey, 2000). In sum, developing countries try to climb to a higher order of the GVC by providing a quality workforce and business environment to convince investing firms of the necessity of further localization, if they want to overcome the race to the bottom. With the technologies and expertise shared by foreign firms, countries need to establish foundations for widely based value-added productions and stability of employment for workers with competencies.

2.2.2.1 Decent Work, Poverty Reduction, and Lifelong Learning

Readers must notice already that the accumulation of competent human capital is important not only for the economic growth of society at large but also for individuals to live safely and soundly. Since we discussed econo-productive factors at the macro and national levels, let us now turn to individual employment.

The International Labour Organization (ILO) (1998) defines decent work as providing productive employment opportunities, offering fair wages, ensuring workplace security, providing social protection for families, and improving prospects for personal growth and social inclusion. It also involves safeguarding individuals' rights to voice their concerns, organize, and take part in decisions impacting their lives while guaranteeing equal opportunities and fair treatment for both women and men. In developing countries, advancing decent work is essential for reducing poverty and achieving sustainable growth. Employment is the primary means through which individuals earn an income, and decent work ensures that this income is sufficient to meet basic needs and contribute to a decent standard of living. Therefore, it will be a proactive solution to the challenges caused by poverty. By having stable and predictable incomes, people can start to plan for the short- and long-term future, spending money for education, health care, and other social services to improve their and their families' well-being. Accordingly, decent work is listed as one of the key targets of the eighth Sustainable Development Goal (SDG8), together with comprehensive and sustainable economic growth.

To achieve this goal, there should be enough job opportunities that match the abilities of people looking for jobs, as well as leading to a stable income for them to sustain their lives. Meanwhile, matching employment opportunities with job seekers' relevant skills and qualifications is often not easy in developing countries. Another important issue, which is the main theme of this volume, is education and training. As for the SDGs, education is listed as the fourth goal (SDG4). The emerging perspective on knowledge for problem-solving, which I discussed in detail in the previous chapter, is also reflected in SDG 4. One of its targets is to achieve lifelong learning, which envisages the learning of not only school-aged children but also adults. As a part of SDG 4, the importance of learning vocational skills is highlighted, although its relation to cognitive and noncognitive abilities to solve problems in the workplace is not made clear.

In a nutshell, the competency development of working adults is the node of social development and individual well-being. Regardless of its importance, as it cuts across different administrative and academic fields, such as education, economics, and labor, there tends not to be a holistic discussion. For example, scholars and practitioners actively involved in the discourse of SDG4 focus predominantly on school education, while those discussing SDG8 rarely pay attention to training and competency formation. Such fragmentation of academic discourse and policy measures makes successful practices in this field difficult. This point will be discussed in more detail in the sections on the structural-regulatory mechanism later in this chapter. In the meantime, let us now turn to the labor market in which individuals are evaluated and selected for employment according to different demands for competencies and skills.

2.2.3 Labor Market Demand for Knowledge and Human Resource Development

However much the government intervenes in the labor market with regulations and incentives aiming to animate the labor dynamics and promote the employment of a skilled workforce, it occurs only where the demands exist. Specialists and practitioners of education and training tend to consider workforce competency development only from the supply side. Supply, in this case, has two meanings; one is that of people with skills for which they will be employed, and another is the provision of services for people to acquire such skills (see Fig. 2.2). Educationists' attention is greatly paid to the latter type of supply. Meanwhile, the value of a worker's abilities is determined by the balance between supply and demand. If more people have similar abilities compared to the employment opportunities requiring them, these abilities are oversupplied in the labor market and valued less. On the contrary, if one can rarely find people with properly matched skills for a job opportunity, those who qualify would be highly valued. Since the value changes according to the balance of supply and demand, no fixed model exists to explain the relationship between the workers, their abilities, and employment. However, certain elements in the

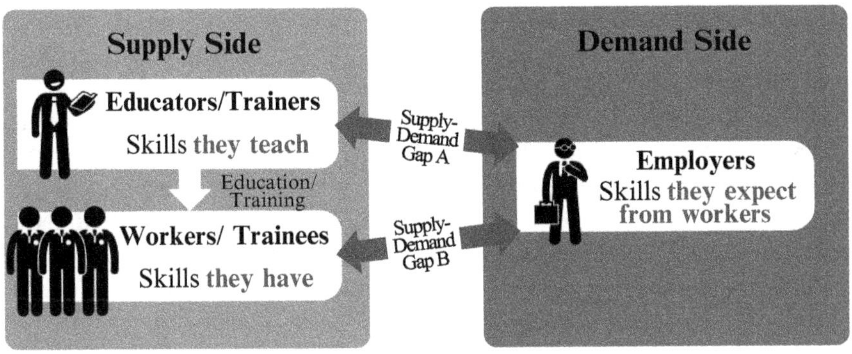

Fig. 2.2 Twin gaps between the supply of and demand for workforces' abilities in the labor market

labor market are likely to influence the individual workers' abilities. To grasp the nature of the econo-productive mechanism affecting respective micro-ecologies of competency development, I will overview some of the key issues related to the labor market.

2.2.3.1 The Twin "Gaps" Between Supply and Demand

According to labor economics, employers offer jobs based on the expectation of the abilities of prospective workers, while their actual performance after employment will be rewarded in the form of wages or promotions. Therefore, the supply-demand matching in the labor market continues throughout a worker's career, seamlessly linking the periods before, during, and after employment. As I stated in the previous chapter, institutionalists conceptualize human activities according to the stages segregated and regulated under function-based institutions. Thus, educationists often treat education as the pre-employment stage, whose transition to the world of work should be designed to be smooth (Faul et al., 2023). Meanwhile, in labor economics, learning during employment is treated as "experience" (Serneels, 2008; Tchernis, 2010). Experience, in most cases, is equated with years of work and does not untangle the contents of competencies acquired through these years. In sum, there are divides among academic disciplines that approach the issues related to competency development from the supply side and those from the demand side, which often hinder our holistic understanding of the ontological reality of micro-ecologies.

People tend to use the concept of the supply-demand gap loosely, which often causes discrepancies in the perceived current situation and challenges among stakeholders. Thus, it would be useful to sort out the dual relationships between supply and demand on workforce abilities here, as shown in Fig. 2.2.

There are two major types of mismatch between the supply and demand sides. One is that of the education programs and the contents taught in educational institutions against the expectations of the employers (Gap A). Another is between the actual abilities of the job seekers and the expectations of the employers (Gap B). As I explained earlier, educationists tend to only look at Gap A, while labor economists focus on Gap B. At the same time, when we hear complaints from private firms that schools do not properly prepare students for the world of work, we notice that employers look to educational institutions responsible for ensuring the quality of their outputs, which are the people they are to employ. Put differently, private sector complaints are about Gap A for not mitigating Gap B.

A structural factor that increases the supply-demand gap is *information asymmetry* (Kar & Datta, 2015). Since it is difficult to shortlist the requirements for workers' abilities precisely and accurately, employers' expectations are often not expressed clearly in the job specifications. Also, it is often the case that education and training institutions are not exposed to the actual situations of the industry and cannot understand the abilities employers seek. It is a form of information asymmetry, a significant background to how Gap A occurs. In addition, there are limited means for job seekers to get information about job vacancies in developing countries. As a result, they often rely on personal connections without having a comprehensive picture of the employment opportunities available to people with the type of expertise and experience they have. This is the nature of information asymmetry affecting Gap B.

Gaps A and B are closely related but distinct. Even if the programs at the educational institutions fully reflect the industry demands and Gap A is minimized, it doesn't guarantee the minimization of Gap B. As learning is a personal process of cognition and adaptation, Gap B is significantly conditioned by the individual's original capacity, psychology, and subjective interpretation of the environment, although the educational programs they attend are important inputs for competency formation. While individual factors are important, we will leave the discussion on them for the following empirical chapters. Here, let us continue the discussion about the labor market mechanism.

2.2.3.2 Variety of Capitalism Approach

Since the turn of the century, political economists have been making efforts to categorize national economies according to the characteristics of labor and productive mechanisms. With the Variety of Capitalism (VoC) approach, Hall and Soskice (2001) proposed to map out national economies along the spectrum between the coordinated market economies (CMEs) and liberal market economies (LMEs). CMEs are considered to be more unionized, where bargaining and decision-making happen at the industrial and national levels, while in LMEs, inter-firm solidarities of workers and employers are less, and decisions take place more at the firm level. It was Estevez-Abe et al. (2001) who applied this VoC approach to explain the specific configuration of skills and labor markets in national economies. They highlight the provision of education and training by the welfare state as central to the competitiveness strategies of national economies. Meanwhile, Lauder et al. (2008) point to the evolving role of multinational corporations (MNCs) in the global economic landscape and their implications for skills demand, regardless of the welfare provision and strategies by the states. While the relative weight of the influence of international investors and the culture of national economies will vary, the VoC framework gives us a lens to analyze the characteristics of skills valued and formulated in specific micro-economies in response to the types of the labor market.

Earlier, I mentioned the differential characteristics of the skills developed in pre- and post-employment education. In general, pre-employment education and training aim to provide students with basic knowledge in their respective fields of specialization and prepare them for the world of work. In contrast, post-employment training tends to be more specific to the workplace or industry. The former are referred to as *generic skills*, the latter as *specific skills*. For example, in the mechanics course of the TVET institutions, students learn theories and basic techniques of handling and repairing machinery. But only after they are employed at firms do they learn to handle machinery for specific industries such as food processing, automotive, or clothing. The more a person's package of abilities becomes specific, the less versatile it may be, but the fit to specific environments would increase.

Demand for these generic and specific skills and the extent to which education and training are provided to develop them differ according to respective firms' styles of human resource management, the industrial structure, and macroeconomic strategies of the countries where they operate. For example, in a workplace that expects workers to be integrated into its culture and be fluent in firm-specific ways of doing things, employers would highly evaluate workers with firm-specific skills and retain them longer compared to the firms that constantly employ new TVET graduates without much additional training.

In the former cases, to incentivize workers to stay instead of moving to another firm, the firms tend to recognize workers' improvements and contributions through generous wage increases and promotions.

As shown in Fig. 2.3, in labor economics, within-firm labor relationships, in which workers' performance is evaluated and reflected in their wages and job rank, are called the *internal labor market*, distinguished from the *external labor market*, in which workers are involved through searching or changing jobs (Deming & Kahn, 2018; Doeringer & Piore, 2020).

Figure 2.3 shows that the internal labor market is characterized by the vertical hierarchy of job ranks. When the internal labor market is closed, employees are expected to acquire many specialized skills. If the workplace is less attractive than elsewhere regarding wages, insurance, or labor relations, or if employees find their skills more highly valued elsewhere, no matter how hard employers try to keep workers, the labor market will become fluid. The greater the chance of better salaries and treatment in the external market, the greater the desire of workers to develop generic skills that are portable and independent of their particular workplace. Portability of abilities is more likely to be appreciated in emerging sectors such as information engineering, where the population with required skills is limited. On the other hand, as work becomes more fragmented and specialized, the range of the external market in which a person can look for other employment opportunities will be narrower. Therefore, in some cases, the external market is fluid only within the same industry, while in other cases, it is transindustrial. The greater the dynamics of the external labor market, the greater the incentive to develop highly portable generic skills.

2.2.3.3 Unique Employment Conditions in the Global South

One of the most pressing drivers of labor market dynamics in the Global South is its unique demographic profile. Many countries in the Global South, particularly in sub-Saharan Africa and parts of South Asia, have young and rapidly growing populations. According to the projection by the United Nations Population (UNP) (2024), in 2050, a quarter of the world's population will

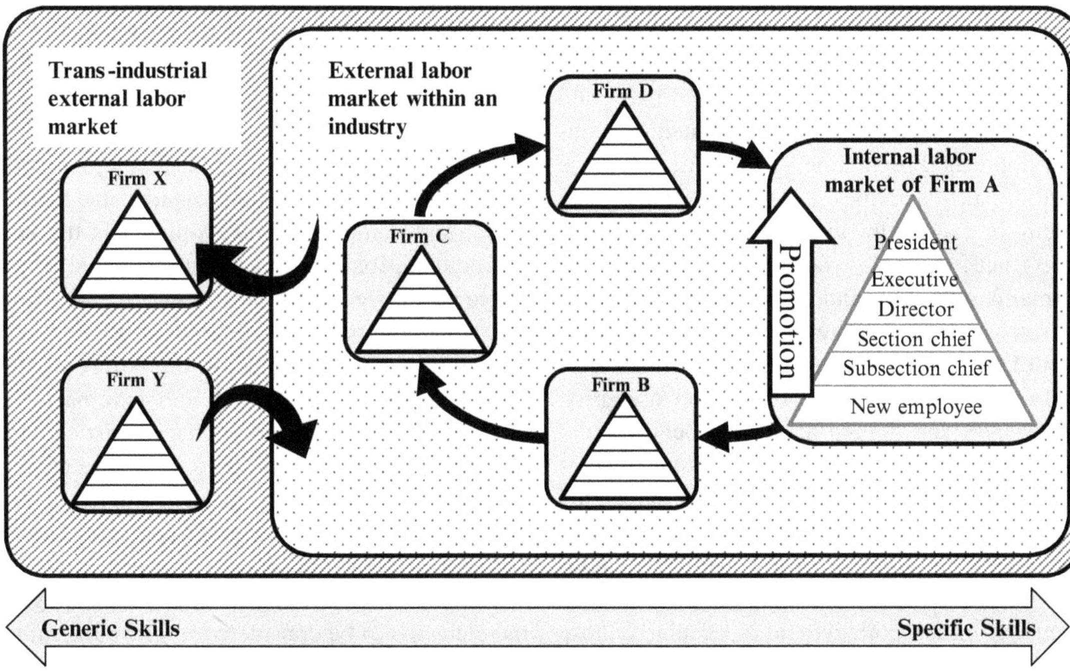

Fig. 2.3 Internal and external labor market and demands for abilities (produced by the authors based on Doeringer & Piore, 2020; reproduced from Yamada & Ohno, 2021, p. 18)

reside in Africa (25.52%), and its share will increase up to 40% in 2100. While Africa gradually takes its share, Asia still occupies half the world's population (54.62%). Europe and North America only comprise 14.41% altogether. This demographic dividend presents both opportunities and challenges. On the one hand, a large, youthful workforce can be a powerful engine for economic growth. On the other hand, unless economic diversification and localization of value-added production are realized, the labor market cannot absorb the increased working-age population, which will result in high unemployment and underemployment. Without creating decent work for them, which provides stable income and livelihood security, and the prerequisite skills development, the benefits of this population growth cannot be exploited.

Another characteristic of developing economies is the large proportion of the informal sector, which encompasses a diverse range of activities that are typically unregulated and untaxed. This sector includes small-scale traders, street vendors, domestic workers, and informal manufacturing, among others. It is estimated that more than 60% of the world's economic activity takes place in the informal sector, although precise data do not exist because governments cannot track the activities of informal and unregistered business entities (United Nations Development Programme, 2022). Also, a large part of such activities happens in the Global South. In a sense, the informal sector serves as a safety net for people who do not have access to formal employment and social security. Despite its role in providing livelihoods for a large portion of the population, employment in the informal sector is often characterized by job insecurity, low wages, and limited access to social protection. In the sense that improved competencies will enhance job security, the situation is the same both in the formal and informal sectors. Given that the majority of the working population is in this sector, it is necessary not only to focus on formal employment, particularly those in export-oriented firms, but also to provide support for the competency development of workers in the informal sector. Chapter 6 of this volume will discuss this issue using our original data from formal and informal sectors in Pakistan and Ghana, which allows us to make rare comparisons of skills development micro-ecologies across these sectors.

Realist-Constructivism considers that the micro-ecologies of competency formation at the firm level cannot be insulated from the influence of the generative mechanisms surrounding them. The subjective motivations of individuals to develop one kind of skill over another, the types of training opportunities provided by employers, and the criteria of promotion are all conditioned by the demands and dynamics of these mechanisms. Based on this understanding, in this section, I focused my discussion on econo-productive mechanisms, one of the three generative mechanisms articulated in Chap. 1. The section confirmed that the influence of econo-productive mechanisms derives from the global, regional, national, and industrial levels. First, I overviewed macroeconomic dynamics, highlighting the relationships with different types of aid-providing agencies and multinational corporations. Reference is also made to the geopolitics caused by the emergence of BRICS and other fast-growing economies from the Global South. I then lowered my gaze to the individuals' labor productivity and employment. Increased labor productivity is essential for both the stable economic development of society and individual employment and livelihood, and competency development is the key prerequisite for these social and personal benefits to be enjoyed. At the same time, the question of 'what competencies should be developed' depends to a large extent on the nature of the labor market (both internal and external). To examine such labor market characteristics, this section introduced some theories that attribute the degree of versatility and specificity of the demanded abilities to state strategies, the nature of firms, and the industry.

Now that we have a general understanding of the elements to be considered to grasp the influence of the econo-productive mechanism on competency development, let us now turn to the structural-regulatory mechanism.

2.3 Structural-Regulatory Mechanism of Workforce Competencies Development

If the labor market were fully open to free competition, supply and demand would naturally be adjusted among educational institutions, employers, and job-seeking individuals. However, as we have seen in the previous section, information asymmetries exist in various parts of the labor market. Therefore, if the supply-demand matching is left entirely to the market mechanism, the investments in human capital development, both by the individuals and the government, may be wasted without being converted to the intended economic growth outcomes. Here emerges the idea that the government should coordinate industrial human resources development to make it work. In other words, it is a welfare state model in that the government proactively plays its role of designing and supervising the regulations, finance, and incentives for the private sector initiatives in human resource development to correct the glitches in the supposedly free and open market.

While it is not just developing country governments that look to models and experiences from elsewhere when they reform their policies and institutions, a peculiarity of developing countries is their oft-heavy reliance on external funding and technical assistance. This resource dependence contributes to the convergence of structural-regulatory mechanisms of countries along the global trend by adopting prescriptions and guidance offered by donor agencies. Therefore, the package of welfare state measures on industrial human resources development is found to be pretty identical in many developing countries. In this sense, the structural-regulatory mechanism in this field is driven more by the global structure of development governance than by the economic, industrial, and labor issues of particular societies. Of course, it is the respective national governments who adapt the popular models by choosing and repackaging specific tools and ingredients from the standardized recipe. Still, there is less room for local variations in the structural-regulatory mechanism than in the econo-productive one.

Based on this understanding, in this section, I will first provide an overview of how the global trends evolved regarding government-led approaches to promoting industrial human resources development. It will then be followed by an exploration of policy measures and methods that constitute the recent model of competency-based training (CBT) and the logic of neoliberalist public management at its basis.

2.3.1 Global Trends in Industrial Skills Development Policies

From the 1950s to the mid-1970s, international development partners heavily promoted Technical and Vocational Education and Training (TVET) to develop human resources in newly independent Global South states. For instance, during 1963–1976, secondary-level TVET received the largest share (23%) of the World Bank's education loans, and TVET overall, including tertiary and nonformal education, garnered more funding (51%) than general education (Jones, 2002). Despite its promising post-WWII beginnings, TVET has been criticized for failing to develop human resources effectively and perpetuating social and economic inequalities by channeling students into disparate and unequal tracks.

In regions where the education system expanded rapidly, schooling is often seen as a pathway to formal sector white-collar jobs (cf. Foster, 1965). Consequently, TVET is perceived as a lesser educational path, which deters good students and their parents (Ozer & Perc, 2020) and leads to poor labor market evaluations (Oproiu & Lițoiu, 2019). These societal perceptions partly explain TVET's limited success. Also, maintaining TVET institutions and updating their facilities to align with workforce demands is costly, raising concerns about the return on investment (Lauglo, 2010; Psacharopoulos, 1993). Another challenge often pointed out by critics is the smooth transition of TVET graduates to the workforce (Faul et al., 2023; UNICEF, 2019), which hinges on both curricular relevance to evolving demands for skills and the alignment between graduates and job opportunities.

As I have commented already, these criticisms against TVET are based on institutionalism, which takes it for granted that the intervention to improve the abilities of industrial human resources should be pre-employment school-based education. Either because the perception that the TVET is an inferior track of education is prevalent or the transition from TVET to work is not smooth, this track of schooling has been criticized for its cost inefficiency and irrelevance, and its institutional failure has often been discussed as if the whole idea of industrial human resources development was problematic.

Because of these negative comments and the lack of clearly successful outputs from the investment in TVET, the priority of international development agencies shifted to basic (primary and lower secondary) education after the 1990s, and international aid to TVET entered a long period of decline. It was only in the 2010s that the attention of policymakers returned to the TVET. As a result of a massive expansion of basic education with focused public investments, a new challenge emerged to provide places for basic school leavers either in the labor market or in school, while youth unemployment rates became high in many countries. That was the background of renewed attention to the TVET.

Whether emphasizing primary education or TVET and higher education, policy priorities shift like a pendulum. The contrast between these two positions can be attributed to the conceived role of government; the former is based on the conception of a distributive welfare state, while the latter is that of a coordinative state. In the following, I will provide an overview of these two state models underlying the policy decisions on human resources development. While they are explained in chronological order, it does not mean that the debate since the 2000s is more advanced than that of the 1990s, as policy has always shifted back and forth between the two models.

2.3.1.1 Distributive and Coordinative Welfare State Models

The Millennium Development Goals (MDGs), adopted by over 200 governments and international organizations in 2000, exemplified a global commitment to poverty reduction, which intends to promote social development in a bottom-up manner. To realize equitable access to basic services, which directly serve to improve the lives of the underprivileged, basic education was brought to the fore together with primary health care.

Following this global focus on basic education, many developing countries adopted *distributive welfare policies*. Basic schools were constructed across the world, and crash courses to certify more teachers were offered to ensure universal access to education. School fees were abolished, as they had excluded the underprivileged population from schooling. All of these were done directly by the government with public funds and personnel.

As I stated above, after a couple of decades of such practices, countries started to experience the backfire of the increased number of school leavers who cannot either go to secondary school or be absorbed in the labor market. Compounding this challenge was the issue of the relevance of school-taught knowledge in a rapidly changing global economy characterized by the rise of information technology and evolving industrial structures. Against this backdrop, in many developing countries, the MDGs' distributive welfare state approach, focused on poverty reduction, began to shift in the mid-2000s. More countries started prioritizing "growth" in their national development plans—a focus that was less prevalent during the MDGs' peak.

In terms of industrial human resources development, two new trends emerged: a focus on fostering problem-solving skills in twenty-first-century learners (Griffin et al., 2012; Yamada, 2016) and increased attention to workplace learning (Mulder & Gulikers, 2011). International aid agencies started to promote activities to intervene in industrial human resources development, driven by labor market analysis, to address unemployment or to boost entrepreneurship.

This led to the emergence of the *coordinative welfare state model*, where the government's role is to facilitate and coordinate rather than directly provide services, thereby harnessing the strengths of private and nongovernmental sectors. This model is based on neoliberal public management, keeping direct government intervention minimal and supporting market-based solutions, contrasting with the distributive model in which the government directly provides services to ensure universal rights. Under this model, the scope of industrial human resources development is expanded beyond traditional TVET institutions to include nonformal education, in-firm training, on-the-job training, and apprenticeships. Unlike earlier policies that predominantly focused on a mid- to high-skilled workforce, these reforms also aim to improve the abilities of informal sector workers and those with limited training, recognizing competency development as an investment in both industrial growth and poverty reduction.

Another characteristic of the coordinative welfare reform of the industrial human resources development system is the emphasis on collaboration between the public and private sectors. To make this happen, many governments adopted the Skills Development Act and set the legal framework, mandating that a portion of corporate taxes be earmarked as a skills development fund, which will then be used for incentivizing companies and educational institutions to commit to training the industrial workforce. Altogether, these measures are intended to create a competitive training market that enhances service quality and reduces the financial burden on governments to fund public TVET institutions solely (Johanson, 2009; Patrinos & Sosale, 2007).

In pursuit of these goals, many countries have established coordinating bodies to mediate between diverse stakeholders involved in industrial human resources development. These bodies are also tasked with leading fundamental curriculum reforms to align education with labor market needs. Through a collective process of developing the assessment framework of job-related competencies, the criteria for certifying individuals' abilities and accrediting TVET institutions are also developed in line with the agreed framework. Altogether, these reforms are known as *competency-based training* (CBT), as they focus on developing workplace competencies matching the supply and demand in the labor market.

2.3.1.2 Measures and Approaches of Competency-Based Training

Table 2.1 summarizes the activities widely recommended to the government under the recent coordinative welfare state model, accompanied by the suggested roles of employers, education and training providers, and individuals, organized by the objectives and actors involved in the activities. To organize scattered practices, I classified them into four categories: (1) enhanced coordination and collaboration among actors, (2) resource utilization for improved effectiveness of the skills development system, (3) formation of a quality skilled workforce, and (4) promotion of employment.

Enhanced Coordination and Collaboration Among Actors

One of the key measures of the coordinative competency-based human resources development system is to establish an independent coordinating body that is not affiliated with any particular ministry. This entity is expected to mediate between the demand for the workforce abilities from industry and the provision of education; between ministries and other governmental offices with different mandates and perspectives involved in industrial human resources development; to provide funding for the system to operate; and to be responsible for standardizing qualifications and accreditation. It is expected to be pivotal to almost all aspects of the system, which is too demanding to be functional in many cases.

This method of multi-faceted coordination has been introduced to overcome the limitations of the two types of divide: one is that between the public and the private sectors, and another is that among sub-governments that touch on the broad field of industrial human resources development, such as ministries of education, labor, industry, and welfare.

As a prerequisite for the establishment of such a coordinating body, the government was also supposed to pass a law regulating the entire

Table 2.1 Types of intervention to promote skills development and the expected role of stakeholders

Objective	Intervention	Role of government	Role of employers	Role of training institutions	Role of learners/ workers
1. Enhanced coordination and collaboration among actors	*Encourage public-private partnerships (PPPs)* to fill the supply-demand gaps	• Establish a *skills development coordination agency* involving multiple government bodies, industries, and training institutions	• Enhance partnerships for various forms of skills development, such as in-firm training, apprenticeship, and public and private TVET • Modernize the apprenticeship system • Bridge the training gaps between formal and informal sectors		
2. Resource utilization for improved effectiveness of the skills development system	Establish a *financial incentive mechanism* to vitalize the training market	• Introduce a levy for skills development • Establish skills development funds • Provide subsidies for companies and training institutions • Offer scholarships for students	• Provide opportunities for skills development, both on and off-site, for employees utilizing the subsidies and loans from the government (for SMEs) • Provide matching funds to accompany government subsidies (for large firms)	• Receive trainees from companies	• Pay tuition for training • Acquire suitable training opportunities using vouchers and other government services • Demand loans and scholarships for continuous learning
3. Formation of a quality skilled workforce	*Offer skills assessment and certification* based on the problem-solving skills required in the world of work	• Establish occupation standards for respective industries and levels of skills • Establish a mechanism to accredit training providers who follow the occupation standards	• Provide input on the needs of employers during the development of occupation standards • Participate as examiners in skills assessments following the occupation standards	• Provide education and training in line with occupation standards • Achieve accreditation from the government for following occupation standards (accredited institutions will have a chance of subsidies)	• Provide education and training in line with occupation standards • Achieve accreditation from the government for following occupation standards (accredited institutions will have a chance of subsidies)

(continued)

Table 2.1 (continued)

Objective	Intervention	Role of government	Role of employers	Role of training institutions	Role of learners/ workers
	Strengthen *practical training*	• Match TVET interns with companies through the skills development coordination agency	• Accept interns (practical trainees) from TVET	• Find companies and workshops at which students can intern • Improve conditions for in-school practical training • Train teachers to catch up with the latest techniques in industries	• Participate in practical training
	Offer public TVET education to *fill the gap* if private TVET and employers do not offer enough training[a]	• Direct management of the public TVET	• Increase open recruitment (reduce closed recruitment)	• Make student and graduate information available to recruiters	• Be proactive in job searches
4. Promotion of employment	*Match recruiters* and job searchers	• Establish an employment agency	• Increase open recruitment (reduce closed recruitment)	• Make student and graduate information available to recruiters	• Be proactive in job searches

Note: Produced by the author based on the review of policy-related materials from international development partners and national governments
[a] Direct provision of TVET is the last resort (minor role of the government)

industrial human resources development system. For example, the Skills Development Act was adopted in South Africa in 1998, and the COTVET (Council for TVET) Act in Ghana in 2006. The contents of the law include specifications for not only the establishment of the coordination body but also the instruments it will oversee, such as levies earmarked for skills development funds, national occupation standards, and a skills qualification framework.

Resource Utilization for Improved Effectiveness of the Skills Development System

In many countries, the lack of an independent budget to fulfill a wide variety of tasks became a significant cause of the malfunctioning of the coordinating bodies, which also meant the de facto failure of the entire human resources development system. Given such experiences, in recent years, international development partners often suggest that governments secure funds that enable the coordinating agency to subsidize training providers and employers. The agency also needs resources to conduct research to develop a national qualifications framework or to hire graders for skills examinations according to the qualification criteria. Flexible funds are also necessary for nonconventional support for workers and small-scale employers. Examples include training for informal workers who need to upskill, and vouchers or study loans for those who cannot afford to pay for their own education or training. Related to this would be financial arrangements to encourage employers to upskill their employees, such as tax exemptions or subsidies for companies that provide training to their employees (Johanson, 2002).

While there are different means to generate funds for these activities, such as donors' assistance or allocation from the ministerial budgets, the most common approach is to institutionalize a levy for skills development, which would be, in many cases, funded by a specific percentage of the total payroll of private companies. Among the four countries we studied, the skills development fund in South Africa is generated through the levy, constituting the budget of 21 Sector Education Training Authorities (SETAs), which I will discuss in more detail in the next section.

Formulating a Skilled Workforce with Better Quality

Skills Assessment and Granting of Qualifications

While coordinating agencies and funding are essential, the ultimate goal in creating these mechanisms is to enable the individual workers to develop their skills more effectively. The industrial skills development systems currently in place in many countries are based on the idea that the system design should start with studying competencies used and required in the actual workplace to solve problems. Then, education and training programs should be envisioned backward from diagnosing the demands in the context.

According to this approach, there should be an objective framework for recognizing the level of competence of people who have studied in different places and by different modes. Even knowledge and skills acquired through apprenticeships or in-firm training should be officially recognized if the holders of such knowledge can pass an assessment in line with this qualification framework.

A unified system of competency-based qualifications, which clearly identifies the type of skills a person has, is supposed to make matching the demand and supply of skills easier. As with individuals' abilities, educational institutions' capacities for providing relevant and quality training should also be evaluated properly. For this purpose, the skills standard and qualification framework are used, rather than evaluating them by the size of inputs or the number of graduates (Castro, 1995). However, a pitfall to this approach is that it is a very demanding task to establish qualification requirements and their measurement criteria for all industries at all levels of competencies, involving both education providers and the industry. For example, South Africa, the first country on the African continent to introduce comprehensive reform of this sort, had more than 10,000 occupational standards as of 2007, a decade after its inception, but according to Allais (2007), less than 10% were based on the skills certification system that had been enacted. It is also not unusual for public TVET institutions to continue to provide education programs based on conventional curricula instead of reconstructing the programs according to new qualification frameworks. In this sense, significant gaps often exist between the structural-regulatory mechanism and operation.

Strengthening Practical Training

In discussing the relevant skills for problem-solving in the work environment, the concept of CBT naturally leads to the view that the content of education and training programs must be practical. The implications of being "practical" may differ according to the types of work. For example, for salespeople, it may mean applying interpersonal skills to customer relationships, while for technicians and artisans in manufacturing, it may mean applying theoretical knowledge about their field of specialization to production.

One of the reasons why pre-employment training at TVET institutions has been criticized for being inappropriate is because it spends a great deal of curricular time teaching theories in the classroom but rarely provides practical training. Because of the required size of investment in machinery and the fast pace of technological changes in the industry, it is difficult for TVET programs, particularly those in manufacturing-related technical sectors, to keep up with the latest technological demands. This is the case even if the schools had initial instalment of the latest equipment and facilities and were backed by a strong political will of the government.

In addition, many TVET teachers are trained to be teachers but have never worked in the industry, so they are often not familiar with the technological demands of the industry. This is why many countries encourage a dual system, whereby internships at companies are included as part of the curriculum, together with on-campus learning. The effectiveness of this dual system has been widely publicized by aid agencies and developing-country governments, and in many national education systems, a significant proportion of the curricular time in TVET schools is now allocated to practical training.

In Ethiopia, a rather extreme policy is being promoted, whereby 70% of the credits required to graduate from secondary-level TVET institutions must be earned through practical training.

The problem is that regardless of the policy enactment, the close collaboration between industry and academia needed to implement it has not been formed satisfactorily (Yamada et al., 2018). To overcome this situation, it is said that public-private partnerships (PPPs) are important not only at the national level but also at the local level.

Operating Public TVET Institutions

The fact that market forces do not work well on public TVET institutions means that they should not be the priority in coordinative welfare state policies but rather supplementary to the training provided by private actors, limited to areas where private actors do not step in.

Nevertheless, due to the history of government-led TVET development, a significant number of teachers and students belong to public TVET institutions in many countries. In addition, when the coordinating bodies for industrial human resources development seek to mediate the supply and demand sides, more often than not, the public TVET institutions are the ones representing the supply side. This is partly because information about private TVET institutions and firm-based training is not readily available and changes frequently. Therefore, it is difficult for the government to know details about training practiced outside of public TVET institutions. In other words, while claiming to create a diverse and dynamic market, the government often has little understanding of what it is trying to coordinate. As a result, ironically, it first involves public TVET institutions, which are least responsive to the changes in the market.

Despite the popular claim that the role of public TVET institutions should remain complementary, I see it necessary to reevaluate their role in fulfilling the human resource needs of small and medium enterprises (SMEs). It is not easy to endogenize a skills development program unless a firm is beyond a certain size. Therefore, in many developing countries, the highest demand for graduates of TVET institutions comes from local SMEs rather than from large MNCs (Yamada & Otchia, 2020). Since they do not have the capacity to train people from scratch, they try to find suitable employee candidates from the pool of people who have already acquired generic skills at pre-employment TVET institutions. Nevertheless, the large supply-demand gap between TVET institutions and employers is causing frustration for SME managers, too. Therefore, aside from some workplace-specific skills, ways to strengthen and utilize TVET will have to be explored.

Promotion of Employment

No matter how well we train people to meet industry demands, the supply-demand gaps will not be filled unless job seekers encounter the appropriate job offerers. In most developing countries, there is no such thing as a job fair or a list of job openings compiled by a job-matching company or agency like those often found in developed countries. In this situation, matching still relies on word of mouth, leading to inequality of opportunity. As a countermeasure, the government may set up job placement agencies. In addition, SMEs often employ interns from TVET institutions after their graduation. SME managers use internships as an opportunity to observe the competence of TVET students on the job so that they can confidently make a judgment about whether to employ them or not. Therefore, good coordination between TVET institutions and SME employers would enhance the effectiveness of skills development programs and the graduates' chances of employment.

Unlike the distributive welfare state model and earlier discussion about TVET, recent policies on industrial human resources development promote the idea that direct provision of technical and vocational education in governmental schools is the last resort only when there are no private schools and workplace-based education does not provide education which meets the labor market demands. Therefore, theoretically, the coordinative welfare state model is supposed to overcome the institutionalist limitations in industrial human resources development. As I have explained with examples from different countries, the realities are not as simple and straightforward as the model is assumed to be. Oftentimes, we observe situations where the structural-regulatory mechanisms remain unchanged in their fundamental nature, and still, a large part of their activities happen in TVET institutions with conventional curricula. One of the reasons for this aversion to change is that governments, educational institutions, and their staff do not really want reforms that require fundamental changes to the way they have been accustomed to and the expertise they have acquired there. Listening to industry people and changing the curriculum and content of education accordingly means restructuring the traditional curriculum from the outside in, which was built up according to the logical sequence of curricular experts. This is a change that not only calls for a fundamental shift in the mindsets of educators, but also, if taken seriously, will affect the way education administration and school management are run. Most countries do not have the political will or resources to go that far, and thus, reforms tend to remain a formality. Governmental policies and systems on skills development are closely related to the individuals' skills acquisition and stakeholders' expectations about skills. In this sense, the influence of structural-regulatory mechanisms on micro-ecologies is significant. The structural-regulatory implications will be discussed in various parts from Chap. 4 onward. In particular, Chap. 5 will highlight them closely in relation to the dynamism among TVET teachers, students, employers, and employees.

2.4 Econo-productive and Structural-Regulatory Conditions of Four Case Countries

In the last part of this chapter, based on what I have described regarding two types of generative mechanisms in global and general terms, I will provide the landscape of the mechanisms surrounding the micro-ecologies in four countries we studied, three in Sub-Saharan Africa and one in South Asia, namely Ethiopia, Ghana, South Africa, and Pakistan. In all of these countries, we focused on workers, employers, and trainers in the same industrial sector: garment production. The reason for focusing on garment production is that it is a labor-intensive industry that hires many working-age people in the Global South. Not only does it employ many relatively low-skilled young workers, but it is also the typical start-up export-oriented manufacturing industry for countries that aim to be competitive in the global value chain. Moreover, it employs predominantly females, who are more vulnerable but whose labor conditions and abilities are less studied than those of their male counterparts. Within the garment production industry, we recruited participants from export-oriented large companies, SMEs selling products mostly to the domestic markets, and small workshops in the informal sector. Therefore, we will be able to examine the different conditions and demands according to the targeted markets and customers, even within the same industry and in the same national economy.

It was around 2014 that our team started its investigation of workforce competencies in Ethiopia. We considered generating more accurate evidence on the skills gap than was available back then, largely driven by the keen interest of the policymakers and company managers whom we met. Earlier in Kumasi, Ghana, I started a survey on the determinants of career choices made by learners in the different tracks of skills development (Yamada, 2017, 2021; the publication was later, but the survey was conducted in 2012–2013). Putting aside the fact that I have years of research experience at both sites, it seemed meaningful to compare situations in two countries in sub-Saharan Africa that adopted the CBT reform on a massive scale in an interval of about a decade; Ghana started it in the 2000s and Ethiopia in the 2010s.

Later in 2018, we added South Africa to our scope of research. In sub-Saharan Africa, South Africa was the first country to introduce the CBT-based skills development system. The ANC (African National Congress) government, which ended apartheid, pushed forward the measures to promote equitable opportunities. As education segregated by race was a symbol of structural discrimination, it was rushed to break down the barrier not only within the education system but also in the labor market after schooling. Competency-based evaluation of people, not by school credentials, was, in the socio-political context of South Africa, of unique value. The Skills Development Act was therefore adopted in 1998, just 4 years after the ANC government came to power. Considering this historical root, the detailed and full-fledged reform the government has gone through for decades, regardless of a lot of challenges and flaws, and accumulated research and operational experiences in this country, it was natural to add South Africa to this cross-country comparative study of work-related competency development in Africa.

Not only in terms of the structural-regulatory mechanisms of workforce competency development, which are driven by the common global trend of CBT, introduced in different periods, but also in terms of the econo-productive mechanisms, the three African countries provide interesting contrasts. As I will discuss soon based on Table 2.2, Ethiopia is a rapidly growing economy, Ghana is a long-time lower-middle income country but is gradually improving with the discovery of oil mines from the beginning of the 2010s, and South Africa has led the regional economy of southern and eastern Africa for decades, but in the middle-income trap with serious unemployment problems.

In addition to these three countries in sub-Saharan Africa and with similar structural-regulatory mechanisms, in 2023, we conducted a survey using the same assessment module in Pakistan. We would not have extended to South Asia unless we were invited. On this matter, we would like to express our gratitude to the Human Development Department of Japan International Cooperation Agency and the Punjab state government. Their request to our team was to identify the training needs of women, both in formal and informal sector employment, in the garment production industry. Given the gendered nature of this industry, it has been our motivation to contribute through the competency assessment to improve the abilities and conditions of female workers, although we did not always make this motivation overt. Therefore, despite it being on a different continent from other cases we studied, we decided to include Pakistan, specifically the Punjab state, in our study. The sociocultural peculiarities of traditional Muslim communities in South Asia added depth to our comparative analysis. Chapter 6 provides a cross-continental comparison of sociocultural and econo-productive mechanisms between Ghana and Pakistan, which is a unique contribution of this volume, particularly as we compared formal and informal sector workers cross-sectionally.

We do not claim our survey participants have representativeness of the garment production industry in the Global South. Regardless, through standardized measurement, we will try to illuminate commonalities across the contexts, which are likely to be found in other micro-ecologies in the Global South, while demonstrating peculiarities.

2.4.1 Comparison of Four Countries by Indicators

In the following sections, I will quickly review the characteristics of four countries according to the development indicators accumulated by the international organizations. Although these indicators do not necessarily capture the realities on

Table 2.2 Indicators of economics, production, employment, and education of the four case countries for the years 2005, 2015, and 2023 (World Bank, 2024)

Indicator	Country	2023	2015	2005
GDP[a]	Ethiopia	112.65	64.59	23.70
	Ghana	70.51	49.41	25.65
	South Africa	362.88	346.71	267.55
	Pakistan	400.17	299.96	210.76
GDP growth[b]	Ethiopia	6.50	10.39	11.82
	Ghana	2.94	2.12	5.90
	South Africa	0.60	1.32	5.28
	Pakistan	0.00	4.22	7.28
Manufacturing, value added[c]	Ethiopia	6.95	18.22	13.03
	Ghana	0.94	3.66	
	South Africa	0.45	–0.19	6.20
	Pakistan	–5.29	4.12	15.73
GDP per person employed[d]	Ethiopia	5949	4369	2262
	Ghana	15,994	14,125	9052
	South Africa	47,905	46,237	38,829
	Pakistan	17,634	15,487	13,785
Unemployment rate[e]	Ethiopia	3.50	2.45	2.50
	Ghana	3.08	6.81	5.82
	South Africa	27.99	22.87	19.56
	Pakistan	5.50	3.57	0.58
Youth unemployment[f]	Ethiopia	5.58	3.83	3.58
	Ghana	5.50	14.27	10.54
	South Africa	49.14	41.99	36.20
	Pakistan	9.65	6.68	0.94
School enrollment, secondary[g]	Ethiopia		34.87	23.44
	Ghana		67.10	37.71
	South Africa		110.17	78.05
	Pakistan		35.17	22.81
School enrollment, tertiary[g]	Ethiopia		9.28	2.85
	Ghana		15.73	5.07
	South Africa		18.86	
	Pakistan		8.61	4.38

[a] Constant 2015 USD
[b] Annual %
[c] % of GDP
[d] Constant 2021 PPP USD
[e] %; ILO estimate
[f] % of total labor force ages 15–24; ILO estimate
[g] % gross

the ground, they are still useful for gaining rough pictures of respective societies in comparison to each other.

Ethiopia has demonstrated a two-digit annual GDP growth rate throughout the 2000s and 2010s (11.82 in 2005 and 10.39 in 2015 in Table 2.2). Although the pace of growth was slowed by the domestic political turmoil and the COVID-19 pandemic, its aspiration to grow fast and join the camp of global diplomatic influencers[5] is a unique background to understand the context of workforce competency formation in its key industry: garment production. GDP has tripled from US $23.7 billion in 2005 (2015 constant) to 112.65 billion in 2023. Labor productivity (represented

[5] Ethiopia became a BRICS Summit member in 2014, as explained in footnote 1.

by GDP per person employed) has also improved by 2.6 times from US $2262 in 2005 (2015 constant) to US $5949 in 2023. However, the contribution of manufacturing to the national economy has not increased, and the economy is still largely dependent on less-value-added agriculture. Regardless of the fast macroeconomic catch-up, there are wide disparities in income and the diffusion of school education and other social services.

In the case of Ghana, although the changes were not as dramatic as in Ethiopia, its economy started to move upward, boosted by the oil processing that started in the early 2010s. Therefore, GDP increased from US $25.65 billion in 2005 (2015 constant) to US $70.51 billion in 2023. Being lower-middle income for years, it accumulated the infrastructure and basis of value-added manufacturing, constituting 11.23% of GDP in 2023, more than twice that of Ethiopia (4.48% in 2023). The labor productivity of Ghana (US $15,994 in 2023) is 2.7 times higher than that of Ethiopia (US $5940). Unemployment rates, both for the total workforce and for youths, have been reducing in tandem with the economic recovery since the 2010s. While the secondary school enrolment rate has been around 30% for years, it became 67.10% in 2015. Accordingly, the higher education enrolment rate also rose to 15.73%.

Despite being a member of the BRICS and an upper-middle-income country for many years, South Africa's economy has stagnated, and its employment prospects are exceptionally poor. The annual growth rate is declining (0.6% in 2023), despite the size of the economy being higher than that of Ethiopia and Ghana (US $362.88 billion in 2023). GDP per worker (labor productivity) is much higher than in other countries (US $47,905 in 2023) but has improved only slightly over the past decade. Youth unemployment is close to 50%, indicating that even though the privileged employed earn more than youths in other countries, many of their peers are left without a livelihood.

A stagnated middle-sized economy also characterizes Pakistan, which has not experienced much growth for two decades. Unemployment rates may not be as alarmingly high as in South Africa (5.5% for the total workforce and 9.65% for youths in 2013), but they are increasing gradually. Value-added manufacturing has not increased. Rather, taking into account the change in currency value, it has declined (–5.29% growth in 2023).

These indicators are good entry points for us to try to understand situations in these countries but are not enough to know their causes and effects on the labor market, employment and lives of individuals, and their relation to the industrial human resources development policies and systems. There is also no indicator about the textile and garment industry on which our study is focused. Thus, in the following, I will briefly describe the characteristics of econo-productive and structural-regulatory mechanisms on industrial human resources development in four countries.

2.4.2 Ethiopia

2.4.2.1 Macroeconomic Outlook and Labor Market

Driven by an intensive public infrastructure program as well as strong service and agriculture sectors, Ethiopia has achieved one of the fastest economic expansions in sub-Saharan Africa, averaging 10.9% per year between 2004 and 2014 (World Bank, 2015). Although the pace of growth slowed, particularly after the political unrest in the north and the COVID-19 pandemic, as of 2023, Ethiopia's GDP growth was reported at 7.2%, with the IMF estimating a slightly lower growth rate of 6.1% (United Nations Development Programme, 2024). This growth was largely driven by the services sector, which now accounts for 40% of GDP. Agriculture remains a significant sector, contributing 32% to GDP, while industry, which includes manufacturing, has grown but still faces challenges, comprising around 28% of GDP. Inflation, while lower than in previous years, remains high at 28.7% in late 2023, down from 34.2% earlier in the year (AfDB, 2024).

In terms of labor market conditions, unemployment remains a persistent issue, particularly for the youth in urban areas. The unemployment rate for persons aged 15–29 in urban areas was 27.2%, higher than the general unemployment rate (18.9 %). Addis Ababa, the capital city, demonstrated the highest youth unemployment rate of 30.0%. The unemployment rate of female youth in urban areas of Ethiopia was two times higher than that of their male counterparts in 2022, at 35%, against 17.2% for males (Ethiopia Statistical Service, 2022). Despite high economic growth, youth unemployment has remained high for a long time, indicating the mismatch between education and the labor market demand.

2.4.2.2 Textile and Garment Industry and Skills Demands

Ethiopia has a long history of manufacturing textiles since the first integrated textile mill factory was established in 1939 in Dire Dawa city. The Ethiopian government considers the textile and garment sector a vital pillar for its ambitious economic industrialization strategy. This is evidenced by the government's rapid expansion of industrial parks to attract foreign investment in the textile and garment industries.

The textile and garment sector has emerged as one of the most significant contributors to value-added manufacturing production and employment (Chang et al., 2016). Staritz et al. (2016) reported an impressive textile export share advancement from US $9 to US $68 million within the 5 years from 2009 to 2014. In 2021, the overall export earnings of the textile and garment manufacturing industry were US $181.4 million, accounting for 46.5% of the total manufacturing sector earnings and 0.6% of the total GDP (Ethiopian Monitor, 2022). According to the Central Statistical Agency of Ethiopia (2018), the textile and garment sector employed around 51,000 workers in 2017.

The garment export from Ethiopia has benefited from the special arrangement of U.S. tariff reduction stipulated in the African Growth and Opportunity Act (AGOA), similar to many other African countries that have attracted multinational corporations in this industry to export products to the North American market at low cost. Ethiopia graduated from AGOA support in 2022, which is considered a significant change in external conditions that could potentially suppress the export capacity of this country.

2.4.2.3 TVET System

The large-scale CBT-based reform of the industrial human resources development system was started in the early 2010s. Education Sector Development Program IV (ESDP VI) emphasized that the outcomes of competency-based TVET were to be assessed based on the occupational standards, which are composed of "units of competence" set for respective levels of qualification from production to management levels (Federal TVET Agency of Ethiopia, 2010; Government of Ethiopia, 2010). Another characteristic of CBT is its emphasis on practical training. Accordingly, in Ethiopia, on-the-job training offered to private sector companies[6] is made obligatory for the TVET diploma.

The number of teachers and students in TVET programs has increased at an annual rate of around 30% since the mid-1990s, having climbed from 106,336 in 2005/06 to 308,501 in 2009/10 and 300,000 by 2017 (Abebe & Tekleselassi, 2022; Krishnan & Shaorshadze, 2013). TVET enrolment has slowed down in recent years, but the share of female students has continued to increase, constituting more than 50% since 2011/12. In tandem with the industrial policy of prioritizing the textile and garment industry, TVET institutions have assigned the largest number of teachers and students to textile-related programs.

Regardless of this emphasis on TVET, the unemployment rate remains high, particularly among TVET graduates. Textile engineering is one of the areas in which more than half of graduates remain unemployed, together with woodworking and carpentry, weaving, and plumbing (Central Statistical Agency of Ethiopia, 2014). Some analysts argue that one of the causes of the

[6]This type of practical training is introduced in many countries under different names. In Ethiopia, it is called cooperative training, in Ghana, industrial attachment, and in South Africa, there are learnerships, apprenticeships and internships with different requirements and conditions.

mismatch between training and employers' expectations is the inability of TVET institutes and their curricula to catch up with the fast pace of change in the economic environment and the consequent changes in demanded skills (Wolter & Ryan, 2011). Others point to problems in the assignment system for students entering TVET programs. Krishnan and Shaorshadze (2013) argue, based on their interviews with TVET graduates, that the Ethiopian government is "command-driven" and assigns students to TVET programs proportionally based on its labor development plan, without considering students' own preferences.

There are some flaws in the assumption that CBT is the magic bullet to solve various problems that lead to the supply-demand gaps of work-related competencies. First, CBT brought about parallel certification systems of, on the one hand, completion of designated school programs and, on the other hand, the actual competency to perform tasks in respective industry contexts. Therefore, completion of TVET courses that prepare students for Certificate of Competency (COC) assessment has not produced very positive results, with a passing rate for COC assessments of less than half (Krishnan & Shaorshadze, 2013). If one accepts these results straightforwardly, TVET institutions in Ethiopia fail to produce many competent graduates. Second, although the training is said to be outcome-based, the current assessment system looks at test takers not in the actual work setting but at the assessment center. Also, although problem-solving skills in the actual work setting comprise not only hands-on vocational skills but also other skills discussed in Chap. 1, assessments still focus on hands-on practices. Because they are based on discrete units of vocational skills to be checked, the occupational standards also fail to address the nexus of contextualized skills.

2.4.3 Ghana

2.4.3.1 Macroeconomic Outlook and Labor Market

The commercial production of oil started in 2012, which then boosted the economy of Ghana. Non-oil industries have also contributed to the recent growth. For example, the share of the service sector grew significantly from 28.8% in 2000 to 44.1% in 2019 (World Bank, 2024). Meanwhile, the contribution of the manufacturing industry to the national economy has been limited (9.0–10.4% in the same period). The share of agriculture has decreased significantly from 35.3% in 2000 to 17.3% in 2019.

In 2001, 10% of the labor force was unemployed, and the unemployment rate of youth between 15 and 24 years old was as high as 15.9%. However, both ratios improved to 4.3% and 9.2% by 2019 (World Bank, 2024). At the same time, employment in the manufacturing sector has shrunk from around 10 to 8.1%, in contrast to the service sector, which expanded with the oil boom (Aryeetey et al., 2014).

This fact indicates that the oil exports increased domestic consumption in the short run, but did not strengthen the basis of value-added production, and that the relative contribution of manufacturing to the national income was reduced. It also suggests that the current growth is fragile, depending on the export price of the raw materials. For long-term and stable economic growth, developing mid- to high-level technicians is considered more significant than ever. The data also shows that a substantial part of the workforce in the agriculture sector has shifted to the service sector, but not so much to the manufacturing sector.

2.4.3.2 Textile and Garment Industry and Skills Demands

The garment production industry in Ghana is mostly dominated by the informal sector (Ghana Statistical Service, 2016; JICA, 2008). Entrance into the business is relatively easy and requires little capital and minimal skills (International Labour Organization, 2016). One merely requires a design flair, sewing skills, and a small working capital to start a business in the garment industry. As a result, garment production dominates Ghana's informal manufacturing economy more than any other industry (Quartey, 2006). Hinshaw (2012) indicates that Ghana used to be a global destination for manufacturing clothes but admits that the team of self-taught needleworkers (informal sector small-scale businesses) lacked skills in mass production.

Studies indicate that the garment industry has gradually declined over the past few years. Estimates suggest that, around the 1960s, the sector comprised over 20 large-scale textile factories and employed over 25,000 Ghanaians. Evidence indicates that the garment industry's total output peaked at about 129 million yards in 1977. This declined to 44 million yards by 2009 and 42 million in 2011. Currently, the garment industry has only four large-scale textile factories and employs less than 2500 workers (Bruce-Amartey et al., 2014).

Recently, this industry has seen some signs of revival, facing the prospect of exporting to the United States with the reduced tariff stipulated in the African Growth and Opportunity Act (AGOA). In 2017, the Association of Ghana Apparel Manufacturers (AGAM) was established to promote the export-oriented growth of this industry. Also, the U.S. Agency for International Development (USAID) launched a program to support this industry in the same year. It provided technical and financial support to a company, which created 1100 new jobs there (USAID, 2017). In sum, although the production size is not significant, there is a growing interest in apparel exports. Together with the informal tailors and workshops, it is important to consider the skills demands in this broad industry that is overarching both the informal and formal sectors.

2.4.3.3 TVET System

Ghana has had a relatively higher level of educational achievements among African countries, being an educational center of British West Africa. As of 2005, its gross primary school enrolment rate was as high as 83.4%, which exceeded 100% in the 2010s. Also, the promotion rate of primary school students to junior high school (JHS) is 93.8%, up to which education is compulsory (Ghana Education Service, 2006, 2015). Meanwhile, those absorbed in TVET institutions are only 12%. Then, more than 60% of the remaining JHS leavers will join informal skills training, or stay not in education, employment, or training (NEET). There is no accurate data on other non-schooled youths, but one can assume that they are either in apprenticeship, informal employment, household work, or idle (Government of Ghana, 2014a). According to an estimation, more than 440,000 youths are learning skills in the informal apprenticeship. If this is true, the ratio of apprentices to TVET students is 4:1 (Darvas & Palmer, 2014; Palmer, 2009).

Not only sites of skills development, but also a large part of employment is in the informal sector. According to the 2010 national census, 93% of employment was in the private sector, out of which 86.1% was informal. Thus, the formal private sector employment was only 7% (Ghana Statistical Service, 2010), and most TVET students take industrial attachment, practical training at the workplace required as a part of the TVET diploma (see footnote 3), in the informal sector. Moreover, it is not common for TVET graduates to get formal sector employment immediately after school. To bridge the polarized economy and to widen the basis of formal sector employment, the government expects TVET to play active roles (Government of Ghana, 2014b). In this situation, TVET institutions promote entrepreneurship for students instead of aspiring to be employed by private companies or governmental bodies. There is grant support for those TVET graduates who fulfill certain conditions and open their businesses (Government of Ghana, 2014a).

2.4.4 South Africa

2.4.4.1 Macroeconomic Outlook and Labor Market

Although it has been the economic center of the southeastern part of sub-Saharan Africa and is a part of the BRICS, the South African economy has stagnated for the past decade and continues to face a complex mix of challenges and opportunities. According to the World Bank (2024), the GDP growth rate for 2024 is projected to be 0.9%. While this reflects a slight recovery from earlier contractions, economic growth remains constrained by energy supply issues, high inflation, and political uncertainty. Persistent power outages due to load shedding continue to undermine industrial productivity, while inflation, driven by rising food and fuel prices, continues, though slightly declining from 2023 levels.

On the labor market front, South Africa continues to grapple with high unemployment rates. As of the first quarter of 2024, the unemployment rate was 32.6%, with youth unemployment remaining particularly problematic at over 60% (Trading Economics, 2024). Structural unemployment, a long-standing issue, is exacerbated by a mismatch between the skills of the labor force and the needs of the economy. Sectors like manufacturing and mining have seen declines in job numbers, while services and retail have shown some resilience.

Government interventions, such as the construction of public infrastructure to address the energy crisis, aim to stimulate growth and job creation, but these initiatives face delays. Moreover, the labor market remains heavily impacted by global economic uncertainties and domestic policy inefficiencies, with investors seeking greater policy stability.

2.4.4.2 Textile and Garment Industry and Skills Demands

The textile and garment industry has experienced a dramatic change associated with policies promoting trade liberalization and a more flexible labor market since the end of Apartheid. Changes in policies and global market dynamics caused a shift from predominantly large factories to small and medium-sized ones, mostly located in the Western Cape and KwaZulu-Natal provinces, with some activity taking place in Gauteng province.

The industry is under severe pressure caused by the massive inflow of cheap textiles and clothes, particularly from China, after its accession to the World Trade Organization in 2001. However, the government is playing a crucial role in promoting local production. It introduced the market-neutral Clothing and Textiles Competitiveness Programme (CTCP) in 2009, which contributed to improving the sector's global competitiveness through a range of structured interventions. Overall, there has been a steady growth in real output since 2000. Although exports have been devastated, production in the domestic market is gradually recovering, with an increase of real output of about 14% from R 26.0 billion in 2009 to R 40.7 billion in 2015 (Government of South Africa, 2017).

Despite the sector being affected by the inflow of cheap products, it is still a significant employer in the manufacturing sector. When cheap imports attacked the country's economy, the number of jobs decreased from over 200,000 in 2002 to about 140,000 in 2012. However, recent employment statistics confirm an increase in employment, from 137,816 people in 2014 to 143,719 in 2015 (Department of Trade and Industry, 2016). Textile and garment manufacturing is a labor-absorbing industry in South Africa, and the majority of its employees are female and low-skilled workers (Fiber Processing & Manufacturing Sector Education & Training Authority, 2014).

2.4.4.3 Skills Development in the Garment Industry

In 1998, the Skills Development Act was adopted, ahead of other countries, requiring employers to pay 1% of their labor costs as a skills development levy. This revenue is allocated to SETAs, which are set up in each of the 21 industrial sectors.

SETAs are funded through a skills development levy, which is then reinvested in skills development programs, with a portion allocated to mandatory and discretionary grants for companies that invest in worker training. These grants are crucial for supporting workforce development, especially in sectors facing acute skills shortages, and labor-intensive manufacturing like garment production is considered the key sector for SETA's intervention. SETAs aim to upskill employees and unemployed individuals, ensuring that South Africa's workforce can meet the evolving needs of its economy.

SETAs are expected to work in partnership with representatives of private enterprises, the government, and education and training institutions to conduct skills development programs according to the demand for skills in each sector and to certify workers according to the criteria the SETAs develop. The definition of *competency* to solve problems at work varies according to the sector and the tasks required at different levels of expertise and experience. Despite the considerable size of its budget, the activities of the SETAs were not clearly defined or supervised. As a result, budgetary control became ambiguous, which encouraged a lot of corruption. Facing a situation where large budgets continue to be spent without producing the intended results from interventions, the South African government has now brought SETAs under the direct oversight of the Department of Higher Education and Training (Kraak et al., 2013). This case indicates that coordinating bodies, which are supposed to be independent and autonomous, are at risk of becoming hotbeds of concessions due to their lack of accountability to the government.

2.4.5 Pakistan

2.4.5.1 Textile and Garment Industry and Female Participation in the Labor Market

The garment and textile production sector in Pakistan, which this study focuses on, is a vital component of the country's economy. It contributes nearly a quarter of industrial value-added products and provides employment to about 40% of the industrial workforce. Additionally, this sector occupies an average share of about 60% of national exports (International Finance Cooperation (IFC), 2020). According to the Pakistani government's national development plan titled Pakistan 2025, the country aspires to achieve an inclusive and equitable economy and become an upper-middle-income country by 2025 (Planning Commission Ministry of Planning Development and Reform Government of Pakistan, 2023). Considering that Pakistan is the nineth largest exporter of garments and the fifth largest producer of cotton in the world, there is no doubt that developing this economic sector is crucial for the country to achieve this goal.

Regardless, women's participation in economically productive activities is quite limited in this country. Despite increases in recent years, female labor force participation in Pakistan is 25%, well below rates for countries with similar income levels (Tanaka & Muzones, 2016). While the garment sector employs 40% of the Pakistani workforce as a whole, females occupy only 30% of it (GIZ, 2024). This ratio is extremely low, considering that the garment and textile industry tends to be female-biased, with 60–80% of the global workforce in this sector being women (ILO, 2023). As a means to mitigate the gender disparity in labor force participation, it will be useful to identify and promote enabling factors for female workers in this sector, where there lies high potential with their strengths to perform well. Such an effort would also contribute to pushing up the productivity of this national flagship industry as a whole.

Based on these observations, I will summarize key issues regarding female participation in the labor market, not only in general but more specifically in the garment sector in Punjab, Pakistan. Since skills development is the critical node of individual and industrial development, the chapter also highlights the role of technical and vocational education and training (TVET) in the growth of the garment and textile sector and female empowerment.

2.4.5.2 TVET Policies and Structure in Punjab and Challenges Faced

After the long neglect of TVET's planning and operation since the 1960s, renewed attention has been paid to this training sector in the last 20 years. The National Vocational and Technical Training Commission (NAVTTC) was established in 2005 to regulate and manage the TVET Sector in Pakistan under the Ministry of Federal Education and Professional Training. Also, the National Skills Strategy (NSS) was developed in 2009, the country's first policy specific to the skills sector. Several actions have already been taken on the recommendations contained in the NSS, which include developing the National Vocational Qualification Framework (NVQF), a national qualifications system for teachers, a code of conduct, an accreditation system, a human resources development policy for TVET, skill standards, and curricula in priority areas (NAVTTC, 2024; Shah & Khan, 2017).

According to its Skills Development Sector Plan 2018, the government of Pakistan recognizes that an important factor hampering the animation of the labor market is low skills and the lack of effective training for improving the capacities of the working age population (15–64 years), particularly young adults aged between 15 and 29 (Government of Pakistan, 2018). According to the Labor Market Survey 2013, among working youths (15–29 years old) in the state of Punjab, more than 40% have an education of less than 12 years (44% of males and 47% of females), out of which the population without any schooling occupies a significant proportion (19 and 30% for respective genders) (Pakistan Bureau of Statistics, 2015).

Given this generally low level of access to school, formal and nonformal TVET and on-the-job skills development are of fundamental importance as a path towards developing human capital. Regardless, only 12% of Punjab's working-age population (15–64 years) have received skills training (Pakistan Bureau of Statistics, 2015).

Challenges persist, including a significant gap between skilled labor demand and supply, highlighted by the annual demand for skilled workers far exceeding enrollment in TVET institutions. The number of enrolments in TVET institutions in 2018 was 433,000, which failed to increase in 2022–2023 (Talat, 2023). Efforts to address this gap face hurdles such as inadequate inclusivity, particularly for marginalized groups like women, the poor, and the disabled. Traditional skills, including garment production, often remain undervalued, hindering their formal training integration. Regardless of its importance, training in the garment and textile sector lags behind the need for female upskilling and companies' labor demands.

2.4.5.3 Skills Development as a Means of Women's Empowerment

Gender disparities in Pakistan are pervasive, as highlighted by the country's low rankings on the Global Gender Gap Index (5th from bottom in 2013). Despite comprising half of the working-age population, women's participation in the labor force remains low, with only 22.5% actively engaged. Urban areas exhibit significantly higher rates of female unemployment compared to rural areas, exacerbating gender inequalities. However, there is growing recognition within government and non-government sectors that this issue should be addressed.

TVET is recognized as a crucial tool for reducing unemployment, empowering women, and alleviating poverty. However, gender disparities persist within the sector, with limited enrollment of women in trades such as dressmaking, embroidery, and beauty services. The TVET provision for females faces numerous challenges, including limited capacity, outdated facilities, and less relevant curricula. Additionally, there is a considerable gender wage gap within the sector, further discouraging women from entering the workforce (Rehman, 2020).

2.5 Synthesis

In this chapter, I discussed the challenges and extrinsic mechanisms that shape the ecologies of workforce competency development in the Global South. According to the Realist-Constructivist conceptual model of competency development, I outlined two primary mechanisms: the econo-productive and the structural-regulatory. These mechanisms influence how competencies are developed and sustained within industrial, national, and global contexts.

The econo-productive mechanism involves how macroeconomic dynamics, trade, and labor productivity impact workforce competency development. I highlighted the historical economic marginalization of the Global South. While some countries have seen rapid growth, many of them still struggle with economic dependency, the export of raw materials, and underdeveloped human capital. Workforce competencies are seen as vital for overcoming these challenges, particularly in attracting foreign direct investment and moving toward value-added production. However, political instability, weak infrastructure, and governance issues often hinder progress.

Despite economic growth, labor productivity in the Global South lags behind more industrialized regions. The chapter explored the factors behind these phenomena, such as resource dependency, lack of export diversification, and a race to the bottom in wages, which do not improve labor conditions. After reviewing these restrictive factors, I turned to the importance of decent work and continuous competency development of individual workers to ensure poverty reduction and self-fulfillment.

The structural-regulatory mechanism involves government-led industrial skills development policies, focusing on competency-based training (CBT) and public-private partnerships. Historically, international aid and policies regarding human resources development have shifted between distributive and coordinative welfare state models. The former tends to prioritize egalitarianism and universal access to basic social services, including education, while the latter emphasizes the government's role in regulating private sector initiatives. The recent policy trend is shifting to the latter, namely the coordinative welfare state model, according to which governments often develop independent agencies to mediate the demand and supply of a skilled workforce. To evaluate the value of the workforce according to their competencies, this model requires the whole human resources development system to be reformed according to the national occupation standards developed in partnership between the public and private sectors. Many Global South countries, particularly those heavily reliant on external financial and technical support, adopt these global trends, although there are significant local variations.

Toward the end of the chapter, I introduced four countries where the survey was conducted: Ethiopia, Ghana, South Africa, and Pakistan. I profiled them in terms of their respective macroeconomic performance, labor market, employment, and competency development systems. Particular attention was paid to the textile and garment industry, for whose workforce competencies we conducted a series of surveys presented in this volume. Now that the mechanisms that are likely to affect the interactions and phenomena in micro-ecologies in respective case countries have been examined, we are almost ready to look at the empirical evidence. Before that, the next chapter will explain the concept, design, and uniqueness of our workforce competency assessment and noncognitive skills training program.

References

Abebe, G., & Tekleselassi, T. G. (2022). *National TVET policies and systems in Ethiopia: Opportunities and issues in challenging times*. Retrieved December 10, 2025, from www.ilo.org/publns

African Development Bank (AfDB). (2024). *African economic outlook 2024, Driving Africa's transformation, The reform of the global financial architecture*. Retrieved September 30, 2024, from https://www.afdb.org/en/countries/east-africa/ethiopia/ethiopia-economic-outlook

Allais, S. M. (2007). Understanding the failures of the South African National Qualifications Framework as the driver of educational reform in post-apartheid South Africa. In *UKFIET conference*.

Appelbaum, R. P. (2005). Fighting sweatshops: Problems of enforcing global labor standards. In R. P. Applebaum & W. Robinson (Eds.), *Critical globalization studies* (pp. 369–378). Routledge.

Aryeetey, E., Baah-Boateng, W., Ackah, C. G., Lehrer, K., & Mbiti, I. (2014). Ghana. In H. Hino & G. Ranis (Eds.), *Youth and employment in Sub-Saharan Africa working but poor* (pp. 36–44). Routledge. https://doi.org/10.4324/9780203798935

BADEA—Arab Bank for Economic Development in Africa. (2024). About BADEA. BADEA—rab Bank for Economic Development in Africa.

Barrientos, S., Mayer, F., Pickles, J., & Posthuma, A. (2011). Decent work in global production networks: Framing the policy debate. *International Labour Review, 150*(34), 297–317. https://doi.org/10.1111/j.1564-913X.2011.00118.x

Bruce-Amartey, E. J., Amissah, E. R. K., & Safo-Ankama, K. (2014). The decline of Ghana's textile industry: Its effects on textile education in Ghana. *Arts and Design Studies, 22*, 36–44. www.iiste.org

Castro, C. (1995). *Training policies for the end of the century*. IIEP-UNESCO.

Central Statistical Agency of Ethiopia. (2014). *The 2014 Urban Employment Unemployment Survey: Statistical Bulletin*. Addis Ababa.

Central Statistical Agency of Ethiopia. (2018). *The 2018 urban employment unemployment survey: Statistical bulletin*.

Chang, H.-J., Hauge, J., & Irfan, M. (2016). *Transformative industrial policy for Africa*. Economic Commission for Africa.

Coe, N. M., Dicken, P., & Hess, M. (2008). Global production networks: realizing the potential. *Journal of*

Economic Geography, 8(3), 271–295. https://doi.org/10.1093/jeg/lbn002

Darvas, P., & Palmer, R. (2014). *Demand and supply of skills in Ghana: How can training programs improve employment and productivity?* The World Bank. https://doi.org/10.1596/978-1-4648-0280-5

Deming, D., & Kahn, L. B. (2018). Skill requirements across firms and labor markets: evidence from job postings for professionals. *Journal of Labor Economics, 36*(S1), S337–S369. https://doi.org/10.1086/694106

Department of Trade and Industry. (2016). *Facts and figures on skills in manufacturing information brief no. 4*. Retrieved December 10, 2025, from www.thedti.gov.za

Dicken, P., Kelly, P. F., Olds, K., & Wai-Chung Yeung, H. (2001). Chains and networks, territories and scales: towards a relational framework for analysing the global economy. *Global Networks, 1*(2), 89–112. https://doi.org/10.1111/1471-0374.00007

Doeringer, P. B., & Piore, M. J. (2020). *Internal labor markets and manpower analysis*. Routledge. https://doi.org/10.4324/9781003069720

Economist Intelligence Unit. (2022, October 12). Emerging markets: will the economic catch-up continue? https://www.eiu.com/n/emerging-markets-will-the-economic-catch-up-continue/

Elbadawi, I. (1999). External aid: help or hindrance to export orientation in Africa? *Journal of African Economies, 8*(4), 578–616. https://doi.org/10.1093/jae/8.4.578

Estevez-Abe, M., Iversen, T., & Soskice, D. (2001). Social protection and the formation of skills: A reinterpretation of the welfare state. In P. A. Hall & D. Soskice (Eds.), *Varieties of capitalism* (pp. 145–183). Oxford University Press. https://doi.org/10.1093/0199247757.003.0004

Ethiopia Statistical Service. (2022). *Statistical report on the 2022 2nd round urban employment unemployment survey*.

Ethiopian Monitor. (2022, September 16). Govt targets $250m annual revenue from textile & apparel exports—Ethiopian Monitor. Retrieved August 4, 2023, from https://ethiopianmonitor.com/2022/09/16/govt-targets-250m-annual-revenue-from-textile-apparel-exports/

Eum, W., & Lee, J. (2022). Alternative paths of diversification for developing countries. *Review of Development Economics, 26*(4), 2336–2355. https://doi.org/10.1111/rode.12915

Farndale, E., Paauwe, J., Morris, S. S., Stahl, G. K., Stiles, P., Trevor, J., & Wright, P. M. (2010). Context-bound configurations of corporate HR functions in multinational corporations. *Human Resource Management, 49*(1), 45–66. https://doi.org/10.1002/hrm.20333

Faul, M. V., Baek, C., & Lee, S. (2023). Foreword. In *The education-training-work continuums: Pathways to socio-professional inclusion for youth and adults NORRAG special issue 08* (pp. 3–5). NORRAG.

Federal TVET Agency of Ethiopia. (2010). Ethiopia TVET system. In *PowerPoint presentation, Federal TVET Agency*. Federal TVET Agency of Ethiopia.

Fiber Processing & Manufacturing Sector Education & Training Authority. (2014). *A profile of the clothing, textiles, footwear and leather sub-sectors*. SETA.

Foster, P. J. (1965). The vocational school fallacy in development planning. In C. A. Anderson & M. J. Bowman (Eds.), *Education and economic development* (Vol. 32, pp. 142–166). Aldine.

Freytag, A., & Pehnelt, G. (2009). Debt relief and governance quality in developing countries. *World Development, 37*(1), 62–80. https://doi.org/10.1016/j.worlddev.2008.01.004

Ghana Education Service. (2006). *Report on basic statistics and planning parameters for education in Ghana 2005-6 academic year*.

Ghana Education Service. (2015). *Report on basic statistics and planning parameters for education in Ghana 2014-5 academic year*.

Ghana Statistical Service. (2010). *Population and housing census 2010: Demographic, social, economic and housing characteristics report*.

Ghana Statistical Service. (2016). *Integrated business establishment survey: Summary report*.

GIZ. (2024). *Pakistan: Inspiring change—Women in action in the textile & garment industry of Punjab*. Deutsche Gesellschaft für Internationale Zusammenarbeit. Retrieved April 21, 2024, from https://gender-works.giz.de/competitions2020/pakistan-inspiring-change-women-in-action-in-the-textile-garment-industry-of-punjab/

Government of Ethiopia. (2010). *Education sector development program IV*.

Government of Ghana. (2014a). How to improve, through skills development and job creation, access of Africa's youth to the world of work. In *2014 ministerial conference on youth employment*. Association for the Development of Education in Africa.

Government of Ghana. (2014b). *Ghana shared growth and development agenda (GSGDA) II 2014-7*.

Government of Pakistan. (2018). *Technical and vocational education and training (TVET-2018) policy for Pakistan: Skills for growth & development*.

Government of South Africa. (2017). *Africa (2017). Industrial policy action plan (IPAP) 2017/18 to 2019/20*.

Griffin, P., McGaw, B., & Care, E. (Eds.). (2012). *Assessment and teaching of 21st century skills*. Springer. https://doi.org/10.1007/978-94-007-2324-5

Hall, P. A., & Soskice, D. (2001). An introduction to varieties of capitalism. In P. A. Hall & D. Soskice (Eds.), *Varieties of capitalism* (pp. 1–68). Oxford University Press. https://doi.org/10.1093/0199247757.003.0001

Hinshaw, D. (2012, November 30). Fast-growing label: Made in Ghana—WSJ. *The Wall Street Journal*. Retrieved November 30, 2019, from https://www.wsj.

com/articles/SB10001424052970204707104578092173528533656
Human Resource Development Council of South Africa. (2022). *The human resource development strategy towards 2030*.
International Finance Cooperation (IFC). (2020). *Textile (value addition) sector profile Pakistan*. International Finance Cooperation (IFC). https://invest.gov.pk/sites/default/files/inline-files/Profile%20-%20Textile%20Sector_new.pdf?gtranslate=en
International Labour Organization (ILO). (1998). *ILO declaration on fundamental principles and rights at work*. International Labour Organization. www.ilo.org/publns
International Labour Organization (ILO). (2016). *Key indicators of the labour market* (9th ed.). International Labour Office.
International Labour Organization (ILO). (2023, March). *How to achieve gender equality in global garment supply chains—InfoStories*. InfoStories. Retrieved April 21, 2024, from https://webapps.ilo.org/infostories/en-GB/Stories/discrimination/garment-gender#introduction
Islamic Development Bank (IsDB). (2024). About IsDB. Islamic Development Bank. Retrieved September 20, 2025, from https://isdb-50.org/about/
Japan International Cooperation Agency (JICA). (2008). *The study and promotion and development of local industries in the Republic of Ghana*.
Johanson, R. (2002). *Sub-Sahara Africa: Regional response to bank TVET policy in the 1990s*.
Johanson, R. (2009). *A review of national training funds* (no. 0922).
Jones, P. W. (2002). *World Bank financing of education*. Routledge. https://doi.org/10.4324/9780203222904
Kar, S., & Datta, D. (2015). Asymmetric information in the labor market. In S. Kar & D. Datta (Eds.), *Industrial and labor economics. India studies in business and economics* (127th ed., pp. 39–86). Springer. https://doi.org/10.1007/978-81-322-2017-6_3
Kpognon, K. D., Atangana Ondoa, H., Bah, M., & Asare-Nuamah, P. (2022). Fostering labour productivity growth for productive and decent job creation in sub-Saharan African countries: the role of institutional quality. *Journal of the Knowledge Economy, 13*(3), 1962–1992. https://doi.org/10.1007/s13132-021-00794-x
Kraak, A., Jewison, R., Pillay, P., Chidi, M., Bhagwan, N., & Makgolane, M. (2013). Review of the current skills development system and recommendations towards the best model for delivering skills in the country. *Skills System Review Technical Task of the Human Resource Development Council of South Africa, 24*.
Krishnan, P., & Shaorshadze, I. (2013). *Technical and vocational education and training in Ethiopia*.
Lauder, H., Brown, P., & Ashton, D. (2008). Globalisation, skill formation and the varieties of capitalism approach. *New Political Economy, 13*(1), 19–35. https://doi.org/10.1080/13563460701859678
Lauglo, J. (2010). Revisiting the vocational school fallacy: a tribute to Philip Foster. *Comparative Education, 46*(2), 223–235. https://doi.org/10.1080/03050061003775546
Mania, E., & Rieber, A. (2019). Product export diversification and sustainable economic growth in developing countries. *Structural Change and Economic Dynamics, 51*, 138–151. https://doi.org/10.1016/j.strueco.2019.08.006
McCormick, D. (2008). China & India as Africa's new donors: The impact of aid on development. *Review of African Political Economy, 35*(115). https://doi.org/10.1080/03056240802011501
Mengistu, A. A., & Adhikary, B. K. (2011). Does good governance matter for FDI inflows? Evidence from Asian economies. *Asia Pacific Business Review, 17*(3), 281–299. https://doi.org/10.1080/13602381003755765
Mulder, M., & Gulikers, J. (2011). Workplace learning in East Africa: A case study. In M. Malloch, L. Cairns, K. Evans, & B. N. O'Connor (Eds.), *The Sage handbook of workplace learning* (pp. 307–318). Sage. https://doi.org/10.4135/9781446200940.n22
National Vocational & Technical Training Commission (NAVTTC). (2024). About us. Retrieved September 20, 2024, from https://navttc.gov.pk/overview/
New Development Bank. (2024). About NDB. Retrieved September 20, 2024, from https://www.ndb.int/about-ndb/
Olney, W. W. (2013). A race to the bottom? Employment protection and foreign direct investment. *Journal of International Economics, 91*(2), 191–203. https://doi.org/10.1016/j.jinteco.2013.08.003
Oproiu, G. C., & Lițoiu, N. (2019). The employers' voice: technical and vocational education and training, where to? *Journal of Educational Science and Psychology, 9*(1), 191–203.
Ozer, M., & Perc, M. (2020). Dreams and realities of school tracking and vocational education. *Palgrave Communications, 6*(1), 34. https://doi.org/10.1057/s41599-020-0409-4
Pakistan Bureau of Statistics. (2015). *Labour force survey 2013–14*.
Palmer, R. (2009). Skills development, employment and sustained growth in Ghana: Sustainability challenges. *International Journal of Educational Development, 29*(2), 133–139. https://doi.org/10.1016/j.ijedudev.2008.09.007
Patrinos, H. A., & Sosale, S. (Eds.). (2007). *Mobilizing the private sector for public education*. The World Bank. https://doi.org/10.1596/978-0-8213-7199-2
Planning Commission Ministry of Planning Development and Reform Government of Pakistan. (2023). *Pakistan vision 2025: One nation, one vision*.
Psacharopoulos, G. (1993). *Returns to investment in education: a global update* (no. WPS1067).
Quartey, P. (2006). The textiles and clothing industry in Ghana. In H. Jauch & R. Traub-Merz (Eds.), *The future of textiles and clothing in West Africa*. Friedrich Ebert Stiftung.

Rehman, A. ur. (2020). *Communication and advocacy strategy for gender mainstreaming in TVET in Pakistan*.

Scullion, H., & Starkey, K. (2000). In search of the changing role of the corporate human resource function in the international firm. *The International Journal of Human Resource Management, 11*(6), 1061–1081. https://doi.org/10.1080/09585190050177166

Serneels, P. (2008). Human capital revisited: The role of experience and education when controlling for performance and cognitive skills. *Labour Economics, 15*(6), 1143–1161. https://doi.org/10.1016/j.labeco.2007.10.003

Shah, S. A., & Khan, M. Z. (2017). *Comparative analysis of TVET sector in Pakistan*. National Vocational and Technical Training Commission. http://tvetreform.org.pk/wp-content/uploads/downloads/pse/Comparative Analysis of TVET Sector in Pakistan.pdf

Staritz, C., Plank, L., & Morris, M. (2016). *Global value chains, industrial policy, and sustainable development—Ethiopia's apparel export sector*. Retrieved December 10, 2025, from https://ucrisportal.univie.ac.at/en/publications/global-value-chains-industrial-policy-and-sustainable-development/

Talat, T. (2023, December 5). *Bridging the skill gap: An analysis of Technical and Vocational Education & Training (TVET) Policy 2018*. Institute for Strategic Studies, Research, and Analysis, Government of Pakistan. https://issra.pk/pub/insight/2023/Bridging--the-Skill-Gap/Bridging-the-Skill-Gap.html

Tanaka, S., & Muzones, M. (2016). *Policy brief on female labor force participation in Pakistan*. Retrieved December 10, 2025, from https://www.adb.org/publications/policy-brief-female-labor-force-participation-pakistan

Tchernis, R. (2010). Measuring human capital and its effects on wage growth. *Journal of Economic Surveys, 24*(2), 362–387. https://doi.org/10.1111/j.1467-6419.2009.00617.x

Trading Economics. (2024). South Africa unemployment rate. Retrieved September 30, 2024, from https://tradingeconomics.com/south-africa

Uganda National Planning Authority. (2020). *National Human Resource Development Plan 2020/21–2024/25: "Positioning Uganda's human resources to deliver the industrialization agenda for inclusive growth, employment, and wealth creation"*.

United Nations Children's Fund. (2019). *Transitions from school to work. UNICEF*. ERIC.

United Nations Development Programme. (2022, June 13). Informal economy data explorer. *Informal economy | Data futures exchange*. Retrieved September 26, 2024, from https://data.undp.org/insights/informal-economy

United Nations Development Programme. (2024). *Quarterly economic profile Ethiopia*.

United Nations Population (UNP). (2024). World population prospects 2024. Retrieved September 26, 2024, from https://population.un.org/wpp/

United States Agency for International Development (USAID). (2017). More than 1,100 new jobs, USAID Ghana apparel manufacturing expansion program. Retrieved November 30, 2020, from https://bit.ly/3qaTOGF

Wolter, S. C., & Ryan, P. (2011). Chapter 11—Apprenticeship. In E. A. Hanushek, S. Machin, & L. Woessmann (Eds.), *Handbook of the economics of education* (Vol. 3, pp. 521–576). Elsevier. https://doi.org/10.1016/B978-0-444-53429-3.00011-9

Woods, N. (2008). Whose aid? Whose influence? China, emerging donors and the silent revolution in development assistance. *International Affairs, 84*(6), 1205–1221. https://doi.org/10.1111/j.1468-2346.2008.00765.x

World Bank. (2015). *Ethiopia's great run: The growth acceleration and how to pace it*. The World Bank Group.

World Bank. (2024). *World development indicators | DataBank*. The World Bank Group. Retrieved September 25, 2024, from https://databank.worldbank.org/source/world-development-indicators#

Yamada, S. (2016). Post-EFA global discourse: The process of shaping the shared view of the 'education community'. In *Post-education-for-all and sustainable development paradigm: Structural changes with diversifying actors and norms* (Vol. 29, pp. 67–142). Emerald. https://doi.org/10.1108/S1479-367920140000029014

Yamada, S. (2017). Skills development paths selected by learners. *Journal of African Studies, 2017*(91), 1–16. https://doi.org/10.11619/africa.2017.91_1

Yamada, S. (2021). Traditional apprenticeship as an educational and life experience: Life stories of young auto repair apprentices in Kumasi, Ghana. In Y. Ofosu-Kusi & M. Matsuda (Eds.), *The challenge of African potentials: Conviviality, informality and futurity* (pp. 181–208). Langaa.

Yamada, S., & Ohno, I. (2021). *Industrial skills development in the developing world: Knowledge and skills in the era of SDGs. Tojyokoku no Sangyo-jinzai Ikusei: SDGs Jidai-no Chishiki to Gino*. Nihon Hyoron Sha.

Yamada, S., & Otchia, C. S. (2020). Perception gaps on employable skills between technical and vocational education and training (TVET) teachers and students: the case of the garment sector in Ethiopia. *Higher Education, Skills and Work-Based Learning, 11*(1), 199–213. https://doi.org/10.1108/HESWBL-08-2019-0105

Yamada, S., Otchia, C. S., Shimazu, Y., Taniguchi, K., & Deresse, F. N. (2018). *Bridging the supply-demand gaps of the industrial workforce: Findings from a skills assessment of garment workers in Ethiopia skills and knowledge for youth research project*. https://doi.org/10.13140/RG.2.2.35481.26728

Realist-Constructivist Evaluation of Work-Related Competencies: Skills and Knowledge for Youth (SKY) Project Modules

3

Shoko Yamada

Abstract

This chapter will introduce the methodology we developed to evaluate and cultivate youths' work-related competencies, operationalizing the theoretical framework of Realist-Constructivism. First, the chapter will introduce the module designed to assess workers' competencies and to uncover the true nature of the "skills gaps" between stakeholders on both the demand and supply sides of the labor market. Drawing on the Realist-Constructivism framework, this module explores the epistemology and ontology of workers' competencies. It does so by combining questionnaires for employers, workers, and educators—gathering their perceptions on detailed skill sets—with tests designed to measure workers' and students' actual abilities. This approach allows for a bottom-up analysis of the diverse realities within the micro-ecologies of these four countries while ensuring comparability across cases. Unlike many critical realist works that remain at the philosophical level, our team's approach makes the concept of abductive reasoning into a set of practical steps. The chapter also explains a unique program we developed to train noncognitive abilities using board games.

Keywords

Skills assessment · Realist-constructivism · Stakeholders' questionnaires · Game-based training · Noncognitive skills · Workforce analysis

3.1 Introduction

In the previous chapters, I explained the theoretical foundations of this volume and the characteristics of econo-productive and structural-regulatory mechanisms affecting the formation of work-related competencies of people in the Global South. Based on them, in this chapter, I am going to introduce the survey modules we developed and used to achieve our Realist-Constructivist goal of describing the nature of workers' competencies precisely while not losing sight of the individuals' subjectivities and social contexts.

As I argued in the introduction chapter, to grasp the nature of what people call "skills gaps" in contextually relevant and meaningful ways, we need to overcome the institutionalist frame of imagination that classifies the formation of people's work-related competencies

S. Yamada (✉)
Graduate School of International Development, Nagoya University, Nagoya, Japan

Graduate School of Asian and African Area Studies, Kyoto University, Kyoto, Japan
e-mail: syamada@nagoya-u.jp

S. Yamada (ed.), *Mitigating the "Skills Gaps"*, Sustainable Development Goals Series,
https://doi.org/10.1007/978-981-95-7968-6_3

between pre- and post-employment, which are administered by different ministries and discussed in different academic disciplines. Based on this argument, I proposed a constructivist approach to examining people's work-related capacities according to the psychology of individuals and their interactions with people in and out of the workplace and the environment. At the same time, however many cases from different countries and workplaces are accumulated, extreme constructivism, which relies solely on individuals' subjective meaning-making and experience, will end up being an epistemological relativism. With such an approach, it is not possible to understand how they are rooted in ontological realities. Here, we notice the necessity of abductive reasoning, which supplements the constructivist examination of working people's competencies with positivism's examination of extrinsic conditions and general patterns of individual reactions to such conditions. Therefore, our team incorporated several conceptual tools from Bhaskar's critical realism. This philosophical stance promotes research practices based on the interplay between ontological reality and epistemological relativism, and to perform abductive reasoning to reach a holistic understanding of the realities (Bhaskar, 1975, 1998; Bhaskar et al., 2017). As I have indicated in Fig. 1.4, inspired by the concepts of "laminations of scale" and "generative mechanisms" from Bhaskar, we conceptualized the work-related competency development as the layer of ecologies from micro to industrial, national, and global ones. Regarding the generative mechanisms composed of the nexus of factors that make us experience the real, we propose three types, namely, econo-productive, structural-regulatory, and socio-cultural mechanisms. Thus, with some conceptual adaptations from critical realism as a starting point, we developed the theoretical model of Realist-Constructivism of work-related competencies.

It was not only Bhaskar who called for abductive reasoning as a philosophical position (for example, Lombrozo, 2012; Walton, 2004). However, not many such metaphysical debates have been reflected in empirical research. One of the significant contributions of Bhaskar, which must be a reason why he has many followers, is his efforts to propose concrete conceptual tools and methodology that bridge positivism and interpretivism in research practices. Still, even among scholars who cite critical realism, their discussions are mostly on its theoretical potential but not much on its application to their own empirical research (Dobson, 2001; Khazem, 2018; Ramsarup et al., 2023).

The surveys we conducted in four countries use the same module, which we developed based on the theoretical consideration of the constructivist notion of competencies, aiming to describe the characteristics of micro-ecology while ensuring cross-sectional comparability. In this sense, we believe it will serve as a strong case of how abductive reasoning can be realized, married with practical tools and analytical methods. Based on this conviction, in the following parts of this chapter, I will explain the design and composition of the data collection modules we developed and used in our series of studies.

In addition to the competency assessment, we also developed a program to train the noncognitive abilities of the workforce using board games uniquely designed according to the behavioral modeling approach. As I wrote earlier, while we conducted the assessments and provided feedback to the governments, industrial associations, companies, and workers, we were almost always requested to conduct training to mitigate the identified "skills gaps." Also, after we analyzed the data from various angles, we came to realize that noncognitive abilities are significant determinants of workplace performance. As I will explain soon, noncognitive abilities appear in diverse ways, according to the characteristics of the micro-ecology, which our assessment module captured. It seemed challenging but fruitful both academically and practically to consider means to train the noncognitive abilities of workers effectively. Depending on the situation, these abilities are formed and utilized differently from individual to individual. However, if standardized training programs can be implemented while accommodating this diversity, they can help companies improve their operations and increase worker motivation. Data obtained from such interventions would also be helpful in deepening our understanding of the nature of work-related abilities.

Based on these considerations, we devised and implemented a 1-day training program consisting of two board games and reflection sessions. The quasi-experiment demonstrated a strong positive effect of this training program by utilizing our competency assessments before and after the training and comparing the test results to measure the training's impact. Not only were the effects statistically significant, but we also received many positive reactions and requests for more training from participants and their employers.

The details of the outcomes and the prospects for further operations of the noncognitive abilities training will be discussed in Chap. 7. Meanwhile, in this chapter, after detailing the competency assessment module and procedure, I will explain the game-based training with its philosophy, design, and contents. It was natural for our Realist-Constructivism that the investigations do not finish by portraying the ecology of work-related competencies conditioned by the specificities of the contexts while being embedded in the meso- and macro-structures. As we closely interacted with people on the ground, we shaped the desire to contribute to their social agenda using our academic expertise. In this sense, the project is becoming a dynamic and participatory Realist-Constructivism, which involves ourselves (researchers) as participants. As we conducted these diverse activities, we called ourselves the Skills and Knowledge for Youths (SKY) project team.

3.2 Our Survey Modules

When I described the econo-productive mechanism in Chap. 2, I mentioned twin gaps between the supply and demand of workforce competencies (see Fig. 2.2). One is the gap between employers and educators in their perceptions of essential abilities for workers, and the other is between the perceptions of employers and job seekers. As I explained earlier, our initial motivation in launching this project was to provide concrete evidence to the policy debates on the "skills gap" because, more often than not, stakeholders blame each other without common ground regarding what they mean by "skills." Another restriction for making evidence-based decisions was that the issues on workforce competencies cut across different sub-governments, such as ministries of labor, education, or industry, and there was no consistent mechanism for collecting comprehensive data about people's abilities before and after employment. By generating detailed data about (1) workers' abilities and (2) differences in expectations among stakeholders, we tried to provide a platform that is not biased by perspectives from any particular position.

Figure 3.1 modifies Fig. 2.2. While the earlier figure described two gaps between the supply and demand sides, in Fig. 3.1, I plotted two gaps within the supply side. One is the gap between educators and workers in *perceptions of essential abilities* necessary to work. Another is the gap between what workers can *actually do* and the perceptions of their abilities among stakeholders, including the workers themselves. In terms of perceptions, first, we have to consider workers' subjective evaluations of their capacities. It is largely a matter of psychology. For example, if a worker considers himself/herself to be good at what s/he considers essential to get a good job, it would positively affect his/her sense of self-efficacy. On the contrary, a person who is not confident in his/her ability in key areas may hesitate to appeal to the supervisor in the workplace. Of course, such assumptions cannot be generalized because a person's behavior is determined not only by confidence in abilities but also by personality, fitness to the required tasks, evaluation by the educator, employer, or other actors around, and many other factors in the micro-ecology. Aside from workers/learners' self-evaluation, educators or trainers in school or training programs have their own criteria for prioritizing what they teach according to their own judgments about curricular objectives and skills needed in the industry. Such criteria by the educator/trainer affect not only their teaching but also their evaluation of their student-workers. Furthermore, on the demand side, as we already saw, employers

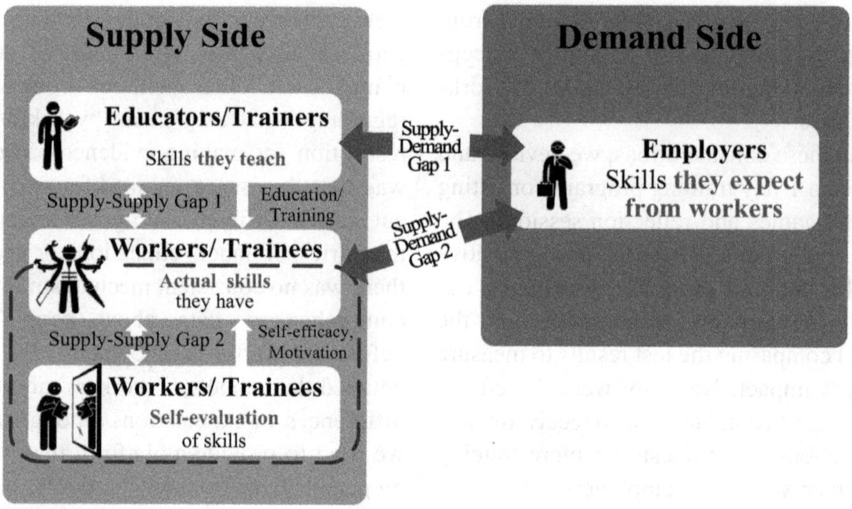

Fig. 3.1 Gaps in stakeholders' perceptions and workers' actual abilities which our module assesses

also have their expectations about the abilities they want to find in their workers.

These varying perceptions should be understood in a constructivist manner without applying any positivistic hypothesis because these actors see the micro-ecology of competency development from their respective vantage points, whose differences are the significant causes of the "skills gap." At the same time, grasping the diverse perceptions about workers' abilities untangles only the epistemological dimension of realities. If we want to reconcile the analysis of epistemology and ontology, we should also capture the actual performance of workers, whose meanings people with different perspectives are talking about. Put differently, examination of the real performance of the workers is the anchor to pin down these perceptions, which are floating in a vague relation to the realities.

To bridge the ontology and epistemology by matching data that allow us to comprehensively describe the actors' perceptions and the workers' abilities, we designed the competency assessment as shown in Fig. 3.2. The module comprises questionnaires distributed to employers, educators/trainers, and workers, as well as written and practical tests for workers. The questionnaires are to know the stakeholders' respective epistemologies, while the tests are to grasp the ontology of what they are talking about. In the following section, I will explain the detailed designs and operational arrangements of the respective instruments constituting the module.

Another point that I need to highlight as a characteristic of our module is that we try to comprehend the competencies in more detail than many other researchers in this field. As I discussed in the introduction, researchers often use the years of schooling or work experience, or at most, written test scores, as a proxy of human abilities, which is far more complex and profound. Our assessment module is designed based on the conception of human abilities according to the taxonomies I presented in Figs. 1.1 and 1.2. More specifically, we measure the workers' performance in cognitive, technical/ vocational, and noncognitive abilities. To be precise, let me provide the working definition of three types of abilities that the SKY assessment module will measure. They follow the definitions in Fig. 1.2, being adapted to the context of working adults in a manufacturing sector.

- *Cognitive Abilities*: Basic knowledge about the specific industry, literacy, and numeracy. The assessment also measures higher-order cognitive abilities for analysis, evaluation, and application of knowledge.
- *Technical and Vocational Abilities*: Operational abilities for production in a spe-

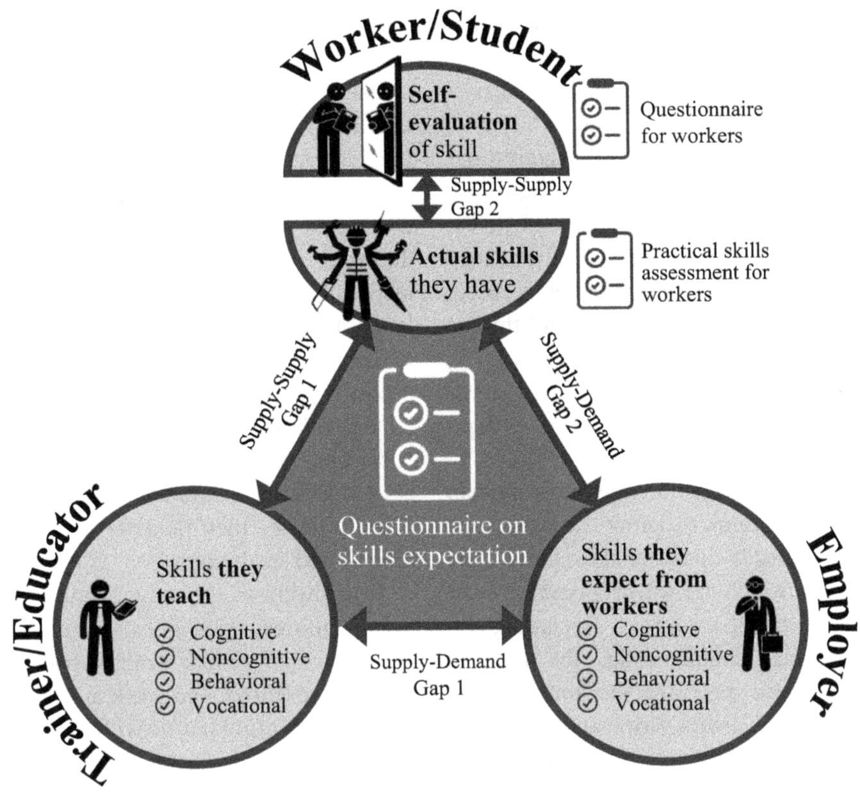

Fig. 3.2 Competency assessment module of the SKY project

cific industry; in the case of this study, it is the garment sector.

- *Noncognitive Abilities*: Abilities to apply knowledge to solve workplace problems, conduct appropriate interpersonal relations, follow rules, and make judgments in order to achieve a required result

Regarding cognitive abilities, we used written tests to assess basic numeracy, literacy, and the capacity to integrate and apply such basic knowledge and theoretical knowledge about textile and garment production. We developed practical tests to assess the technical and vocational abilities and asked educators and employers to grade them. The objective of involving the actors from both the demand and supply sides was to contrast their evaluation criteria of the same workers' performances (extensively discussed in Chap. 5). Lastly, noncognitive abilities were grasped through the questionnaire distributed to the workers, which included, aside from a psychological scale on personality traits, question items about their workplace behavior, which we composed in consultation with Japanese and Ethiopian experts in garment factory production management. We also referred to the national occupational frameworks for the garment production industry from multiple countries, especially South Africa, Ethiopia, Ghana, and India.

3.2.1 Constructs of the Assessment Module

In this section, I will detail the respective instruments constituting the SKY assessment module.

3.2.1.1 Questionnaire

We have five types of questionnaires: (1) for human resources managers of companies; (2) for production managers of the companies; (3) for educators/trainers in TVET institutions, in-house training centers, or any other training centers which the entities who invited our team want to be involved in the assessment; (4) for workers in the companies where managers who answer questionnaires (1) and (2) work. The fifth type of questionnaire is for students of TVET institutions where teachers who answer questionnaire (3) work. Since we mostly worked in response to the requests from the industry side, questionnaires (1), (2), and (4) are the most frequently used, while (3) and (5) were also conducted in Ethiopia in 2016, South Africa in 2018, and Ghana in 2018–19. We also conducted an educators' questionnaire (3) in Pakistan in 2023, but without involving students in the survey.

The questionnaire given to companies' human resources managers aims to know the workplace factors that extrinsically condition the nature of the micro-ecology in which the workers develop their abilities and are being evaluated. Regarding the companies' business characteristics, the question items included those regarding the annual sales, types of products and clients, hiring and promotion of the workforce, and demography of the workers by age, schooling, type of work, and rank.

The production managers' questionnaire focuses more on their perceptions of the workers' abilities. While human resources (HR) managers generally oversee HR-related matters, production managers supervise the factory production floors directly. Therefore, they have more concrete ideas of what they expect workers to be able to do and what kind of attitude they appreciate. Following the basic questions about managers themselves, in some sections of the questionnaire, they are asked about the perceived level of importance of the listed abilities for workers with less than 3 years of experience. Respondents are asked to grade each listed ability on the Likert Scale by selecting one of five points from "1—not important at all" to "5—extremely important". In the section on cognitive abilities, 10 items are listed to be graded. The following section on technical and vocational abilities has 40 items. Regarding personality traits, which are a part of the noncognitive skills according to my classification in Fig. 1.2, we request production managers to rank desirable ones from the list of Big Five personality traits according to the psychological definitions: extraversion, agreeableness, openness to experience, conscientiousness, and neuroticism. Lastly, there is also a section about workplace behavior (socio-emotional aspect of noncognitive skills) comprising 27 items.

For the sake of comparing the perceptions about desirable abilities among stakeholders with different perspectives, the items that ask the respondents to grade the listed abilities by the level of importance are made identical across the questionnaires (2), (3), (4), and (5). While the production managers of the company (2) and educators/trainers (3) were asked only to grade according to the degree of importance, the workers (4) and school students (5) were asked additionally to rate their own performance according to their self-evaluation.

In addition to the main sections about workforce abilities, each questionnaire asked about the respondents' demographic background, education, household, and work and training experience, which provided us with the information to analyze the determinants of the differential perceptions about workforce abilities.

3.2.1.2 Written Tests

The workers and students were given 90 min to complete reading, mathematics, integrated skills, and vocational knowledge tests. The initial three tests on reading, mathematics, and integrated skills had 20 items each, while only the last test on vocational knowledge had 40 items. All exam questions were multiple-choice items, where respondents had to choose one option out of four.

The overall objective of the written tests was to capture test-takers' cognitive abilities, which are necessary for the production process in the garment industry. A fundamental difference between our written tests and those for school students is that ours are made to evaluate the test takers' cognitive abilities in the context of work, regardless of their school education records. Accordingly, we tried to design the tests to capture the ability to apply knowledge for problem-solving. For example, in the reading section, the materials to read included an imaginary announcement posted on the factory notice board, a letter by a company staff to another organization, or a text message on the phone. Similarly, in the integrated skills section, the questions require test-takers to collect information from graphs and tables that record the numbers for different types of products and groups of workers and decide how much they have to produce or what materials to procure. The vocational knowledge section directly relates to the industry in which they work but assesses how much they have theoretical and cognitive knowledge, unlike our practical test, which assesses hands-on skills.

When we analyze the participants' scores from written tests, to avoid the bias caused by the variations in the level of difficulty among test items and make each person's performance comparable, we applied the Item Response Theory, which will be explained in detail in relation to the analysis presented in empirical chapters from Chap. 4 onward.

As we will discuss later, there are certain tendencies in how the performance in cognitive tests in different fields reinforces each other. Advanced cognition in reading and mathematics contributes to the performance of integrated skills, which also relates to the achievement of the vocational knowledge test. At the same time, such patterns in cognitive tests relate differently to the practical test and other factors contributing to the overall effectiveness at work.

3.2.1.3 Practical Tests

The practical test aims to capture workers' advanced garment-producing skills comprehensively. In designing the practical test, we applied the same philosophy as that for written tests to assess the abilities of workplace problem-solving, but not of reproducing the same technical tasks as shown. In developing this set of modules, we got some ideas from the literature on learning trajectories in developmental psychology. We also collaborated with experts in manufacturing production management who have rich experience in factories in the Global South.

The test is composed of five different activities: (1) pattern making, (2) analysis of garment structure, (3) machine sewing, (4) ironing (10 min each), and (5) the advanced activity (20 min).

In the practical skill assessment, assessors from the employer and the TVET trainer sides concurrently graded the same examinees' vocational skills (workers and trainees). While questionnaires allow us to compare each stakeholder's perception, knowing "what they think" is not enough unless we examine how it is translated to the actual performance and evaluation. Thus, one of this study's methodological strengths is that its design allows us to contrast the actual performance of workers and their evaluation by people from both the supply and demand sides of the labor market. It also makes it possible to contrast the workers' claims about what they can do and the evaluation of their performance by third parties.

Figure 3.3 summarizes the structure of the assessment module and the roles of participating entities. Production managers of companies and educators are assigned two roles: respondents to questionnaires and examiners of practical tests. Workers and students participate in all three forms of data collection, namely, the questionnaire, written, and practical tests.

3.3 Our Unconventional Training Program

As I have discussed earlier, many scholars and practitioners point out the importance of noncognitive abilities in achieving high performance at work. Our team's assessments in different settings kept indicating that noncognitive abilities are significant determinants of wages (for example, Otchia & Yamada, 2021; Yamada & Otchia, 2022). Being requested to provide some training to mitigate the "skills gaps" identified by our competency assessments, we started to consider the best form of our contribution as an academic team, composed predominantly of educationists. Out of cognitive, technical & vocational, and noncognitive abilities that constitute human competencies, the one for which effective training programs did not exist was the noncognitive. For the cognitive and technical & vocational abilities, we can introduce appropriate training providers and schools to those individuals and employers who request our assistance in mitigating the iden-

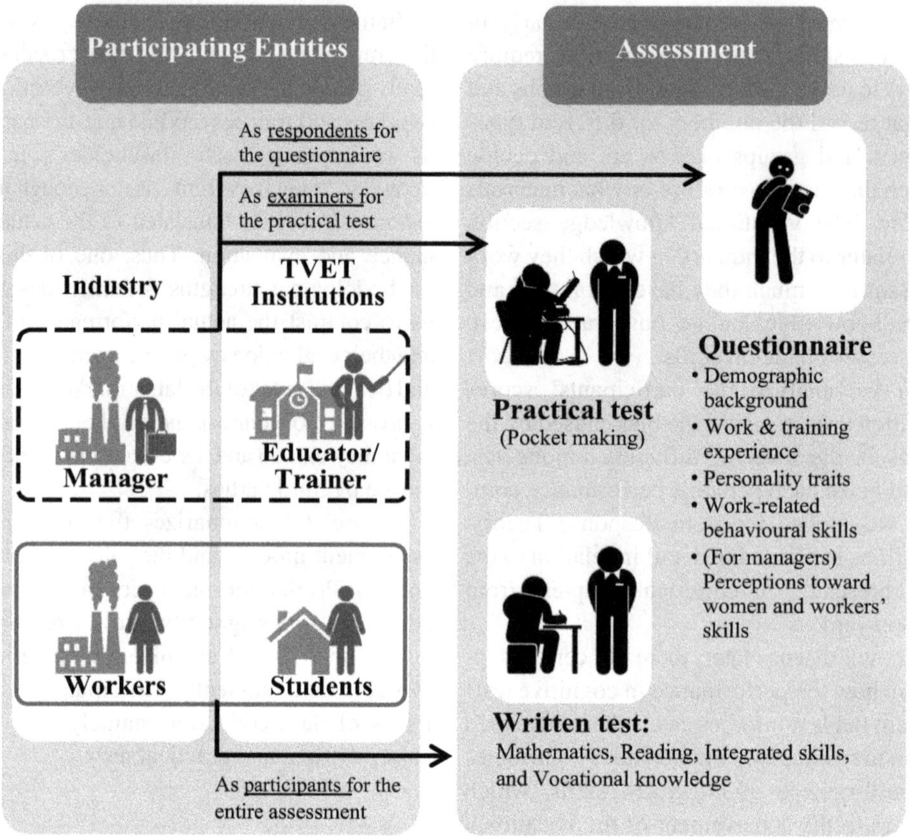

Fig. 3.3 Components of assessment and roles of the participating entities

tified "skills gaps". Then, these institutions would be able to either let the workers participate in their regular programs or modify these programs to attend to their specific needs. However, training in noncognitive abilities requires pedagogical innovations rather than the knowledge of the contents to be taught. This task was challenging but suited our expertise. It also met the practical needs in situations where the importance of noncognitive abilities is discussed greatly, without effective and feasible means to improve them.

3.3.1 Game-Based Noncognitive Abilities Training for Workers

Since I have already explained extensively the nature of noncognitive abilities, I will not repeat it here. The point I want to clarify here is that out of the vast domain of noncognitive abilities, we focused mainly on cultivating the socio-emotional aspect. As Fig. 1.2 shows, noncognitive abilities are composed of socio-emotional and psychological aspects. The latter relates to the personalities of individuals, which are, of course, important determinants of how people interact with others and perform their tasks. At the same time, psychological traits are difficult to train directly through exogenous interventions. Thus, we tried to develop a training program to improve their socio-emotional skills, which would, in turn, positively affect the participants' psychology. To some extent, such positive impacts were observed through the positive comments and proactive attitudes among training participants.

3.3.1.1 Socio-emotional Abilities Identified Through Workplace Analysis

The nature of socio-emotional skills, which are often called "soft skills," is significantly influenced by the culture of the contexts where they are demanded and evaluated (Zhou, 2017). From 2020 to 2021, we collected information about existing socio-emotional skills (or more popularly called "soft skills") training for working youths in Ethiopia. The issue was hot (and still is), and several development agencies and civil society organizations were offering training in the same garment production sector as we do.[1] However, a few training programs whose course design and contents we looked at are all composed of lectures and group discussions in the meeting room, segregating participants from their daily work environment. For participants in such training, it would be difficult to connect general ideas about soft skills to specific events at the workplace. Moreover, knowledge in declarative form acquired in traditional training, such as lectures, tends to fade away after some time.

Socio-emotional abilities are exercised through people's behavior. A behavioral ability is expressed adaptively in response to the reality in front of a person, and the essence of such an ability lies in the reasoning behind it and the achievement of aimed outcomes, rather than the action itself. Therefore, listing the actions that may appear on the surface and letting training participants memorize them would not lead to mastering this ability unless they internalize the reasons behind them (Kechagias, 2011).

After reviewing the existing training programs and considering the nature of socio-emotional abilities, we decided to design the program based on workplace observations and consultation with experts in the manufacturing process. We collected many photos and videos provided by the experts and listened to their explanations about why the phenomena and situations captured in the photos are desirable or undesirable in the production sites. We classified desired/undesired behaviors of workers thematically and constructed five groups of socio-emotional skills desired for workers with less than 3 years of experience in garment production companies. These are (1) Occupational health and safety, (2) Tidiness and cleanliness, (3) Efficiency, (4) Quality control, and (5) Teamwork.

Under respective categories of socio-emotional skills, there are six to seven examples of workers' behaviors, including positive and negative models. These examples, identified through the analysis of photos and videos, were then incorporated into the games. In some cases, they were directly cited in the soft skills cards, while in many other cases, we reflected them in the rules and arrangements of the games so that the participants would encounter situations where they had to think of their actions to overcome the challenges in the game.

3.3.1.2 Theory of Behavioral Modeling

As I discussed in the introduction, Behavior Modeling Training, also known as BMT, is grounded in Bandura's (1977) social learning theory. Based on individuals' learning in the social context, social learning theory emphasizes that humans learn by observing others' behaviors. A well-known experiment by Bandura et al. (1961), the Bobo doll experiment, found that after having a group of children watch a video of an adult assaulting a blowup doll, the children performed the same assaulting actions on the doll when left to play with it without guidance. This experiment concludes that observing social models influences individuals' behavioral changes. The social learning theory not only focuses on observational learning but also on the modeling process. Observed behaviors are not effectively learned unless the observation goes through *model observation, rehearsal of actions according to the observed model, application of the actions, and reflection*.

After reviewing the literature, we identified four crucial conditions for maximizing participants' socio-emotional abilities through BMT, which we reflected in our game-based training. First, before observing models, participants should be given learning points in the form of

[1]For the sake of anonymity, I will not name the organizations whose training programs we examined. Apart from whether they provide soft skills training, there are many development agencies that are active in the field of industrial human resources development, including the World Bank, International Labor Organization, GIZ (German agency), and Swiss, Dutch, Swedish, Japanese, South Korean, and Chinese governments.

rule codes, which greatly enhance the effect of training (Bryant & Fox, 1995). Second, the opportunities to rehearse the action in their minds before physical practice (*symbolic or mental rehearsal*) increase the retention of learning (Taylor et al., 2005). Third, mental rehearsal, which is closely related to real-life situations, contributes to greater effects of BMT (Law et al., 2018; Taylor et al., 2005). Lastly, participants' motivation or willingness to practice the learned key behaviors is associated with the presence of positive *social and intrinsic reinforcement*, such as reward or a sense of achievement (Decker & Nathan, 1985; Taylor et al., 2005).

The BMT approach is proven to enhance both declarative knowledge (knowledge of what) and procedural knowledge (knowledge of how, sometimes referred to as skill reproduction). Because of such an advantage, BMT is applied to various fields such as leadership training (Waldman et al., 2013), parental skills training (Gelatt et al., 2010; Law et al., 2018; Webster-Stratton, 1982), and cross-cultural skills training (Harrison, 1992). As I stated, we aimed to design training that does not dwarf the behavioral nature of socio-emotional abilities into memorization but contributes to the mindset changes that lead to problem-solving. For this reason, we embrace the BMT as a theoretical foundation of our game-based training.

3.3.1.3 Game-Based Behavior Modeling

Recently, the attention to socio-emotional learning through participation in games has been sharply increasing (Armstrong & Landers, 2018). Games create opportunities for players to exercise newly learned behaviors in the virtual or simulated world. It also reduces the risk of real-life damage and allows players to repeatedly explore different possibilities of the consequences of behavior through a trial-and-error process in a gamified setting. For instance, although business games mimic the market's aggressive and competitive nature, the players may make mistakes and learn throughout the gaming, without the real cost of failure. By practicing through games, the employees will know proper behavior when encountering real-life challenges. Hence, many enterprises currently utilize gamified training to coach their employees' noncognitive abilities (Merkuryev & Bikovska, 2012). In fact, many studies found that noncognitive skills are better learned in workplace-related or simulated scenarios to be reproduced in real-life events (Dawe, 2002; Shuman et al., 2005; Talavera & Perez-Gonzalez, 2007).

3.3.2 Game-Based Training Program Design and Content

As more details will be presented in Chap. 7, our socio-emotional skills training package consists of six sessions, including two board games, which represent BMT's five steps: (1) the introduction session, (2) Game I, (3) reflection session on Game I, (4) Game II, (5) reflection session on Game II, and (6) the wrap-up session. It is a 1-day program. Sessions up to (3) are conducted in the morning, and the remaining are in the afternoon. One of the significant reasons for making it 1 day is that a more extended program would (a) exhaust the participants and result in reducing the effect of training, and (b) company managers are often reluctant to take workers away from production duties for too long, even for the sake of improving their capacities. Therefore, to enhance the motivation of both workers and employers, finishing the training in 1 day on the weekend was quite significant. Company managers appreciated this training program, and we quickly gave feedback based on the findings from the workers' competency assessments. Regardless, for the private sector managers who pursue economic efficiency, the value of training is judged based on the opportunity costs of hours and salaries of the workforce.

3.3.2.1 Beneficiaries

This training program is designed for garment manufacturing workers, from recently employed line operators to supervisors of production lines. In this program, we define the supervisors as those working with other line operators on the ground. Their role is that of line leaders and should be differentiated from factory managers, who work at the management level, for whom we are developing a different set of games. Both supervisors and less-experienced line operators must develop the capacity and motivation to contribute to collective productivity. Therefore, our training program is designed to foster workers' individual socio-emotional skills by considering their commitment as members of the firm, leading to a more significant contribution to the line and the firm's shared goals.

3.4 Participants and Schedule of Assessment

In this section, I will provide details on the participants and schedules of the survey conducted in four countries. As explained above, we have two types of activities: skills assessment and game-based noncognitive skills training. The latter is a recent activity that is only conducted in Ethiopia in 2022, as detailed in Chap. 7. Otherwise, the surveys detailed in this section were of the former type, which aimed to assess skills gaps by conducting questionnaires, as well as written and practical tests.

3.4.1 Ethiopia

There are two major datasets from Ethiopia. The first dataset was gathered in 2016 and aims to identify gaps between the skills supplied by TVET institutions and workers' actual skills and the demand from employers and firms. The second dataset collected in 2022 deals with exploring the impact of a game-based training program grounded in the behavioral modeling theory on workers' self-efficacy and soft skills.

In 2016, the SKY Project conducted fieldwork in Ethiopia to determine the kinds of mismatches that exist between employers, training providers, and workers. The study involved the participation of 13 production managers, 591 workers from 13 domestic Ethiopian garment firms, and 19 human resource managers from FDI firms; 83 trainers and 162 students from seven TVET colleges also participated in the study. Participating garment firms were taken from a list of firms under the Ethiopian Textile and Garment Manufacturers Association. Initially, 35 firms located in and around the vicinity of Addis Ababa were asked to participate. Of the 35 firms contacted, 13 agreed to participate in the study. However, only 7 of the 13 firms allowed workers (N = 116) to participate in the assessment. To obtain the views of TVET trainers and students, the five largest TVET institutions out of the 27 public institutes in Addis Ababa were selected to participate in the study.

Table 3.1 provides a summary of the data collected and a timeline. Data was collected during two periods for this assessment. During the first period (Jan 2016), a survey was given to factory production managers (Table 3.1, row 1). The production managers were then asked to nominate a mix of workers with or without a TVET background who are relatively new to the firm to take part in the skills assessment (Table 3.1, row 3) during the second data-gathering period (Sept 2016). To obtain the views of TVET providers, 30 TVET trainers were surveyed during the first assessment period, with an additional 53 during the second assessment period (Table 3.1, row 2). TVET trainers were asked about their demographic information, views about the curriculum and cooperative training, and their expectations and evaluation of trainees' skills. The workers who participated in the skills assessment were asked to answer questionnaires informing us of their socioeconomic and demographic background, personality, job aspirations, and self-evaluation of work attitudes and skills. For the second data collection period (Sept 2016), we also surveyed TVET trainees on their demographic and socioeconomic information, job aspirations, perceptions, and opinions about the TVET curriculum, cooperative training, and important workplace skills. We also asked TVET students to evaluate their skills and personal performance (Table 3.1, row 5). To further enrich the data collected, we asked human resource managers from 19 FDI firms regarding their factory characteristics, demography of workers, and training provision (Table 3.1, row 6) to compare small and medium domestic manufacturers that

Table 3.1 Summary of collected data for the 2016 Ethiopia assessment

Row #	Period conducted	Survey type	Contents	Participant (sample size)
1	January 2016	Questionnaire	Factory characteristics Demography of employees Training of workers Expectation and evaluation of the worker's skills	Production managers (N = 13)
2	January & September 2016	Questionnaire	Demography of trainers Curriculum Cooperative training Expectation and evaluation of trainee's skills	Jan: TVET Trainers (N = 30) Sep: TVET Trainers (N = 53)
3	January 2016	Practical Test	Four activities related to: • Sewing • Pattern-making • Garment structure • Ironing, finishing	Workers (N = 116); Assessors (N = 9)
4	January 2016	Questionnaire	Socioeconomic background Personality Job aspirations Self-evaluation of work attitudes Self-evaluation of skills	Workers (N = 591)
5	September 2016	Questionnaire	Job aspirations Curriculum perception Cooperative training perception Opinions about important skills Self-evaluation of skills and performance	TVET Students (N = 162)
6	October-November 2016	Questionnaire	Factory characteristics Demography of employees Training of workers	Human resource managers (N=19) of FDI firms

Note: Data from the Skills and Knowledge for Youth Program assessment
TVET technical and vocational education and training

participated in the first data-collection period with FDI factories found in industrial parks.

The characteristics of the participants for the 2016 dataset are summarized in Table 3.2. An overwhelming majority of the study participants are female. About 8 out of 10 (84%) of TVET trainees are women. A similar ratio of employees that participated were women (85%). The average age of TVET students is 19.6 years old whereas their counterparts in the garment firms are 22.1 years old on average. Regarding experience before entering TVET, none of the students said they had worked before. Meanwhile, 31.6% of the employees surveyed said they had worked before joining their current jobs. About 35.6% of garment firm employees reported having at least a senior high school education, most of whom hold TVET certifications.

For the second data set, we had another separate skills assessment of Ethiopian garment workers between October and December 2022 to conduct a longitudinal study to explore how game-based training grounded in the behavioral modeling theory would help improve the soft skills of garment workers. Before the fieldwork, we conducted multistage cluster sampling from a list of 389 firms operating in Addis Ababa, with a total of 31,838 employees provided by Ethiopian Enterprise Development; 21 firms (N_{small} = 15, N_{medium} = 5, and N_{large} = 1) were randomly selected proportional to their firm size based on the current number of workers at the time of sampling: 6–50 (small), 51–300 (medium), and more than 300 (large). After contacting the garment firms and obtaining their consent to conduct fieldwork, we requested a list of full-time employees from which we randomly selected participants proportional to the firm's size; 504 workers were selected and then randomly assigned to the treatment group or the comparison group. For this fieldwork, we limited the sample population to full-time employees mainly because of the relatively high labor turnover rate in Ethiopia's garment sector and the longitudinal nature of the study. A summary of the collected data and timeline is presented in Table 3.3.

Table 3.2 Background information on participants for the 2016 Ethiopia assessment

Variable	Trainee N = 162	Employee N = 591
Female	84.0%	85.3%
Age[a]	19.6	22.1
Family in garment industry	19.0%	20.7%
Previous work experience[b]	–	31.6%
Education level		
No formal education	–	0.80%
Primary (Grades 1–8)	–	54.7%
Junior high (Grades 9–10)	–	8.8%
Senior high (Grades 11–12)	–	9.8%
Tertiary	–	4.4%
TVET (Levels 1–4)	100%	21.4%

Note: Data from the Skills and Knowledge for Youth Program assessment. Dashes indicate no respondents
TVET technical and vocational education and training
[a]Average age, in years
[b]Average for 44 participants who answered the question item

Baseline data was collected from October to November 2022 to obtain workers' demographic information and baseline self-reported work-related soft skills, vocational skills, and noncognitive skills (Table 3.3, row 1). Table 3.4 shows a summary of the participants' demographic data. Most of the respondents were female, at 81.8%. This reflects the dominance of female workers in Ethiopia's garment sector, where most rank-and-file laborers are women, while men primarily dominate supervisory and managerial positions. The average age of the participants was 25.9 years (with a standard deviation of 5.99). The average household size is 4.1 persons per family. A third of the participants surveyed had an upper secondary education, TVET, or tertiary education. The rest of the participants received education up to grade 10. Line workers make up about 81.7% of the participants. Regarding receiving in-house training, roughly 55% of the participants reported not receiving on-the-job training.

Table 3.3 Summary of collected data for the 2022 Ethiopia game-based training intervention

Row #	Period conducted	Survey type	Contents	Participant (sample size)
1	Oct–Nov 2022	Baseline Questionnaire	Socioeconomic background Self-reported work-related soft skills Self-evaluation of vocational skills Self-evaluation of noncognitive skills	Garment workers (N = 504)
2	Oct–Nov 2022	Written Examination	Reading test Mathematics test Integrated skills test Vocational knowledge test	Garment workers (N = 504)
3	Oct 2022	Questionnaire	Factory characteristics Demography of employees Training of workers	Human resource managers (N = 21)
4	Oct 2022	Questionnaire	Demography of managers Expectations on workers' cognitive, behavioral, and vocational skills Expectation of types of personality traits valued	Production managers (N = 21)
5	Nov–Dec 2022	Post-intervention Questionnaire	Self-reported work-related soft skills Self-evaluation of vocational skills Self-evaluation of noncognitive skills	Garment workers (N = 504)

Note: Data from the Skills and Knowledge for Youth Program assessment.
TVET technical and vocational education and training

A visual summary of the data is presented in Fig. 3.4.

After obtaining workers' demographic information and baseline self-reported work-related soft skills, vocational skills, and noncognitive skills, we conducted written examinations (Table 3.3, row 2) to test garment workers' reading and mathematics proficiency, integrated skills, and vocational knowledge. The examination aims to determine if there is any link between workers' cognitive functions and level of soft skills.

Post-intervention data was collected from November to December 2022 on treatment and comparison groups after the game-based training to capture changes in garment workers' self-efficacy on various work-related soft skills. (Table 3.3, row 5). By collecting data after the game-based training intervention, we hope to capture the differences between groups—treatment and comparison—and make meaningful inferences on individual workers' growth and changes in attitudes and behavior before and after the training. The strength of this methodological design is that we could make valid inferences about the actual effect of the training program/intervention.

Similar to the earlier study, human resource and production managers' data were obtained. One human resources manager from each of the 21 garment firms was asked to answer questionnaires to provide firm-level data, employee demographic information, and training information (Table 3.3, row 3). The questionnaires would provide insight into the characteristics of each worker's respective workplace and the kind and nature of the training they are provided and determine if there is any link with soft skills development. Finally, we surveyed one production manager from each firm to answer questionnaires on the manager's demographic information and their expectations of workers' cognitive, behavioral, and vocational skills (Table 3.3, row 3). By comparing the manager's expectations with the worker's self-evaluated skills, we hope to identify gaps in soft skills perception between the supply side (garment workers) and the demand side (production managers). With this, we can determine which skills are valued in the workplace and should be given priority in the various training programs provided to the workers.

Table 3.4 Background information on participants for the 2022 Ethiopia game-based training assessment

Variable	Participants N = 504
Female	81.9%
Age	25.9
Household Size	4.1
Line worker	81.7%
Previous work experience	68.3%
Education level	
Below Grade 11	65.9%
Above Grade 11	33.9%
OJT	44.3%

Note: Data from the Skills and Knowledge for Youth Program assessment
OJT on-the-job training

3.4.2 Ghana

The Ghana study conducted a skills assessment between November 2018 and February 2019 involving 331 student trainees and 8 trainers from four TVET institutions, 71 workers from two factories, and 92 informal workers from workshops that belong to the Union of Informal Workers Associations (UNIWA) to contrast the skills possessed by workers to the demands of the employers and with what is taught in TVET institutions. A total of four TVET institutions agreed to participate in the assessment. Three TVET schools provide National Qualifications Framework (NQF) levels 1–4, and a technical university provides NQF level 5. The participating TVET institutions are located within and around the vicinity of Accra city. The two domestic factories are located in Accra, and both export products mainly to the United States and/or the United Kingdom. Informal workers who are members of UNIWA from workshops in the Accra vicinity participated in the study. Participants were selected using random sampling from a complete list of students and workers provided by the TVET schools, companies, and UNIWA to reduce selection bias.

The first data collection phase was done in November 2018, involving TVET students and trainers. The second data collection phase was

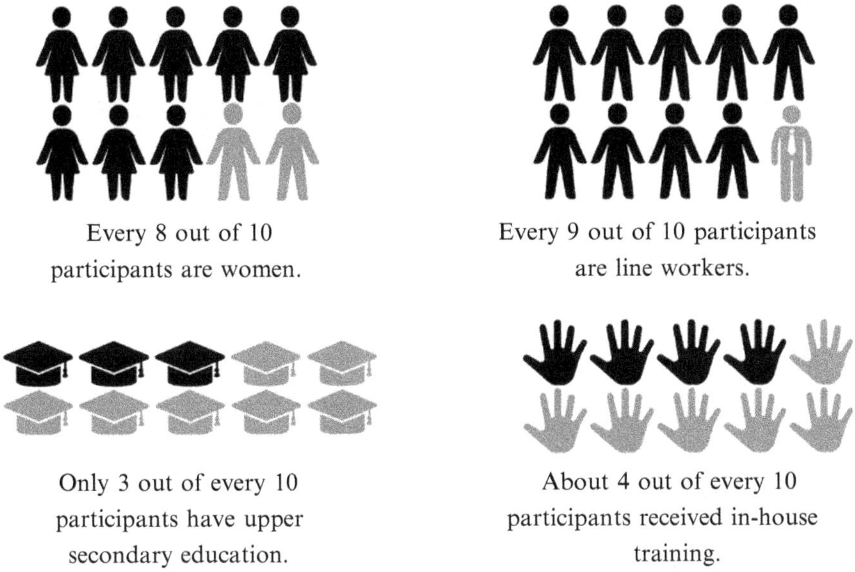

Fig. 3.4 Background information on participants for the game-based training assessment

conducted in February 2019 and primarily involved factory employees and informal workers. Table 3.5 summarizes the data collected and the timeline. First, TVET students were asked to answer questionnaires (Table 3.5, row 1) to obtain information about their demographic information, personality, job aspirations, perception of the curriculum, and self-reported skills. A similar questionnaire was provided to factory and informal workers during the second phase (Table 3.5, row 5), replacing curriculum perception with their self-reported work attitudes. After the questionnaire, all groups were given the written examination (Table 3.5, rows 2 & 6). A practical test was given to a randomly selected subset of the participants (Table 3.5, rows 3 & 7) to obtain information on their level of garment-related skills. The smaller sample size for the practical test was primarily due to limitations on the venue, equipment, materials, examiners, and time needed to ensure the quality of the data collected. Lastly, a questionnaire was provided to TVET trainers to obtain data on the demography of trainers, TVET curriculum, and their expectations and evaluation of the trainee's skills (Table 3.5, row 4). Factory production and human resource managers were also asked to provide information on factory characteristics, employee demography, training provision, and their expectations and evaluations of the workers' skills (Table 3.5, row 8).

Table 3.6 provides a summary of the participant characteristics. In terms of gender, about 9 out of 10 (87%) of participants are female (Fig. 3.4). There is a slightly higher concentration of female participants in TVET schools and informal workers (90% and 89%, respectively) than factory employees (80%). On average, informal workers are much older (35.70 years old) than their counterparts in the factory (29.63 years old) and TVET schools (21.16 years old), who are in their 20s. At least seven out of ten informal workers have family members working in the garment industry. This contrasts with factory workers and TVET students, who have only about four out of ten and five out of ten family members in the industry, respectively. Household economic levels were measured from an aggregate score of whether or not participants own or have the following items at home: DVD/CD player, TV, cell phone, computer, car, motorcycle, and refrigerator/freezer. Factory employees have the highest socioeconomic levels at 6.72 points, followed by TVET students at 6.13 points, and finally, informal workers at 5.88 points. Regarding work experience, only 35% of TVET students have experience working before

Table 3.5 Summary of collected data for the 2018–2019 Ghana assessment

Row #	Period conducted	Survey type	Contents	Participant (sample size)
1	November 2018	Questionnaire	Socioeconomic background Personality Job aspirations Curriculum perception Self-evaluation of skills	TVET Students (N = 331)
2	November 2018	Written Examination	Reading test Mathematics test Integrated skills test Vocational knowledge test	TVET Students (N = 331)
3	November 2018	Practical Test	Four activities related to: • Sewing • Pattern-making • Garment structure • Ironing, finishing	TVET Students (N = 160)
4	November 2018	Questionnaire	Demography of trainers Curriculum Expectation and evaluation of trainee's skills	TVET Students (N = 8)
5	February 2019	Questionnaire	Socioeconomic background Personality Job aspirations Self-evaluation of work attitudes Self-evaluation of skills	Employees (N = 71), Informal workers (N = 92)
6	February 2019	Written Examination	Reading test Mathematics test Integrated skills test Vocational knowledge test	Employees (N = 71), Informal workers (N = 92)
7	February 2019	Practical Test	Four activities related to: • Sewing • Pattern-making • Garment structure • Ironing, finishing	Employees (N = 71), Informal workers (N = 91)
8	February 2019	Questionnaire	Factory characteristics Demography of employees Training of workers Expectation and evaluation of worker's skills	Factory employers (production manager/human resource manager)

Note: Data from the Skills and Knowledge for Youth Program assessment
TVET technical and vocational education and training

admission to their current schools. On the other hand, almost nine out of ten (87%) factory workers have prior experience, while only about four out of ten (39%) of informal workers have worked in the garment industry before their current jobs. The age, work experience, and family members in the industry of informal workers are possible indications that most of them (about 61%) had their first and current jobs in the informal business sector, possibly continuing or participating in the family-run business. On average, about six out of ten (62.3%) of factory employees attained at least upper secondary education (Fig. 3.5). Meanwhile, only one out of ten (13%) informal workers went to upper secondary education and above, with most of them (68.02%) stopping after finishing or reaching lower secondary.

3.4.3 South Africa

The assessment in South Africa was conducted twice in 2018 and 2023, as presented in Table 3.7. In 2018, we conducted the assessment with 122

Table 3.6 Background information on participants for the 2018–2019 Ghana assessment

Variable	Trainee N = 331	Employee N = 71	Informal N = 92	Total N = 494
Female	90%	80%	89%	87%
Age[a]	21.16	29.63	35.70	26.35
Family in garment sector	46.8%	36.7%	71.4%	49.9%
Household economic level[b]	6.13	6.72	5.88	6.21
Previous work experience	35%	87%	39%	43%
Education level				
No formal education	–	0.16%	3.34%	1.83%
Primary	–	0.32%	15.55%	8.30%
Junior high	–	37.22%	68.02%	53.35%
Senior high	–	36.10%	10.03%	22.45%
Tertiary	–	20.13%	2.03%	10.65%
TVET (Levels 1–4)	–	2.56%	1.02%	1.75%
Other	–	3.51%	0.00%	1.67%
Father's education				
JHS and below	42.3%	44.1%	64.8%	47.9%
SHS and above	57.7%	55.9%	35.2%	52.1%
Mother's education				
JHS and below	65.5%	65.0%	87.7%	70.3%
SHS and above	34.5%	35.0%	12.3%	29.7%

Note: Data from the Skills and Knowledge for Youth Program assessment. Dashes indicate no respondents
TVET technical and vocational education and training, *JHS* junior high school, *SHS* senior high school
[a]Average
[b]Aggregate factor score of DVD/CD player, TV, cell phone, computer, car, motorcycle, and refrigerator/freezer

students from the University of Technology (UoT) and a technical and vocational education and training (TVET) institute. Eighty of them were from the university, while 42 of them were students from the TVET college. The education levels of the students at the point of survey are illustrated in Fig. 3.6. The data indicates that TVET Level 1 holds the largest share at 35.34 %, with UoT Level 2 following at 21.55%. The remaining levels exhibit similar proportions, falling within the range of approximately 12–15%.

As shown in Table 3.8, around 58% of the students are female. Their average age is 23.7 years. We found that around eight out of ten students (76.9%) attained pre-primary education. Regarding family background, students have approximately five siblings, including themselves. The economic level of the household was estimated based on the aggregation of ten items the household owns. The items consist of a DVD/CD player, television, mobile phone, computer, vehicle, motorcycle, and refrigerator/freezer. The average socioeconomic status of the students is 4.86 (See Table 3.8). Moreover, the findings indicate that 27.3% of the students have at least a family member employed in the garment industry. Regarding work experience, four out of ten trainees (44.5%) possess prior work experience before joining the current school.

During the second fieldwork, which took place between June and July 2023, another assessment was conducted with 239 workers from eight garment factories in Gauteng and Kwazulu-Natal Provinces. Table 3.9 illustrates the demographic information of the participants. We found that eight out of ten participants are female (80.3%). The average age of the workers is 39.9 years. Regarding education level, as shown in Fig. 3.6, around six out of ten workers (56.6%) attained at least upper secondary education. Household economic status was assessed based on a cumulative score reflecting the ownership of the following items: DVD/CD player, television, mobile phone, computer, vehicle, motorcycle, and refrigerator/freezer. The average socioeconomic status of the workers is measured

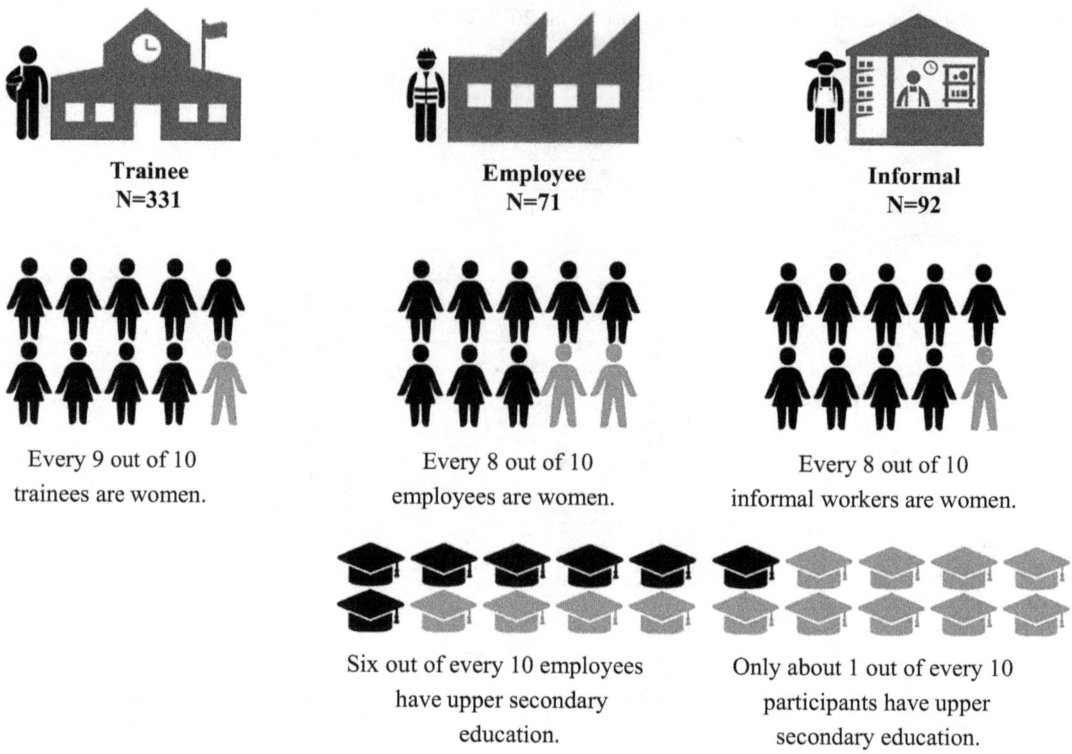

Fig. 3.5 Demography of Ghana participants

at 4.18 points. In terms of the average household size, we found that the participants have approximately six members in the family. Moreover, three out of ten participants have at least a family member working in the garment industry.

In terms of work experience, we discovered that participants typically began their careers at about 19 years old. About six out of ten workers (63.2%) reported having previous work experience prior to their current position, according to Fig. 3.7. Regarding their current employment, their estimated monthly salary is roughly 4528 South African Rand, with an average of 5.4 working hours each day.

3.4.4 Pakistan

Between August and September of 2023, we administered the skills assessment to 220 home-based informal workers and 205 formal workers from 17 garment factories in Lahore, the capital city of Punjab, Pakistan. Production managers from each participating firm were invited to answer the questionnaire in this fieldwork. Table 3.10 demonstrates the participants' demographic information, comparing informal to formal workers. We found that their characteristics are widely different in a few aspects. On average, informal workers were approximately 5 years older than factory workers. In terms of income, home-based workers earned around 40% of the average monthly income of those who worked in the factory. However, factory workers worked around 2.5 h more than home-based workers.

Both groups have similar characteristics in terms of the family backgrounds, including household size and the family's economic status. Each group of workers' families consists of approximately six members. The family's economic status was determined by adding up scores based on the household's ownership of items, including a DVD/CD player, TV, cell phone, computer, internet, bank account, car, motorcycle, bicycle, and refrigerator/freezer. The factory

Table 3.7 Summary of collected data for the 2018 and 2023 South Africa assessment

Row #	Period conducted	Survey type	Contents	Participant (sample size)
1	November 2018	Questionnaire	Socioeconomic background Personality Job aspirations Curriculum perception Self-evaluation of skills	UoT and TVET Students (N = 122)
2	November 2018	Written Examination	Reading test Mathematics test Integrated skills test Vocational knowledge test	UoT and TVET Students (N = 122)
3	November 2018	Questionnaire	Demography of trainers Curriculum Expectation and evaluation of trainee's skills	TVET Trainers ($n_{UoT} = 6$; $n_{TVET} = 2$)
4	June–July 2023	Questionnaire	Socioeconomic background Personality Job aspirations Self-evaluation of work attitudes Self-evaluation of skills	Employees (N = 239)
5	June–July 2023	Written Examination	Reading test Mathematics test Integrated skills test Vocational knowledge test	Employees (N = 239)
6	June–July 2023	Practical Test	Pocket sewing	Employees (N = 239)

Note: Data from the Skills and Knowledge for Youth Program assessment

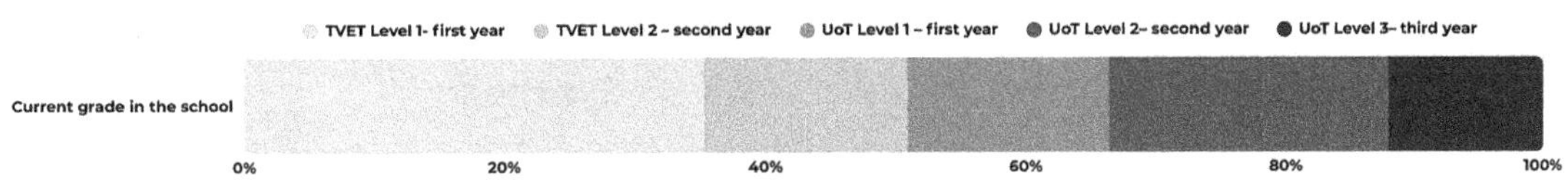

Fig. 3.6 Participants' percentage of current education level

and home-based worker groups both rated their family's economic status at around 3.2 points.

Furthermore, both groups of workers reside in similar types of communities. The variable "community type" indicates the categorization of participants' residential areas, with rural and semi-urban areas coded as 0 and urban areas coded as 1. The average score for both groups was approximately 0.8, indicating that the majority of participants live in urban areas.

Figure 3.8 depicts the comparison between factory and home-based workers in terms of their experiences in work and training. In Lahore, women typically begin their first job at around the age of 19 (refer to Table 3.10). However, the percentage of factory workers with prior work experience is slightly higher than that of home-based workers. We found that 46.1% of factory workers had work experience before their current job, while only 31.4% of home-based workers had previous work experience. On the other hand, both factory and piece-rate workers have similar levels of experience in on-the-job training (OJT) opportunities. According to the results, 37.1% of factory workers and 33.8% of home-based workers reported having OJT experience.

As indicated in Table 3.11, there are no discernible differences between home-based workers and factory workers regarding educational background. Both groups have diverse academic backgrounds. In general, while approximately a quarter of female workers did not attend formal schooling, over 30% completed at least 10 years of education.

Table 3.8 Background information on participants for the 2018 South Africa assessment

Variable	Trainees N = 239
Female	58.3%
Age	23.7
Pre-primary education	76.9%
Sibship size	4.86
Family in garment industry	27.3%
Household economic level[a]	4.31
Previous work experience	44.5%
Education level	
TVET Level 1—first year	35.34%
TVET Level 2—second year	15.52%
UoT Level 1—first year	15.52%
UoT Level 2—second year	21.55%
UoT Level 3—third year	12.07%

Note: Data from the Skills and Knowledge for Youth Program assessment
TVET technical and vocational education and training, *UoT* University of Technology
[a] Aggregate factor score of DVD/CD player, TV, cell phone, computer, car, motorcycle, and refrigerator/freezer

Table 3.9 Background information on participants for the 2023 South Africa assessment

Variable	Trainees N = 239
Female	80.3%
Age	39.78
Education level[a]	56.6%
Household size	5.52
Family in garment industry	27.7%
Household economic level[b]	4.18
Age at first work	18.9
Wage, in ZAR	4528.2
Work hours per day	5.44
Line worker	45.4%
Previous work experience	63.2%

Note: Data from the Skills and Knowledge for Youth Program assessment
ZAR South African Rand
[a] Above senior high school
[b] Aggregate factor score of DVD/CD player, TV, cell phone, computer, car, motorcycle, and refrigerator/freezer

Figure 3.9 demonstrates the characteristics of the participating firms. There were eight small firms, four medium-sized firms, and five large firms. The size of the firms is determined based on the number of employees defined by the Small and Medium Enterprises Development Authority (SMEDA) of Pakistan (Cited in Raza et al., 2018). Over 90% of the firms offered on-the-job training (OJT) to their employees. The percentage of female workers in the firms varies significantly, ranging from 4 to 100%. On average, four out of ten workers were female. Only 35% of the companies reported engaging with TVET institutions when hiring employees.

3.4.5 Summary

Table 3.12 presents a summary of the assessment module constructs utilized for each country study and the participants involved. Depending on the objective, we utilized different constructs of our unique assessment modules with different sets of participants. However, one thing remains the same throughout our exercise on the use of our assessment modules: we aim to identify gaps between the demand side and supply side of skills and, at the same time, work with individuals on the ground on providing research-based solutions that would address the gap in skills expectations.

3.5 Synthesis

In this chapter, I introduced two main sets of instruments we used in the surveys conducted in four countries. One is the module to assess the competencies of workers and identify the real nature of "skills gaps" that lie among stakeholders in the demand and supply sides of the labor market. Based on the Realist-Constructivism framework theorized in Chap. 1, the module is made to examine the epistemology and ontology of workers' competencies by combining the questionnaire for employers, workers, and educators, which asks perceptions about detailed lists of abilities and tests to grasp the actual abilities of workers. With this module, diverse realities of micro-ecologies in four countries can be analyzed bottom-up in a constructivist manner while maintaining the comparabilities across the board. Unlike many scholarly works that discuss it at the philosophical level, this approach devised by our team makes abductive reasoning a sequence of practical steps to follow.

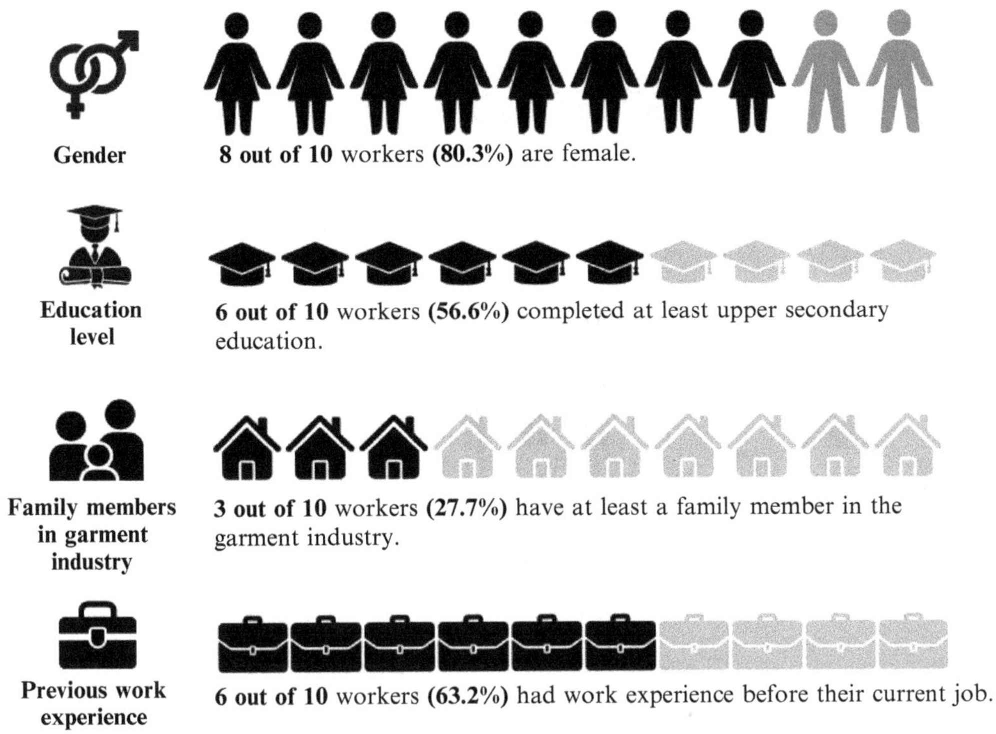

Fig. 3.7 Demography of South Africa participants in 2023

Table 3.10 Background information on participants for the 2023 Pakistan assessment

Variable	Home-based worker (N = 220)	Factory worker (N = 205)
Female	100%	100%
Age	33.9	28.5
Household size	6.38	6.48
Family in garment industry[a]	3.17	2.71
Urban residence	83.0%	78.5%
Household economic level	3.20	3.20
Age at first work	18.9	19.8
Wage, PKR	8277.8	20,679.4
Work hours	5.44	8.06
Work days	5.40	5.97

Note: Data from the Skills and Knowledge for Youth Program assessment
PKR Pakistani rupee
[a] Aggregate factor score of DVD/CD player, TV, cell phone, computer, car, motorcycle, and refrigerator/freezer

Another instrument we developed is a program to train noncognitive abilities using board games designed with a behavioral modeling approach. Our competency assessments conducted in four countries identified noncognitive skills as significant factors in workplace performance. While the importance of these abilities is highlighted widely by scholars and policymakers, there has not been an effective means for training workers in the noncognitive abilities that greatly depend on behavioral applications. Grounded on the psychological theory of behavioral modeling, we developed a training program composed of two board games that help participants consider their behavior in a simulated situation.

Our project started as an exercise to describe work-related competencies' ecology precisely at the micro-level, but in the nexus of influences from macro, national, and industrial levels. However, through close interactions with individuals on the ground, it evolved into a dynamic, participatory form of Realist-Constructivism, where we, as researchers, are actively involved as providers of innovative training.

In the following three chapters (Chaps. 4, 5, and 6), we present the findings from the stan-

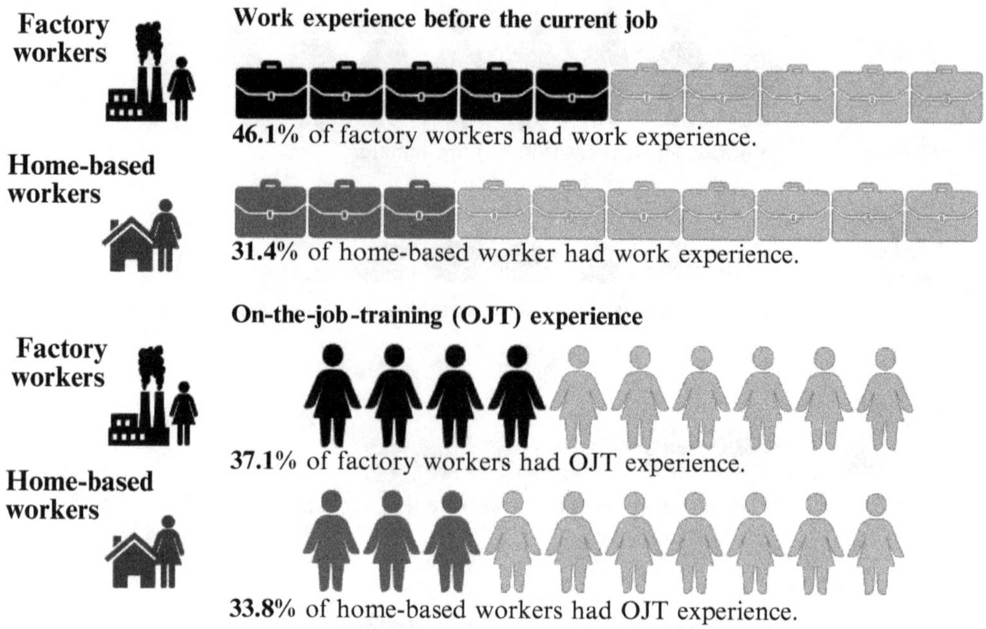

Fig. 3.8 Participants' work and OJT experience by affiliation for Pakistan assessment

Table 3.11 Participants' percentage of attained education level by affiliation for the Pakistan assessment

Education level	Home-based worker (%)	Factory worker (%)
No formal schooling	23	28
Primary education (Grade 1–5)	23	16
Lower secondary education (Grades 6–8)	16	16
High school/Matric (Grades 9–10)	20	27
Intermediate/ FA/ FSc	10	9
TVET	1	0
Tertiary (Diploma, BA/ BSc, MA/MSc, PhD)	4	3
Others[a]	2	0

Note: Data from the Skills and Knowledge for Youth Program assessment
FA faculty of arts, *FSc* faculty of science, *BA* bachelor of arts, *BSc* bachelor of science, *MA* master of arts, *MSc* master of science, *PhD* doctor of philosophy
[a] *Others* refers to certification that cannot be categorized under the national education system

dardized skills assessment in four countries. Chapter 4 discusses the findings from the cross-sectional comparison of micro-ecologies across countries and workplaces; Chap. 5 focuses on a country—Ethiopia—and closely describes the mutual enforcement of various factors, such as perceptions of different actors, unique characteristics of workplaces, and econo-productive, structural-regulatory, and socio-cultural mechanisms, in determining the types of work-related competencies values in specific national ecology of Ethiopia. Then, in Chap. 6, while using the data from multiple countries, instead of comparing across countries, we highlight the characteristics of workers' abilities according to their work styles, namely informal and formal employment. As mentioned earlier, the situation in the informal sector is difficult to capture as the business entities in this sector are not formally registered and are changing rapidly. Accordingly, generating data on workers' capabilities in both formal and informal sectors at once is difficult. Since an advantage of our dataset is that it includes workers in both work styles, we will discuss our unique findings from that.

After these chapters, which discuss findings from multi-country competency assessments, in Chap. 7 results from the game-based training will be presented. We will also share the prospects of our ongoing training interventions.

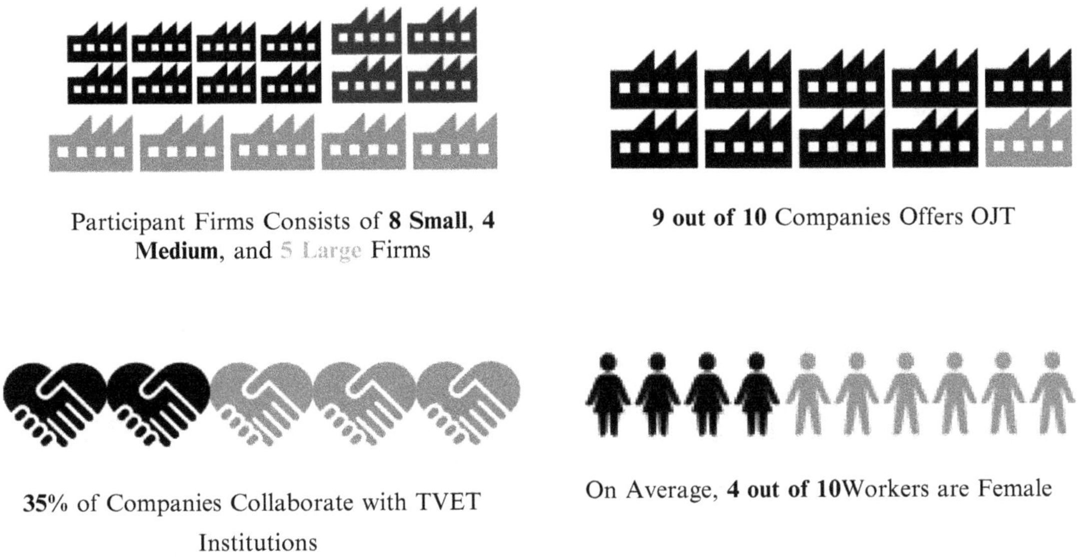

Fig. 3.9 Characteristics of participating firms for the Pakistan assessment

Table 3.12 Summary of assessment module constructs utilized and participants

Instrument *Participant*	ETH 2016–2017	GHA 2018–2019	ETH 2022	ZAF 2018	ZAF 2023	PAK 2023
Questionnaire						
Production Managers	○	○				○
HR Managers	○	○	○		○	○
Workers	○	○	○		○	○
TVET Trainers	○	○		○		
TVET Trainees	○	○		○		
Written test						
Workers	○		○		○	○
TVET Trainees				○		
Practical test[a]						
Workers	○				○	
TVET Trainees						

Note: Data from the Skills and Knowledge for Youth Program assessment
ETH Ethiopia, *GHA* Ghana, *ZAF* South Africa, *PAK* Pakistan, *HR* human resources, *TVET* technical and vocational education and training
[a] Pocket making

References

Armstrong, M. B., & Landers, R. N. (2018). Gamification of employee training and development. *International Journal of Training and Development, 22*(2), 162–169. https://doi.org/10.1111/ijtd.12124

Bandura, A. (1977). *Social learning theory*. Prentice Hall.

Bandura, A., Ross, D., & Ross, S. A. (1961). Transmission of aggression through imitation of aggressive models. *The Journal of Abnormal and Social Psychology, 63*(3), 575–582. https://doi.org/10.1037/h0045925

Bhaskar, R. (1975). *A realist theory of science*. Verso. https://doi.org/10.4324/9780203090732

Bhaskar, R. (1998). Philosophy and scientific realism. In M. Archer, R. Bhaskar, A. Collier, T. Lawson, & A. Norrie (Eds.), *Critical realism* (p. 32). Routledge. https://doi.org/10.4324/9781315008592

Bhaskar, R., Danermark, B., & Price, L. (2017). *Interdisciplinarity and wellbeing: A critical realist general theory of interdisciplinarity*. Routledge. https://doi.org/10.4324/9781315177298

Bryant, S. E., & Fox, S. K. (1995). Behavior modeling training and generalization: interaction of learning point type and number of modeling scenarios. *The Psychological Record, 45*(3), 495–503. https://doi.org/10.1007/BF03395157

Dawe, S. (2002). *Focussing on generic skills in training packages*. NCVER.

Decker, P. J., & Nathan, B. R. (1985). *Behavior modeling training: Principles and applications*. Praeger.

Dobson, P. J. (2001). The philosophy of critical realism—An opportunity for information systems research. *Information Systems Frontiers, 3*(2), 199–210. https://doi.org/10.1023/A:1011495424958/METRICS

Gelatt, V. A., Adler-Baeder, F., & Seeley, J. R. (2010). An interactive web-based program for stepfamilies: development and evaluation of efficacy. *Family Relations, 59*(5), 572–586. https://doi.org/10.1111/j.1741-3729.2010.00624.x

Harrison, J. K. (1992). Individual and combined effects of behavior modeling and the cultural assimilator in cross-cultural management training. *Journal of Applied Psychology, 77*(6), 952–962. https://doi.org/10.1037/0021-9010.77.6.952

Kechagias, K. (2011). Teaching soft skills. In K. Kechagias (Ed.), *Teaching and assessing soft skills* (p. 189). 1st Second Chance School of Thessaloniki (Neapolis). https://web.archive.org/web/20150807162639/http://mass.educational-innovation.org/attachments/396_MASS-wp4-final-report-part-1.pdf

Khazem, D. (2018). Critical realist approaches to global learning: A focus on education for sustainability. *International Journal of Development Education and Global Learning, 10*(2). https://doi.org/10.18546/IJDEGL.10.2.02

Law, G. C., Neihart, M., & Dutt, A. (2018). The use of behavior modeling training in a mobile app parent training program to improve functional communication of young children with autism spectrum disorder. *Autism, 22*(4), 424–439. https://doi.org/10.1177/1362361316683887

Lombrozo, T. (2012). Explanation and abductive inference. In K. J. Holyoak & R. G. Morrison (Eds.), *The Oxford handbook of thinking and reasoning* (pp. 260–276). Oxford University Press. https://doi.org/10.1093/oxfordhb/9780199734689.013.0014

Merkuryev, Y., & Bikovska, J. (2012). Business simulation game development for education and training in supply chain management. In *Proceedings—6th Asia international conference on mathematical modelling and computer simulation, AMS 2012* (pp. 179–184). https://doi.org/10.1109/AMS.2012.12

Otchia, C. S., & Yamada, S. (2021). Interactions between vocational and attitudinal skills in labour market outcomes: findings from the skills' assessment of garment factory workers in Ethiopia. *Journal of Vocational Education & Training, 73*(1), 24–46. https://doi.org/10.1080/13636820.2019.1652675

Ramsarup, P., McGrath, S., & Lotz-Sisitka, H. (2023). Reframing skills ecosystems for sustainable and just futures. *International Journal of Educational Development, 101*, 102836. https://doi.org/10.1016/j.ijedudev.2023.102836

Raza, S., Minai, M. S., Zain, A. Y. M., Tariq, T. A., & Khuwaja, F. M. (2018). Dissection of small businesses in Pakistan: Issues and directions. *International Journal of Entrepreneurship, 22*(4), 1–13.

Shuman, L. J., Besterfield-Sacre, M., & McGourty, J. (2005). The ABET "professional skills"—Can they be taught? Can they be assessed? *Journal of Engineering Education, 94*(1), 41–55. https://doi.org/10.1002/j.2168-9830.2005.tb00828.x

Talavera, E. R., & Perez-Gonzalez, J. C. (2007). Training in socio-emotional skills through on-site training. *European Journal of Vocational. Training, 40*(1), 83–102. Retrieved December 11, 2025. https://www.cedefop.europa.eu/files/etv/Upload/Information_resources/Bookshop/468/40_en_repetto.pdf

Taylor, P. J., Russ-Eft, D. F., & Chan, D. W. L. (2005). A meta-analytic review of behavior modeling training. *Journal of Applied Psychology, 90*(4), 692–709. https://doi.org/10.1037/0021-9010.90.4.692

Waldman, D. A., Galvin, B. M., & Walumbwa, F. O. (2013). The development of motivation to lead and leader role identity. *Journal of Leadership & Organizational Studies, 20*(2), 156–168. https://doi.org/10.1177/1548051812457416

Walton, D. N. (2004). *Abductive reasoning*. The University of Alabama Press.

Webster-Stratton, C. (1982). The long-term effects of a videotape modeling parent-training program: Comparison of immediate and 1-year follow-up results. *Behavior Therapy, 13*(5), 702–714. https://doi.org/10.1016/S0005-7894(82)80026-9

Yamada, S., & Otchia, C. S. (2022). Differential effects of schooling and cognitive and non-cognitive skills on labour market outcomes: The case of the garment industry in Ethiopia. *International Journal of Training and Development, 26*(1), 145–162. https://doi.org/10.1111/ijtd.12252

Zhou, K. (2017). Non-cognitive skills: Potential candidates for global measurement. *European Journal of Education, 52*(4), 487–497. https://doi.org/10.1111/ejed.12241

4 Cross-Sectional Analysis of Workforce Competencies at the Intersection of Ecologies and Generative Mechanisms

Shoko Yamada

Abstract

This chapter applies a Realist-Constructivist approach to cross-national survey data on competency development among working youth, focusing on the garment sector. Using six datasets from Ethiopia, Ghana, South Africa, and Pakistan (2016–2023), the analysis examines perception gaps between employers, employees, TVET trainers, and students regarding the desirable skills for work, compared to the workers' actual skills as assessed by written and practical tests. The assessment module developed uniquely by the author's group allows for meaningful comparisons across firms, countries, and TVET institutions. Results show that firm-level contexts often matter more than country-level differences as wage determinants, although in some aspects, countries reveal distinctive socio-cultural and econo-productive mechanisms that condition the competency development by workers. Perceptions of skill needs vary among stakeholders, reflecting micro-ecologies shaped by the firms' ownership (e.g., foreign-invested vs. local) structures and local environments. Overall, practical and noncognitive abilities are important determinants of wages across ecologies. At the same time, noncognitive abilities demonstrated high context-specificities. On the side of the TVET, a challenge to the policymakers is identified. Despite governments promoting TVET as a means of mitigating skills gaps, TVET students who participated in our surveys are not necessarily keen on employment in the industry for which they are trained, and different career orientations coexist among them.

Keywords

School vs. skills effects · Wage determinants · Cross-sectional analysis · Global South · Noncognitive skills · Multiple imputations · Item response theory

4.1 Introduction

Based on the discussion of the theoretical framework and methodologies in the earlier three chapters, from this chapter on, we will present findings from the series of our empirical surveys. As the first chapter to apply the Realist-Constructivist approach to the analysis of competency development among working youths, this chapter presents findings from cross-sectional comparisons of

S. Yamada (✉)
Graduate School of International Development, Nagoya University, Nagoya, Japan

Graduate School of Asian and African Area Studies, Kyoto University, Kyoto, Japan
e-mail: syamada@nagoya-u.jp

S. Yamada (ed.), *Mitigating the "Skills Gaps"*, Sustainable Development Goals Series,
https://doi.org/10.1007/978-981-95-7968-6_4

survey data from multiple countries. This chapter demonstrates how context-relevant analysis of varieties of skills can be conducted without compromising the generalizability of its findings.

I used six datasets presented in Table 3.12. Particularly, for the analysis of employers and employees (namely, Supply-Demand Gap 2 and Supply-Supply Gap 2 in Fig. 3.1), data from surveys in Ethiopia 2016–2017, Ghana 2018–2019, Ethiopia 2022, South Africa 2023, and Pakistan 2023 are used. Meanwhile, for the analysis of TVET trainers and trainees (namely, Supply-Supply Gap 1 and 2 in Fig. 3.1), I used data from Ethiopia (2016–2017), South Africa (2018), and Ghana (2018–2019). While the assessment module was composed of multiple questionnaires and tests, as explained in Chap. 3, not the whole package was implemented in the respective surveys. As a small Japan-based research team, we could not administer the process all by ourselves, and our operation always depended on the requests and support of the national partners and coordinators. Therefore, sometimes, the survey focused only on employers and employees in the companies, while other times, we worked with the Ministry of Education, which is more interested in the effectiveness of TVET, and helped us to conduct only part of the module related to it. Admittedly, the datasets analyzed here have limitations caused by such operational conditions. The statistical approaches I could use for this chapter's analysis were restricted by the lack of full matches among sub-datasets. Still, I consider that the analysis presented in this chapter demonstrates that our module provides the data to meet the objective of Realist-Constructivist analysis of the ecologies of competency development, using the garment production sector as the manufacturing case in multiple contexts in the Global South.

The comparison is made not only between countries but also at the level of firms to investigate how different levels of ecologies affect evaluations of workforce abilities. Differences in perceived needs of various types of skills among stakeholders suggest the nature of the intra-firm and industrial environment in which workers are evaluated and develop their own package of skills to be successful. After standardizing wages for currency and inflation, country differences in wage determinants became less important than firm-level variations. Still, I found a peculiar tendency among survey participants in Pakistan, attributed to the socio-cultural mechanism and the econo-productive mechanism, represented by the macroeconomic position of the garment industry of this country. The chapter will also discuss the factors that contribute to the differences in firm-level micro-ecologies by comparing the foreign-invested and domestic firms. How does the nature of ecologies surrounding competency development affect psychology and behavior in the workplace? I try to consider this question by closely examining the variables of socio-emotional skills and personality traits while also paying attention to those of school education, cognitive and practical skills, and the socio-economic backgrounds of workers.

The chapter will also discuss the learning ecologies of TVET institutions by comparing the perceptions of TVET teachers and students. What kind of skills do students consider necessary to be employed in the formal sector firms, in contrast to being self-employed? How do the perceptions about the necessary abilities for employment differ between teachers and students, and what causes such differences? These questions will be considered using data from surveys in TVET institutions.

One of the challenges I faced in the analysis was that, although the assessment module is designed to grasp the perception gaps of multiple groups of stakeholders, bridging the supply and demand sides, the dataset that allowed us to do it directly was only that from Ethiopia in 2016/17. Composed of multiple surveys conducted at different times and with different populations, the Ethiopia data showcase how the full-fledged implementation of our module will allow us to grasp a national ecology of workforce competency development in its totality, which will be presented in Chap. 5 in detail. Meanwhile, the cross-national analysis I present in this chapter is based on separate analyses of supply and demand sides, supplemented by circumstantial evidence from econo-productive and structural-regulatory mechanisms to make a comprehensive discussion to connect both sides.

At the end, this chapter will synthesize the findings on competency development ecologies of firm, country, and TVET by presenting factors that are common and peculiar to the different ecologies. The influence of econo-productive, structural-regulatory, and socio-cultural mechanisms will also be considered. Practical and noncognitive abilities are important determinants of wages across ecologies, while cognitive abilities are related to different factors. Also, noncognitive abilities demonstrated high context-specificities. In a broad sense, employers agree on the importance of socio-emotional and problem-solving skills, but the connotations of such skills are very different according to the culture and workplace environment.

4.2 Methodology and Data

4.2.1 Samples Used

As mentioned above, data from surveys conducted in Ethiopia in 2016/17, Ghana in 2018/19, Ethiopia in 2022, South Africa in 2023, and Pakistan in 2023 are used to analyze workplace ecologies involving employers and employees. Meanwhile, to analyze TVET ecologies, I utilized survey data from teachers and students in Ethiopia (2016/7), South Africa (2018), and Ghana (2018/9). In this chapter, I will refer to the former as Dataset 1 and the latter as Dataset 2. The number of participating individuals and organizations (private companies and TVET institutions) is listed in Table 4.1. For Dataset 1, employees' data are matched with those from their companies and their managers. Similarly, in the case of Dataset 2, students' data are matched with those of their institutions and trainers.

The sizes of the samples differ from survey to survey because of the conditions we faced in the respective operations. Also, the survey years stretched from 2016 to 2023. We had to handle statistically these heterogeneities of sample size and years across datasets, which I will discuss soon. Before that, let me present the conditions that affected the data collection.

In the case of Ethiopia, we consistently had strong local support, and, as we will present in Chap. 5, we devoted ourselves to developing comprehensive datasets to examine the nature of the national ecology from multiple perspectives. However, in Ghana, the number of formal companies in the garment production industry was small to begin with. As detailed in Chap. 2, the formal garment production industry has declined because of the cheap imported products since the early 2000s, and the workforce in this field is mostly in the informal sector. A positive effect of this industry characteristic was that we managed to acquire an interesting dataset on informal sector workers in Ghana, which is used for the analysis in Chap. 6. Meanwhile, the formal sector samples ended up being small: two companies and their 62 employees.

The TVET-side surveys were conducted only in three countries: Ethiopia, Ghana, and South

Table 4.1 Samples used for the analysis in this chapter

	Dataset 1		Dataset 2	
Surveys	Employees	Companies	TVET trainees	TVET institutions
Ethiopia 2016/17	591	16		
Ethiopia 2022	504	19		
Ghana 2018/19	62	2		
South Africa 2023	240	7		
Pakistan 2023	205	8		
Ethiopia 2016/17			162	7
Ghana 2018/19			331	4
South Africa 2018			127	2
Total	1602	52	620	13

Note: Data from the Skills and Knowledge for Youth Program assessment

Africa. In Pakistan, the Punjab state agencies, which invited us to conduct the survey, did not consider it relevant to give questionnaires and tests to TVET students, and we only received a couple of trainers' responses and talked with students in some classes. While in Ghana, we had more TVET participants than from companies; in Ethiopia and South Africa, the number of TVET participants was smaller than in the private sector. It was because the number of programs and students majoring in the garment and textile industries was not concentrated in TVET institutions in the cities where the surveys were conducted.

4.2.2 Data Handling Methods and Descriptive Statistics

4.2.2.1 Multiple Imputation

When datasets have small samples or uneven representations of subpopulations, multiple imputation can be a powerful tool, compared to ad-hoc fixes such as listwise deletion or single imputation. Listwise deletion removes entire cases with any missing data, which is a simple approach but reduces the analyzable number of samples, thereby weakening statistical power. In contrast, multiple imputations replace missing values with plausible estimates multiple times, creating several complete datasets to analyze. It is a more robust and effective method that uses all available information and better accounts for uncertainty. This is especially important when subgroups have different sample sizes and variables from parts of the survey instruments that do not fully overlap, which is precisely the case of our datasets. In summary, multiple imputation enables us to utilize all available data, accurately reflect uncertainty, and make more equitable comparisons across subgroups with uneven sample sizes or conditions. It avoids the double penalty of biased estimates and reduced power that often occurs when one relies on listwise deletion in unbalanced data structures (Little & Rubin, 2019; Rubin, 1987). Based on Little's test of missing completely at random, the pattern of our missing data was missing at random (MAR). When there is no consistent tendency in missing data and it occurs entirely at random, it means there is no systematic bias in the data. This missingness pattern is considered to be handled effectively by multiple imputation. Accordingly, I dealt with the data by imputing it 30 times for each exploration of statistical modeling.

4.2.2.2 Item Response Theory: Test Scores Standardization

Regarding the written test scores, instead of using the raw scores, I standardized the respondents' answers to respective test items along a comparable gridline. Each item has a different level of difficulty, resulting in the diversity of test items' capacities to discriminate among the respondents' abilities. That is, too-easy questions tend not to have a high probability of distinguishing individual abilities because almost anybody can answer them. Meanwhile, items with excessive difficulty for the general abilities of respondents would also have limited capacity to discriminate, with too few correct responses. Likewise, the level of difficulty and discriminative capacity of each item vary. As a result, a simple comparison of individuals' raw score points becomes an unreliable approach to assessing their abilities (Noguchi & Watanabe, 2015). Therefore, we ran the two-parameter model of Item Response Theory (IRT). IRT is based on the idea that the probability of a correct response to an item is a mathematical function of the person and item parameters. Based on overall performance on the test, the person parameter is construed as the latent trait of an individual (*theta*; θ), and the item parameter is represented by the location on the difficulty range of all items (item difficulty).

In this chapter, variables on written tests (both the overall total and section total scores) utilize *theta*s derived through the IRT procedure (Tables 4.2 and 4.3). For all test score variables, IRT was run, including all participants regardless of country or year of survey. By standardizing the scores across the board, an individual's performance in the written test, which represents his/her work-related cognitive abilities, became comparable without being bound by the characteristics of national and firm-level ecologies.

Table 4.2 Descriptive statistics of industry-side participants

Variable	N	M	SD	Min	Max
Background of respondents					
Log (Age)[a]	1571	3.25	0.277	2.56	4.16
Female	1579	0.849	0.36	0.00	1.00
Household economic level[b]	1500	0.00	1.00	−1.68	4.91
Education level[c]	1537	0.42	0.49	0.00	1.00
Previous work experience	1572	0.51	0.50	0.00	1.00
Respondents' experience at work					
Wage[d]	1051	0.00	1.00	−1.63	7.73
Supervisor	1549	0.14	0.35	0.00	1.00
Work hours per day	1455	2.10	0.23	0.00	6.91
Advice	1543	0.78	0.41	0.00	1.00
Promoted	1568	0.07	0.25	0.00	1.00
OJT attendance	1543	0.43	0.49	0.00	1.00
Characteristics of the company					
Foreign-invested firm	1602	0.37	0.48	0.00	1.00
Total employees[e]	1377	5.50	1.80	1.61	8.33
OJT frequency[f]	986	5.15	2.18	0.69	10.31
Abilities and perceptions of respondents					
Cognitive skills					
Cognitive ability[g]	1602	0.00	0.93	−3.34	2.81
Vocational ability[h]	1602	0.00	0.76	−2.07	2.58
Socio-emotional skills					
Self-assess: Behavior[i]	918	0.00	1.00	−5.03	3.17
Gap: Behavior[j]	205	0.00	1.00	−3.82	1.68
Personality traits					
Openness	1565	3.89	0.83	1.00	5.00
Personality[k]	1377	0.00	1.00	−4.49	1.81
Vocational skills					
Self-assess: Vocational[l]	1345	0.00	1.00	−3.60	2.93
Gap: Vocational[m]	493	0.00	1.00	−2.54	2.26

Note: Data from the Skills and Knowledge for Youth Program assessment
N observations, *M* mean, *SD* standard deviation, *OJT* on-the-job training
[a] Log-transformed age
[b] Standardized household socio-economic level
[c] 1, if education is senior secondary or above

(continued)

Table 4.2 (continued)

[d] Standardized wage after adjusting for inflation
[e] Log-transformed total number of employees
[f] Log-transformed frequency of OJT provision
[g] Standardized theta scores of the written test
[h] Standardized theta scores on vocational knowledge
[i] Principal component of self-evaluated workplace behavior
[j] Principal component of the employer-employee perception difference on workplace behavior
[k] Factor variable of self-reported personality
[l] Principal component of self-evaluated vocational skills
[m] Principal component of the employer-employee perception difference on vocational skills

Table 4.3 Descriptive statistics of TVET-side participants

Variable	N	M	SD	Min	Max
Background of respondents					
TVET level[a]	566	0.378	0.485	0	1
Female	601	0.827	0.379	0	1
Log (Age)[b]	562	3.028	0.159	2.639	3.871
Household economic level[c]	523	0.000	0.998	−2.954	2.188
Previous work experience	597	0.342	0.475	0	1
Actual and perceived abilities of respondents					
Integrated reading-math[d]	620	0.001	0.706	−2.597	1
Vocational[e]	620	0.000	0.762	−2.547	2.302
Practical ability[f]	157	−0.000	0.964	−3.182	2.182
Self-assess: Vocational TV[g]	266	0.000	1	−3.989	2.581
Career aspirations and school choice					
Reason: TVET school[h]	457	0.000	1	−1.125	4.497
Career prospect[i]	470	0.000	1	−.916	4.019
Internship	591	0.404	0.491	0	1
Reason: Internship[j]	248	0.000	1	−2.756	1.673

Note: Data from the Skills and Knowledge for Youth Program assessment
N observations, *M* mean, *SD* standard deviation, *OJT* on-the-job training
[a] 1, if attended the TVET beyond middle level
[b] Log-transformed age
[c] Standardized household socio-economic level

(continued)

Table 4.3 (continued)

[d] Standardized theta scores of the written test on integrated reading and math
[e] Standardized theta scores of the written test on vocational knowledge
[f] Standardized theta scores of the practical test
[g] Principal component of self-evaluated vocational skills
[h] Principal component of reason for choosing the current TVET school
[i] Principal component of the career prospects
[j] Principal component of trainees' perception of internship

4.2.2.3 Constituting Skills Variables

In addition to the scores of the written test, which measures the cognitive skills of workers and TVET trainees, there are variables on vocational/technical skills and noncognitive skills, as conceptualized in Fig. 1.2. While there are various possibilities for processing skills-related data to construct variables for different analytical purposes, in this chapter I constructed several variables related to noncognitive skills and perceptions of skills. As the details of the module for collecting these data were presented in Chap. 3, I will simply explain here how I processed them to be incorporated into the analysis as variables.

Noncognitive skills encompass both socio-emotional and psychological aspects. In terms of socio-emotional skills, our module features a 27-item scale, which is used identically in questionnaires for different groups of stakeholders, including employers, employees, TVET trainers, and students. In general, I constructed factor variables to represent socio-emotional skills by conducting principal component analysis (PCA). In Table 4.2, the variable *"Self-assess: Behavior"* represents employees' self-evaluation of their own socio-emotional skills, while *"Gap: Behavior"* is based on the comparison of employers' expectations and employees' self-evaluations.

Regarding the psychological aspect of noncognitive skills, we adopted the established scale of the Big Five personality traits and asked respondents 24 questions. There is a standard formula for calculating the scores for the five personality traits. However, we often encountered situations where most of the personality variables constructed in this way did not demonstrate any meaningful impact on the models. Meanwhile, when we developed factor variables using 24 personality items, they often showed significant results. Several studies have highlighted the limitations of using the Big Five scale with participants from non-Western societies (Cheung et al., 2001; Fetvadjiev et al., 2015; Gurven et al., 2013). In a similar vein, I acknowledge the possibility that the scale may not fully capture the personalities of the participants in this study. Therefore, while I attempted to utilize the variables representing five personality traits in their original constructs, I also developed factor variables using the same 24 items through PCA. The variable *"Openness,"* as shown in Table 4.2, was the only Big 5 item that demonstrated statistical significance in the models tested in this chapter. Otherwise, I used the variable of personality traits derived from the PCA named *"Personality."*

In Table 4.2, I have another category of skills-related variables: perceptions of vocational skills. Similar to the variables on socio-emotional skills explained above, variables named *"Self-assess: Vocational"* and *"Gap: Vocational"* are constructed through the PCA of 40 question items about vocational skills. *"Self-assess: Vocational"* represents employees' self-evaluation of their vocational skills, while *"Gap: Vocational"* indicates gaps between employers' expectations and employees' self-evaluation. *"Self-assess: Vocational TV"* in Table 4.3 is the TVET trainees' self-evaluation of their vocational skills.

Still another group of perception-based variables using the PCA factor points is shown in Table 4.3. Variables named *"Reason: Internship"* show TVET students' perceptions about important aspects of internship, namely, the practical training at the industrial sites. Also, *"Reason: TVET school"* is a factor variable that represents the respondent's reason for selecting the TVET institution they belong to. And *"Career prospect"* is the principal component of the respondents' career prospect after graduation from the current TVET institution.

4.2.2.4 Socio-Economic Index and Standardizing Monetary Variables

The socio-economic background of the household often influences the opportunities and experiences that young workers and students have. At the same time, it is difficult for young people to report the total income of their households in cash values. To overcome this challenge, a common practice in social surveys is to provide a list of home appliances and commodities from which respondents select those their families possess. Following the approach of Vyas and Kumaranayake (2006), I conducted a PCA of the 10 items[1] whose possessions were reported by respondents. Then, the predicted primary factor variable was standardized by country (the variable named *"Household economic level"* in Table 4.2).

Another group of variables that required standardization was those in monetary values. Salaries are important variables to determine the labor market outcomes of workforce competencies. To make them comparable, I first adjusted the salaries for inflation using the respective currency's rate. Then I converted them to U.S. dollars at the 2023 exchange rate, the year when the latest surveys were conducted. The variable named *"Wage"* is thus created.

Companies also provided information in monetary terms, such as sales and costs. Although I used other variables to indicate workplace characteristics, I did not incorporate these monetary variables into the analysis presented in this chapter but they would have required similar cross-currency standardization if I had decided to use them.

4.2.2.5 Descriptive Statistics

Tables 4.2 and 4.3 show all variables used for the statistical models presented in this chapter. Table 4.2 summarizes the variables from the survey datasets of companies and their employees, while Table 4.3 presents those from TVET institutions and their students. Except for the variables whose constitution processes are explained above, there are variables related to individual respondents' backgrounds and the characteristics of micro-ecologies of competency development.

For the analysis of company employees, I used variables of their age, gender, educational background, and previous work experience. Regarding their experience after being employed in the current company, several variables are used. They include: whether they have ever been promoted, whether they receive regular advice from superior staff, whether they are ranked as a supervisor or higher, and their weekly work hours. Furthermore, variables indicating company characteristics are also included, such as whether the company is foreign-invested or local, the total number of employees, and the frequency of on-the-job training offered.

Regarding TVET students, I also included the variable of their academic year (grade level) in the TVET program in the analysis.

The age of the participants varied from 13 to 64, with the highest average age in South Africa at 30.78 compared to the overall average of 26.82. Except for Ethiopia, where the majority of employees are young females with less than 5 years of standard deviation (SD), in three other countries the SD reaches as high as 8.5–10 years, including significant outliers. This fact suggests the relative homogeneity of Ethiopian participants, who included many people drafted from rural communities after completing basic education to work at large export-oriented companies. At the same time, to avoid the inconsistent effect of the variable *"Age,"* I converted its values into logarithms. As for TVET trainees, the age disparities were much smaller, with a mean of 20.95 and an SD of 3.76 years. However, for the sake of standardization between Dataset 1 and Dataset 2, I also converted the TVET trainees' *"Age"* values into logarithms. In addition, I rescaled the raw values into logarithms for company-provided variables, namely, *"Total employees,"* and *"OJT frequency,"* so that relationships become more linear, interpretable, and statistically well-behaved.

[1]These are: (1) DVD/CD player, (2) Television, (3) Cellular phone, (4) Computer, (5) Bank account, (6) Refrigerator/freezer, (7) Internet, (8) Bicycle, (9) Motorcycle, and (10) Car.

Another variable that would require precaution is *"Female"* which reflects the industry's globally common characteristic; 84.9% of employees and 82.7% of TVET students are female. Due to this significant female dominance, as I will discuss later, the variable *"Female"* did not signal any unique effects on the patterns of competency development within this industry.

4.2.3 The Analytical Framework

First, this chapter attempts to test, using cross-sectional data, whether the types of abilities rewarded in the labor market, in the form of wages, are similar to those taught in school, and if there are any differences, what makes such differences. In an earlier paper (Yamada & Otchia, 2022), using our data from the 2016/17 Ethiopia survey, we demonstrated the differential impacts of the years of education and various skills on the labor market outcomes (wages) of survey participants. The results indicated that the schooling record is a significant determinant of the level of basic cognitive skills. Meanwhile, labor market outcomes are more dependent on the employees' noncognitive and practical skills. Given that one of the objectives of our project was to provide an evidence-based and detailed discussion of the impacts of pre-employment school-based education and work experience separately, the publication of this paper marked a significant milestone for us. At the same time, our discussion was limited to one survey conducted in a particular country. It remains to be examined whether the patterns we found with the 2016/17 Ethiopian samples are generalizable across the board. Therefore, the following two hypotheses are to examine the generalizability of our earlier findings:

Hypothesis 1

Education before employment and learning at work have different impacts on labor market outcomes, and this is so across contexts

Hypothesis 2

Noncognitive and practical abilities are stronger predictors of labor market outcomes, while the individuals' levels of cognitive skills are linked more closely with pre-employment education

The above two hypotheses are deductive, oriented to confirm what can also be safely assumed in other Asian and African countries, based on the cross-sectional analysis of surveys from four countries. Meanwhile, another appeal of Realist-Constructivism, which I repeated in the earlier part of this volume, is its ability to match them with inductive analysis of diverse micro ecologies. It is not common for a constructivist scholar to provide hypotheses because imposing assumptions based on findings and observations elsewhere on the unique cases is considered a sign of deduction. However, to enhance the clarity of my discussion, I will provide a set of perspectives on inductive exploration, somewhat parallel to the two hypotheses above.

Exploratory Perspective 1

Socio-cultural, econo-productive, or structural-regulatory mechanisms contribute to the uniqueness of some national- and firm-level ecologies on individuals' competency development

In an earlier paper (Yamada, 2023), I compared the skill compositions and their relationships to the labor market outcomes of formal sector employees in Ghana (2018/19) and Ethiopia (2016/17). While its findings about the effects of cognitive and technical skills are consistent not only between the two countries but also with other analyses by our team, a unique contribution of this paper was its discussion about characteristics of noncognitive skills, which are found and evaluated differently according to the contexts, because of the culture, work environment, and employers' expectations. At that time, I could not delve deeper to untangle the kind of generative mechanisms that cause such differences in noncognitive skills between participants from two countries. With samples from two more countries, in this chapter, I will try to examine the determinants and nature of variations more closely.

Another explorative perspective relates to the psychology of stakeholders, which determines the nature of micro-ecologies of competency development. A unique feature of Realist-Constructivism is its attention not only to the ontology of competency development but also to its epistemology. Human abilities are developed based on the career aspirations and self-evaluation of individuals, in response to social norms and expectations from peers and supervisors, which are transmitted through interactions. How people perceive the necessity and quality of each other's abilities are important determinants of what is actually conducted and experienced. As shown in Tables 4.2 and 4.3, we have many variables that represent the perceptions of different groups of participants regarding various types of skills. They will allow me to investigate the epistemological aspects of competency development. Accordingly, my second explorative perspective reads as follows:

Exploratory Perspective 2

The psychology of stakeholders and their mutual influence determines the nature of micro-ecologies and the abilities of the workforce appreciated within them.

To test Hypotheses 1 and 2 through deductive analysis, I developed statistical models using ordinary least squares (OLS). Each OLS model is imputed 30 times, as explained above, to avoid the bias caused by differences in subgroup sizes and variable coverage. To compare the determinants of outcomes in the labor market and school-based education, I run two parallel regression models—one using the wage as the dependent variable (Model a) and another using the total written test score as the dependent variable (Model b). In these models, wages and test scores are considered proxies for the outcomes of exposure to the labor market and education, respectively. For these models, I adopted 2-stage OLS to address firm-level endogeneity. It was done so that, in the course of analysis, the firm variable was noticed to cause significant bias to the experience and abilities of the workforce. It suggests the importance of micro-ecologies of competency development. At the same time, this fact becomes noise when one tries to grasp the general picture. Therefore, while I developed the third model (Model c) to examine the firm micro-ecologies, which I will explain soon, the two models to examine the general patterns of labor market and educational outcomes I controlled for the firm-level effects.

Models a and b are estimated according to the following equation:

$$\text{Structural}: y_{ic} = X_{ic}^{'}\beta + \theta q_{j(i)} + \mu_c + u_{ic}$$

$$\text{First stage}: q_{j(i)} = Z_{ic}^{'}\pi + X_{ic}^{'}\gamma + \mu_c + v_{ic}$$

$$\text{Yielding } \hat{q}_{J(i)}$$

$$\text{Second stage}: y_{ic} = \boldsymbol{X}_{ic}^{'}\beta + \theta\hat{q}_{J(i)} + \boldsymbol{\mu}_{c} + u_{ic}$$

where the model indicates the outcome y of individual i in firm j in country c. The outcome is the wage of an individual in the case of Model a and the test score in the case of Model b. Exogenous variables are represented by X_{ic}, which include demography, experience, education, and abilities. An endogenous regressor is the individual's firm assignment. Country fixed effects are indicated by μ_c.

In addition to Model a and b, I run the third model to examine the characteristics of firms that frequently conduct on-the-job training (Model c). Much literature suggests that on-the-job training has positive effects on improving the noncognitive and technical abilities of the workforce in the Global South (Adhvaryu et al., 2023; Menzel, 2005). However, the effects of such interventions by firms to promote learning at work have not been examined in comparison to other conditions that enable the young workforce to develop their competencies. Therefore, the third model attempts to unravel the characteristics of the micro-ecologies within firms, which, according to the literature, are conducive to developing employees' competencies. The equation is as follows:

$$y_{ij} = \alpha + F_j'\beta + X_{ij}'\gamma + \mu_c + e_{ij} \left(Model\, C \right)$$

Outcome variable y_{ij} is the frequency of on-the-job training offered by the company to which the individual belongs. F_j represents firm-level covariates and X_{ij} indicates individual covariates.

As it was difficult to conduct close examinations of the ontology and epistemology of micro-ecologies using OLS, I also employed inter-group comparisons of Cohen's d means and factor loadings of principal components of perceptions on different types of skills. Cohen's d is a standardized measure of the difference between two means. Unlike t-tests or ANOVA,[2] which report statistical significance of group differences based on raw data, it expresses the magnitude of the difference between groups in terms of standard deviations. Standardized differences allow comparisons across datasets with different scales, which is effective for this cross-sectional study.

In the following sections, I will first discuss the findings in relation to the deductive hypotheses and then gradually shift attention to the meso- and micro levels to identify some factors that make certain ecologies peculiar based on the two exploratory perspectives provided above. In addition, while the majority of the discussion will focus on the industry-side ecologies, the chapter will also explore the perceptions of TVET trainers and students regarding employable skills and the efficacy of industry-attached internships.

4.3 How Country- and Firm-Level Contexts Shape Skills

This section focuses on the findings from industry-side data (Dataset 1 in Table 4.1), while the discussion in Sect. 4.4 will be based on TVET-side data (Dataset 2 in Table 4.2). As I mentioned at the beginning of this chapter, our module is designed to grasp the multi-directional influences of ecologies and generative mechanisms, encompassing not only ontological factual data but also detailed data on perceptions from multiple groups of stakeholders, thereby bridging the supply and demand sides, as well as ontology and epistemology. Due to the operational conditions, we were only able to obtain the dataset that enables us to conduct such linked analysis directly in Ethiopia, which will be presented in Chap. 5. Meanwhile, what I present in this and the next sections of this chapter are separate analyses of the supply and demand sides. In addition to data directly produced through our module, we collected numerous policy documents and observed firms and schools, as presented in Chap. 2, which serve as rich circumstantial evidence to support a comprehensive discussion. Therefore, I will synthesize the findings from both sides after respective discussions.

4.3.1 Wage Determinants: School vs. On-the-Job Training

First, using Dataset 1, I will discuss the findings from three OLS models and consider Hypotheses 1 and 2. Table 4.4 shows the factors closely related to the wage amount, the written test score, and the frequency of on-the-job training (OJT) that the company provides for its employees. For these models, I used most of the variables categorized under the respondent's background, work experience, company characteristics, and cognitive skills, as shown in Table 4.2. Skills-related variables other than cognitive ones will be ana-

[2] Analysis of variance.

Table 4.4 Determinants of wage, test scores, and firm-level ecologies

	Coefficients		
	(a) Wage	(b) Cognitive ability	(c) OJT frequency
Age	0.013* (0.008)	–0.005 (0.004)	0.003 (0.003)
Female[a]	–	–	–
Household economic level	0.019 (0.068)	–0.03 (0.051)	0.002 (0.006)
Education level	–0.093 (0.12)	0.269*** (0.061)	0.032 (0.041)
Previous work experience	0.273** (0.122)	–0.068 (0.063)	–0.034 (0.043)
Supervisor	0.582* (0.35)	0.041 (0.124)	0.093 (0.083)
Work hours per day	0.507* (0.264)	–0.079 (0.176)	0.354*** (0.119)
Advice	0.045 (0.107)	–0.002 (0.007)	0.27*** (0.038)
Promoted	0.581** (0.25)	0.086 (0.143)	–0.016 (0.096)
OJT attendance	–0.006 (0.06)	0.041 (0.029)	0.31*** (0.019)
Total employees	0.018 (0.067)	–0.006 (0.034)	0.186*** (0.023)
Vocational	0.246** (0.096)	0.549*** (0.037)	–0.01 (0.025)
Openness	0.235*** (0.08)	0.221*** (0.036)	–0.023 (0.024)
Pakistan	0.615** (0.286)	–1.14*** (0.078)	–.157*** (0.052)
Constant	-3.786*** (0.693)	–0.426 (0.374)	–0.591** (0.252)
No. of imputed cases	1602	1602	1602
Prob > F	0.000	0.000	0.000

Notes: Standard errors in parentheses. No. of imputations = 30

* $p < 0.1$

** $p < 0.05$

*** $p < 0.01$

[a] Omitted in all models due to the lack of variation

lyzed later, in relation to Exploratory perspectives 1 and 2. These skills and stakeholders' perceptions about them are more context-dependent and better suited for inductive exploration than for inclusion in deductive modelling.

Model a, which uses the wage as the dependent variable, shows that the labor market rewards the workers for their experience and vocational knowledge. The employees who receive higher wages are older, with the variable *"Age"* being significant (0.03 at $p < 0.1$). These older employees are rewarded because they have more experience. Having worked in the same industry before being employed at the current company is a significant predictor of higher wages (*"Previous work experience"* being significant with a coefficient of 0.273 at $p < 0.01$). In addition to the experience, they possess good theoretical knowledge of their vocational field (*"Vocational ability"*; 0.246 at $p < 0.05$). They are also characterized by the personality that looks for new and diverse opportunities and is too creative to maintain familiar routines (*"Openness"*; 0.235 at $p < 0.01$). While it is not hard to imagine their mutual relationship, people with better wages tend to have experienced promotion in the current company (*"Promoted"* 0.581 at $p < 0.05$), and being in a supervisory position (*"Supervisor"*; 0.582 at $p < 0.1$). They also work longer hours than others (*"Work hours per day"*; 0.507 at $p < 0.1$). Years of education (*"Education level"*) or households' socio-economic background (*"Household economic level"*) do not affect the individuals' evaluation in the garment production firms in the surveyed four countries.

Now, let's turn to Model b, which investigates the determinants of the total scores on the written test. Interestingly, most of the variables that demonstrated their significance in Model a did not have any impact on Model b, except for the theoretical knowledge (*"Vocational ability"*; 0.549 at $p < 0.01$) and openness to new and creative experience (*"Openness"*; 0.221 at $p < 0.01$). Among many other insignificant variables, *"Education level"* stood out to be a strong predictor of written test score (0.269 at $p < 0.01$). In sum, determinants of the total test score are contrasting to those of wage. People who get high scores in the written test (which is the measurement of cognitive skills) are those who stayed longer in school, which is the pre-employment education. Employees who are good at the written test have no guarantee of being successful in the labor market, except that the test scores from the section on vocational knowledge alone have a positive effect on wages. As I have explained in Chap.

3, the written test consists of four sections: basic mathematics, reading, integration of math and reading, and vocational knowledge. At first, I included the scores for each of these four sections in the models sequentially. In terms of Model a, all scores other than that for vocational knowledge (*"Vocational ability"*), including the total of four sectional ones, were insignificant. Meanwhile, for Model b, as a matter of course, four sections of the written test scores are significantly related to the total score and multicollinear, because the latter is the sum of the former, including that on vocational knowledge.

It is noteworthy that the personality trait of *"Openness"* is a significant predictor of both the labor market outcomes (wage) and educational outcomes (test score). In fact, this personality trait is found to be significant throughout our study (see, for example, Chap. 6 of this volume). Earlier in this chapter, I questioned the applicability of the Big Five personality scale and its formula to constitute indicators of the personality traits in non-Western contexts. Thus, I decided to develop factor variables through the PCA of 24 personality-related question items to capture local realities more closely. Meanwhile, the fact that *"Openness"* was the only variable that was constituted according to the Big Five calculation formula and demonstrated statistical significance across the board suggests its universal importance for success in either a work or academic environment.

Lastly, Model c will provide us with insights into the micro-ecologies within the firms regarding on-the-job training. The firms that offer OJT opportunities more frequently are likely to have workers who ask for advice from their superiors and colleagues (*"Advice"*; 0.354 at $p < 0.01$) and have attended a variety of OJT programs (*"OJT attendance"*; 0.31 at $p < 0.01$). The workers in the companies which offer OJT frequently tend also to work longer hours (*"Work hours per day"*; 0.344 at $p < 0.01$). Such companies tend to be big in scale (*"Total employees"*; 0.186 at $p < 0.01$), including many export-oriented foreign-invested firms. As I will discuss later, whether a firm is export- or locally oriented is a significant determinant of its micro-ecology. Here, we confirm that the company's commitment to OJT is a significant enabler for employees to seek opportunities for learning by asking for advice and becoming more involved in their work. Such an environment is likely to be found in large export-oriented ones.

The above findings from three regression models support Hypotheses 1 and 2. Models a and b indicate the differential determinants of labor market outcomes and educational outcomes (Hypothesis 1). In terms of categories of human abilities, in the workplace, rewards are determined by technical and vocational knowledge, practical skills developed through experience, and noncognitive skills, such as openness to learning new things and innovating. Meanwhile, for the sake of acquiring higher-level cognitive skills, education before employment is a significant determinant (Hypothesis 2). Additionally, the frequent provision of OJT by firms is a strong predictor of enabling micro-ecologies, where employees are motivated to learn and adapt to the environment proactively.

Now that I have confirmed the two hypotheses to be generally applicable to the garment production industry in the Global South, it is time to discuss contextual variations and their determinants.

4.3.2 Context Matters for Skills Development

Exploratory perspective 1, which I presented above, is to untangle socio-cultural, econo-productive, or structural-regulatory mechanisms that contribute to the uniqueness of some national- and firm-level ecologies on individuals' competency development. In this section, I will examine the factors that cause differences among subgroups using statistical data from four countries, employing different classifications, such as country, firm ownership, or employment status.

4.3.2.1 Country-Level Contexts

One thing I haven't discussed so far, despite its obviousness in Table 4.4, is the peculiarities exhibited by the variable *"Pakistan"* in all three models. The reason for not discussing it was that a sign of the uniqueness of a national ecology was not a focus of the deductive testing of Hypotheses 1 and 2. Variables representing all four countries are included in the estimations, but only that for *"Pakistan"* remained significant throughout (0.614, –1.14, and –.157 at $p < 0.01$ for Models a, b, and c). It is also notable to see that in Model a, the *"Pakistan"* factor was strongly positive, whereas in the two other models, it was strongly negative. In a nutshell, the ecology of the Pakistani garment production industry depicted by these models is that it rewards the workforce highly by experience, job-related knowledge, and work hours, whose employees' level of cognitive skills is significantly lower than their counterparts in other countries, and relatively fewer companies are enthusiastic about on-the-job training for employees.

Here, to avoid misunderstanding, I would like to clarify that exploration is not to judge the overall quality of a country's workforce or industry. What is described here is the nature of the ecology surrounding the skills development of garment production workers, as shared among Pakistani firms that participated in the survey.

To closely examine the characteristics of Pakistan's national ecology, Fig. 4.1 compares the means of the listed variables between Pakistan and three other countries, using Cohen's d value. As explained above, Cohen's d values are suitable for comparing variables across different scales in a standardized manner. If the boxes are plotted between the two reference lines—the gray null-effect line and the red lines indicating the overall statistical significance threshold—there is no statistically significant difference between the groups (in this case, the samples from Pakistan and those from other countries). On the other hand, if the boxes are situated out-

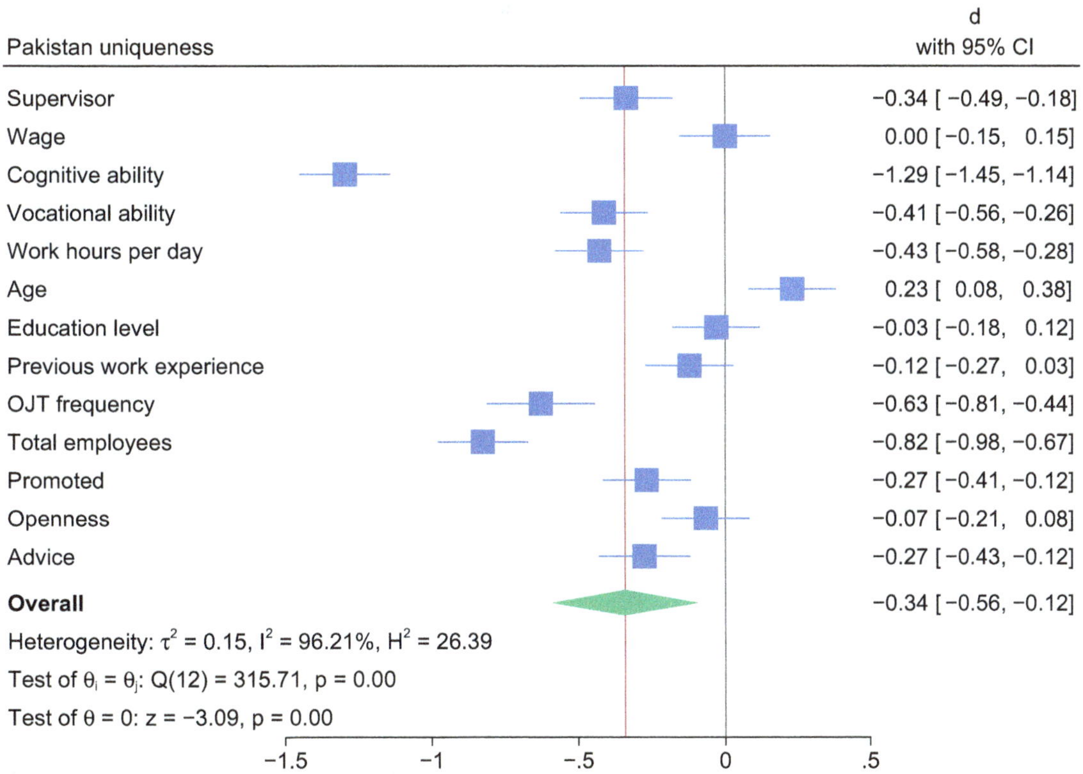

Fig. 4.1 Comparison of skills determinant between Pakistan and the other three countries. Plotted boxes indicate Cohen's d values for respective variables

side the range of these reference lines, the difference between the groups for that particular variable is significant. When they are placed left of the areas between reference lines, it means the effect of the variable is negative. Meanwhile, the boxes on the right sides are positively significant.

As is already evident in Model b of Table 4.4, the total scores of the written test (*"Cognitive ability"*; –1.29) are significantly lower among Pakistani participants. In a way, it reflects the fact that Pakistan's school enrolment rates are lower, as discussed in Chap. 2. However, the general trends of secondary and tertiary education gross enrolment in Pakistan are not so different from those in Ethiopia (35.17 vs. 34.87 for secondary; 8.61 vs. 9.28 for tertiary) (see Table 2.2). Regardless, Pakistani participants' cognitive skills are significantly lower. One may attribute this to the unique socio-cultural mechanism of Pakistani society, which tends to discourage females from engaging in activities outside the home, including learning. This topic will be discussed in more detail in Chap. 6.

Another notable characteristic is that Pakistani companies, which participated in the survey, are generally smaller in size than those in other countries (*"Total employees"*; –0.82). As I discussed regarding Model c of Table 4.4, smaller companies tend not to offer their employees many opportunities for OJT (*"OJT frequency"*; –0.63). On the one hand, the environment is conducive for workers who make efforts, as it promotes and pays relatively higher wages compared to the majority of companies in other countries. On the other hand, they tend not to be large enough to regularly and systematically implement OJT for their employees internally. Based on observations in various locations, I have repeatedly drawn attention to the fact that the small and medium enterprises (SMEs) tend not to have capacity to provide employee training on their own and are the primary clients of on- and off-the-job training offered by formal educational institutions, such as technical and vocational education and training (TVET) (for example, Yamada, Otchia, Shimazu, et al., 2018). This is so because large companies, particularly those foreign-invested and incorporated into the global value chain, train their own employees according to their specific technical and behavioral requirements. This is the case of a tight internal labor market, as explained in Sect. 2.2 in Chap. 2.

Here we see the intersection between econo-productive and structural-regulatory mechanisms on workforce competency development. While it is generally observed that the major clients of TVET-based training are SMEs, the positions of SMEs in the industry vary across different national economies. A characteristic of the Pakistani garment industry is that, although garment production is the driving force behind exports, employing 40% of the labor force, it is largely engaged by SMEs rather than mega foreign direct investment (FDI) companies. Meanwhile, in other countries, particularly in Ethiopia, the industry is dualized between the domestic and export markets, with the former occupied by SMEs and the latter by large companies. In summary, as widely promoted by international agencies, enhancing the synergy between educational institutions and the industry is crucial, particularly by refining TVET programs for SMEs (see Sect. 2.3 in Chap. 2). This is a matter of structural-regulatory mechanisms. Meanwhile, the types and levels of abilities required for employees are determined by the business relationships in which the company is enmeshed. Alignment of TVET programs with SMEs' demands would mean different orientations depending on the positions of SMEs, which require a close understanding of the econo-productive mechanisms.

As explained in Chap. 3, half of our Pakistani survey participants are home-based informal workers, whereas the other half are full-time employees of formal companies. For the analysis in this chapter, I included only those who were employed full-time. However, the significant contribution of home-based informal workers in this industry's workforce should be considered as an element characterizing the Pakistani ecology and its econo-productive and socio-cultural mechanisms.

4.3.2.2 Variations of School Effects

According to the analysis presented in Table 4.4, in general, years of schooling did not significantly influence wages. However, unlike vocational and noncognitive skills, whose significant impact on wages is constantly confirmed, the years of schooling are found to have mixed effects when comparing countries. For example, when I compared the 2016/17 Ethiopian and 2018/19 Ghanaian data, the *"Education level"* variable demonstrated a significant impact on wages in Ghana, but not in Ethiopia (Yamada, 2023). Since garment production is a labor-intensive industry that employs a large number of less-schooled people, particularly in the countries where this industry is export-oriented and a part of the global value chain, such as Ethiopia and Pakistan, the influence of *"Education level"* on wages is muted. Meanwhile, in Ghana and South Africa, where garment exports are less dominant and school education is more prevalent, we see greater diversity among employees in terms of educational backgrounds. Evidencing this observation, in Dataset 1, 59.3% of Ghanaian participants attended senior secondary education or higher, followed by 55.4% in South Africa, 40.3% in Pakistan, and 38.5% in Ethiopia.

The wage effects of years of schooling are primarily attributed to the fact that it is often used as a criterion for hiring and salaries (Keep & James, 2010), particularly when employers cannot precisely evaluate the abilities of individuals. Therefore, when the workforce has diverse educational backgrounds, the level of certificates tends to affect the level of initial salaries. Moreover, because it is unlikely that salaries increase steeply in a short period, the initial amount decided based on years of schooling has lasting effects on intra-firm wage differences. At the same time, as I demonstrated (Yamada, 2023), wage increases after employment are determined by vocational and noncognitive skills, as well as experience. In sum, initial salary tends to be influenced by the signaling effect of educational certificates, whereas vocational performance, job-related attitudes, and skills determine the rewards after employment.

When educational opportunities are unequal and vertical dispersion is high, school education variables affect wages. Given that wage increases after employment are determined by abilities rather than a record of education, one can say that the maturity and prevalence of the education system influence the initial conditions of labor market outcomes. The education system is a key building block of the structural-regulatory mechanism. This fact suggests that the structural-regulatory conditions of respective countries significantly influence the nature of national ecologies.

4.3.2.3 Firm-Level Contexts: Company Owners' Characteristics

Ethiopian participants in our surveys involved workers from both foreign-invested large companies in the industry parks and SMEs. Investors originate from diverse backgrounds and bring their own cultural perspectives on employee management, including training and promotion. Therefore, comparing the companies by ownership, specifically whether they are foreign-invested or locally owned, provides us with interesting insights into firm-level ecologies regarding workforce competency development. For other countries, we don't have as comprehensive data on FDI companies as we do in Ethiopia, but we can still make some firm-level comparisons cross-sectionally.

Figure 4.2 presents a similar comparison to Fig. 4.1, showing the mean difference, this time, between FDI and domestically owned companies using Cohen's d values. In general, FDI companies employ a larger number of people (*"Total employees"*; 2.4), which is associated with frequent offers of OJTs (*"OJT frequency"*; 2.96). This situation aligns with the portrayal of *"OJT frequency"* companies in Model c, as presented in Table 4.4, and contrasts with the situation of SMEs described above. Meanwhile, the employees of FDI firms are younger (*"Age"*; –0.97) than those of domestic firms, with less education (*"Education level"*; –0.20) and less work experience (*"Previous work experience"*; –0.65). They also demonstrate a little less *"Openness"* to the changes and innovations (–0.29).

The situation that we can delineate from this is that many young girls with less education

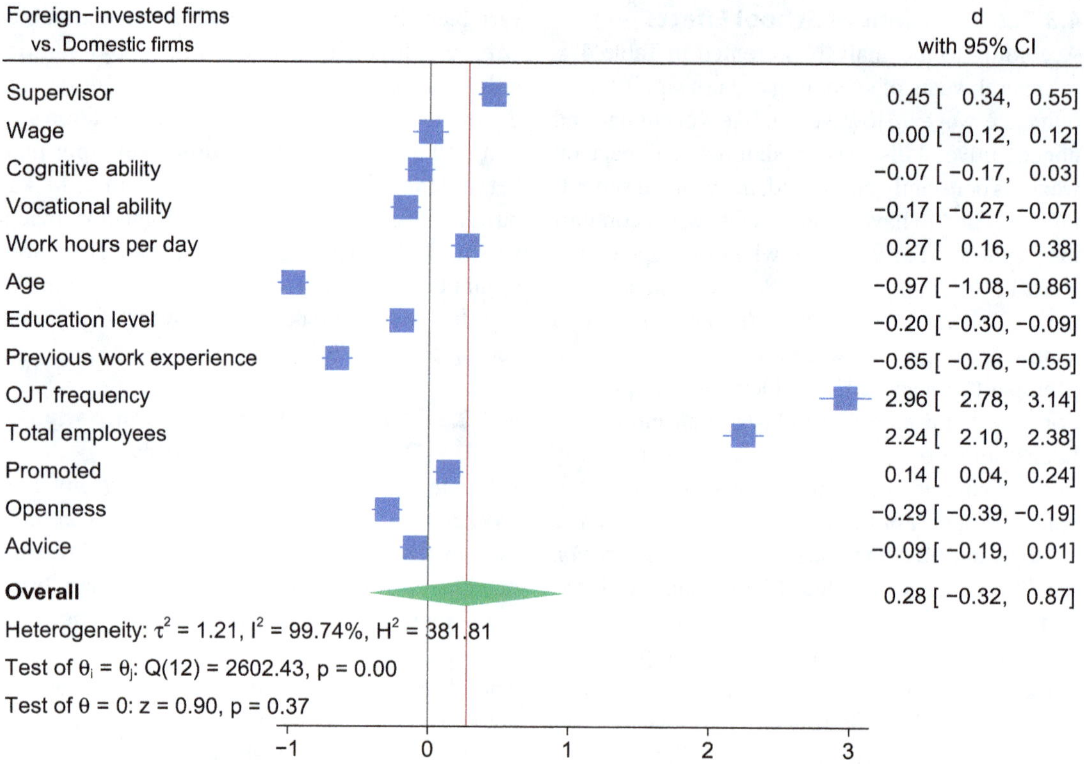

Fig. 4.2 Comparison of foreign-invested firms' skills development ecologies and domestic ones. Plotted boxes indicate Cohen's d values for respective variables

and experience are employed in groups, receive intensive training, and are assigned to work on the large floor alongside other workers. Workers are relatively passive and tend to follow orders rather than suggest improvements. It is a phenomenon that has been reported for years from different parts of the world, particularly in labor-intensive light export industries such as garment production. It is sometimes criticized for offering low wages and harsh labor conditions, which can lead to high employee turnover (Anner, 2020; Hale & Wills, 2005). Our data does not provide us with any details about the employees' living conditions and career prospects. However, we have heard from Ethiopian officials about the challenges of high workforce turnover in industrial parks, which are not often discussed in relation to SMEs. They highlight the role of training in enhancing the motivation and capacities of employees, so that they will be promoted and stay longer in FDI firms. Here, the expectations for training programs differ fundamentally from those for SMEs, which predominantly focus on the technological and vocational aspects of competencies.

Now, after comparing domestic and FDI firms, I will proceed one step further to examine the differences within the category of FDI firms. Figure 4.3 shows the Cohen's d values of firms owned by East Asian investors in contrast to other FDI firms in Ethiopia. It is only for Ethiopia that we have information on the investors' country of origin. Therefore, the firms described in Fig. 4.3 are FDI firms in Ethiopia alone, excluding non-FDI and non-Ethiopia-based firms. Out of 12 companies whose detailed data were available, six were from East Asia (one from China, one from Hong Kong, two from South Korea, and two from Taiwan). The other three came from Sri Lanka, two from India, and one from the United Arab Emirates.

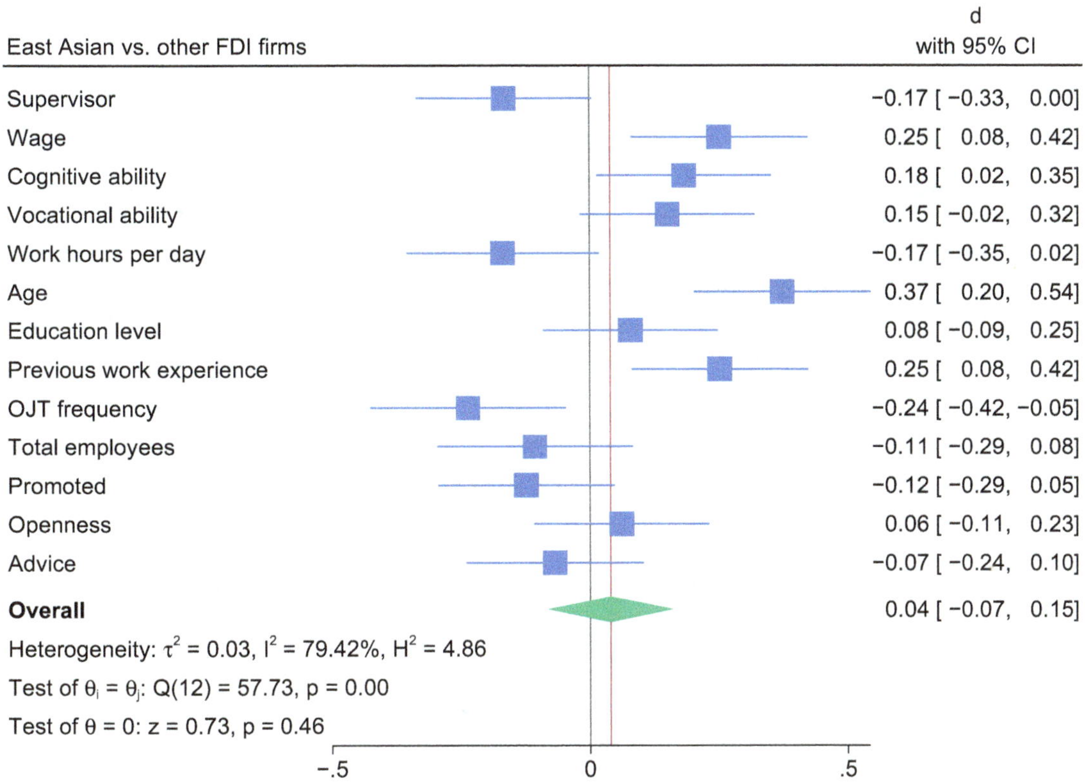

Fig. 4.3 Comparison of micro-ecologies of East-Asian invested firms and those of other investors in Ethiopia. Plotted boxes indicate Cohen's d values for respective variables

In contrast to the overall pattern of FDI firms employing younger and less educated youths with lower wages, East Asian investors exhibit unique characteristics. Employees of East Asian investment firms are older (*"Age"*; 0.37), with higher levels of education (*"Education level"*; 0.08) and longer previous work experience (*"Previous work experience"*; 0.25). In line with the findings from Model b in Table 4.4, the higher level of education is associated with better test scores (*"Cognitive ability"*; 0.18 and *"Vocational ability"*; 0.15). Their wages tend to be higher than those of other FDI firms (*"Wage"*; 00.25). While East Asian investment firms are likely to employ people with higher levels of previous education and experience, offering better salaries, they invest less in OJT (*"OJT frequency"*; –0.24). The chance of promotion after employment is less, too (*"Supervisor"*; –0.17 and *"Promoted"*; –0.12). To summarize, East Asian investors appear to prefer having better-prepared individuals from the outset, with good initial salaries. However, the upskilling seems to be the responsibility of individual workers rather than that of the employer, as there is a lower chance of OJT and promotion. In such a case, the internal labor market of the firm will be less tight, and employees tend to be motivated to develop more generic skills to appeal to the external labor market for job opportunities (Fig. 2.3 in Chap. 2).

The magnitude of such differences within the group of FDI firms would be smaller than the general contrast between SMEs and FDI firms. Additionally, the East Asian investor characteristics captured here may not align perfectly with the stereotype of their corporate culture, which is often described by a commitment to lifelong employment and extensive in-house training (Koike, 1997; Rubin, 1987). Probably, the practices of East Asian investors in the Ethiopian garment industry are influenced by the specific positions of their production bases in the global value chain or the strategy of the multinational corporate network. While it is beyond the scope of this volume to specify the causes of these characteristics of multinational businesses, it is noteworthy that the micro-ecologies of firms differ not only between domestic and FDI firms, but also among FDI firms, and that such characteristics are somewhat shared among investors from the same region. It is another case of firm-level variations caused by a socio-cultural mechanism, which is, at the same time, conditioned by an econo-productive mechanism that determines the firms' positions in the global market. Lauder et al. (2008) highlighted the roles of multinational corporations (MNCs) in shaping the nature of the labor market within the global economy. Based on the analysis of our data, I would like to call attention to the fact that there are significant variations among the labor markets and skills demands created by MNCs, which cannot be explained by the general interaction of state policies and MNCs' strategies.

In summary, the comparative findings presented in this section demonstrate how the development of competency among garment workers is influenced by the broader ecologies in which firms and workers are embedded. The Pakistani case highlights how socio-cultural norms and SME-dominated industrial structures can limit both cognitive skill formation and opportunities for systematic on-the-job training, while still rewarding experience and effort within firms. By contrast, large foreign-invested firms tend to organize labor through group recruitment and standardized training regimes, although often under conditions associated with high turnover rates. Meanwhile, variation among FDI firms themselves—such as the preference of East Asian investors to recruit more educated and experienced workers while offering limited internal skill upgrading—demonstrates that firm-level strategies are also conditioned by owners' cultural orientations and positions in global value chains. Together, these patterns underscore that workforce competencies are co-constructed through the interaction of national education systems, firm size, ownership structures, and the demands of global production networks. Recognizing these layered mechanisms is therefore essential when considering how skill development policies and training interventions can be effectively aligned with the realities of different industrial and institutional contexts.

Now, based on these observations of country- and firm-level ecologies conditioned by generative mechanisms, I will consider the psychologies of stakeholders in the next section. Supported by evidence, the section aims to deepen the discussion about Exploratory perspective 2 I presented earlier, namely, "The psychology of stakeholders and their mutual influence determines the nature of micro-ecologies and the abilities of the workforce appreciated within them."

4.3.3 Psychology of Abilities and the Epistemology of "Skills Gap"

The differences in perceptions of skills among stakeholders lead to divergent understandings of the same realities surrounding workforce competency development, resulting in epistemological "skills gaps". Initially, "gaps" are predominantly epistemological. As much as the human abilities themselves are intangible, their gaps are too. However, the mismatch of such imagined needs and expectations for "employable" abilities constitutes the characteristics of the micro-ecologies and takes the ontological shapes of operational measures and arrangements for promotion, training, or discipline. This, in turn, will affect the psychology of workers/learners willing to align with expectations and achieve better outcomes. Thus, the analysis of psychology regarding work-related abilities is an important building block for Realist-Constructivism, which abductively links the ontology of competency development with its epistemology. For the analysis in this section, I used variables that represent the perceptions of different groups of survey participants regarding various types of skills, as shown in Table 4.2.

Similar to the previous section, which discussed the general trends regarding the effects of generative mechanisms and national- and firm-level ecologies, this section will begin with deductive findings, followed by a more nuanced and inductive discussion of the psychology of abilities in different contexts. For the former discussion, I will use principal components of questionnaire items as skills-related variables, which depict their latent commonalities. Meanwhile, in the latter analysis, I will examine the questionnaire items more closely to unravel the different positionalities of employers and employees, as well as the national characteristics.

4.3.3.1 Perceptions and Labor Market Outcomes

Table 4.5 continues the approaches of the three OLS models presented in Table 4.4, using wage, total score of the written test, and frequency of OJT offered by firms as dependent variables. This time, the analyses focus on the relationship among employees' self-evaluations of their abilities, employers' expectations, and labor market outcomes, as well as test results.

Variables on perceptions about skills, which I used for this analysis, are: *"Self-assess: Behavior," "Gap: Behavior," "Personality," "Self-assess: Vocational,"* and *"Gap: Vocational"* (Table 4.2). Variables with the prefix *"Self-assess"* indicate that they are the principal components of employees' self-evaluation of their abilities. Meanwhile, those with the prefix *"Gap"* are the principal components of the difference between the employer's and employee's response, which shows the perception gap between the two. *"Self-assess: Behavior"* and *"Gap: Behavior"* are based on the 27 questionnaire items regarding the socio-emotional skills (behavior) at the workplace. *"Self-assess: Vocational"* and *"Gap: Vocational"* are constituted from 27 items on vocational skills. And *"Personality"* is the principal component of the 24 items on personality traits. As for *"Personality,"* we only have a self-evaluation variable because it is not feasible to ask employers to specify their expectations for employees' personality traits generally.

Table 4.5 Influence of workers' self-evaluations and employers' expectations on labor market outcomes

	Coefficients		
	(a) Wage	(b) Cognitive ability	(c) OJT frequency
Self-assess: Behavior	0.167** (0.08)	0.014 (0.046)	–0.158 (0.104)
Self-assess: Vocational	0.137* (0.071)	0.03 (0.041)	–0.214** (0.098)
Gap: Behavior	–0.186* (0.11)	–0.009 (0.064)	0.282* (0.145)
Gap: Vocational	–0.324*** (0.088)	0.079 (0.05)	0.328** (0.126)
Personality	0.249** (0.099)	0.134** (0.057)	–0.227* (0.124)
Constant	–0.026 (0.094)	–0.863*** (0.055)	1.524*** (0.122)
No. of cases imputed	1602	1602	1602
Prob > F	0.000	0.000	0.000

Notes: Standard errors in parentheses. No. of imputations = 30
* $p < 0.1$
** $p < 0.05$
*** $p < 0.01$

In Table 4.5, Model a demonstrates that higher self-evaluations of workplace behavior (0.167, $p < 0.05$) and vocational skills (0.137, $p < 0.1$) positively contribute to the wage. At the same time, the gap between these employees' self-evaluation and employers' expectations has an adverse effect (–.186 at $p < 0.1$ for behavior and –.324 at $p < 0.01$ for vocational skills). Personality is also a significant determinant of wage (0.249 at $p < 0.05$). In sum, having confidence in one's socio-emotional and vocational skills is a positive predictor of wage; meanwhile, if such confidence is not in line with the expectations of the employers, it leads to a mismatch of expectations ("skills gap") and negatively affects the labor market outcomes.

Confirming the findings in Table 4.4, Model b again shows that written test scores (cognitive skills) have little to do with intra-firm dynamics and the psychologies of stakeholders. It is only the personality of the individuals that positively correlates with the test scores.

Model c provides an interesting contrast to Model a. Model a suggests that the bigger expectation gaps at the level of individual employees have a negative impact on their own reward in the form of wages. On the other hand, when the skills gaps are large but employees are not confident that they have enough abilities, the companies tend to offer more OJT. Thus, the dependent variable *"OJT frequency"* is positively correlated with two "Gap" variables (*"Gap: Behavior,"* 0.282 at $p < 0.1$ and *"Gap: Vocational,"* 0.328 at $p < 0.05$) but negatively correlated with employees' self-evaluation. The variable *"Self-assess: Vocational"* is significant at $p < 0.05$ level with the coefficient of –0.214. While the coefficient of another self-evaluation variable, *"Self-assess: Behavior,"* is not statistically significant, it is also negatively correlated. Furthermore, it is noteworthy that the *"Personality"* variable is negatively correlated with the likelihood that the company offers the OJT. What does it mean that the *"Personality"* positively affects the wages but negatively predicts the frequency of companies' OJT offers? I will investigate this question in the following sub-section.

So far, we have found a general picture that perception gaps regarding important skills between employers and employees are significant determinants of both individual wages and the nature of the firm's micro-ecology. At the same time, the mechanisms by which perception gaps affect wages and the companies' human resources development are contrasting. On the one hand, individual employees' confidence in their capacities positively predicts their wages, while the larger skills perception gaps negatively impact their wages. On the other hand, companies become more willing to provide OJT when there are larger perception gaps and lower confidence among employees. Meanwhile, employees' cognitive skills appear not to be influenced by the workplace environment or the expectations of employers, at least in the case of floor workers in the garment production industry.

4.3.3.2 Skills Perceptions as the Ecological Characteristics of Firms and Countries

Let us now consider more details of these perceptions of skills. Tables 4.6, 4.7, and 4.8 present the

Table 4.6 Differential perceptions of workplace behavior in firm- and country-level ecologies

Question item		Workplace behavior	Factor loading				
			Self-assess: Behavior	Gap: Behavior	Pakistan	Ethiopia	South Africa
15	I can read the market trends.	Business management	***0.7139***	0.544	0.1395	0.0422	0.5049
1	I can do the work with accuracy and good quality.	Accurate & quality work	***0.7106***	0.3975	0.4445	0.1818	0.5945
7	I can find solutions to the problems I face at work.	Problem-solving	***0.6107***	0.765	0.5395	0.1051	0.6386
5	I can oversee the whole workplace.	Interpersonal relationship	0.5545	***0.8114***	0.1834	0.0989	0.4412
2	I always keep time and do not delay.	Disciplined subordination	0.47	***0.8496***	0.3085	0.104	0.5923
9	I can finish the task in time.	Accurate & quality work	0.2426	***0.8186***	0.5623	0.3184	0.6694
26	I help a co-worker who has too much to do.	Interpersonal relationship	0.2189	N/A	0.782	***0.6401***	0.6998
22	I receive recognition for a job well done.	Sense of fit	-0.0125	N/A	0.7815	***0.5094***	0.5068
23	I am satisfied with my job.	Sense of fit	0.322	N/A	***0.8418***	***0.5568***	0.6023
24	My skills align with the job I am doing.	Sense of fit	0.2194	N/A	***0.8176***	0.3249	0.5548
17	I am good at working collaboratively in a team.	Interpersonal relationship	-0.127	0.3531	***0.7864***	0.4899	***0.7398***
16	I follow the direction given by the supervisor.	Interpersonal relationship	0.3328	0.1441	0.6431	0.108	***0.7728***
13	I make sure that the work environment is safe.	Attention to the work environment	0.1613	0.6974	0.7811	0.0717	***0.7247***

Notes: Values in cells are factor loadings for the principal component. Items with the three largest factor loadings are highlighted for each respective column

Notes: Values in cells are factor loadings for the principal component. Items with the three largest factor loadings are highlighted for each respective column

Table 4.7 Differential perceptions of workplace behavior in firm- and country-level ecologies

		Level of occupation standard	Factor loading					
			Self-assess: Behavior	Gap: Behavior	Pakistan	Ethiopia	Ghana	South Africa
33	Conduct appropriate sampling for quality audit	IV	***0.7193***	0.333	0.1738	0.2121	0.4462	0.7116
31	Carry out relevant visual inspections of materials, parts, and final products	IV	***0.7162***	0.1744	0.1278	0.1911	0.5915	0.726
29	Monitor production as per the plan and consider alternative processes	III	***0.716***	0.2616	0.2225	0.279	0.3525	***0.7943***
34	Maintain records and prepare reports on quality assurance	IV	0.6968	0.2853	0.1925	0.2435	0.4323	***0.7864***
32	Develop checkpoints where quality control has to be exercised	IV	0.6841	0.2091	0.146	0.215	0.5104	***0.8061***
15	Produce a pattern using a CAD system	II	0.2578	***0.8749***	0.1565	0.5012	0.1174	0.2834
11	Use electronic fashion design tools to create the required designs or patterns	II	0.1953	***0.793***	0.1671	0.5768	0.3159	0.235
12	Grade flat or 2D patterns used for garment production	II	0.1797	***0.8312***	0.2107	0.5513	0.254	0.1579
08	Measure and cut custom-made garments	I	0.1818	0.2937	***0.7836***	0.7146	0.5561	0.2781
06	Lay up, mark, and cut complicated fabrics and lays.	I	0.0851	0.2435	***0.7711***	0.6849	0.669	0.102
03	Carry out and analyze body measurements	I	0.1928	0.1026	***0.7634***	***0.7273***	0.39	0.2667
02	Have knowledge of fabrics and trims	I	0.1362	0.3083	0.6948	***0.7749***	-0.0189	0.153
04	Research on fashion trends and identify emerging themes	I	0.1926	0.2288	0.6495	***0.7588***	0.4603	0.2728
22	Identify faults, spots, and marks and take appropriate actions.	III	0.3179	0.1087	0.1278	0.0848	***0.806***	0.3065
24	Know different types of customer labels, washing labels, size labels, tags,	III	0.2415	0.1531	0.0697	0.2862	***0.8124***	0.2455
40	Carry out preventive machine maintenance	IV	0.2054	0.2257	0.1268	0.1845	***0.7573***	0.2445

Notes: Values in cells are factor loadings for the principal component. Items with the three largest factor loadings are hilighted for each respective column
CAD computer-aided design

Notes: Values in cells are factor loadings for the principal component. Items with the three largest factor loadings are highlighted for each respective column
CAD computer-aided design

Table 4.8 Differential perceptions of workplace behavior in firm- and country-level ecologies

	Question item	Big Five classification	Factor loading				
			Personality	Pakistan	Ethiopia	Ghana	South Africa
11	Are you very interested in learning new things?	Openness	***0.667***	0.5451	0.575	0.3004	0.6082
16	Are you very polite to other people?	Agreeableness	***0.638***	***0.6259***	***0.6019***	0.426	0.574
17	Do you work very well and quickly?	Conscientiousness	***0.7096***	***0.6901***	***0.6004***	0.5204	***0.6955***
9	Do you forgive other people easily?	Agreeableness	0.6145	***0.6258***	0.5774	0.407	0.4819
21	Do you think carefully before you make an important decision?	Conscientiousness	0.5792	0.5903	***0.5973***	0.2642	***0.6888***
23	Do you ask for help when you don't understand something?	Agreeableness	0.3042	0.4265	0.4822	0.1278	***0.7236***
10	Do you tend to worry?	Neuroticism	0.1666	0.4611	0.2331	***0.6298***	0.3504
4	Do you like to keep your opinions to yourself?	Extraversion	0.0973	0.1419	0.221	***0.6409***	0.084
12	Do you prefer relaxation more than hard work?	Conscientiousness (reverse)	-0.1573	0.1505	0.1148	***0.6347***	0.1698

Notes: Values in cells are factor loadings for the principal component. Items with the three largest factor loadings are highlighted for each respective column. Item 12 is a reverse question, which means that the larger the value, the less the person is characterized by this item

Notes: Values in cells are factor loadings for the principal component. Items with the three largest factor loadings are highlighted for each respective column. Item 12 is a reverse question, which means that the larger the value, the less the person is characterized by this item

factor loadings of the questionnaire items, which suggest the latent nature of the skills-related variables using principal components. Table 4.6 compares the factor loadings of the "behavior" (socio-emotional skills) variables. Similarly, Table 4.7 compares the factor loadings of items related to vocational skills, and Table 4.8 highlights the inter-group differences in personality attributes.

These tables list the questionnaire items that have high factor loadings for different groups of participants. The designs of the tables are identical. The first column indicates the highly loaded items that constitute the variables for all employee participants, namely, *"Self-assess: Behavior"* for Table 4.6, *"Self-assess: Vocational"* for Table 4.7, and *"Personality"* for Table 4.8. The second column represents the components of the overall difference in perceptions between employers and employees, namely, *"Gap: Behavior"* and *"Gap: Vocational"*. From the third to the rightmost column, I provided the results of the PCA on employees' self-evaluations for the national subgroups, namely, Pakistan, Ethiopia, Ghana, and South Africa.[3] By conducting this series of PCAs for different subgroups, I aimed to highlight the characteristics of socio-emotional, personality, and vocational skills, which tend to be influenced by human interactions embedded in the socio-cultural, econo-productive, and structural-regulatory environment.

As discussed throughout the volume, atmospheres of micro-ecologies are shaped by a complex interplay of generative mechanisms. Particularly, the differences demonstrated in this section are predominantly psychological and thus also cultural in nature. In their efforts to gain more opportunities and rewards, humans tend to internalize the socially shared norms and values. In firms, employees who meet the expectations of employers, namely with fewer perceived "skills gaps," have a better chance of success. Such familiarity with social values can be considered the possession of "cultural capital" according to Pierre Bourdieu's theory (1986), which is a socio-cultural mechanism in Realist Constructivism. Some aspects of employers' expectations are unique to firms, such as the cases of East Asian investors discussed earlier. Meanwhile, there would be some commonalities in a society at large. This will be revealed by comparing the national tendencies in employees' self-evaluations.

In all three tables, I highlighted items with the top three most significant factor loadings for the respective subpopulations. Upon a quick glance, readers would notice that the patterns of highly loaded items differ across countries and between employers and employees. This fact supports my argument that vocational and noncognitive skills, the latter being composed of socioemotional skills and personality traits, are context-dependent.

Workplace Behavior: Socioemotional Skills

Let us examine each table closely. In Table 4.6, the descriptions of workplace behavior added to the right of the question items are the categories used to develop the question items. As explained in Chap. 3, we established these categories after close consultation with experts and observations of workplaces. While they helped us at the stage of designing the module, guiding us to consider questionnaire items systematically and deductively, these categories may not readily explain the diverse realities in respective ecologies. Still, they would suggest some patterns to us.

First, the highlighted items constituting the variable *"Self-assess: Behavior"* suggest that, in general, workers tend to consider their workplace behavior in terms of their capacities to perform tasks autonomously, by predicting market trends (0.7139), solving work-related problems (0.6107), and producing accurate and high-quality outputs (0.6107). Meanwhile, the firm managers (*"Gap: Behavior"*) are not looking for such autonomy but expect them to work well as members of the organization, with good interpersonal relationships (0.8114), being well-disciplined (0.8496), and completing the required tasks on time (0.8186). Here, we can

[3]Items on behavioral skills were not included in the questionnaire for the 2019 survey in Ghana. Accordingly, Table 4.6 does not have the column for Ghana.

see the contrast in orientations between employees and employers. Employees want to see themselves as independent planners and implementers, while employers expect them to adapt well to workplace demands and human relationships.

Against the generally different positionalities between the two sides of employment, let us now examine the country-level variations. The variables *"Pakistan," "Ethiopia,"* and *"South Africa"* in Table 4.6 suggest that the employees' self-evaluations reflect the atmosphere in which they work. Across three countries, good interpersonal relationships and the feeling of being a good fit and acknowledged in the workplace appear to influence their self-evaluation. While the question items that constitute their culturally embedded psychology about workplace behavior differ, we also observe similarities among the three countries. Collaboration with colleagues and compliance with orders are commonly adopted workplace attitudes. A slight difference is that workers in Pakistan and Ethiopia tend to prioritize fitting the employers' expectations, whereas South Africans emphasize their abilities to ensure safety at work.

Vocational Skills

Let us now turn to Table 4.7. Out of 40 question items regarding practical vocational skills on garment production, each of which the respondents are to rate, the table only shows those whose factor loadings are among the top three for any of the six subgroups provided. In the case of employees, they are requested to rate their own abilities, while the employers answered the degree to which they consider these items important. The former category of responses is used for variables *"Self-assess: Vocational," "Pakistan," "Ethiopia," "Ghana,"* and *"South Africa,"* while the latter is used for *"Gap: Vocational"*.

The column named "Level of Occupation Standard" refers to the Occupation Standards of India, South Africa, and Ethiopia, based on which these question items are developed. Level I is the most basic, where workers perform straightforward, repetitive tasks and rely on close guidance. Level II is that of semi-skilled workers, who can perform tasks independently once instructed, but work remains routine. Level III is equivalent to experienced workers who can conduct complex tasks and make informed judgments, and may occasionally supervise others. Level IV is the technician level, where the person can lead and make decisions, in addition to their technical expertise.

Similar to the case with the workplace behavior discussed above, workers tend to evaluate themselves as good at high-level autonomous work. In Table 4.7, two items among the top three factor loadings for *"Self-assess: Vocational"* are classified in Level IV, while another is in Level III. This is a clear contrast to the expectations of employers, as indicated by the items that characterize the variable *"Gap: Vocational,"* which are all at Level II, a level more basic than Levels III and IV. Following the case of workplace behavior, we again notice a "skills gap" in the perceptions of workers and employers regarding vocational skills. Employers consider that the important skills for their employees require some experience and training, but are still routine; whereas workers consider themselves ready to supervise others and make decisions, having sufficient technical expertise. When the gaps are not too large, having high self-esteem is not necessarily a bad thing, as such a person would likely be motivated to work, which may lead to better job prospects and potentially higher wages. However, when the gaps between their self-esteem and employers' expectations become significant, it may be perceived as culturally uprooted arrogance and negatively affect labor market outcomes.

When it comes to the country-level ecologies, the employees' self-esteem appears to be influenced by the econo-productive mechanisms in which the firms are situated. Average monthly wages of the survey participants are $77.20 for Pakistan, $44.61 for Ethiopia, $97.97 for Ghana, and $246.87 for South Africa. Ethiopian participants are the least paid, followed by Pakistani, Ghanaian, and, with a considerable interval, South African. This order roughly corresponds to that of

GDP[4] per person employed, an indicator of labor productivity, in Table 2.2, except for Pakistan ($17,634, $5,949, $15,994, and $47,905 for Pakistan, Ethiopia, Ghana, and South Africa, respectively). In Pakistan, female labor market participation and educational levels are lower due to socio-cultural mechanisms that tend to discourage women's activities outside the home, regardless of the country's average labor productivity. Pakistani female workers in the garment production industry are likely to be paid significantly less than the national average.

In a nutshell, due to the conditions of the garment production industry and socio-cultural mechanisms surrounding the female workforce, expectations for their practical production skills are determined. In Pakistan and Ethiopia, where a large part of the companies are involved in the global value chain and engage in export-oriented mass production, workers tend to be paid less and are expected to have only simple skills sufficient for routine tasks. Accordingly, the items with higher factor loadings for predicting the self-evaluation of workers in these two countries, as shown in Table 4.7, are all at Level I. As they are not expected and not trained for more advanced techniques, they are only confident about basic skills. In Ghana, out of the top three items, two are at Level III and one is at Level IV. In South Africa, two are at Level IV, with one Level III item. One of the common characteristics of Ghana and South Africa is that these countries have better-developed national economies, and wage standards are higher. Another more important factor is that, in these countries, the garment production industry is not particularly successful in exports, and products are primarily intended for the domestic or regional market. This fact suggests that production is less divided, and a worker is often required to engage in multiple tasks. Multi-tasking suggests not only that a worker must cover a wider range of technical areas but also that s/he must be able to make decisions and prioritize tasks at hand. These are more advanced skills than those for simple routine responsibilities.

Personality Traits

As the final part of the exploration of psychological determinants of competency development, Table 4.8 unravels the latent characteristics of personality traits as reported by employees. As stated above, we don't have a variable to show the employer's expectations here, because it was not feasible to ask them their preferred personality types for workers in a general term, while personalities are unique to individuals. Also, while the question items are adopted from the established Big Five personality scale, as I stated earlier, out of the five personality traits calculated according to the provided formula, it was only *"Openness"* that had effects on estimation models. That's why I provide the factor loadings of question items here. At the same time, I provide the Big Five categories (next to the question items) in Table 4.8 to guide the discussion on contextual characteristics of personalities.

The *"Personality"* variable represents the overall tendency of self-reported personality across four countries. Here again, an item to measure a person's *"Openness"* is one of the top three determinants (0.667). Another one represents *"Agreeableness"* (0.638) and the third one is about *"Conscientiousness"* (0.7096). Agreeableness is a personality trait that aligns with the culture of the society, facilitating effective collaboration with others. The fact that *"Agreeableness"* turned out to be a pillar of the *"Personality"* variable shows the synergy with the finding that collaborative interpersonal relationships were important characteristics of workplace behaviors. "Conscientiousness," which indicates an organized, responsible, and self-disciplined personality, is still another important common characteristic.

Regarding the national characteristics of personality traits, the patterns for the four countries are not so clearly different, except for Ghana. As for Pakistan, Ethiopia, and South Africa, general patterns are not so different from the overall trend, where *"Agreeableness"* and *"Conscientiousness"* are the primary determinants of the characteristics.

The Big Five scale allocates the same number of question items to each personality trait,

[4]Gross domestic product.

which is three. In Table 4.8, original three items respectively to estimate *"Agreeableness"* and *"Conscientiousness"* are all retained. Meanwhile, for *"Extraversion," "Neuroticism,"* and *"Openness,"* only one item each has survived. This fact suggests that demonstrating the personality traits of *"Agreeableness"* and *"Conscientiousness"* contributes to success in the labor market of the garment production industry in these countries.

Ghana is a very peculiar case. While items related to *"Agreeableness"* and *"Conscientiousness"* do not significantly affect national characteristics, *"Extraversion," "Neuroticism,"* and the reverse item of *"Conscientiousness"* collectively determine the personality trend of the Ghanaian participants. To make any conclusive arguments, the data is limited. *"Neuroticism"* and *"Extraversion"* appear to indicate opposite types of personality. Meanwhile, an extrovert who is relaxed and sits back (the opposite of being conscientious) may seem to align with a Ghanaian stereotype for some comparative culturalists. Or, the difference may be attributed to the econo-productive mechanism, which enables Ghanaian workers to perform their tasks more independently based on their own pace. However, this explanation contradicts the earlier observation of vocational skills, in which the econo-productive mechanisms in Ghana and South Africa appear to affect them similarly. In terms of personality traits, South African participants are more similar to Pakistanis and Ethiopians than to Ghanaians.

Altogether, the comparative analysis of perceptions of socioemotional skills, vocational skills, and personality traits highlights that perceptions are not simply individual attributes but are shaped by the interactions and shared psychologies of employers and employees within specific organizational and national contexts. Employees tend to want to perceive themselves as autonomous contributors, capable of problem-solving and executing high-level tasks, while employers prioritize reliability, disciplined coordination, and interpersonal harmony. The resulting perception gaps influence both wages and firms' decisions to invest in training, thereby shaping the operational and developmental character of workplace micro-ecologies.

National patterns further demonstrate how broader socio-cultural and econo-productive conditions shape the psychology of ability. In Pakistan and Ethiopia, where production remains highly segmented and wages are lower, workers' self-evaluations tend to focus on basic routine skills. In Ghana and South Africa, with more diversified production and expectations of multitasking, workers report confidence in higher-level, decision-oriented competencies. Personality traits likewise reflect the cultural ecology of work: agreeableness and conscientiousness—traits that support cooperative and reliable participation—are widely valued, while Ghana shows a distinctive configuration shaped by different workplace social dynamics.

Taken together, these patterns directly support my *Exploratory Perspective 2: the psychology of stakeholders and their mutual perceptions actively shape the micro-ecologies of workplaces, influencing which abilities are recognized, rewarded, and developed.* "Skills gaps" are therefore not merely technical deficits but socially and culturally constituted phenomena. The abilities appreciated within any firm are co-produced through ongoing interactions between employers' expectations, employees' self-understandings, and the wider environments in which they are embedded.

Section 4.3 has demonstrated that workforce competency development in the garment industry arises from complex interactions among national contexts, firm characteristics, and workplace-level micro-ecologies. Labor market rewards are shaped less by formal educational attainment than by vocational knowledge, accumulated experience, and noncognitive dispositions such as openness, while the acquisition of cognitive skills is more closely tied to pre-employment schooling. The availability of structured on-the-job training likewise varies significantly, with larger export-oriented firms fostering environments in which workers seek advice, learn from peers, and participate more actively in production processes, in contrast to the more constrained training ecologies of SMEs and informal-sector workplaces. Cross-country and ownership-based comparisons further reveal that broader industrial structures and the firms' positions in global value chains condition employers' skill expectations and human resources management. Socio-cultural mechanisms of the society in which the firms are located and those of the original societies of investors would also affect the nature of micro-ecologies.

The analysis also shows that employers' and employees' psychological orientations toward skills—how they value, interpret, and internalize expectations—play a constitutive role in shaping micro-ecologies. Differing perceptions of abilities among stakeholders shape what is commonly understood as the "skills gap" and influence the nature of competency development ecologies. Such gaps are initially epistemological—rooted in subjective interpretations of what counts as competent workplace behavior, vocational proficiency, and desirable personality traits. However, these differences in perception become ontological when they materialize in organizational practices such as wage setting, promotion, and training. Such is the way that epistemology and ontology shape the micro-ecologies of competency development, which are experienced by the participants as real.

Taken together, these findings suggest that competency development is not a linear function of training provision but a dynamic process shaped simultaneously by socio-cultural norms, structural-regulatory arrangements, production demands, and the psychological negotiations of workplace actors. Building on this insight, Sect. 4.4 turns to the TVET sector to examine the functions that educational institutions play in preparing the workforce's skills and how such practices relate to the demands of the labor market.

4.4 The Pre-Employment TVET Paradox

The dataset used for this section's analysis is Dataset 2, detailed in Table 4.1. As mentioned earlier, the sampling of TVET participants was less comprehensive than that of the industry side, lacking matching data from Pakistan, and the total number of participants was only 620 from 13 TVET institutions in Ethiopia, Ghana, and South Africa. Thus, Dataset 2 has considerable limitations for cross-sectional analysis. Instead of trying to force an analysis on a fragile basis, I will state only what can be asserted to a reasonable reliability. In our earlier publications, using data from Ethiopia, we evidenced significant divergences in perceptions between TVET trainers and trainees (Yamada & Otchia, 2020) and between TVET trainers and employers (Yamada, Otchia, & Taniguchi, 2018). However, such detailed comparisons of positionalities and causes of disparities seem not to be feasible with Dataset 2. Thus, I will defer demonstrating the full capacity of our module in analyzing the multi-faceted "skills gaps" until Chap. 5, which focuses on the national ecology of Ethiopia. Even within the constraints of cross-sectional data, I believe the analysis can effectively showcase the potential of the data, which encompasses both the supply and demand sides of the skills market, as collected through standardized instruments, in achieving the goal of Realist Constructivism.

4.4.1 TVET, Gender, and Labor Market Mismatch

Table 4.9 presents the OLS model, which indicates the factors characterizing female TVET students, using *"Female"* as the dependent variable. As has been discussed, garment production is an industry in which the majority of employees are female. While 84.9% of the employees who participated in our survey are female (Table 4.2), this proportion is also similar to that of female participants from TVET institutions (82.7% in Table 4.3). Therefore, it is not relevant to assume that the female students are a minority in garment-related programs in TVET institutions. Nevertheless, the female students portrayed in Table 4.9 differ from the stereotype of TVET students, at least as imagined by the policy makers, as they appear to be less keen on vocational preparation and less skilled than their male counterparts.

Table 4.9 Characteristics of female TVET students

DV: female	Coefficients
Age	−2.304*** (0.557)
Previous work experience	0.044 (0.109)
Household economic level	0.158* (0.079)
Practical ability	−0.569*** (0.078)
Integrated Reading-Math	0.501*** (0.125)
Vocational	−0.066 (0.084)
Self-assess: Vocational	−0.209*** (0.058)
Reason: TVET school	−0.095* (0.046)
Career prospect	−0.006 (0.039)
Internship	1.974*** (0.388)
Reason: Internship	0.178 (0.099)
Constant	6.147*** (1.466)
No. of cases imputed	620
Prob > F	0.0023

Notes: Number of imputations = 30. Standard errors are in parentheses
DV dependent variable, *TVET* technical and vocational education and training
* p < 0.1
** p < 0.05
*** p < 0.01

Compared to male students, who constitute only about 17% of the population, female students are significantly younger (*"Age"*; –2.304 at p<0.01) and from better-off families (*"Household economic level"*; 0.158 at p < 0.1). Their written test scores on integrated mathematics and reading strongly positively characterize them (*"Integrated reading-math"*; 0.501 at p < 0.01). In contrast, the results of the practical skills tests are significantly lower than male participants (*"Practical ability"*; –.569 at p < 0.01) and self-evaluation of their vocational skills are also lower (*"Self-assess: Vocational TV"*; p < –0.209 at p < 0.01).

In the countries where our surveys were conducted, internships (which are referred to by different names in respective countries, such as industrial attachment or cooperative training) arranged by the school are a requirement for completing the TVET diploma. Therefore, many students have participated in internships, including females (*"Internship"*; 1.974 at p < 0.01). However, female students don't consider any aspect of training in the industry to be relevant and are not particularly motivated to participate in them (*"Reason: Internship"* is not statistically significant). These girls are neither characterized by their experience of previous work (*"Previous work experience,"* which is not significant) nor by their scores on the written test of vocational knowledge (*"Vocational,"* being insignificant).

The portrait of the female students here is that they are younger and have proceeded to the TVET institutions soon after junior secondary school, without prior work experience. They perform better academically than their male counterparts, but significantly less well in vocational skills. They are also indifferent to a career in the garment production industry (the variable *"Career prospect"* regarding post-graduation career, which does not show statistical significance, indicates their lack of interest in companies in this field).

An interesting trend is the strongly negative relationship between being female and the reason for choosing this school (*"Reason: TVET school"*; –0.095 at p < 0.1). *"Reason: TVET school"* is a factor variable derived from principal component analysis (PCA). The question items that characterize this variable (items with higher factor loadings) include: "because school has a good reputation," "school is known for good teachers," "school has a high pass rate of national competency examination," and "it has good facilities and equipment". The strongly negative effect of this variable suggests that female students are dissatisfied with their schools, teachers, facilities, and reputation. In other words, they wanted to attend secondary schools with higher academic reputations and considered their current school to be an inferior option in the education system. While they don't feel the necessity of vocational preparation for future employment in the garment production industry, it would also not have been an option for them to start work without proceeding to the TVET program. The desire to stay longer in the education system for higher certification can be partly explained by the fact that these girls' families are in a relatively better economic status and, presumably, more willing to invest in their children's education.

As I discussed in Chap. 2, there is a die-hard popular belief prevalent in many societies that vocational tracks are an unfavorable alternative to the general education track, which is the option for those whose exam scores were not enough to enter the general courses. Such an idea is said to be found in societies where the history of school education is shorter and access to education has spread in close ties with job opportunities for schooled people (Dore, 1976). As gaining a better diploma is itself a preparation for employment, regardless of the content of knowledge learned in school, learning vocational techniques in school tends not to be a major objective for people with such an attitude (Foster, 1965). As discussed earlier, the shared belief in society affects not only the choices and attitudes of students and their parents, but also the employers' criteria of hiring (Keep & James, 2010). It is one of the effects of socio-cultural mechanisms on competency development ecologies, both in TVET and industry. The discrepancy in perspectives between female TVET students and company employees suggests that, even though policymakers conceptualize them as being part of the same continuum of pre- and in-employment workforce in the same industry, in reality, TVET students rarely consider themselves a part of the garment industry ecosystem.

The analysis of Table 4.9 also suggests a contrasting picture of male TVET students. Male students tend to have relatively higher practical skills and are older, often with more prior work experience. This portrait indicates the possibility that male students enrolled in TVET have different motivations and backgrounds than their female counterparts. Dataset 2, used for this chapter's analysis, does not allow us to compare motivations for enrolling in the current TVET institutions with those of cohorts who chose different educational and training institutions. However, my past research in Ghana, which tried to untangle the strategies adopted by students of different types of TVET institutions in the same city (one under the Ministry of Labor and three under the Ministry of Education), demonstrated the differential tendency of students' motivations by the types of TVET institutions and by their own experience, age and socioeconomic backgrounds (Yamada, 2017). In a crude summary, older students with more experience tend to attend school to enhance their prospects for business success with school certificates, although they already possess sufficient technical and business expertise. Meanwhile, younger students, particularly those enrolled in technical high school, consider their school as one of the options within the education system, a stepping stone to the polytechnics or universities. In Table 4.9, using Dataset 2, such differences in motivation coincided with gender, where female, younger students appeared to be oriented toward school-based career development, while male, older students returned to school after accumulating experience and techniques.

Here, we observe the complex relationship between the labor market and education, which challenges the underlying assumptions behind the structure and regulations aimed at mitigating the "skills gaps" in multiple ways. On the one hand, students who desire to acquire higher educational credentials, what matters is that the institution is part of the education system, but curricular content targeted at employment in specific industries is not the central issue of concern. On the other hand, students who return to school to enhance the market value of their expertise and experience with a school credential are not in need of learning outside of their work. Ironically, neither of them takes the technical and vocational skills taught in these schools very seriously. It is an inherent structural-regulatory issue with government-led competency development schemes in many countries of the Global South. Also, it is fundamentally inseparable from the mass distrust in TVET, which is a matter of the Socio-cultural mechanism.

4.5 Synthesis

This chapter has examined how competencies among young workers in the garment production industry are formed and valued at the intersection of education systems, firm-level structures, and broader socio-economic environments. By applying a Realist-Constructivist framework to cross-national data from Ethiopia, Ghana, South Africa, and Pakistan, the analysis demonstrated consistent evidence supporting the differential impacts of pre-employment schooling and work-based learning on labor market outcomes. While schooling contributes to cognitive skills, especially those captured in standardized written tests, wages and labor force mobility are more strongly determined by vocational knowledge, practical experience, and noncognitive abilities, including the personality trait commonly identified as openness. These findings reinforce Hypotheses 1 and 2, underscoring that competency development is cumulative and context-dependent, shaped by the combination of learning experiences before and after employment.

At the same time, the inductive exploratory analyses revealed important variations in micro-ecologies, formed through the interaction of socio-cultural, econo-productive, and structural-regulatory mechanisms. The case of Pakistan illustrates how lower cognitive skills and limited firm-based training coexist with relatively high rewards for experience, reflecting broader patterns of educational access, gender norms, and SME-dominated industrial structures. Comparisons of domestic and foreign-invested firms further highlighted how the structure and scale of firms condition opportunities for skill development, shaping whether learning occurs through systematic OJT or through individual adaptation. Moreover, differences among foreign investors—particularly East Asian firms—illustrated how organizational cultures, managerial norms, and global value chain positions shape expectations regarding autonomy, training, and promotion, thereby creating distinct competency pathways even within the same national context.

A central contribution of this chapter is the clarification that competency development is not solely an ontological process of acquiring skills, but also an epistemological process shaped by how abilities are perceived, recognized, and rewarded. The analysis of employer–employee perception gaps revealed that self-confidence in abilities can lead to better labor market outcomes, provided that this self-assessment aligns with employer expectations. Conversely, mismatches in perceived readiness or performance standards generate forms of the widely discussed "skills gap," which can manifest as either wage penalties or increased demand for OJT. These findings suggest that competency development is deeply epistemological, as it depends on how individuals internalize workplace norms, negotiate expectations, and orient themselves toward recognition and progression.

The last section of the chapter provided the analysis of TVET-side data. TVET often functions more as a continuation of schooling than as preparation for employment. Many students enroll in TVET to remain within the education system rather than to develop vocational skills, and their attitudes and motivations are loosely connected to the realities of work in the garment industry. As a result, the alignment assumed between TVET institutions and labor market needs is weak, and the system struggles to make a meaningful contribution to reducing skills gaps.

Taken together, the cross-national and firm-level comparisons suggest that national education systems, industrial structures, labor market institutions, and cultural norms jointly configure the ecologies of competency development. The implications extend beyond diagnosing mismatches: they point toward context-sensitive strategies for aligning TVET systems, firm-based learning, and workers' career aspirations. In particular, interventions must take into account whether firms operate in tight or loose internal labor markets, the extent to which learning is collective or individualized, and how socio-cultural expectations shape both workers' behavior and employers' evaluations.

This synthesis sets the stage for Chap. 5, which examines the full, integrated dataset from Ethiopia, where both industry-side and TVET-side data were collected concurrently. That chapter will show how national-level competency development ecologies can be captured more holistically when multiple stakeholder groups are examined together, enabling a more complete account of how structural, institutional, and interpersonal mechanisms interact to shape youth skills formation and labor market integration.

References

Adhvaryu, A., Kala, N., & Nyshadham, A. (2023). Returns to on-the-job soft skills training. *Journal of Political Economy, 131*(8), 2165–2208. https://doi.org/10.1086/724320

Anner, M. (2020). Squeezing workers' rights in global supply chains: purchasing practices in the Bangladesh garment export sector in comparative perspective. *Review of International Political Economy, 27*(2), 320–347. https://doi.org/10.1080/09692290.2019.1625426

Bourdieu, P. (1986). The forms of capital. In J. G. Richardson (Ed.), *Handbook of theory and research for the sociology of education* (pp. 241–258). Greenwood Press.

Cheung, F. M., Leung, K., Zhang, J.-X., Sun, H.-F., Gan, Y.-Q., Song, W.-Z., & Xie, D. (2001). Indigenous Chinese personality constructs. *Journal of Cross-Cultural Psychology, 32*(4), 407–433. https://doi.org/10.1177/0022022101032004003

Dore, R. (1976). *The diploma disease: Education, qualification and development*. Allen and Unwin.

Fetvadjiev, V. H., Meiring, D., van de Vijver, F. J. R., Nel, J. A., & Hill, C. (2015). The South African Personality Inventory (SAPI): A culture-informed instrument for the country's main ethnocultural groups. *Psychological Assessment, 27*(3), 827–837. https://doi.org/10.1037/pas0000078

Foster, P. J. (1965). The vocational school fallacy in development planning. In *Education and economic development* (Vol. 32, pp. 142–166). Aldine.

Gurven, M., von Rueden, C., Massenkoff, M., Kaplan, H., & Lero Vie, M. (2013). How universal is the Big Five? Testing the five-factor model of personality variation among forager–farmers in the Bolivian Amazon. *Journal of Personality and Social Psychology, 104*(2), 354–370. https://doi.org/10.1037/a0030841

Hale, A., & Wills, J. (2005). *Threads of labour: Garment industry supply chains from the workers' perspective*. Blackwell.

Keep, E., & James, S. (2010). *Recruitment and selection—The great neglected topic* (No. 88).

Koike, K. (1997). *Human resource development*. Japan Institute of Labour.

Lauder, H., Brown, P., & Ashton, D. (2008). Globalisation, skill formation and the varieties of capitalism approach. *New Political Economy, 13*(1), 19–35. https://doi.org/10.1080/13563460701859678

Little, R., & Rubin, D. (2019). *Statistical analysis with missing data* (3rd ed.). Wiley. https://doi.org/10.1002/9781119482260

Menzel, A. (2005). *Organizational learning: Experimental evidence from Bangladeshi garment factories background—Sewing lines and learning*. Retrieved December 11, 2025, from https://assets.publishing.service.gov.uk/media/57a0895a40f0b64974000030/Research-Note_2005_Menzel_Organizational-Learning.pdf

Noguchi, H., & Watanabe, N. (2015). *Soshiki Shinri Testing no Kagaku: Komoku Hanno Riron niyoru Soshiki Kodo no Tankyu (Science of organizational and psychological testing: Investigation of organizational actions with item response theory)*. Hakuto Shobo.

Rubin, D. B. (1987). *Multiple imputation for nonresponse in surveys*. Wiley. https://doi.org/10.1002/9780470316696

Vyas, S., & Kumaranayake, L. (2006). Constructing socio-economic status indices: how to use principal components analysis. *Health Policy and Planning, 21*(6), 459–468. https://doi.org/10.1093/heapol/czl029

Yamada, S. (2017). Skills development paths selected by learners: *Journal of. African Studies, 91*, 1–16. https://doi.org/10.11619/africa.2017.91_1

Yamada, S. (2023). Constructivist analysis of cross-sectional data on varieties of skills: Contextualities and generalities of skills packages and rewards to them in Ghana and Ethiopia. *International Journal of Educational Development, 102*(Skills for Development Revisited). https://doi.org/10.1016/j.ijedudev.2023.102851

Yamada, S., & Otchia, C. S. (2020). Perception gaps on employable skills between technical and vocational education and training (TVET) teachers and students: the case of the garment sector in Ethiopia. *Higher Education, Skills and Work-Based Learning, 11*(1), 199–213. https://doi.org/10.1108/HESWBL-08-2019-0105

Yamada, S., & Otchia, C. S. (2022). Differential effects of schooling and cognitive and non-cognitive skills on labour market outcomes: The case of the garment industry in Ethiopia. *International Journal of Training and Development, 26*(1), 145–162. https://doi.org/10.1111/ijtd.12252

Yamada, S., Otchia, C. S., Shimazu, Y., Taniguchi, K., & Deresse, F. N. (2018). *Bridging the supply-demand gaps of the industrial workforce: Findings from a skills assessment of garment workers in Ethiopia skills and knowledge for youth research project*. https://doi.org/10.13140/RG.2.2.35481.26728

Yamada, S., Otchia, C. S., & Taniguchi, K. (2018). Explaining differing perceptions of employees' skill needs: the case of garment workers in Ethiopia. *International Journal of Training and Development, 22*(1), 51–68. https://doi.org/10.1111/ijtd.12118

Ethiopia's National Ecology of Workforce Competency Development

5

Shoko Yamada, Christian S. Otchia, and Fekadu Nigussie Deresse

Abstract

This chapter analyzes Ethiopia's national ecology of workforce competency development through a Realist-Constructivist framework, drawing on the richest and most comprehensive datasets among the four surveyed countries, which encompass FDI and domestic firms, TVET institutions, trainers, and students. By comparing parallel micro-ecologies shaped by distinct econo-productive mechanisms, the chapter demonstrates how employers' skill demands, training practices, and evaluation criteria diverge sharply between export-oriented and domestic firms and between employers and TVET trainers. Using cognitive, practical, and noncognitive skills assessments, it reveals that labor market rewards are driven primarily by vocation-specific and practical skills, while cognitive test performance reflects different developmental trajectories. Analyses of trainers', employers', and students' perceptions show that "skills gaps" arise from epistemological mismatches. At the same time, multi-dimensional analysis of Ethiopian national ecology revealed that competence does not reside solely within individuals, but it emerges from dynamic interactions among actors' perceptions, institutional structures, and the socio-economic mechanisms of their micro-ecologies. The chapter also identifies conditions under which TVET contributes positively to skill formation. Overall, it illustrates how Realist-Constructivism enables an abductive understanding of a complex competency formation mechanism of a country, using Ethiopia as a case.

Keywords

Ethiopia · FDI vs. SMEs · Dual labor markets · TVET · On-the-job training · Skills gaps

---

This chapter is based on and extends the analysis presented in earlier publications from the team as follows: Yamada, Otchia, and Taniguchi 2018; Yamada, Otchia, Shimazu, et al. 2018; Yamada and Otchia 2020; Otchia and Yamada 2021; Yamada and Otchia 2022; Yamada 2023

S. Yamada (✉)
Graduate School of International Development, Nagoya University, Nagoya, Japan

Graduate School of Asian and African Area Studies, Kyoto University, Kyoto, Japan
e-mail: syamada@nagoya-u.jp

C. S. Otchia
Graduate School of International Development, Nagoya University, Nagoya, Japan

F. N. Deresse
Ethiopia Investment Commission, Addis Ababa, Ethiopia

S. Yamada (ed.), *Mitigating the "Skills Gaps"*, Sustainable Development Goals Series,
https://doi.org/10.1007/978-981-95-7968-6_5

5.1 Introduction

Following the cross-national comparison in Chap. 4, this chapter provides a close examination of a national ecology of workforce competency formation in the garment production industry, using Ethiopia as a case study. In 2016, our team initiated an effort to develop a module to measure workforce abilities, which are highly intangible yet require detailed analysis to contribute to academic discussions on human capital and to provide evidence for the improved relevance of policy measures. Since then, while we extended our activities to three other countries, Ethiopia has always been the site where we tried the most cutting-edge interventions and involved different types of stakeholders. Due to these continuous activities and relationships, our datasets of Ethiopian participants enable us to provide the most comprehensive and multifaceted analysis, along with contextual details about the national ecology, compared to any other participating country. We hope that this chapter will further demonstrate the potential of Realist-Constructivism in connecting abductively between induction and deduction, as well as epistemology and ontology, not only at the theoretical level but also in research practice, utilizing substantial instruments of data collection and analysis.

As Sect. 3.4 of Chap. 3 has detailed, the data collection in Ethiopia was conducted in multiple phases involving different participants, namely employers and employees in both export-oriented large companies and small- and medium-sized enterprises, as well as technical and vocational education and training (TVET) students and teachers. With the datasets yielded from them, the authors have published several journal articles, policy papers, and briefs, which discussed the perceptions of important abilities by different stakeholders, the differential effects of abilities and schooling on labor market outcomes, and policy implications of our analysis to mitigate "skills gaps". Thus, the arguments presented in this chapter are not entirely new, but rather a synthesis of existing ones restructured through the Realist-Constructivist lens, with some new analysis added. When published earlier, these papers focused on narrower research questions, linked to literature on specific research interests, so that they fit the scope and requirements of peer-reviewed journals. These journals offer a vital platform for publication, guided by peer scholars and adhering to the standards of their respective academic fields. However, they cannot serve as a venue for expressing the fundamental purpose or philosophical orientation that underlies multiple papers. Therefore, we still consider it indispensable to include findings and discussions presented in earlier papers on Ethiopia in this chapter, so that, not only empirical, but also theoretical and methodological messages from our team will become clear.

Ethiopia is one of the fastest-growing economies on the African continent, with the textile and garment industry being a highly prioritized sector. In 2021, the overall export earnings of the textile and garment manufacturing industry accounted for 46.5% of the total manufacturing sector earnings and 0.6% of the total GDP[1] (Ethiopian Monitor, 2022). According to the Central Statistical Agency of Ethiopia (2018), the textile and garment sector employed around 51,000 workers in 2017. Thus, the government assigns the largest number of trainers and students to textile-related TVET programs. Regardless of this emphasis on TVET, the unemployment rate remains high, particularly among TVET graduates. This brief description of the labor-industry-education context would suffice to indicate the relevance of our study to the needs of policymakers and practitioners, as more details are provided in Chap. 2.

One of the unique aspects of the Ethiopian national ecology of competency development is the coexistence of the export-oriented and domestic garment industries, whose labor demands and relationships with the formal TVET system differ. As Chap. 4 has discussed, we found a cross-national trend that foreign direct investment (FDI) firms tend to hire a large number of younger and less educated people to be trained on-the-job after employment, although the chapter also revealed that such a general trend among FDI firms does not apply uniformly, depending on the investor's country of origin and the firm's posi-

[1] Gross domestic product.

tion in the global value chain. Thus, while it is important to be sensitive to the intra-group variations among FDI firms, it would be meaningful to examine FDI firms and small and medium enterprises (SMEs) as parallel ecologies driven by different econo-productive mechanisms.

Based on this consideration, after explaining the datasets and samples, the chapter presents a comparison of workforce demographics and firm characteristics between FDI firms and SMEs. After that, the chapter will proceed to a deeper analysis of workers' abilities, their evaluations by employers, and ecologies of competency development in the workplace. One of the strengths of our Ethiopian datasets is the capacity to directly compare the perceptions of employers and TVET trainers on the actual performance of workers on practical tests. Therefore, in the latter part of the chapter, we will contrast the perspectives of stakeholders, not only between employees and employers, but also between trainers and employers, as well as between TVET trainers and their students. The findings from statistical datasets are matched with those from interviews and observations conducted throughout our multi-year surveys and a participatory workshop held in August 2017, which enable us to provide a vivid picture of what was actually happening in the Ethiopian ecosystem.

5.2 Samples and Descriptive Statistics

As shown in Table 5.1, the main datasets used for the analysis in this chapter were collected in 2016, 2017, and 2022. For detailed explanations of these datasets, the readers are encouraged to refer to Chapts. 3 and 4.

The surveys conducted in 2016 and 2017 were divided into multiple phases, with smaller subgroups of participants, as our exercises were still at the trial stage. Thus, some of the analyses presented in this chapter, particularly those in Sects. 5.5 and 5.6, use such subgrouped samples. Since it would be confusing for readers to see statistical details for different sets of analysis altogether, the descriptive statistics and analytical models will be provided in later sections as part of the explanation for the respective analyses.

Instead, in this section, we will provide a brief overview of the characteristics of stakeholder groups that participated in our surveys, specifically workers in FDI and domestic firms, TVET trainers, and students.

5.2.1 FDI vs. Domestic Firms

Among the above-mentioned datasets from Ethiopia, the one conducted in 2017 involved FDI firms. The total number of participating firms across different phases of the study was 37, out of which 19 are foreign-invested and located in one of two industrial parks, namely Hawassa and Bole Lemi I.

According to the information provided, the majority of surveyed FDI firms began operating in Ethiopia after 2014 as part of the global apparel supply chain, exporting to 19 different buyers in eight countries, among whom H&M,[2] PVH,[3] and TCP[4] are the top three buyers. At the time of the 2017 survey, these firms employed 21,372 workers, of whom 97% were Ethiopian nationals. The remaining 3% of employees were expatriates, whose top three nations of origin were Sri Lanka (26% of all non-Ethiopian employees), China (19%), and India (18%). There was only one European employee and none from Africa outside Ethiopia. On average, there were 2042 workers per firm, although with a wide range of variation from 320 to 4142.

Unlike FDI firms, which were established less than 3 years before the surveyed year, domestically owned Ethiopian firms outside of industrial parks, which we surveyed in 2016 and 2022, were more diverse in terms of their operating periods. The oldest had been operating for 45 years, and the newest was 3 years old, with a median period of 10 years. Domestically owned firms are also diverse in terms of size, ranging from the smallest, which employs only six workers, to the largest, which has 430 employees, with

[2] H & M Hennes & Mauritz AB.

[3] PVH Corp., formerly known as the Phillips-Van Heusen Corporation.

[4] The Children's Place.

Table 5.1 Ethiopian samples used for the analyses in this chapter

	Employees	Companies	TVET trainees	TVET trainers	TVET institutions
2016–2017	591	16			
2016			162	53	7
2022	504	19			
Total	1095	35	162	53	7

Table 5.2 Samples from TVET by school and enrolled program

	Teachers		Students	
TVET college	Total number in garment programs	Research participants	Total number in “basic apparel production” courses (Levels 1 and 2)	Research participants
A	8	8	N/A	29
B	6	6	44	21
C	8	8	78	14
D	9	8	64	28
E	14	12	68	36
F	7	6	N/A	11
G	5	5	40	23
Total	57	53	N/A	162

Sources: Addis Ababa City Administration TVET Agency, 2015; Yamada & Otchia, 2020

an average of 154. Unlike FDI firms, which are typically 100% exporters, these domestic firms utilize multiple channels for selling their products. In response to the question about the channels through which they sell their products, which allowed multiple responses, each of the 18 firms reported doing business with several different types of sales partners, varying from private individuals (15.91%) to small businesses (13.64%) to government agencies and public enterprises (13.64%) to international clients (13.64%). Eight firms—fewer than half of the 18 firms surveyed—reported exporting some portion of their products, but these exports were not constant.

5.2.2 TVET Institutions and Their Students

TVET-side data were collected at seven public TVET colleges in Addis Ababa. After our first-round survey in January 2016, we did a second round of data collection in September 2016, at seven TVET colleges, distributing questionnaires to 162 students and 53 trainers. The selected colleges were those with the highest enrollment in garment-related programs (Table 5.2).

Participating students were enrolled in the programs of Levels 1 and 2. There are five levels of garment certificates, according to the competencies defined by the occupational standards, ranging from Level 1, subordinate workers with basic production skills, to Level 5, production managers. In the case of garment production, Levels 1 and 2 highlight sewing skills more than design or management, and are considered to be at the competency level of production workers. Level 3 involves more supervisory roles, combined with a few advanced production skills such as computer-based design and embroidery. As of 2015, in Addis Ababa, 43.88% of students in textile-related courses were pursuing Level 2 certification, followed by Level 3 (27.44%) and Level 1 (27.37%) (Addis Ababa City Administration TVET Agency, 2015).

The following sections present distinct analyses, each drawing on specific subsets of the datasets described above. To maintain analytical clarity and avoid redundancy with other chapters, we present methodological details, variable construction procedures, and descriptive statistics within each analytical section where they are directly relevant.

5.3 Ethiopia's Dual Labor Market and Skills Development

To understand how Ethiopia's dual labor market influences opportunities for workforce competency development, particularly through on-the-job training, this section begins by comparing the basic characteristics of domestically owned and foreign-invested (FDI) firms, as well as the workers they employ. Drawing on firm-level survey data, we explore the differential skills demands between two categories of firms and their implications for the opportunities available to workers.

5.3.1 Foreign-Invested and Domestically Owned Firms

As discussed in Sect. 4.3 of Chap. 4, FDI firms across four countries have distinct characteristics that are not found in domestic firms. The picture shown in Fig. 4.2, which compares firm-level ecologies across countries, generally aligns with the situation in Ethiopia.

To understand the differential characteristics of the workforce and micro-ecologies between domestically owned and foreign-invested firms, Table 5.3 presents the results of the t-test, which compares the means of variables related to employees' demographics and experience, as well as those indicating the characteristics of the firms for which they work. Except for the households' economic standard (variable named *"Household economic level"*), the attributes of workers and firms all demonstrated statistically significant differences between the two groups of firms. Similar to the pattern identified in the cross-country analysis, FDI firms in Ethiopia tend to hire individuals who are younger (*"Age"*), less educated (*"Education level"*), and without prior work experience (*"Previous work experience"*). Meanwhile, employers in FDI firms commit more to training their employees after hiring (*"OJT frequency"*) and providing advice during work (*"Advice"*) than their domestic counterparts. The size of the workforce in FDI firms is significantly larger than in domestically owned ones (*"Total employees"*).

In summary, generally speaking, FDI firms do not expect their workforce to be fully prepared for work when they are employed; rather, they provide on-the-job and off-the-job training after employment. In other words, they internalize the interventions to develop the capacities of their workforce, rather than expecting formal pre-employment educational institutions to prepare them for the world of work. It is possible because these companies are larger and have more financial and technical means to do so. Meanwhile,

Table 5.3 Comparison of characteristics between domestically owned and foreign-invested firms in Ethiopia (two-sample *t*-tests with equal variance)

	Obs1 Domestic	Obs2 FDI	Mean1 Domestic	Mean2 FDI	Diff	St. Err	*t* value
Age	507	585	25.840	22.072	3.768***	0.276	13.65
Education level	506	587	0.419	0.356	0.063**	0.03	2.15
Household economic level	506	509	−0.141	−0.213	0.072	0.054	1.35
Previous work experience	507	583	0.678	0.318	0.361***	0.029	12.75
Supervisor	507	586	0.103	0.237	−0.135***	0.022	−5.95
Work hours per day	505	482	2.091	2.146	−0.054***	0.013	−4.2
Advice	507	574	0.708	0.758	−0.05*	0.027	−1.85
OJT frequency	258	436	1.806	3.454	−1.648***	0.036	−45.3
Total employees	466	436	153.895	2041.567	−1887.7***	57.443	−32.85

Diff difference, *St. Err* standard error, *FDI* foreign direct investment, *OJT* on-the-job training
* $p < 0.1$
** $p < 0.05$
*** $p < 0.01$

smaller domestic firms tend to hire pre-trained personnel, partly because they cannot afford to train them in-house. At the same time, such discrepancies between the two groups of firms in their hiring and training orientations suggest factors that cause perceived "skills gaps" and a misfit in the human resources development mechanisms. Based on this consideration, let us now examine the nature of the intra-firm training in two groups of firms and its implications for our understanding of the Ethiopian structural-regulatory mechanism of workforce competency development.

5.3.2 Determinants of On-the-Job Training

In response to our questionnaire survey, all firms confirmed that they provide training opportunities for their workers. Again, the gross number of training participants (including multiple counts of individuals who took part in more than one program) varies both within and between the two categories of firms. First, the average number of training participants per firm was 1497 for the FDI category, but only 74.1 for the domestic firm group. Regarding the intra-category variation, the smallest number of training participants per domestic firm was two, with a maximum of 120. Meanwhile, among the FDI firms, the number of participants per firm ranged from 240 to 3500.

5.3.2.1 Role of Management

Generally, the size of the company and the frequency of training opportunities are correlated (overall correlation coefficient is 0.78). As we examined earlier, the firms' commitment to in-house training largely depends on their technical and financial surplus capacities to allocate resources for activities not directly related to production, including staff training, which are closely linked with the size of their business. At the same time, the significant intra-group variations suggest that the training provision is determined not only by the firms' capacities and types of business but also by the managerial will.

Regarding the FDI firms, the general trend is that they employ younger, less experienced people, but provide more training after hiring. However, investors from East Asia have demonstrated a significantly different pattern of hiring and training. Since Sect. 4.3 of Chap. 4 extensively discussed this point using Ethiopian data, we will not repeat it here. However, we would like to draw the readers' attention to the fact that the differential management traditions brought by investors from their society of origin, along with the firms' positions in the global value chain, cause variations in the intra-firm labor market and skills demands (see also Yamada, 2023).

Meanwhile, as for the domestic firms, variations in the on-the-job training (OJT) provision seem to be attributed more to the management wills of respective firms. Out of 18 domestic firms surveyed, only four (three from the 2017 survey and one from the 2022 survey) had a training participation rate exceeding 100% in the past year. In these four firms, all workers had at least one training opportunity. While the average annual training participation ratio for 18 firms was 66.4%, it varies from 0.4% to 146%.

Interestingly, the correlation between firm size and OJT provision is lower for domestic firms than for FDI counterparts (the correlation coefficient for domestic firms is 0.57). Some smaller firms conduct on-the-job training more actively than larger ones. One such firm, whose general manager has a training facility and is very committed to developing the skills of its employees, even allows employees of other firms to attend its training programs. As discussed later in this chapter, according to our skills assessment conducted with workers from domestic firms, their practical skills are significantly related to the firms they work for, and those employed in the firms that are serious about training demonstrate higher performance.

5.3.2.2 Contents and Business Environment

The study also reveals differential emphases on training content between FDI and domestic firms. Our questionnaire asked firm managers to report the frequency of training programs they offered, by the content taught. As shown in Fig. 5.1, the items on training content, which allowed for multiple responses, ranged from cognitive to technical to noncognitive skills. Firstly, the t-test of the mean of the training offered demonstrated statistically significant differences for all listed content items between domestic and FDI firms. Given the existence of differential focus, Fig. 5.1 visually presents the nature of employees' abilities that the respective categories of employers try to cultivate. The content coverage does not equal the frequency of training offered, as the firms may cover multiple content in a single training program. Although it is a subjective report by the managers, we consider it useful to understand the managers' perceptions of necessary skills and their reflection in the OJT practices.

One evident contrast is that the domestic firms' coverage of training content is wider than that of the FDI firms. Although employees in domestic firms have higher average years of education, employers still provide basic training in literacy and numeracy. Additionally, managers in domestic firms strive to upgrade the technical abilities of their employees at all stages of garment production, from cutting the fabric to making patterns, sewing, and designing. They also expect their employees to possess various noncognitive abilities, including communication, work ethic, and safety considerations.

In contrast, managers of FDI firms tend to have more focused expectations on employees' abilities. While they tend to employ less educated people, unlike domestic firm managers, they do not provide any training on cognitive skills. Meanwhile, they focus on training technical skills, predominantly in sewing, followed by cutting. Sometimes, they provide training on pattern making and quality control, but only for a smaller group of employees. In large firms where the division of labor is advanced, quality control is typically performed by relatively experienced line supervisors. Furthermore, when a company produces garments according to the designs and specifications provided by clients, as is often the case in export-oriented foreign-invested enterprises, they don't need an in-house capacity for pattern-making and designing. In summary, their technical demands for entry-level floor workers focus rather exclusively on sewing and cutting. Similarly, the noncognitive skills trained in FDI firms are less comprehensive than those in domestic firms and receive significantly less attention than technical upskilling.

The differences in training focus reflect the business environment in which the respective categories of firms operate: one faces the global export market, while the other predominantly serves the domestic market. It is evidence that the econo-productive mechanisms condition the training ecologies of firms. Domestic and smaller firms require workers to attend to multiple tasks, while the mass production firms divide tasks and train workers for effectiveness in a limited number of specified tasks.

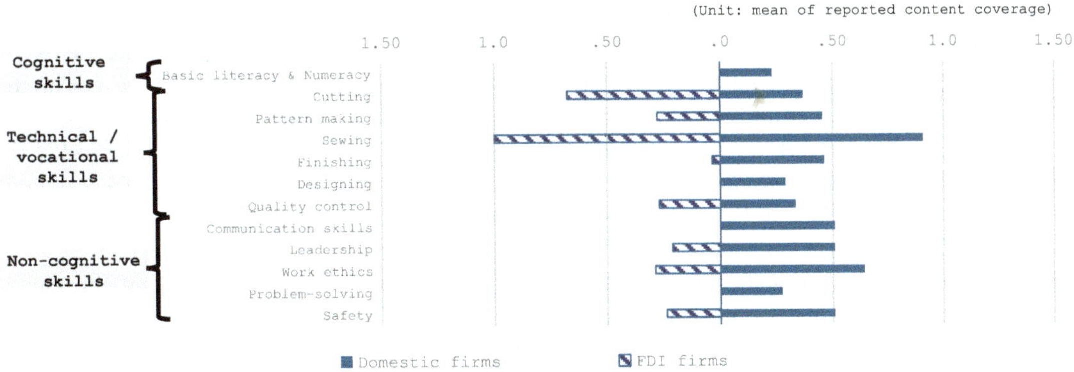

Fig. 5.1 Contents of on-the-job training offered by firm type

5.3.3 Implications of the Dual Labor Market on Policy

One of the challenges of the skills development structure regulated by the national government, as detailed in Sects. 2.3 and 2.4 of Chap. 2, is that it aims to cover comprehensively the potential skill demands in diverse forms of employment, which naturally require very different capacities. As we reviewed above, the skills development ecologies of domestic and FDI firms are different because of the econo-productive mechanisms in which they operate. On the other hand, the government-led structural-regulatory skills development framework is not focused on any specific work context but is designed to meet the demands with the greatest common denominations of the diverse workplaces within the same industry. The individuals who try to find jobs and develop their careers have to find the balance between the contextual demands in specific micro-ecologies, which are determined by the demands from econo-productive mechanisms, and the structural-regulatory mechanism of the country, which sets the standards of formal school-based education, evaluation, and acknowledgement of skills acquired through such education. There is also a twist between the national skills development framework, which aims to equip the workforce with employable skills, and FDI firms, which do not typically look for people with pre-employment technical training.

We will come back to this point regarding the disjuncture between econo-productive and structural-regulatory mechanisms later, with more evidence on expectation gaps between formal school teachers and employers. Meanwhile, let us now turn to the effects of various skills on labor market outcomes. Although there is a general agreement that the skills are important determinants of labor market outcomes, it would be important to disaggregate the effects of respective types of skills, as well as those of schooling.

5.4 Differential Effects of Skills and Schooling on Labor Market Outcomes

As was discussed in Chap. 4, the cross-sectional analysis of the four countries' data revealed that the labor market outcomes measured by the amount of wages are determined by the practical skills and knowledge directly related to the vocation, in this case, garment production, and noncognitive skills, particularly the socio-emotional aspect of it. In this section, we will examine whether these findings can be confirmed using data from Ethiopia.

The following questions will be addressed: Are there any differential effects of schooling and skills on labor market outcomes? If so, how are they different? Then, what kind of combination among cognitive, noncognitive, and functional skills is likely to be rewarded in the labor market? To answer these questions, let us now turn to the data and its analysis.

5.4.1 Data and Methodology

5.4.1.1 Construction of Variables and Descriptive Statistics

Table 5.4 shows the descriptive statistics for the variables used for the analysis. First, we constructed variables to represent individuals' cognitive capacity.

As explained in Sect. 4.2 of Chap. 4 in detail, we employed the Item Response Theory approach to standardize the scores of individual respondents to each test item. The variable "*Cognitive*" is the aggregation of the standardized theta yielded by the one-parameter model of IRT. In addition to the aggregate score of the written test, we also included the aggregate scores of the vocational knowledge section in the written test (variable named "*Vocational*").

To examine the effect of practical operational abilities, we included the aggregate scores of the practical test as well ("*Practical*").

Table 5.4 Descriptive statistics for the analysis of Sect. 5.4 (reproduced from Yamada & Otchia, 2022)

Variable	N	M	SD	Min	Max
Wage[a]	591	7.14	0.50	6.21	8.99
Cognitive[b]	591	0.00	0.94	−4.41	2.30
Vocational[c]	591	0.00	0.03	−0.08	0.10
Practical[d]	591	0.00	1.00	−0.47	4.39
Accurate-Certain[e]	591	0.00	0.91	−4.79	1.84
Leadership-Innovation[f]	591	0.00	0.91	−3.11	2.33
Education level[g]	591	0.36	0.48	0.00	1.00

N observations, *M* mean, *SD* standard deviation
[a] Log-transformed wage
[b] Standardized theta score of the total written tests
[c] Standardized theta scores on vocational knowledge
[d] Standardized total score of the practical assessment
[e] Noncognitive ability (1): being accurate and certain about the task
[f] Noncognitive ability (2): taking leadership and being innovative
[g] Years of education are more than 11

Regarding the socio-emotional aspect of the noncognitive skills, we constructed two variables—*"Leadership-Innovation"* and *"Accurate-Certain"*—using principal component analysis on 26 questions from the questionnaire, which asked respondents to self-rate various aspects of their attitudes as workers and employees.

Further, we included variables for salary, workplace position (a manager or not), and level of education (above grade 11 or not).

5.4.1.2 Analytical Framework

Based on our interest in examining the effects of cognitive, noncognitive, and practical skills on wages, we run two regression models in parallel—one using wage as the dependent variable (Model a) and another using total score on the written test (Model b). The comparison of these models enables us to assess the cognitive capacities required for effective reward in the workplace against those that yield good scores on the written test. As we discuss later, the analyses demonstrate different patterns. We thus estimate the following equation:

$$y_i = \alpha + \beta Cong_i + \tau Nonc_i + \gamma Pract_i + \rho Educ_i + \varepsilon_i$$

where y_i is the outcome indicator of interest (wages in the case of Model a, and written test score in the case of Model b); *Cong* measures the cognitive ability regarding vocational theories; *Nonc* is a vector of noncognitive skills variables, namely being accurate and certain about the tasks, and taking leadership and being innovative; *Pract* represents practical skills; *Educ* takes 1 if educational attainment is grade 11 or above and 0 otherwise; and ε is the error term. We employ gradient boosting regression to estimate these relationships because skills and knowledge domains exhibit complex interdependencies that linear specifications may not fully capture. Cognitive abilities intersect with vocational knowledge acquisition, while noncognitive traits interact with both domains in ways that condition their labor market effects. This analytical approach is particularly appropriate in our context, where practical skills may yield differential returns depending on workers' levels of noncognitive discipline, or where vocational knowledge may require threshold levels of general cognitive ability to translate into workplace productivity. We supplement the gradient boosting results with analysis of variable importance measures to understand the relative contribution of each skill domain to wage and test score outcomes, thereby maintaining our commitment to linking epistemological frameworks with ontological realities in workforce competency.

5.4.2 Determinants of Labor Market Outcomes and Cognitive Skills

Table 5.5 presents the outcomes of the two regression models, which examine the complex relationships among schooling and different types of skills—cognitive, noncognitive, and practical—as contributors to workers' labor market outcomes.

Table 5.5 Determinants of labor market outcomes and cognitive skills

	(a) Wage Model	(b) Written Test Model
Education level	0.0511	0.0321
Leadership-innovation	0.2313	0.1611
Accurate-certain	0.3060	0.2498
Practical	0.1093	0.0903
Vocational	0.3023	0.4667

Note: This table reports variable importance measures derived from gradient boosting regression models predicting (a) wages and (b) written test scores. The values represent standardized importance scores on a scale from 0 to 1, where higher values indicate greater predictive power

Let us first examine the effects of various skills on wages, as shown in Model a. In terms of cognitive skills, knowledge of vocational theory is the strongest predictor of wages. The results indicate that employers evaluate and reward their workers based not on cognitive reasoning, but on vocation-specific knowledge.

Another important finding is that employers place a heavy weight on skills that visibly and directly contribute to productivity. Like proficiency in vocational theory, performance on the practical test is a significant determinant of wage. To be competent in the workplace, workers—even those on production lines—should be able to process information and make informed judgments to find optimal solutions within their context. However, such workplace reasoning capacity appears to differ from that which the written test of one's reading or mathematics ability can measure. With experience, workers likely develop work-related problem-solving capacity, which compensates for the lack of capacity to process information in written form.

A further critical issue is reward for noncognitive skills. As Table 5.4 shows, two variables representing noncognitive skills are included in this analysis. The variable "Leadership-Innovative" denotes a proactive disposition, as one would see in a worker who is prone to thinking innovatively, proposing changes, and leading the group. The other variable, *"Accurate-Certain,"* denotes an inclination to carefully and accurately complete given tasks, ensuring that one does what is expected. The analysis shows that self-reported noncognitive skills contribute to wages to a lesser extent than vocational knowledge and practical skills. Regardless, employers tend to reward a disposition toward obedience and accuracy more than an inclination toward leadership. This tendency was observed not only in the case of machine operators working on production lines but also among those in supervisory positions. It indicates that employers have little use for workers who extoll their potential for leadership and independence.

Now we turn to Model b and examine the determinants of written test scores. Practical skills and self-reported noncognitive skills exert minimal influence on test performance. An essential difference between Models a and b regarding the *"Vocational"* variable is that it is a much stronger predictor of a dependent variable (*Test score*) in Model b than (*Wage*) in Model a. In other words, written tests and workplace success both demand diverse cognitive skills but weigh them differently. Tests emphasize theoretical vocational knowledge most heavily, while the workplace distributes importance more evenly across theory, accuracy, leadership, and practical skills. Rather than requiring fundamentally different abilities, the two domains reward overlapping competencies with different relative priorities. Here, we observe a consistent yet fundamental contrast in epistemology regarding workforce abilities between individuals who view learning as a holistic growth of cognition and those who prioritize immediate practicality, which surfaced in many different places throughout this volume. Such epistemic differences are, of course, subjective and personal, but, as the analysis in this section demonstrates, reside in the institutional micro-ecologies that have their distinct culture and orientations.

Lastly, we discuss the effect of schooling, which is denoted by the variable *"Education level."* We should highlight that the level of school certificate has little to do with the score on the written test. Although the study was conducted with relatively new employees (less than 3 years of employment) in labor-intensive export factories, a sizable number of participants (40.22%) had finished more education than lower secondary, such as upper secondary (grades 11–12; 9.34%), tertiary (4.84%), and TVET (26.04%). The test was translated into the national language, Amharic, and the questions were based on primary and lower secondary curricula. Still, as we see above, there was a significant divergence in written test performance.

Table 5.5 suggests that school certificates have a greater impact on labor market outcomes than on written test scores. Possessing practical skills and having knowledge of vocational theory, for which the labor market rewards workers, are not as much the result of schooling as they are of having cognitive skills. Regardless, those workers who received an education above grade 11 tend to have higher wages. This is, as discussed in various parts of this volume, the signal effect of the educational credential, while it has a less significant impact on the evaluation after being employed.

5.4.3 Synthesis

The findings of this section's analysis empirically support the position championed by some academics that the labor market effects of schooling and skills are different. The school variable is influential not because it represents an individual's capacity but because employers treat it as the screening criterion for hiring and promotion. It follows, then, that policymakers and other stakeholders should consider the effects of schooling and skills separately. In addition, one should not automatically assume that the effect of the school variable is equivalent to the effect of education, given that performance on the written test was not strongly correlated with the school certificates the participants held.

Second, skills cannot be considered monolithically. Different types of skills—cognitive, non-cognitive, and vocation-specific—have varying effects. Therefore, on the one hand, it is important to consider the holistic nature of competence. On the other hand, for a precise understanding of the nature of holisticity in this context, we consider the Realist-Constructivist approach to be promising, which untangles the skills into specific dimensions and examines their contribution to overall competence and labor market outcomes.

Lastly, we would like to point out that our Realist-Constructivist approach to skills assessment is particularly relevant in situations where realities of competency development are difficult to capture. Unlike in developed economies, where the underemployment of the overeducated population is a major issue for human resources development, in societies of the Global South, where the average years of education are relatively less, with slimmer chances of formal-sector employment, a large part of learning and career development happens outside of the scope of governmental planning and record-taking. In such situations, whereas pre-employment training is important, the learning and skills acquisition that takes place after graduation is too important to be neglected in evaluating the workforce's abilities. The workers' learning trajectories are determined by the interaction of their subjective motivation and the social requirements, which can only be grasped through the analysis of microscopic data on multifaceted skills.

5.5 Epistemology of "Skills Gaps"

As explained in Chap. 1 and other parts, for Realist-Constructivism, it is essential to consider the psychology of people who are involved in evaluating workers' abilities, designing the training programs based on such evaluation and judgment about necessary skills, as well as the self-evaluation of workers who try to improve their abilities, responding to the social norms and values surrounding them. Thus, from the very beginning of the study, we attempted to investigate people's perceptions about workforce abilities in diverse ways. We even considered that the "skills gaps" are predominantly a matter of psychology until we theorized the mutual enforcement between stakeholders' perceptions and econo-productive, socio-cultural, and structural-regulatory mechanisms in specific micro-ecologies. Put differently, this research, which eventually led us to the theory of Realist-Constructivism, evolved from close observations of epistemology in the effort to construct our understanding of reality based on the subjectivities of individuals.

Due to this history, in Ethiopia, where the project originated, we collected data on the perceptions of various stakeholders in multiple phases and with close attention. In this section, we will present our findings on contrasting perceptions. Section 5.1 compares the perceptions of domestic firms' managers and TVET trainers, and Sect. 5.2 compares those of TVET trainers and students. Both are based on relatively small sample surveys conducted in 2016.

5.5.1 Employers vs. Trainers: Expectations and Evaluation

As explained in Chap. 3, our assessment module has attempted to match the data of the employers' and trainers' expectations with the workers' test scores, which indicate their actual abilities, ensuring that the study does not focus solely on epistemology but is linked with the ontology of workers' abilities. Such relationships between epistemology and ontology were easier to establish regarding cognitive skills, as the correct answer for each item in the written test is unchangeable and applies across differences in contexts. Meanwhile, evaluation of noncognitive and technical/vocational skills is influenced by the socio-cultural and econo-productive mechanisms in and around the micro-ecologies. I have extensively discussed the contextual characteristics of noncognitive skills and their ontological meanings in Chap. 4. Regarding technical/vocational skills, it was only in Ethiopia in 2016 and Ghana in 2018 that we managed to involve both firm managers and TVET trainers in evaluating the practical test performance of workers onsite simultaneously. We hypothesized that the evaluation criteria differ between the two groups of graders due to their backgrounds. It became possible to highlight these differences only by giving them the same checklist and asking them to grade the performance of the same group of examinees.

The investigation aimed to clarify the nature of the supply-demand gap in expectations for workers' skills. Specifically, the questions were (1) whether the expectations from the labor market and from the training institutions correspond to their evaluation of workers' abilities, and (2) whether stakeholders' demographics and professional backgrounds affect their perceptions of skills.

The design of the practical test, along with its objectives, is detailed in Sect. 3.2 of Chap. 3. Here, we will only remind readers that there are four areas of performance check, constituting 20 items in total: pattern development, analysis of garment structure, machine sewing, and garment finishing. Assessors used a five-point Likert scale, ranging from 1 (very unsatisfactory) to 5 (highly satisfactory), to grade the performance of workers. In addition, assessors responded to questionnaires designed to enable us to analyze their grading patterns in relation to their respective backgrounds. For this purpose, the questionnaire for factory managers and TVET trainers contained identical question items regarding expectations for various skills.

5.5.1.1 How Graders' Experience and Context Shape Skills Evaluation

Fig. 5.2 contrasts the grading patterns of trainers and employers. We standardized the average scores for each category of tasks, plotted them for two groups of assessors—trainers and employers—based on their distance from the overall average. Fig. 5.2 demonstrates TVET trainers' general tendency to give higher scores for the performance of workers. In contrast, employers tended to be critical, scoring lower, even though both groups of assessors were evaluating the performance of the same group of workers concurrently. In other words, the actual performance, the workers to be evaluated, and the context of the assessment were all the same. Therefore, this clear and consistent tendency in grading can be

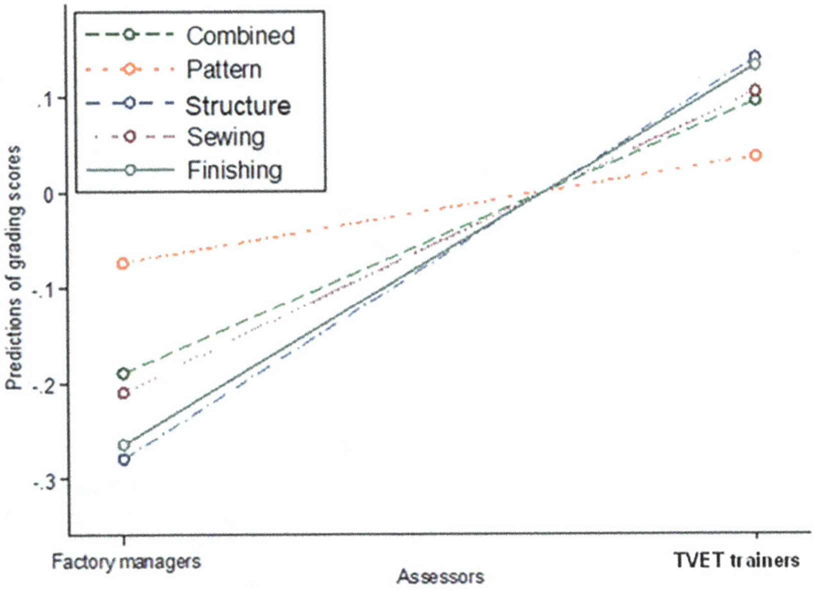

Fig. 5.2 Supply-demand gaps in expectations of garment production skills

considered to represent a difference in expectations when each respective group evaluates the tasks performed by workers. In addition, the slopes of the lines are steeper for garment structure, sewing, and finishing, meaning that the mismatch in expectations between the supply and demand sides is bigger in these domains of skills.

In our earlier publication (Yamada, Otchia, & Taniguchi, 2018), we suggested that the differential work environments of employers and trainers led to their discrepancies in evaluating the workers' practical skills. TVET colleges' training aims to develop all-rounders who can follow the steps of garment making, from measuring a customer's body to creating a pattern, sewing, and finishing the garment, so that trainees can be either self-employed or employed in a factory. For instance, the TVET model curriculum for Level 1, used in sample schools, allocates 24.28% of total time to pattern making and fabric layout and cutting, 25.97% to sewing, and 8.72% to noncognitive (soft) skills, among others. Level 2 allocates no time to sewing but places more emphasis on pattern making and finishing, which account for 39.92% and 30.11%, respectively, of the total time (Addis Ababa City Administration TVET Agency, 2015). Meanwhile, when factories employ new workers, they provide initial intensive training that normally lasts for approximately 2 weeks. After that, workers are mainly initiated into sewing. Workers acquire additional skills, such as ironing and embroidery, as they gain more experience. Therefore, the larger the factory, the less exposure newer workers have to patterns and structures, whereas those in smaller factories tend to perform a wider variety of functions.

These differences in the focus and mode of training reflect the differing expectations in the school and in the factory. Since they assess the quality of work according to commercial standards, factory managers tend to be strict in their evaluation, particularly in the sewing department. TVET trainers, on the other hand, are educators who assess performance in comparison with the average of the cohort and based on the criteria of the Ethiopian Occupational Standards, which are quite comprehensive.

Second, the differences in education and work experience between trainers and employers seem to be another cause of the gap in their assessments of skills in structure, sewing, and finishing, as well as combined skills. When trainers were asked about their work experience in a factory, the majority reported having none, a common pattern among TVET trainers, who mostly transitioned directly from their own education. Conversely, many current employers have long experience working on the production line, having climbed the ladder to become a supervisor and then a manager. Some of them also serve as trainers in their firms, given the high demand for production skills, particularly in sewing.

5.5.1.2 Graders' Beliefs and Skills Evaluation

Having confirmed that the influence of trainers' and employers' contrasting work contexts has affected their evaluation of workers' practical skills, we will now consider how the assessment of workers' actual skills is related to the assessor's expectation of young workers' skills in general, as expressed in the questionnaire. Put differently, it is an investigation to see if epistemology determines one's judgment about ontology and actions based on such judgment. The analysis of such direct linkage between epistemology and ontology is, as we stated earlier, the strength of this dataset.

As explained in earlier chapters, the questionnaire asked employers and trainers to report the expected level of abilities for workers with less than 3 years of experience. After conducting the t-test, we recognized statistically significant differences in means exist between perceptions of firm managers and TVET trainers across four domains of vocational skills and for all domains combined. Therefore, not only in terms of grading behavior, but also in terms of general expectations for workforce abilities, we confirmed that there are differences between these two groups. Such collective differences can be attributed to the differences in generative mechanisms and the experiences they have accumulated accordingly.

In addition to this group comparison, we also examined whether the expectation affects the grading behavior of individual assessors, regardless of their affiliation. The reason for conducting such an analysis is that subjectivity resides in the individual mind. Regardless of the collective orientation generated by socio-cultural and econo-productive factors, each assessor has acted on their own values. Thus, by segregating the individual orientation from the collective one, we can truly examine the linkage between epistemology and ontology without being influenced by surrounding conditions.

Table 5.6 displays the results of an Ordinary least squares (OLS) analysis using the five categories of skills as dependent variables to determine whether assessors' general expectation of garment workers' abilities affects their grading of the performance of actual workers. In conducting this analysis, we statistically control for the effects of individual workers' experience, age, gender, and education, as well as the organiza-

Table 5.6 Effects of general expectations of workers' skills on grading scores (reproduced from Yamada, Otchia, & Taniguchi, 2018)

	(1) Combined	(2) Pattern	(3) Structure	(4) Sewing	(5) Finishing
Impression of workers' skills in general	0.384** (0.181)	0.014 (0.206)	0.202** (0.100)	0.674*** (0.140)	0.551* (0.133)
Worker control	Yes	Yes	Yes	Yes	Yes
Factory control	Yes	Yes	Yes	Yes	Yes
Constant	−1.848** (0.730)	−0.897 (0.735)	−1.179*** (0.444)	−1.892*** (0.600)	−1.305** (0.569)
N	171	171	171	171	171
R^2	0.669	0.686	0.667	0.683	0.718

Note: All estimates control for years of experience, age, gender, education, and factory where employed. Robust standard errors in parentheses

* $p < 0.1$

** $p < 0.05$

*** $p < 0.01$

tions they work for, so that we can examine, without being affected by other factors, the interaction between assessors' grading of assessment takers' actual skills and their general impression of workers' capacity. Table 5.5 shows that the assessors' expectations of workers' abilities in general significantly affect their grading for sewing, finishing, and the four domains combined. The lack of statistical significance in pattern making arises from the fact that even the TVET trainers recognize the low demand for these skills in the labor market.

5.5.1.3 Epistemology and Ontology of Competency Evaluation

This section demonstrates how our team's assessment module effectively operationalizes Realist-Constructivism by linking epistemology and ontology within the micro-ecologies conditioned by generative mechanisms, such as socio-cultural, econo-productive, and structural-regulatory ones. The arrangements to have multiple graders from both the industry and TVET sides, together with workers taking the practical test, at the same venue with the necessary machines and equipment, were not easy. Thus, with our limited means, it was not possible to involve a larger number of samples or duplicate the same operation in multiple countries with acceptable, comparable quality. Regardless, with the questionnaire asking about expectations of the workforce's abilities and scores from actual grading practices, it was demonstrated that the acts of grading, which create the ontological experiences of workers being evaluated by supervisors and teachers, are driven by the perceived needs of certain sets of abilities. While individual perceptions determine their actions, these perceptions are conditioned by the environment in which they view the entire ecology of competency development.

Thus, in addition to the close connection between perceptions and graded scores, we also noticed the significant collective differences between TVET trainers and employers. Standardized grading patterns show that trainers consistently give higher scores, while employers are more critical, despite assessing the same workers under identical conditions. The largest expectation gaps appear in sewing, analysis of garment structure, and finishing tasks. These differences stem from contrasting work environments: TVET programs train all-rounders across many tasks based on comprehensive occupational standards, whereas factories emphasize narrow, production-oriented skills—especially sewing—with stricter commercial quality expectations. Trainers also tend to have limited factory experience, while employers often possess extensive hands-on production backgrounds.

The tendency to expect all-around technical capacities found among TVET trainers may correspond to the tendency observed in domestic firms, particularly those with smaller sizes, where employees must engage in multiple tasks with a limited division of labor. This fact suggests the influence of various sources on the expectations for the workforce's abilities. First, as discussed in Sect. 5.3 of this chapter, SMEs and large, often export-oriented, firms are operating in different econo-productive mechanisms. One requires accurate but obedient line workers, while another needs multi-skilled workers who can solve problems. Meanwhile, TVET teachers are trained to teach according to curricula based on national occupational standards. They are educators, not businesspeople. As educators, they value general comprehensive knowledge for students to acquire. Here, the differences of econo-productive conditions faced by large firms and SMEs intersect with the structural-regulatory framework of the TVET system. TVET trainers embody the structure, regulation, and curriculum. Thus, the mismatch between TVET trainers and employers can be considered as the one between the structural-regulatory and econo-productive mechanisms. Ethiopian Occupation Standards (EOSs) may meet industry-side demands sporadically.

Particularly for the lower-skilled workforce, equivalent to Levels 1 and 2 of TVET, the industry's demands focus on specific techniques, and the expectation gaps from TVET are notable. Still, the demands are not uniform, depending on the size of the firms and the market they serve. A related challenge is that a significant proportion of TVET graduates become self-employed rather than being employed in firms, which we will discuss further soon. While the skills required for self-employment differ from those needed in firms, the EOSs seem to try to kill multiple birds with one stone.

Now that we have examined the causes of "skills gaps" between the industry and TVET sectors, let us turn to the intra-dynamics within TVET institutions, which are more strongly conditioned by the structural-regulatory mechanism than private firms.

5.5.2 TVET Trainers vs. Students

In this section, we will focus on the perceptions of the contents of education in TVET in relation to the respondents' perceptions about important skills for employment after graduation. Comparison will be made between questionnaire returns from TVET trainers and students.

5.5.2.1 Teaching Priorities vs. Student Goals

Fig. 5.3 shows the domains of skills that TVET trainers prioritize in teaching. We asked trainers to select, from a list of noncognitive and vocational skills, the top three types of skills they highlight in teaching students who are training for Levels 1–3. We aggregated the points respondents gave to each domain of skills to understand the general pattern of prioritization by trainers in the seven sample TVET colleges. As Fig. 5.3 shows, the kinds of skills trainers emphasize are basic vocational skills, such as body measurement, laying out and cutting fabric, sewing, and pattern making. Meanwhile, the kinds of skills that are not emphasized are those necessary for running a business, such as formulating a work plan, leadership, management, and entrepreneurship.

These trainers' teaching priorities demonstrate a stark contrast to what students want to learn. Our study found that students want to learn skills to run a business, such as entrepreneurship and making a work plan. Our interpretation of this result is that students do not value these basic production skills as much as trainers do because most students aspire to be self-employed. Of 162 students surveyed, more than 60% mentioned that they are likely to be self-employed after graduating from the TVET course. At the same time, fewer than 10% of students predicted they

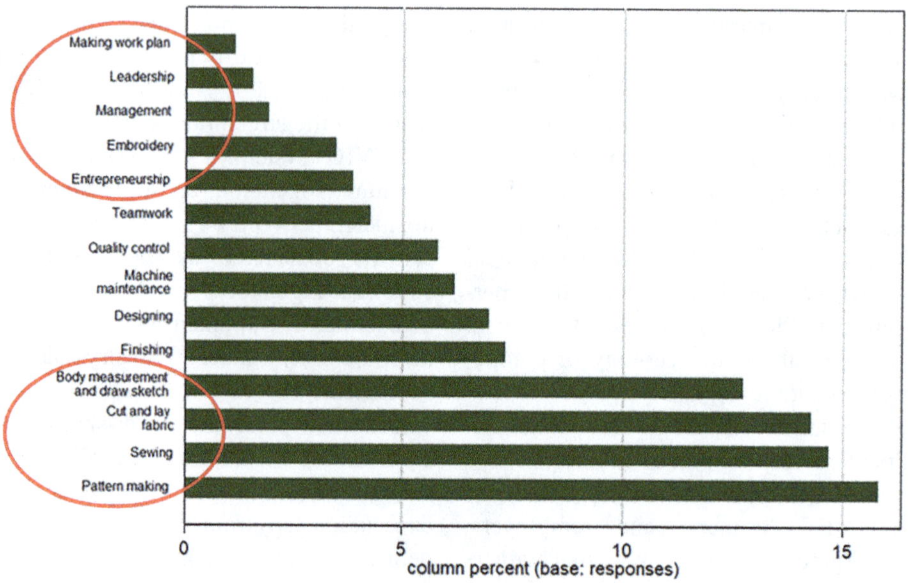

Fig. 5.3 Teachers' priorities in teaching Levels 1–3 students

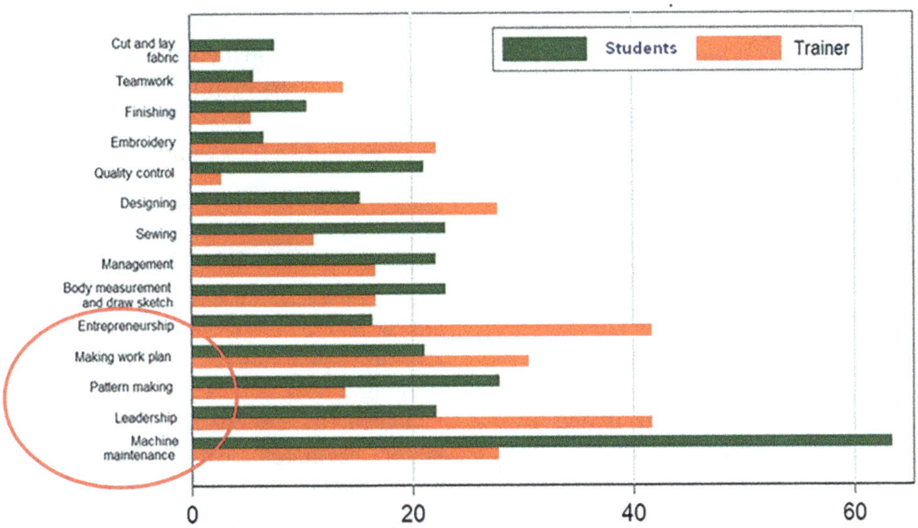

Fig. 5.4 Most difficult skill to teach for trainers and to learn for students

would be employed in the factories. These job aspirations may be related to the fact that a large portion of TVET students come from relatively well-off families and have parents and siblings who tend to hold leadership positions in offices or run their own businesses.[5] This observation is consistent with students' preference for supervisory skills.

Whereas Fig. 5.3 focuses on the skills that respondents prioritize or consider important, Fig. 5.4 illustrates the skills they perceive as difficult—both for trainers to teach and for students to learn. The bigger the difference in length between the green bar and the orange bar in Fig. 5.4, the greater the perception gap on the difficulty of that particular domain of skills. Significant differences are found in perceptions regarding skills in machine maintenance, leadership, and entrepreneurship. In particular, trainers consider entrepreneurship, creating a work plan, and leadership to be challenging topics to teach; yet, as we discussed above, students consider these the most important topics to learn. Overall, trainers are more confident in teaching production-related skills, particularly these basic ones.

Here, one can observe several gaps in perception between TVET trainers and students, as well as between TVET trainers and employers. In TVET, students aspire to be self-employed or in a supervisory position, yet trainers are not confident about teaching entrepreneurship and leadership. Trainers are confident about teaching basic production skills, which students are not very excited about. Meanwhile, in the garment industry, the workforce demand is mostly for machine operators on the production line, rather than designers or pattern makers, and, needless to say, supervisors. With such multiple mismatches of expectation, the structure designed to create a supply-demand partnership for training a skilled workforce is standing on shaky ground, with none of these stakeholders fully committed to the prospects raised in government policy.

5.5.2.2 Satisfaction Levels with Cooperative Training

The Ethiopian Ministry of Education made it compulsory that 70% of a TVET program be provided in private-sector firms, leaving only 30% to take place in the TVET colleges. The goal is to

[5]This tendency that female TVET students tend to come from relatively well-off households and are not much interested in garment firm employment is not confirmed.

equip students with practical skills in a real-world work environment. In Ethiopia, such workplace training is referred to as "cooperative training," which requires a strong partnership between TVET colleges and the firms that accept student trainees. According to the questionnaire responses, however, more than half (54%) of factory managers reported that they had never cooperated with TVET colleges, and only 23% said they accept TVET students for cooperative training. Despite the policy intentions, therefore, there appear to be significant challenges in establishing positive relationships between firms and TVET colleges to train the workforce jointly.

Then, how do students consider their experience of cooperative training? As shown in Fig. 5.5, students' average level of satisfaction with cooperative training was 3.12 on a scale of 1–5, just around the middle. At the same time, their level of satisfaction varied largely by school. Fig. 5.5 shows the level of satisfaction with cooperative training among students in seven sample schools. The Figure also presents, for comparison, the perceptions of trainers in the respective schools. Overall, trainers are less satisfied than students; however, the relative level of satisfaction by school demonstrates a similar pattern for both trainers and students. Our analysis indicates some relationship between a school's teaching methods and the quality of its cooperative training. First, students tend to express higher satisfaction with cooperative training setups by schools that use more participatory approaches in their in-school practical training (e.g., by demonstrating the way things are done). Also, schools with a greater proportion of trainers holding higher-level certificates are likely to have greater student satisfaction with their cooperative training.

During the cooperative training itself, several factors seem to affect the level of satisfaction. First, students value the experience of operating specialized industrial machines. With TVET colleges lacking adequate equipment, both TVET trainers and students praise factories that provide access to modern machines or hand tools, as these complement the basic knowledge learned in TVET colleges with industry-based skills. At the same time, many teachers complain that factories involved in cooperative training do not understand the competencies that the EOS requires workers to have and do not train students systematically according to these requirements. According to them, cooperative training would

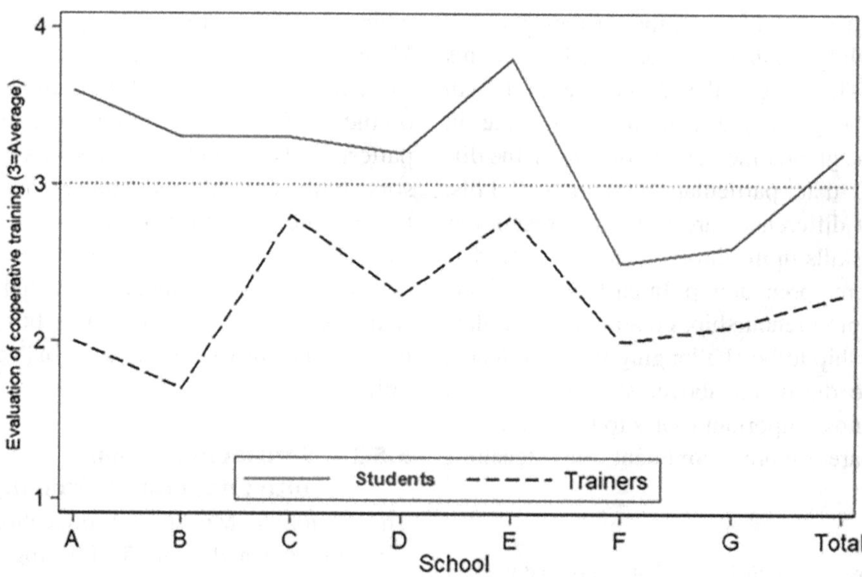

Fig. 5.5 Level of satisfaction with cooperative training, by school

become more effective if factory supervisors were more willing to follow the EOS requirements.

5.5.2.3 Missing Links Between TVET System and Labor Market Realities

TVET institutions are part of the national education system. As a result, they attract students who desire to pursue further education or inherit or own a business under their family's auspices. As argued in Chap. 5, it is an ironic twist that, despite the intention of the structural-regulatory framework for national skills development, TVET institutions often fail to prepare and provide a trained workforce for the specified industries, as it does not align with the perceived needs for competencies of any stakeholders. The perception gaps between TVET trainers and students suggest that students lack interest in the major channel of employment, which is the private firms of the garment production industry. Additionally, TVET trainers are often not equipped to prepare future workers with up-to-date technical skills, as they lack industry experience. They sometimes do not even consider it necessary, as they view teachers as privileged in not getting their hands dirty.

In addition to the gap between students' aspirations and structural-regulatory assumptions, there is also a stakeholders' lack of interest in supporting the firm-TVET partnership demanded to effectuate the national skills development structure. The responses to the questionnaire items on cooperative training suggest the absence of cooperation between the two sides. As we collected the voices of stakeholders from ministries of education and labor, TVET institutions, and firms during a participatory workshop organized in 2017, we gained insight into how they envision different dreams within the same framework of "workforce competency development" (see Yamada, Otchia, Shimazu, et al., 2018). To detail their mutual blame is not the objective of this chapter. However, one thing would be worth pointing out from the Realist-Constructivist perspective. The structural-regulatory mechanism of competency development tends to be imposed based on armchair theories. However, stakeholders' epistemology and ontology of competency development operate with different sets of gears than institutionalist beliefs on "education-to-work transition" (see Sect. 1.1 of Chap. 1 for our theoretical argument on this point).

5.5.3 Synthesis

Section 5.5 has demonstrated that what is commonly referred to as a "skills gap" is not merely a deficit in workers' abilities, but a consequence of deeply rooted epistemological differences among stakeholders who evaluate, train, and employ the workforce. By examining how employers, TVET trainers, and students perceive vocational skills, and how these perceptions shape their concrete actions—grading behaviors, teaching priorities, and job aspirations—we demonstrated that stakeholders operate within distinct socio-cultural, econo-productive, and structural-regulatory environments that shape their expectations in systematically different ways.

The contrast between employers and TVET trainers revealed that assessments of the same workers diverge sharply depending on the assessor's work context and professional experience. The comparison between TVET trainers and students adds an additional layer of mismatch. Trainers prioritize basic production skills, while many students, aspiring to self-employment or supervisory roles, seek entrepreneurial and managerial abilities that trainers often feel unprepared to teach. Common interests as the precondition for firm-TVET partnerships seem to be slim.

Taken together, these findings demonstrate that "skills gaps" emerge from the misalignment of perceptions and practices across stakeholder groups, each shaped by different generative mechanisms. The structural-regulatory framework assumes a unified pathway from training to employment, but in practice, stakeholders interpret and enact competency development through their own lenses. Understanding these mismatches—epistemological, institutional, and econo-productive—is essential for reframing skills development policies in ways that meaningfully align with the realities of Ethiopia's labor market and the subjective worlds of those who inhabit it.

5.6 TVET's Strength in Preparing the Workforce

Given the epistemological and ontological "skills gaps", we may jump to the conclusion that pre-employment education in TVET is generally irrelevant to the skills demands outside of the school system. In fact, as Sect. 2.2 of Chap. 2 has reviewed, criticism of TVET for being cost-inefficient and unable to respond to skills demands in a timely manner has recurred throughout the post-World War II period. Due to this widespread concern about TVET's capacity to meet labor market demands, the recent global trend in skills development policies promotes a more market-driven training mechanism, in which governments play a role in coordination and incentivization. According to this popular model, direct government operation of TVET should be kept as a last resort, provided only when and in areas where private training providers cannot step in (see Table 2.2, Chap. 2).

However, in many countries, TVET-based pre-employment vocational education has a history of several decades, and it is not possible to dismiss teaching staff, discard the familiar curriculum for competency-based training (CBT), or retrain all teaching staff to change their mindsets and attitudes overnight. Thus, setting aside the ideals of global trends and the pressures of external development partners, the realities of the national ecology of competency development do not allow new policies to abruptly break away from the existing structural and regulatory framework. Here again, we notice the limitation of the structural-regulatory mechanism, introduced in a top-down manner without considering the nexus of generative mechanisms, epistemologies, and micro-ecological contexts.

One of the authors of this chapter has pointed out the problems caused by applying cookie-cutter, standardized models of reform to aid-dependent countries elsewhere (Yamada, 2010). CBT is one such global trend. While we will refrain from discussing this point further here, a task of Realist-Constructivist scholars would be not just to discuss its limitations, but to shed light on the aspects of the structural-regulatory mechanism that work in synergy with other generative mechanisms in the national ecology. Thus, in this section, we will consider the positive effects of TVET education on the workforce abilities, in contrast to those who haven't experienced TVET.

5.6.1 Differential Environment of Learning Practical and Noncognitive Skills

According to the objective stated above, this section aims to consider the determinants of practical and noncognitive skills, with a particular focus on the differences between workers who graduated from TVET and those who did not. The question to be investigated is: are there any comparative advantages of pre-employment TVET education over on-the-job training offered by firms in upgrading workforce abilities? If yes, in developing which type of abilities?

As we discussed earlier, unlike foreign-invested firms, which prioritize employing younger people with less education, smaller domestic firms are more likely to accept cooperative trainees from TVET institutions and employ some of them, if they match their expectations. SMEs have limited means to train their employees in-house. In addition, they require a more multi-skilled workforce than in large firms. Such conditions of SMEs may potentially match well with characteristics of education in TVET, which tend to be comprehensive and general. Of course, for such a match between SMEs and TVET institutions to bear fruit, there should be well-designed arrangements to meet the expectations and resources on both sides. This section will set aside such operational concerns, focusing instead on the determinants of ability formation.

5.6.2 Data and Methodology

5.6.2.1 Construction of Variables

The dataset used for this analysis is part of a 2016–2017 survey that involved domestic firm workers.

The variables representing noncognitive skills, similar to those created in Chap. 4, are generated through principal component analysis of ten questionnaire items that assess the socio-emotional aspects of noncognitive skills. Table 5.7 presents the question items that demonstrated high factor loading in constituting the variables. Factor 1 was able to explain 70.60% of the socio-emotional skills of all sampled workers. This high proportion justifies using Factor 1 as the representative variable of noncognitive (socio-emotional) skills for further analysis.

The items that turned out to constitute the relevant noncognitive skills of garment-sector workers are those related to maintaining a clean, tidy, and organized workplace; being disciplined; and regularly reporting to supervisors on the progress of work and any problems related to it.

Regarding practical vocational skills, we aggregated the scores for 20 checkpoints given by respective assessors and averaged them for each test taker. The design of the practical test is the same as the dataset used for the analysis in Sect. 5.1; however, for the current analysis, we use the total score instead of the scores for each of the four domains separately, namely, pattern development, analysis of garment structure, machine sewing, and garment finishing.

The variables used for the Ordinary Least Squares models to examine the determinants of (a) vocational skills and (b) noncognitive skills are shown in Table 5.8.

Table 5.7 Question items that constitute noncognitive skills

Question item	Factor 1	Uniqueness
I will continue a routine task even if there are some defects. (reverse question)	0.2228	0.9092
I wash my hands when I return from a break.	0.3177	0.7002
I report any problem with the sewing machine to the leader.	0.3585	0.5710
I can tell whether the sewing machine is in good or bad condition.	0.5051	0.6218
I clean the sewing machine regularly.	0.5030	0.6557
I clean the workplace at the end of the day's work.	0.6037	0.5397
I report unsafe working conditions to my supervisor.	0.2402	0.6865
Eigenvalue	1.20935	
Proportion (%)	70.60	

Table 5.8 Descriptive statistics of data used for the analysis

Variable	M	SD	Min	Max
Vocational skills[a]	0.00	1.00	−2.32	2.31
Noncognitive skills[b]	0.00	1.26	−2.55	1.73
Previous job experience[c]	0.37	0.48	0.00	1.00
In charge of sewing[d]	0.89	0.31	0.00	1.00
OJT[e]	0.21	0.41	0.00	1.00
Export firm[f]	0.58	0.50	0.00	1.00
TVET[g]	0.37	0.48	0.00	1.00
Household size[h]	1.28	0.46	0.00	2.40
Household economic level[i]	0.00	1.71	−6.79	1.60
Family in garment sector	0.16	0.37	0.00	1.00
Father's education[j]	1.63	0.48	1.00	2.00
Mother's education[j]	1.68	0.57	1.00	3.00
School was in Addis Ababa	0.63	0.48	0.00	1.00

M mean, *SD* standard deviation, *OJT* on-the-job-training, *TVET* technical and vocational education and training
[a] Combined score on the vocational knowledge test
[b] Factor score
[c] 1 if have worked before, 0 otherwise
[d] 1 if main task is sewing, 0 otherwise
[e] 1 if firm provides OJT, 0 otherwise
[f] 1 if firm exports to other countries, 0 otherwise
[g] 1 if TVET graduate, 0 otherwise
[h] Log-transformed household size
[i] Factor analysis of household items
[j] 1 no education, 2 primary or secondary, 3 TVET
[k] 1 if school was in Addis Ababa

Table 5.9 Determinants of vocational and noncognitive skills

Determinant	Model (a): Vocational skills		Model (b): Noncognitive skills	
	(1) Factors of direct influence	(2) TVET graduate or not	(3) Factors of direct influence	(4) TVET graduate or not
Job experience	0.292 (0.186)		1.694*** (0.174)	
Main task is sewing	−0.508* (0.264)		0.530* (0.293)	
OJT	0.727*** (0.184)		0.011 (0.377)	
Export firm	−1.321*** (0.182)		1.376*** (0.184)	
TVET	0.065 (0.172)		1.129*** (0.401)	
Household size		0.148** (0.072)		0.188*** (0.063)
Household economic level		0.157*** (0.014)		0.148*** (0.019)
Family in garment sector		−0.373*** (0.065)		−0.282*** (0.079)
Father's education: Primary[a]		−0.664*** (0.062)		−0.559*** (0.092)
Mother's education: Primary[b]		0.233*** (0.079)		0.209** (0.082)
Mother's education: TVET[c]		−0.454*** (0.080)		−0.674*** (0.078)
School was in Addis Ababa		0.610*** (0.052)		0.576*** (0.074)
Constant	0.748*** (0.287)	0.161** (0.063)	−2.309*** (0.441)	0.075 (0.059)
Observations	171	171	171	171

Note: Robust standard errors in parentheses
TVET technical and vocational education and training, *OJT* on-the-job training
* $p < 0.1$
** $p < 0.05$
*** $p < 0.01$
[a]1 if father's highest education level is primary or secondary, 0 otherwise
[b]1 if mother's highest education level is primary or secondary, 0 otherwise
[c]1 if mother's highest education level is TVET, 0 otherwise

5.6.3 Determinants of Noncognitive Skills and Practical Skills

Table 5.9 presents the results of OLS, Model (a) using *"Vocational skills"* as the dependent variable, and Model (b) using *"Noncognitive skills."* In the process of analysis, we found that the educational background of workers (whether TVET graduates or not) is closely linked with the variables that indicate their socioeconomic background, such as household size, wealth, parents' education, and migratory history (whether they are originally from Addis Ababa or migrated from elsewhere). Including variables that are endogenous to educational background in further analysis, alongside other variables, would increase the error of the analysis due to multicollinearity. Therefore, we conducted this analysis in two steps. The first step is shown in columns (2) and (4) of Table 5.9, which uses workers' educational background (TVET or not) as the endogenous variable and socioeconomic conditions as exogenous variables. Doing so controls for the effect of socioeconomic factors, which are not the direct determinants of skills themselves but indirectly influence skills through the TVET variable. Therefore, the second level of analysis, shown in columns (1) and (3), indicates the magnitude of influence from factors that directly influence the levels of practical vocational skills and noncognitive skills, respectively.

5.6.3.1 Background of TVET Graduates

First, we will examine the factors determining the educational backgrounds of workers. As explained earlier, all participants in the skills assessment were female. Those with formal education through TVET were generally from relatively better-off families and grew up in Addis Ababa and its vicinity. Columns (2) and (4) of Table 5.8 indicate a strong positive correlation of having graduated from TVET with the variables *"Household economic level"* (0.157 and 0.148 under Models 1 and 2, respectively) and *"School was in Addis Ababa"* (0.610 and 0.576, respectively), all at the significance level of $p < 0.01$. On the other hand, having a family member who works in the garment industry (−0.373 and −0.282 under Models 1 and 2, respectively) and having a mother who graduated from TVET (−0.454 and −0.674, respectively) both demonstrate a negative correlation with the worker being a TVET graduate (all at $p < 0.01$). This result means that there is no atmosphere of artisanship at home, such as working in garment factories or managing a tailor shop in town, that prompts these women to attend TVET. Finally, the fathers of TVET graduates have a relatively high level of education. The variable *"Father's education: Primary"* shows a negative correlation with TVET graduation (−0.664 under Model 1 and −0.559 under Model 2, at $p < 0.01$), implying that father's education is secondary or higher.

This picture aligns with our earlier discussion in this chapter and Chap. 4, which suggests that TVET students, who tend to come from more affluent socioeconomic backgrounds, have different career aspirations than those who enter the workforce directly from basic education. In households where members have higher levels of education, parents tend to allow children to continue formal education beyond basic education. Those whose examination results do not permit access to the academic track go to TVET. The Ethiopian government is significantly increasing the intake of TVET students, and it assigns students to their school and major in a top-down manner, resulting in some students being allocated to programs for which they have no passion. Some observers argue that under these circumstances, students' motivation for learning will be lower, and even once they are employed, their commitment to work will be diminished (Edukans Foundation, 2009; Hailu, 2012).

5.6.3.2 Predictors of Noncognitive vs. Vocational Skills

Next, we examine factors related to the competencies—both production and noncognitive—of workers, including educational background. Model (a) shows that TVET education is not a significant determinant of production skills, whereas the effect of on-the-job training on practical skills is significant (0.727, $p < 0.01$). Although TVET offers a broad curriculum, an education in TVET does not appear to predict high practical test scores among factory workers. Rather, those who work in factories that actively train their workers score higher in skills assessments.

Meanwhile, the determinants of noncognitive skills (Model (b)) differ significantly from those of vocational skills. Firstly, TVET graduates and workers with longer experience exhibit better noncognitive skills (1.129 and 1.694, respectively, at $p < 0.01$). Under the strong initiative of then-Prime Minister Meles, the Ethiopian government has been enthusiastic about adopting KAIZEN, the Japanese model of production improvement. A significant part of KAIZEN activities involves training workers to adopt an attitude of safety, tidiness, punctuality, and other essential attributes necessary for enhanced productivity. These KAIZEN activities are implemented not only in enterprises but also in TVET colleges. In the TVET colleges we visited, the slogan of the five S's—*seiri* (sorting out), *seiton* (setting in order), *seiso* (cleaning), *seiketsu* (neatness), and *shitsuke* (discipline)—is raised frequently in classrooms and workshops to convey the importance of tidiness, cleanliness, discipline, and safety. Such school-based promotion of Kaizen appears to influence the development of socio-emotional skills appreciated in the workplace among TVET graduates. The attitudinal capacities that KAIZEN involves, unlike production skills, which are to be ingrained in bodies, are changes in values and judgment, which are difficult to achieve overnight.

As argued in various parts of this volume, noncognitive skills, particularly the socio-emotional aspects of them, are a sign of cultural exposure and willingness to adapt to the common values of the environment. Therefore, while the schools and factories aim to establish such a KAIZEN or attitudinal culture in their organizations, students and workers internalize these values. It may be a peculiar context in Ethiopia that the strong government-led promotion of KAIZEN activities creates a socio-cultural mechanism that transcends schools and workplaces, preparing TVET students to seamlessly fit into the workplace culture. At the same time, it suggests the possibility that TVET can play a role in preparing the workforce's socio-emotional capacities by promoting common work ethics, as those expected in the world of work.

Lastly, it is worth noting that factories that export some of their products tend to have workers with higher noncognitive (socio-emotional) skills (1.376, with $p > 0.01$). Exporting firms must fulfill the detailed product specifications and quality standards required by client firms, resulting in tighter quality control in the workplace. These specifications require not only quality in the products but also efficiency and accuracy in production procedures, as well as discipline among the workers involved in production. As discussed in Chap. 7, our training program, designed to improve noncognitive skills, also yields higher outcomes in larger export-oriented firms. Seen from a different angle, in large firms, employees are daily exposed to managers' and peers' expectations of effective and efficient work, which constitute the socio-cultural environment of the firm's micro-ecologies.

In sum, noncognitive skills are dependent on the socio-cultural context, whether it is in schools or in firms. Since people are exposed to the intangible expectations and norms of the micro-ecologies they belong to through interactions with peers and superiors, in environments where greater interaction occurs, individuals have a higher chance of improving their socio-emotional aspects of noncognitive skills.

Meanwhile, the acquisition of practical skills is directly linked to opportunities for practice, which tend to be limited in schools compared to the workplace, despite the fact that TVETs are designated to teach vocational skills. Considering that SMEs have demands for pre-employment vocational training, as mentioned earlier, there is a need to improve the quality and fine-tune practical vocational training in TVET to meet the needs of SMEs.

5.7 Conclusion

With comprehensive datasets from one country, Ethiopia, this chapter has demonstrated how a Realist-Constructivist approach enables us to grasp a national ecology of competency development through abductive reasoning that links epistemology and ontology with the generative mechanisms shaping the country's labor market. The diverse information from datasets allowed us to operationalize the book's central theoretical claim: competence does not reside solely within individuals, nor can it be reduced to formal schooling or firm-level training alone; rather, it emerges from dynamic interactions among actors' perceptions, institutional structures, and the socio-economic mechanisms of their micro-ecologies.

Our comparison of FDI and domestic firms revealed two distinct econo-productive mechanisms—one driven by global value-chain imperatives and narrow task specialization, the other by multi-task demands and limited training resources. These different mechanisms create divergent ontological realities for skill requirements, which the structural-regulatory framework of the national TVET system cannot uniformly address. This finding reinforces the book's argument that structural-regulatory systems—no matter how well designed—cannot function effectively when they fail to account for the micro-ecological contexts in which competencies are enacted.

The analysis of cognitive, practical, and non-cognitive skill determinants further underscored the inadequacy of conventional human capital assumptions. Cognitive test scores depend on layered combinations of reading and mathematical capacities, reflecting an epistemological trajectory shaped by schooling. Yet wages—the ontological reality of labor market reward—respond primarily to vocation-specific knowledge, practical skills, and socio-emotional dispositions such as accuracy and discipline.

Section 5.5 made visible the epistemological foundations of "skills gaps." Employers, TVET trainers, and students evaluate worker ability through distinct interpretive frames shaped by their socio-cultural and institutional environments. These perceptions are not mere noise or bias; they are generative mechanisms that shape real decisions—such as grading, teaching priorities, hiring, and workplace evaluation. In Ethiopia, such epistemological differences directly translate into ontological consequences, including mismatched training content, inadequate cooperative training, and divergent job aspirations.

Finally, the analysis of the potential strengths of TVET revealed that the structural-regulatory mechanism can contribute positively to competency development—but only when its comprehensive, all-round training aligns with the needs of specific micro-ecologies, such as domestic SMEs that require versatile workers. As argued throughout the volume, mechanisms do not operate uniformly; their interaction effects depend on ecological configurations.

Taken together, the chapter shows that Ethiopia's "national ecology" of competency development is not a linear supply–demand mismatch, but a complex landscape where perceptions, institutional histories, labor market structures, and socio-economic imperatives reinforce or contradict one another. By bringing epistemology, ontology, and generative mechanisms into a single analytical frame, Realist-Constructivism enables us to see why global prescriptions or standardized reforms consistently fail to close skills gaps. Effective policy must instead emerge from an understanding of how competencies are constructed, recognized, and enacted within the lived realities of Ethiopia's diverse micro-ecologies.

References

Addis Ababa City Administration TVET Agency. (2015). *Enrolment of trainees 2005 E.C.* Addis Ababa, Ethiopia.

Central Statistical Agency of Ethiopia. (2018). *The 2018 urban employment unemployment survey: Statistical bulletin*. Addis Ababa.

Edukans Foundation. (2009). *Technical vocational education and training in Ethiopia mapping Learn4Work Schokland programme on TVET*. Addis Ababa. https://www.academia.edu/33126633/Technical_Vocational_Education_and_Training_in_Ethiopia_Mapping_Learn4Work_Schokland_Programme_on_TVET

Ethiopian Monitor. (2022, September 16). *Govt targets $250m annual revenue from textile & apparel exports—Ethiopian monitor*. https://ethiopianmonitor.com/2022/09/16/govt-targets-250m-annual-revenue-from-textile-apparel-exports/. Accessed 4 August 2023.

Hailu, E. T. (2012). *Analysing the labour outcomes of TVET in Ethiopia: Implication of challenges and opportunities in productive self-employment of TVET graduates*. Institute of Social Studies.

Otchia, C. S., & Yamada, S. (2021). Interactions between vocational and attitudinal skills in labour market outcomes: Findings from the skills' assessment of garment factory workers in Ethiopia. *Journal of Vocational Education & Training, 73*(1), 24–46. https://doi.org/10.1080/13636820.2019.1652675

Yamada, S. (2010). *Multiple conceptions of education for all and EFA development goals: The processes of adopting a global agenda in the policies of Kenya, Tanzania, and Ethiopia*. VDM Verlag Dr. Müller.

Yamada, S. (2023). Constructivist analysis of cross-sectional data on varieties of skills: Contextualities and generalities of skills packages and rewards to them in Ghana and Ethiopia. *International Journal of Educational Development, 102*(Skills for Development Revisited), 102851. https://doi.org/10.1016/j.ijedudev.2023.102851

Yamada, S., Otchia, C., Shimazu, Y., Taniguchi, K., & Deresse, F. N. (2018). *Bridging the supply-demand gaps of the industrial workforce: Findings from a skills assessment of garment workers in Ethiopia skills and knowledge for youth research project*. Nagoya. https://doi.org/10.13140/RG.2.2.35481.26728

Yamada, S., & Otchia, C. S. (2020). Perception gaps on employable skills between technical and vocational education and training (TVET) teachers and students: The case of the garment sector in

Ethiopia. *Higher Education, Skills and Work-Based Learning, 11*(1), 199–213. https://doi.org/10.1108/HESWBL-08-2019-0105

Yamada, S., & Otchia, C. S. (2022). Differential effects of schooling and cognitive and non-cognitive skills on labour market outcomes: The case of the garment industry in Ethiopia. *International Journal of Training and Development, 26*(1), 145–162. https://doi.org/10.1111/ijtd.12252

Yamada, S., Otchia, C. S., & Taniguchi, K. (2018). Explaining differing perceptions of employees' skill needs: The case of garment workers in Ethiopia. *International Journal of Training and Development, 22*(1), 51–68. https://doi.org/10.1111/ijtd.12118

Economic Informality and Gendered Perspectives on Skills: Micro-Ecological Variations in Pakistan and Ghana

6

Pimmada Charoensilp, Emmanuel Estrellado, and Shoko Yamada

Abstract

According to the Realist-Constructivist perspective, the global ecology of skill formation is surrounded by a nexus of generative mechanisms. Using cross-national data from Pakistan and Ghana, this chapter examines how generative mechanisms, particularly those related to economic and socio-cultural aspects, influence the skill formation of female workers across different micro-ecologies. This chapter examines variations in skills and characteristics between formal and informal workers in the two countries. The results from the logistic regression models showed significant demographic and skill divergences between Ghanaian informal and formal workers in most domains, whereas these differences were not observed among Pakistani workers. The heterogeneity observed in Ghana is attributed to the intersection of greater market opportunities for microentrepreneurship in the garment sector and less restrictive gender norms in society, compared to those in Pakistan. Instead, the variation in skill formation among Pakistani female workers is rather associated with conditions within the micro-ecology. The results of an ordered logistic model indicated that the firm's characteristics and decisions regarding skill development, as well as supervisors' perceptions of skills and women's social roles, were significant factors. Taken together, these phenomena explain how generative mechanisms, which constitute the outermost layer of the framework, shape narratives within micro-ecologies and facilitate skill formation at the individual level.

Keywords

Cross-sectional comparison · Economic informality · Informal workers · Gender stereotypes · Industry profiles · Interlinked mechanisms of skills acquisition

P. Charoensilp
Center of Excellence on Migration and Development, Institute of Asian Studies, Chulalongkorn University, Bangkok, Thailand
e-mail: pimmada.c@chula.ac.th

E. Estrellado (✉)
Graduate School of International Development, Nagoya University, Nagoya, Japan

S. Yamada
Graduate School of International Development, Nagoya University, Nagoya, Japan

Graduate School of Asian and African Area Studies, Kyoto University, Kyoto, Japan
e-mail: syamada@nagoya-u.jp

6.1 Introduction

Earlier chapters of this book have drawn empirical evidence to discuss how the nexus of generative mechanisms and local dynamics influences the nature of competencies and the process of

S. Yamada (ed.), *Mitigating the "Skills Gaps"*, Sustainable Development Goals Series,
https://doi.org/10.1007/978-981-95-7968-6_6

their formation in respective micro-ecologies. Unlike other chapters that describe the details of the workers' competencies and their differences across countries and workplaces, this chapter untangles how seemingly global norms and social orders affect the formation of workers' competencies differently, because of micro-ecological conditions. This chapter will walk the readers through a cross-sectional comparison of skills formation between formal and informal workers, explained by the econo-productive and socio-cultural mechanisms of two countries, namely Pakistan and Ghana.

In these countries, workers in both formal and informal sectors participated in the survey. That gave us a rare opportunity to compare the workforce competencies across formal-informal boundaries based on the same standard. Measuring the abilities of working adults is not easy in general, unlike school students who learn according to the common curricula and take tests on them. It is particularly true in the informal sector, where the details of business entities and their employees are not fully grasped. In this chapter, using the datasets, including detailed information from the informal sector in both countries, we will discuss the characteristics, cognitive, noncognitive, and technical skills of workers with different types of employment, but commonly in the garment industry. This will allow us to synthesize how the generative mechanisms revolve around the variation of individuals' skills formation and career choice in two different national contexts.

In the latter part of this chapter, we will go further down to the firm-level, where workers have direct day-to-day interactions with supervisors and peers. Particular focus will be given to the experiences of women in formal sector firms in Pakistan, in contrast to informal sector counterparts. The survey questionnaire for the company managers included items about their perceptions of suitable work for women. By incorporating company managers' perspectives into analysis, we examine whether supervisors' attitudes and workplace environment affect women's skills development, such as the opportunities for on-the-job training and their motivations to upskill. At the micro level of the workplace, we still recognize the influence of socio-cultural norms about gender, which serve as a form of generative mechanism for skills formation.

6.2 Realist-Constructivism on Competencies

There are some cultural norms that overshadow how industrial human resources development is conducted in different societies around the world. Gender ideologies would be among them. Cultural norms about the nature of women influence how families, local communities, and employers conceive of "suited work" for them, which in turn conditions the choices and attitudes of female individuals themselves. In considering the ecosystem of skills formation, we cannot overlook this issue, particularly as the garment and textile industry, which this book focuses on, is known for its heavy female bias, with the majority of the workforce being female in the Global South.

Regardless of such globally shared concerns about gendered cultural norms, conditions of employment, and socio-cultural contexts vary, and there seems not to be a common path for these women to formulate their competencies. Variation in socio-cultural norms, economic conditions, and institutional regulations significantly affects events experienced by workers in different national frameworks. This chapter is framed around the realist-constructivist approach to grasp the multi-layer phenomenon linking productive capabilities and labor segmentation among female workers with a more comprehensive lens. This framework helps us to identify the hidden generative mechanisms that possibly explain specific outcomes in the labor market. Our inquiry aims to understand how actual skill development opportunities for women on the ground are shaped by and interact with national- and firm-level social and economic conditions.

The concept of Realist-Constructivism, introduced in Chap. 1 of this book, offers a means to unpack the complex mechanisms of how people conceive of, value, and learn competencies. It makes sense of the micro-level phenomena and practices comprehensively, as socially embedded experiences of subjective agents, while at the same time, inseparable from the greater societal system. Applying this Realist-Constructivism to skill development in the labor market, we will go deeper than simple observations of firms or learning sites and investigate how workers acquire particular types of skills rather than others, why specific job types are more common among particular demographic or characteristic groups, and how cultural narratives, such as gender ideology, surface themselves into the actual practices in the workplace. This chapter will discuss the influence of generative mechanisms, both socio-cultural and econo-productive, on the variation of competencies among workers with different forms of employment in Pakistan and Ghana.

6.2.1 Econo-Productive Mechanism in the Garment Industry

For many developing countries whose economy is at an early stage of participation in the global value chain, the garment and textile industry is critical, taking advantage of comparatively low labor costs. One of the common characteristics of the sector observed across countries is the significant proportion of female employment. With its low entry barriers, the industry attracts many youths, particularly those who are less educated and from rural areas. The flip side of this easy entry is the oft-criticized minimal payment, poor working conditions, and the lack of career prospects, which result in high turnover. For retaining those workers, providing proper training together with opportunities for promotion and salary raises is considered important. Also, aside from those employed in formal sector firms, informal labor accounts for a significant proportion of this industry in both Pakistan and Ghana. Those informal workers include those who own or work for small tailor shops or take piecemeal work from formal firms, such as sewing or embroidering. In sum, this industry employs many vulnerable youths, ranging from export-oriented formal firms and local small and medium enterprises (SMEs) to the informal sector.

In Pakistan, the garment industry is crucial to the national economy. The share of the garment and textile industry was nearly a quarter of the value-added manufacturing. Likewise, around 60% of the national exports were retrieved from this industry (IFC, 2020). As one of the top ten largest global exporters of garment and textile products, Pakistan exports more than $16.5 billion USD in fiscal year 2022–2023 (TDAP, 2024), involving both SMEs and large-scale firms capable of mass production following the order of the multinational apparel brands. Informal workers are almost all female. Meanwhile, unlike in many other countries, a unique situation in Pakistan's garment industry is that the proportion of male workers is visibly larger than that of female workers in factories (Ruwanpura & Hughes, 2016). Despite their potential for a significant economic contribution, women are not yet commonly included in formal employment opportunities. Given these conditions, female informal workers are typically home-based and receive piecemeal orders from nearby factories.

The Ghanaian garment industry presents a different picture. In recent decades, the garment and textile industry was once a major contributor to total manufacturing output during the 1970s and 1980s. However, this industry faced several economic challenges, which has led to a severe decline (Bruce-Amartey et al., 2014). As of 2019, the garment industry accounted for only about 0.5% of Ghana's GDP.[1] Despite challenges as detailed in Chap. 3, the Ghanaian government has made efforts to revitalize the industry through several policies to attract investment, boost exports, and implement other initiatives. Given the limited export opportunities and the breakdown of the local market, the scale of this industry is far smaller than before. Thus, the informal segment maintains the market by filling the gaps of both production and employment left by the minimal presence of large-scale factories (Sandefur, 2010).

6.2.2 Socio-Cultural Mechanisms and Gender Stereotypes

When we try to understand the nature of the micro ecosystem for industrial skills formation, particularly for female workers, we cannot ignore

[1] Gross domestic product

social norms and ideologies. For example, gender stereotypes serve as the foundation for shared beliefs regarding the roles and capabilities that individuals are expected to possess based on their gender. Social ideology about gender is embedded in every institution, including families, educational systems, media, and the workplace, and characterizes the socio-cultural mechanism of the micro ecosystem (Ellemers, 2018). It shapes not only female workers' agencies but also judgments about them by their families, communities, employers, and even governments.

Pakistan and Ghana present meaningful cases for comparison. They both have the garment and textile industry, which employs many female workers, with a substantial share of informal sector employees. However, they seem to have distinctive characteristics in terms of gender values. Culturally, Ghana has some ethnic groups with matrilineal traditions and has had many females in leading positions. Meanwhile, Pakistan is known for its strict Muslim tradition, which discourages female involvement in productive and external activities (Takyi & Gyimah, 2007). Given such differences in females' socio-cultural position, it is not surprising to see that, in the 2023 Global Gender Gap Index (World Economic Forum, 2023), Pakistan ranked 142nd out of 146 countries, while Ghana was in 100th place. Such divergence in the global index may indicate the existence of differences not only in people's minds but also in the structure of both countries, particularly in terms of female economic participation.

In the case of Pakistan, being ranked almost at the bottom of the global index, less than 5% of female employment is in senior professional positions. The patriarchal norms strictly control gender roles, suggesting the tight association between women and domestic responsibilities, which limits them to informal and low-status jobs. At the same time, this socio-cultural condition further stigmatizes working women, restricting them from feeling confident and emotionally supported (Maqsood et al., 2024).

In Ghana, conservative gender norms still exist. However, they are less solidly enforced compared to Pakistan, especially in urban areas. Women were observed to be customarily engaged in economic activities, particularly at the micro-level, such as owning small-scale enterprises and serving as middlemen in the market (Sowatey et al., 2018). Still, it is worth noting that women have less access to formal education, technical training, and formal business networks than men (Nartey et al., 2023). The diverging social norms and gender ideologies between Pakistan and Ghana provide an interesting opportunity to examine how the underlying socio-cultural mechanisms influence female workers' choices in economic participation and skill development.

6.2.3 Formal vs. Informal Work

Informal work often refers to labor activities that are independent of having formal contracts with employers. Workers of this type are usually not protected by regulations and do not benefit from social services. In developing countries, informal work occupies the majority of employment. In sub-Saharan Africa, for instance, nearly 85% of the total employment is informal (ILO, 2018). Moreover, in both Ghana and Pakistan, as in other African and South Asian countries, women comprise a larger proportion of the informal sector workforce than men (ILOSTAT database, 2020).

The nature of informal work varies significantly in terms of required production-related skills and the demographic profile of the labor. Typical modes of acquiring skills for informal workers are apprenticeship, self-learning, or through social connections (Regel & Pilz, 2019). Skills and knowledge acquired as such are different in nature from those that would be learned in schools or formal vocational education. The flexibility in learning paths is likely to lead to differences in the type and depth of skills of informal workers from their formal-sector counterparts.

Likewise, studies suggest that one of the crucial determinants of whether a woman would go for the formal or informal sector is the demographic background of job seekers, such as age, marital status, and educational attainment (Dadheech & Sharma, 2023; Fadliyanti et al.,

2023). According to existing literature, young Pakistani single women have more discretion to join formal employment. Yet, when they are married, their participation in the formal sector tends to decline and shift toward informal jobs (Khan et al., 2023). In contrast, in Ghana, marital status is positively associated with female labor force participation. This signifies that women tend to remain in the labor market throughout their life course, encompassing both formal and informal segments. However, limited opportunities for education were one of the most significant factors predicting women's informal employment in this country because of its lower entry barrier (Abraham et al., 2017). Given these contrasts regarding female informal work, it is worthwhile investigating the similarities and differences in the characteristics of skills and the environment to acquire them among women across the two countries with distinct social norms and economic structures.

The main objective of this chapter is to explore the differences in characteristics, personality traits, skills, and work-related experience between informal and formal factory workers in the garment and textile sector of Pakistan and Ghana. Against the different socio-cultural and economic mechanisms in these two countries, we examine context-specific as well as cross-cutting patterns of skills formation, focusing on demographic characteristics and demands for skills in respective environments, which overshadow individuals' career paths and learning.

We initially hypothesize that characteristics of skills differ not only between formal and informal sectors but also between Pakistan and Ghana. First, we assumed that the ways these two economic sectors attract workers are closely related to individuals' educational and economic conditions, resulting in differential demands for skills. Second, we considered that the different socio-cultural values of the two countries would also make the patterns of skills formation different between them. If this hypothesis is rejected, it means that there are other determinants of skills formation than we hypothesize, and we need further investigation to find an alternative explanation.

6.3 Skills Comparison of Informal and Formal Sector Workers: Pakistan and Ghana

The first half of this chapter will explore the variations in the characteristics of skills and work-related experiences between informal and formal workers in the garment and textile industry in Ghana and Pakistan. As explained in Chap. 2, the SKY team was requested to assess the skills of workers in Lahore, Pakistan, in order to grasp the existing skills gap and provide some insights for training needs. As stated above, there was a shared assumption that skills between formal and informal workers were likely to be different both qualitatively and quantitatively. Therefore, this section will investigate whether the assumption is valid based on scientific evidence collected from both groups of workers. Likewise, with the availability of data from informal workers in Ghana, we decided to take advantage of this rare opportunity to explore whether the assumption holds true across heterogeneous economic and cultural contexts.

6.3.1 Descriptive Statistics and Data Handling Methods

All participants involved in the SKY assessment have taken part in our standardized skills assessment, which is designed to comprehensively capture competencies in multiple aspects anchored in their work environment. The detailed process of our measuring tool development and data collection in both countries is presented in Chap. 2. In this section, we will analyze the data from the questionnaire administered to workers who participated in the assessment, along with their scores on the written and practical tests. The variables are categorized into five groups: demographic characteristics, practical skills, cognitive skills, personality traits, and work-related experiences. The descriptive statistics of the samples from Pakistan and Ghana are presented in Table 6.1.

Table 6.1 Demographic information of participants in Pakistan and Ghana

	Pakistan						Ghana					
Variables	*N*	*M*	SD	Min	Max	Missing (%)	*N*	*M*	SD	Min	Max	Missing (%)
Demography												
Formal sector	425	0.48	0.50	0.00	1.00	0.0	154	0.40	0.49	0.00	1.00	0.0
Age	421	31.29	10.98	13	85	0.9	151	33.13	8.85	20	81	2.0
Female	425	1	0.00	1	1	0.0	153	0.84	0.37	0	1	0.7
Education level[a]	411	0.38	0.49	0	1	3.3	147	0.33	0.47	0	1	4.6
Household size	419	6.43	3.05	1	40	1.4	150	7.07	6.58	1	50	2.6
Household economic level[b]	425	−0.34	0.69	−1.31	3.23	0.0	147	0.99	1.09	−1.08	3.34	4.6
Practical skills[c]												
Practical skills	425	−0.08	0.80	−2.33	2.65	0.0	154	0.24	1.30	−2.37	2.39	0.0
Cognitive skills[c]												
Reading	425	−0.20	0.78	−1.95	1.87	0.0	154	0.54	0.99	−2.29	2.00	0.0
Mathematics	425	−0.29	0.76	−1.89	1.86	0.0	154	0.79	0.82	−2.09	1.87	0.0
Integrated reading-math	425	−0.22	0.70	−1.65	1.99	0.0	154	0.61	0.98	−1.67	2.65	0.0
Vocational knowledge	425	−0.24	0.61	−1.83	1.42	0.0	154	0.67	0.98	−1.69	2.44	0.0
Cognitive skills	425	−0.33	0.70	−2.11	1.99	0.0	154	0.92	0.97	−2.97	2.78	0.0
Personality traits[d]												
Extraversion	409	3.38	0.93	1.33	5.00	3.8	153	3.08	0.75	1.00	5.00	0.7
Conscientiousness	409	3.98	0.79	1.67	5.00	3.8	153	4.13	0.68	1.33	5.00	0.7
Openness	409	3.88	0.89	1.00	5.00	3.8	153	4.26	0.64	2.00	5.00	0.7
Emotional stability	409	3.28	1.05	1.00	5.00	3.8	153	2.88	0.77	1.33	5.00	0.7
Agreeableness	409	4.22	0.76	1.00	5.00	3.8	153	4.18	0.65	1.67	5.00	0.7
Grit	409	3.94	0.85	1.00	5.00	3.8	152	3.71	0.77	1.67	5.00	1.3
Decision making	408	4.15	0.78	1.00	5.00	4.0	153	4.16	0.70	2.00	5.00	0.7
Neuroticism	409	3.54	1.08	1.00	5.00	3.8	152	3.08	1.00	1.00	5.00	1.3

(continued)

Work-related experience												
Wage[e]	408	9.15	1.03	5.30	11.17	4.0	123	5.94	0.79	3.91	8.70	20.1
Wage increase[f]	410	0.71	0.45	0	1	3.5	141	0.82	0.38	0	1	8.4
Work hours per day	411	6.72	2.85	0.00	19.00	3.3	128	8.57	1.71	3.00	18.00	16.9

N observations, *M* mean, *SD* standard deviation

[a] Participant attained education level: 1 if equal to or above lower secondary level, 0 otherwise

[b] Principal component on ten household assets (DVD/CD player, TV, cell phone, computer, internet, bank account, car, motorcycle, bicycle, and refrigerator) standardized across two countries

[c] Practical skills and cognitive skills were constituted by the item response theory (IRT) approach. IRT was framed based on the idea that each test item functions across different populations differently. To standardize Ghana and Pakistan's scores on a comparable scale, instead of using raw scores, we estimated participants' latent ability (theta score) of each subject based on the test items' information and characteristics. Theta (θ) is standardized with a mean of 0 and a standard deviation of 1. IRT can be applied to both binary and ordinal data. For binary or dichotomous items, we fitted a 2-Parameter Logistic (2PL) Model, which includes the parameters of item difficulty and item discrimination into account. On the other hand, the Graded Response Model (GRM) is an extended form of 2PL for estimating theta when test items are in polytomous or ordinal form (Tay et al., 2015)

[d] Constituted based on the formula of the Big 5 scale

[e] Log-transformed wage

[f] Participant experience of wage increase: 1 if experience of wage increase, 0 otherwise

Demographic information explained the characteristics of our sample in the two countries with four essential variables. First, according to Table 6.1, the average age of Pakistani participants was 31.29 years, while Ghanaian participants were aged around 33.13 years on average. Second, the percentage of individuals who completed lower secondary education in Pakistan (38%) was slightly higher than that of Ghana (33%). Third, the average number of family members in both countries was approximately six to seven people. Lastly, we constituted the variable named "*Household economic level*" as the proxy of the economic level of the individual's household. Since it is difficult to obtain accurate, objective information about households' economic standards from stakeholders' questionnaires, the technique of asking about the possession of different types of assets is often used in social surveys (Ware, 2019). As Footnote b of Table 6.1 explains, we constructed the household economic level variable by conducting principal components analysis (PCA) using a set of 10 binary asset-possession indicators (each coded 1 = yes, 0 = no). The first principal component was used as the index score, representing a weighted sum of the asset indicators in relation to the distribution of each asset across the sample (Vyas & Kumaranayake, 2006). Thereafter, the index was standardized across two countries. Ghanaian participants scored 0.99 on average, whereas participants from Pakistan achieved −0.34. To summarize, there were no significant demographic differences between participants from Pakistan and Ghana, except that the household economic level was higher in Ghana. Regarding the gender composition of the sample population, we will discuss it in detail shortly.

Practical skills were measured by the practical test as detailed in Chap. 2. This practical test assigned each worker to a shirt pocket according to the sample within a set period of time. During the test, assessors rated each worker's performance and the final product on 11 different criteria (e.g., "*Backstitch both ends of the pockets to strengthen*" and "*Work station is cleaned after work completion*"). For each criterion, assessors could assign a score from 1 (Could not do at all) to 5 (Excellent).

Given that this chapter focuses on a comparative study between two different countries, we employed the IRT, fitting the graded response model (GRM), to combine the scores for each of the 11 test criteria. The practical skills variable in this section referred to a standardized theta across the two countries that we obtained from the IRT. According to Table 6.1, the average standardized score of Ghana ($\bar{x}$ = 0.24) was higher than that of Pakistan ($\bar{x}$ = −0.08). At the same time, the standard deviation was greater in Ghana (S.D. = 1.30), indicating that this type of skill was more varied there, while it was more clustered in Pakistan (S.D. = 0.80).

Cognitive skills encompassed four aspects of cognitive skills and knowledge for garment production, including reading, mathematics, integrated cognition, and vocational knowledge. As it was one of the core parts of the SKY assessment, details of the contents and arrangement should be found in Chap. 2. To standardize participants' test scores across two national contexts on a comparable scale, we conducted an IRT analysis, fitting two-parameter logistic (2PL) models to estimate a latent ability (theta) for each participant, accounting for each test item's difficulty and discrimination.

According to Table 6.1, participants from Ghana outperformed their counterparts from Pakistan in all domains of the written test. In the reading test, the mean score for Ghanaian participants was 0.54, while Pakistani counterparts achieved −0.20. As for mathematics, they scored 0.79 and −0.29, respectively, for integrated cognition, 0.61 and −0.22, and for vocational knowledge, 0.67 against −0.24. At the same time, the standard deviations of all subjects in Pakistan were smaller than those in Ghana, indicating that the scores clustered more in Pakistan than in Ghana.

Personality traits were classified into eight, according to the Big Five personality scale, adapted from the World Bank STEP Skills measurement survey by Pierre et al. (2014). The traits included extraversion, conscientiousness, openness, emotional stability, agreeableness, grit, decision-making, and neuroticism. They were measured using a 26-item scale that asked respondents to rate the frequency with which they conduct stated actions. Then, participants' responses to respective items were calculated into corresponding domains, following the set formula of the Big Five scale. While the mean scores from participants of the two countries mostly ranged from 3 to 4.5 (except for "*Emotional stability*" for Ghanaians with 2.88 points), standard deviations varied, and the patterns seemed to differ between Pakistani and Ghanaian groups. We will investigate these differences in personality tendencies later in relation to other variables.

Work-related experiences were composed of variables that would unpack the circumstances survey participants encountered with regard to their wages, experiences with wage increases, and daily work hours. On average, we found that workers experienced a wage increase of 82% in Ghana compared to 71% in Pakistan, which is about 10% higher. The chances of a wage increase seemed to be accompanied by longer average work hours in Ghana. Ghanaian workers generally work 2 hours longer than their Pakistani counterparts. In sum, the Ghana dataset observed 154 workers in total ($n_{\text{formal}} = 62$; $n_{\text{informal}} = 92$), while the Pakistan dataset included 425 observations ($n_{\text{formal}} = 220$; $n_{\text{informal}} = 205$).

The samples used for the analysis here were female workers from both the formal and informal sectors of Ghana and Pakistan. In Pakistan, the original purpose of the survey was to assess female workers' skills and employability; therefore, no male participant was involved. However, in the case of Ghana, female participants comprised up to 84% of the total sample ($n = 128$), while male participants accounted for only around 16% ($n = 25$). Even though the majority of the participants were female, to discuss the gender aspect of skills formation and compare Ghana and Pakistan on it, we needed to examine whether Ghanaian male participants demonstrate any significantly different characteristics that require separate treatment. To confirm whether male and female participants can be generalized across a range of demographic information, cognitive skills, and personality traits, we conducted a series of multivariate analyses of variance (MANOVA), which compares the means of two groups across multiple dependent variables (Bray & Maxwell, 1985). If we identify any statistically significant differences between groups, we cannot treat them as the same. Conversely, we do not need to treat them separately without a statistically significant difference. As shown in Table 6.2, the results of three models tested, (1) demographic information ($p = 0.268$), (2) personality traits ($p = 0.995$), and (3) cognitive skills ($p = 0.110$), indicated that there were no significant multivariate gender differences among Ghanaian participants. Given that the homogeneity of covariance matrices was violated when we estimated Model 1 using Box's M test, we switched to Pillai's Trace to confirm the absence of significant group differences, which is robust to violations (Meyers et al., 2016). These results signified that the examined variables were similar between Ghanaian male and female workers. Therefore, with the generalizability across genders, it was reasonable to involve male groups for subsequent logistic regression analyses, securing an adequate sample size.

Table 6.2 The results of multivariate analyses of variance using Ghana participants

Table model	Dependent variables	Pillai's trace	*F* (df)	*p*-value
1. Demography	Age, education, household size, household economic level, wage, wage increase, work hours	0.08	$F(7,103) = 1.28$	0.268
2. Personality traits	Extraversion, conscientiousness, openness, emotional stability, agreeableness, grit, decision, hostile	0.07	$F(8,142) = 0.14$	0.995
3. Cognitive skills	Practical skills, Reading, mathematics, integrated cognition, vocational knowledge	0.06	$F(5,147) = 1.83$	0.110

df degrees of freedom

6.3.2 Pathways into Formal and Informal Work

To test our hypothesis, we ran identical logistic regression models side by side for the respective countries. The dependent variable used in these models was "*Formal sector*", a dummy variable that categorizes the samples according to their forms of employment. This statistical approach estimates the likelihood or probability of a binary outcome explained by one or more observed independent variables. It is applied when the dependent variable is a categorical or dichotomous variable, containing two possible values, typically labeled as 0 and 1 (Gudivada et al., 2016). In this case, being a formal factory worker was coded as 1, while being an informal worker was coded as 0.

Missing data was observed during the data collection in the fields due to a wide range of reasons (e.g., nonresponse due to misunderstanding, technical problems of the online survey platform, and data entry errors). According to Table 6.1, missing rates in Ghana ranged from 0.7% to 20.1%, while those of Pakistan were between 0.9% and 4%. Based on Little's test of missing completely at random, the pattern of our missing data was missing at random (MAR). When there was no consistent tendency in missing data, and it occurred entirely at random, it means there was no systematic bias in the data. This missingness pattern was considered to be handled effectively by multiple imputation, which replaced each missing value with multiple plausible estimates based on the distribution and relationships among the available data. Then, the analysis would be conducted across all generated datasets and combined at the end (Hughes et al., 2019). For this section of this chapter, we ran the logistic regression models across 50 imputed datasets to enhance the accuracy of the results.

Fig. 6.1 illustrates the results of the logistic regression models using multiple imputation, with the independent variables located on the left side, which were analyzed for their statistical relationship with the dependent variable (informal or formal worker). The pooled Wald test ($F(20, 35944.2) = 1.99$, $p = 0.005$ for Ghana's and $F(20,895203.7) = 3.97$, $p = 0.000$ for Pakistan's model) indicated that the independent variables jointly improved model fit. The square and circle markers represent the coefficient of each variable for Pakistan and Ghana, respectively. The lines extending horizontally from each marker indicate the 95% confidence interval range between the lower and upper limits. When the line does not cross the zero point on the x-axis, the coefficient of the concerned variable is statistically significant. Significant coefficients are all written out in the figure, accompanied by asterisks that indicate the significance level of respective independent variables' contributions to predicting the outcome. One, two, and three asterisks (*, **, ***) signify that the level of probability that the variable is not associated with the dependent variable is lower than 5%, 1%, and 0.1%, respectively. When the marker is positioned on the negative side (the coefficient is below zero), a one-unit increase in a particular predictor raises the probability that the respondent will be an informal worker. In contrast, the positive coefficient indicates that when there is a one-unit increase in the independent variable, if a case is selected randomly from all participants, the probability is higher that the person works in the formal sector.

The results showed that in both countries, the probability of randomly selecting an informal worker from all participants significantly increased as her age increased by 1 year. The probability rose by about 2.1% in Ghana and 1% in Pakistan. In other words, formal sector workers were younger in both Ghana and Pakistan. Compared to formal employment in factories with concrete labor regulations, informal jobs required less strict conditions. Older workers might have been in the formal sector earlier, but when they got married and were tied to domestic and caregiving responsibilities, flexible and periodic informal employment might become a more feasible option for them. This career pattern was often found in Pakistan (Khan et al., 2023). Putting aside tendencies dependent on the lifecycle trajectories, younger people had less difficulty entering the formal sector than older ones, who faced various entry barriers. Formal factory

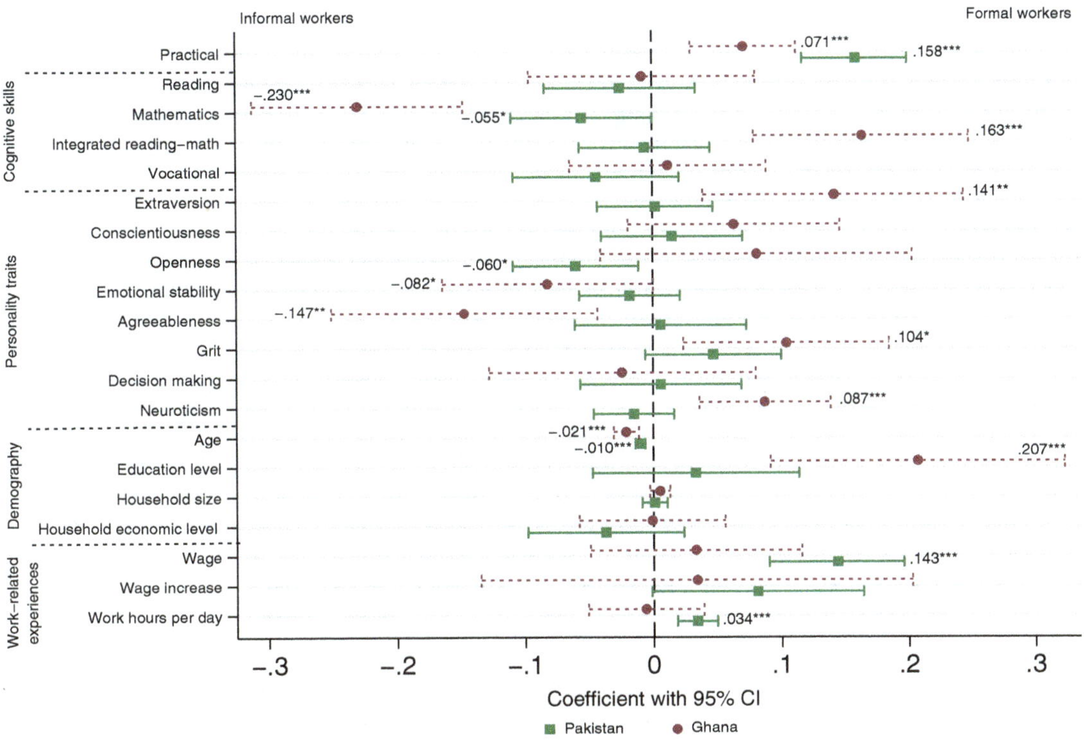

Fig. 6.1 The results of logistic regression models of Pakistan and Ghana. The coefficient values are presented in the form of average marginal effects (AME). $*p < 0.05$, $**p < 0.01$, $***p < 0.001$

jobs often required a certain level of education, knowledge, and physical endurance. In developing countries, these qualities were more likely to be found among younger people with increased availability of formal education, training opportunities, and health care in recent decades (Schofer & Meyer, 2005). Given this, one may assume that school attainment directs how individuals choose their work segment, either formal or informal.

Nevertheless, based on our findings, this assumption did not apply to Pakistan. The completion of lower secondary education was associated with the probability of being employed in the formal sector only in Ghana. Graduating from this level of school or above increased the chances of being a formal worker by around 20.7%. This fact suggested the possibility that hiring in the formal sector in Ghana depended on educational credentials. On the other hand, in Pakistan, better educational credentials did not necessarily mean an advantage for women in gaining jobs in the formal sector. Similar situations were reported from India, where the beliefs regarding women and their gendered roles shared many commonalities with those of Pakistan (Mahapatro, 2019). This situation in Pakistan, clearly contrasting to that in Ghana, can be discussed on multiple fronts. It could be a restriction of female intake by the employer, either tacitly or knowingly, preventing women's employment even for those having adequate qualifications. Simultaneously, it could also be on the side of the female job seekers themselves that they subjectively decided not to seek formal employment. Both the regulation on the employer side and the career decisions made by women can result from people's shared conceptions about the characteristics of women and their position in society. In other words, the patriarchal system controlled women at both macro (laws, labor regulations, or organization rules) and micro levels (within oneself, families, communities, or local organizations) (Hunnicutt, 2009). To elaborate further, at the micro-level, patriarchal practices limited women's freedom through the concepts of family honor and self-virtue (Hadi, 2017).

In contrast, in Ghana, women's participation in the labor market reflected both a strong entrepreneurial spirit and increasing opportunities in formal employment. As we mentioned earlier, the root of such an open environment for female labor participation might be found in the history of this country, which had many matrilineal clans. Evidence from the Global Entrepreneurship Monitor showed that Ghanaian women were even more likely than men to engage in early-stage entrepreneurial activity, with women owning nearly 70% of the country's SMEs (Owusu et al., 2014; Wang et al., 2023). While historically a large part of this participation had been in the informal economy, educational attainment had enabled women to join formal employment, broadening their economic roles (Abraham et al., 2017). At the corporate level, Ghanaian women increasingly occupy managerial and executive positions, with research demonstrating both their resilience in navigating organizational barriers and the positive performance impact of women in top management (Amakye et al., 2022; Nyeadi et al., 2021). These patterns were reinforced by policy and institutional shifts, such as the passage of Ghana's Affirmative Action Gender Bill in 2024, which mandates a minimum of 30% female representation in governance roles (Reuters, 2024).

Taking the contrasting phenomenon in Pakistan and Ghana as showcases, we can see that the socio-cultural mechanism regarding gender ideologies hidden in the background did play a vital role in regulating the labor market outcomes. This mechanism, certainly, functioned differently according to cultural contexts. Thus, in Pakistan, where female participation in economic activities was restricted, the survey participants' experience was found to be very different from that in Ghana, which was more open for women to be involved in entrepreneurship and leadership roles.

Apart from demographic characteristics, our dataset observed a remarkable distinction in cross-sectional skills formation between the two cultural contexts. In brief, although in Pakistan, the characteristics of skills, composed of cognitive, noncognitive, and technical skills, did not demonstrate statistically significant distinctions between formal and informal workers, the situation was different in Ghana. We found some clear divergence between the two groups of Ghanaian participants regarding personality traits, skills profiles, and job-related experiences. Given these observations, in the next section, we will unravel the mechanisms underlying people's perceptions about their realities and about the necessary abilities for people to live and work there. The contrast in skills profiles between female workers from formal and informal sectors in the two countries will be explained through the interplay of two key generative mechanisms: the econo-productive and socio-cultural mechanisms.

6.3.3 The Nature of the Garment Industry as the Econo-Productive Mechanism

The econo-productive mechanism concerns how the nature of the economic structure, commercial practices, labor market dynamics, and other bodies related to the economy of particular societies or countries may shape the way workers' demographic and psychological profiles are valued, demanded, and developed. For instance, practical skills were more closely associated with formal workers in both Pakistan and Ghana. Given that workers in formal firms benefited from structured training, access to up-to-date machinery and innovation, and institutionalized regulatory oversight to meet standardized production requirements, they tended to have higher practical skills than their informal counterparts. At the same time, it is essential to note that the practical test required the participants to use industrial sewing machines, which were not familiar to some informal workers and disadvantaged them.

On the other hand, in both countries, the performance in the mathematics test was more closely associated with informal workers. This finding might be attributed to the nature of work in the informal segment. Informal sector workers have to be responsible for business comprehensively, not only making clothes but also estimating costs and accounting for sales and profits, unlike their formal sector counterparts, who are assigned specific tasks and receive monthly salaries.

In terms of personality traits, we observed clear differences between formal and informal workers in Ghana. In four personality traits, we found statistically significant associations with their sector of employment. When the *extraversion, grit*, and *neuroticism* increased by one unit, there was an increase in the probability of being a formal worker with the coefficients of 0.141, 0.104, and 0.087, respectively. While being an *extrovert* appeared to be a strong determinant of being in the formal sector, the range of coefficients at a 95% confidence level was wider than that of other personality traits. It means that, regardless of the general inclination of being outgoing, there were naturally great variations. *Grit* refers to perseverance and passion for long-term goals. *Neuroticism* is the measure of the tendency to perceive others' behavior as hostile to oneself. In sum, according to our survey, Ghanaian participants employed in the formal companies tended to be more extroverted and suspicious. Also, they were more likely to be perseverant workers.

On the other hand, holding all other variables constant, each additional unit in *agreeableness* and *emotional stability* raised the probability of being an informal worker, with coefficients of −0.147 and −0.082, respectively. People with high *emotional stability* are said to remain calm, resilient, and secure even under stress. They experience fewer negative emotions, such as anxiety, sadness, anger, or irritation. Meanwhile, *agreeableness* suggests that the person is warm, empathetic, and cooperative. They value social harmony and are motivated to help others. It suggested that a personality well appreciated in the Ghanaian informal sector was collaborative and consistent.

In Ghana, despite the increasing interest of the government in joining the global value chain as an apparel exporter, the export conditions were not favorable, as discussed in Chap. 2. With the limited size of growth in the manufacturing industry, the informal sector currently plays a dominant role in the garment industry. Given the minimal presence of large-scale manufacturers, it had deeply settled in the country's local economy in terms of both production and employment (Sandefur, 2010). Compared to other types of commercial manufacturing, the garment industry embraces a more significant share of informality as it requires less sophisticated working capital to start small-scale businesses. Therefore, the female workforce in the informal sector has been involved in a wide range of independent entrepreneurial activities, such as seamstresses, tailors, and dressmakers, for decades (Amu, 2005).

The nexus of these economic structures and commercial practices allows for skill-oriented entrepreneurship, where individuals acquire competencies and skills through apprenticeship systems rather than formal education. In this cultural context, the econo-productive mechanism drives a stratified informal sector where skills are divergently demanded and formed based on how individuals experience work-related circumstances, such as the nature of local clients and market competition in the surrounding community (Yamada, 2021). Different circumstances could lead to a wide range of skill formation paths among informal workers. However, we found some interesting patterns among them in our data. Informal work appeared to attract workers with specific psychological profiles, particularly those characterized by *agreeableness* and *emotional stability*. By regularly encountering inconsistent and unpredictable events in the business environment, such as negotiating the fluctuating prices of raw materials with suppliers, informal workers may have embodied the ability to maintain calmness and resilience in such situations. Likewise, it makes sense that they cultivated a personality trait of being agreeable, as the success of micro-businesses closely relies on relationships with clients.

In contrast to the variety in the informal segment, formal workers in factories encounter a limited range of tasks, as their duties are highly restricted to the routinized mass production process dictated by employers' expectations. This nature could possibly curtail the variation in skills formation among factory workers. As discussed above, among Ghanaian factory workers, *extraversion, grit,* and *neuroticism* were more prevalent. These characteristics were appreciated by employers, or perhaps both employers and peer workers, as they contributed to working under team-based and hierarchical environments that reward efficiency, hard work, and determination. Neuroticism may be developed as a response to pressures in the workplace, such as perceived unfair treatment (Judge et al., 2006). In summary, given the diverse types of tasks they encounter, Ghanaian informal workers seemed to go through unique paths of skills development and, in the course of their work, develop their own aspirations differently from their formal sector counterparts.

Contrary to the situation in Ghana, there was little contrast in characteristic and skill profiles between informal and formal worker participants from Pakistan. Among eight personality traits, *openness* was the only trait that demonstrated some difference between the two groups. We found that a one-unit increase in openness raises the probability of being an informal worker by around 6% points. Unlike Ghana, the garment industry plays a crucial part in Pakistan's economy as a whole. Its contribution share accounts for nearly 25% of the value-added products of manufacturing, with approximately 60% of the national exports deriving from this sector (International Finance Cooperation (IFC), 2020). Being one of the most powerful exporters of garment products globally, Pakistan undoubtedly is home to a substantial number of garment factories to absorb a large part of the workforce. Given that the econo-productive mechanism of this particular industry is vertically integrated into the global value chain, unlike in Ghana, where the employment basis of the industry is widely stretched and flat with a large informal sector, it is challenging for micro or independent entrepreneurs to enter and succeed in the market (Chemin, 2010). Instead, informal workers in this cultural context are typically low-skilled home-based pieceworkers who are outsourced by factories (Akhtar, 2020). They often lack adequate skill training opportunities and growth potential, left out of the skills development ecosystems of formal factories (Mullan & Rolleston, 2020). They are also not rewarded in terms of wage, as we found that participants who have higher wages (0.143 at $p < 0.001$) are more likely to be in the formal sector.

However, while there are apparent differences in the work environment and support for skills development between the formal and informal workers, their individual background and inherent capacities seemed not to be very different, with insignificant divergence in demographic, psychological, cognitive, and noncognitive characteristics. Since there are not many female business owners in Pakistan, in both formal and informal sectors, their tasks are similar in nature, basically recurring and routine. What made them significantly different was the number of hours they worked.

Despite some significant contrasts in the skills development ecosystems in Pakistan and Ghana, both countries still exhibited common demographic patterns and the influence of econo-productive mechanisms. Those variables that did not show any statistically significant differences and centered around a zero coefficient in Fig. 6.1 are the ones that do not differ between informal and formal sector workers. There were a couple of variables like that commonly for both countries, namely "*Household size*" and "*Household economic level*". It suggested that, among the participants of this survey, the households' demographic and household economic level did not dictate whether a person got formal or informal employment in either Ghana or Pakistan. Put differently, we could infer that household economic level did not vary the form of employment. It was a unique contribution of our survey that we could attribute the differences of employees in two economic sectors in two countries not to their socioeconomic and demographic backgrounds but to their packages of skills, composed of practical, cognitive, and personality (noncognitive) skills, which were shaped in response to the social and workplace demands in different ways.

6.3.4 Cross-Sectional Comparison of National and Sector-Level Ecosystems of Skills Development

Based on empirical data collected from two countries where the informal sector significantly contributes to the garment industry, in Section 6.2 we observed results from cross-sectional comparisons among workers with two different forms of employment, namely, formal and informal. This analysis highlighted how socio-cultural and econo-productive generative mechanisms interplay differently within distinct cultural contexts.

In Ghana, formal and informal workers displayed distinct skills and traits. Formal employees tended to be more extraverted, conscientious, gritty, and less hostile, fitting the demands of structured factory work. Informal workers, by contrast, scored higher on agreeableness and emotional stability, qualities that support resilience and client relations in entrepreneurial activities such as tailoring. These differences reflected Ghana's economy, where informality dominates due to the small scale of manufacturing in the garment industry, and where women's participation was supported by matrilineal traditions and educational credentials that increased access to formal jobs.

Pakistan showed a different pattern. Despite the garment industry's central role and integration into global value chains, few distinctions existed between formal and informal workers, with openness being the only trait linked to informality. Informal workers were often low-paid pieceworkers, while formal factory jobs dominated due to the sector's export orientation. Unlike in Ghana, education did not increase women's chances of formal employment, as patriarchal norms and employer bias limited their participation and often pushed women to leave work after marriage.

Overall, the contrast underscored how economic structures and socio-cultural mechanisms intersect differently in each country. Activities linked to production and employment were closely intertwined with cultural values. This interaction between the economic-productive and socio-cultural mechanisms explained the observed divergence in demographic profiles, skills, and personalities between individuals who built their careers in different national ecosystems and in informal and formal sectors.

6.4 Firm-Level Ecosystems of Skills Formation in Pakistan: Determinants of Practical Skills

From here, our primary mission is to untangle what was unsolved in the first part of this chapter. We will explore factors that explain the variation in practical skills observed among female factory workers in Pakistan. So far, the national and sector-level comparisons have not provided us with a close understanding of *how* skills are developed in the respective workplace. The reason to focus on the practical skills is that they help us to consider individual workers' skills in relation to the firm's productivity. To understand how workers' practical skills may differ depending on the firm they were employed by, we conducted an ordered logistic regression after categorizing firms into three groups: highly skilled, moderately skilled, and less skilled. The classification was based on the ranking of their workers' average practical skills. The part of the data we used for this analysis included 205 female workers from 17 firms. The firms that were in the top five were grouped as 'highly skilled firms,' while those in the bottom five were grouped as 'low-skilled firms.' The other seven firms in the middle position were categorized as 'moderately skilled firms.' Ordered logistic regression will inform us which factors are most likely to predict the membership of firms in these groups (Williams, 2016). The findings from this analysis should provide important insights into improving the workforce's skills to achieve higher collective productivity, tailored to firms at different developmental stages.

6.4.1 Descriptive Statistics and Data Handling Methods

For this analysis, we used independent variables that came from three different sources. The first set of variables was derived from the workers' questionnaire, representing the characteristics of individual workers across three firm categories. The second set of variables was derived from questionnaires completed by managers in charge of production, while the third set, firm-level information, was provided by a human resources officer from each firm. Descriptive statistics of each category of firms are presented in Table 6.3.

Worker variables This set of variables represents workers' individual information. The variables can be divided into (1) practical skills, (2) cognitive skills, (3) personality traits, and (4) demographic and work-related information. Practical and cognitive skills were handled a little bit differently from the way we did in the prior analysis, given that this analysis unit concentrated on a single country's data. During the practical skill test, each worker's performance was assessed by two to three assessors over 11 criteria. To adjust for the differences in assessors' leniency or toughness, we standardized each assessor's scores to a comparable scale at a mean of 50 and a standard deviation of 10. Then, the standardized scores for each item were averaged across all assessors for each examinee before all items were aggregated and rescaled (divided by 100) to generate a total practical skills score. The practical skills score ranged from 6.25 (high-skill firm), 5.73 (middle-skill firm), to 5.40 (low-skill firm).

For cognitive skills, we conducted IRT, fitting 2PL models for each subject as we did in the prior analysis unit. However, instead of using theta to estimate the latent ability, we estimated a predicted probability for each item. Thereafter, we summed them to obtain a more interpretable expected total score. According to Table 6.3, "*Reading*" was the only subject where the highest scores respectively decreased from the high-skill firm ($\bar{x} = 8.87$) to the middle-skill firm ($\bar{x} = 8.82$) and the low-skill firm ($\bar{x} = 6.78$) group. In contrast, the score ranking of the other three subjects did not consistently follow the order. The middle-skill firm group has both the highest "*Mathematics*" and "*Integrated reading-math*" scores of 6.71 and 4.95, respectively. The low-skill firm ranked highest in "Vocational knowledge," with a mean score of 8.87.

In terms of non-cognitive competencies, we focused on five main personality traits, or the Big 5, in this analysis unit. These included "*Extraversion*", "*Conscientiousness*", "*Openness*", "*Emotional stability*", and "*Agreeableness.*" Personality traits were measured and converted into corresponding domains using the Big Five scale formula, as we did in the analysis we conducted in the first half of this chapter. Across five domains, the scores ranged between 3.14 and 4.34. The ranking of personality trait scores across different firm categories did not generally follow the order, except for "*Openness*" and "*Emotional stability.*"

The variables regarding individual workers' demographic and work-related information were mainly the same as those included in the prior analysis presented above, namely, "*Age*", "*Education level*", "*Wage*", and "*Work hours per day.*" One difference was that we additionally paid close attention to the workers' motivation for the current job. To generate the "*Job motivation*" variable, we first conducted a principal component analysis (PCA) to extract components from a multiple-choice question asking participants to provide reasons for choosing their current jobs (e.g., "Income is good", "Employers provide transportation", and "Family encouraged me to do it"). The first component, with the highest eigenvalue, which indicated the strongest underlying pattern, grouped three reasons together: "Employers provide training opportunities", "I can become more confident", and "Opportunity to connect with people". From that, we computed factor scores of the first component to represent the "*Job motivation*" scores. Therefore, this variable captured participants' motivation to improve their confidence, skills, and connections through work. In other words, in terms of mindsets, workers with a higher "*Job motivation*" score were more oriented toward gaining learning opportunities than toward other kinds of benefits, such as financial gains or welfare. Based on Table 6.3, workers from the high-skill firm group had the highest mean ($\bar{x} = 0.21$), followed by workers from the middle-skill ($\bar{x} = -0.04$) and low-skill ($\bar{x} = -0.17$) firms, respectively.

Table 6.3 Descriptive statistics across three groups of firms

Variable	Low-skill firm					Moderate-skill firm					High-skill firm				
	N	*M*	SD	Min	Max	*N*	*M*	SD	Min	Max	*N*	*M*	SD	Min	Max
Practical skills[a]															
Practical ability	58	5.40	0.47	4.21	7.07	80	5.73	0.48	4.47	7.19	67	6.25	0.64	3.61	7.28
Cognitive skills[b]															
Reading	58	6.78	2.84	2.65	11.7	80	8.82	2.58	2.74	12.4	67	8.87	2.52	3.28	13.0
Mathematics	58	6.14	2.07	2.71	11.5	80	6.71	2.40	2.95	12.2	67	6.41	2.39	2.65	12.2
Integrated reading-math	58	4.64	1.39	2.28	9.36	80	4.95	1.63	2.68	9.91	67	4.84	1.47	2.72	9.91
Vocational	58	8.87	1.00	7.75	11.2	80	8.64	0.75	7.73	11.8	67	8.64	0.92	7.72	11.5
Personality traits[c]															
Extraversion	58	3.26	0.95	1.67	5.00	78	3.36	0.86	2.00	5.00	66	3.24	0.91	1.33	5.00
Conscientiousness	58	4.01	0.76	2.67	5.00	78	4.00	0.78	1.67	5.00	66	4.09	0.75	1.67	5.00
Openness	58	3.97	0.74	2.00	5.00	78	3.83	0.92	1.00	5.00	66	3.74	0.84	1.00	5.00
Emotional stability	58	3.33	1.17	1.00	5.00	78	3.30	1.02	1.00	5.00	66	3.14	0.87	1.67	5.00
Agreeableness	58	4.34	0.51	3.00	5.00	78	4.21	0.73	1.00	5.00	66	4.26	0.73	1.67	5.00
Demographic and work-related information															
Age	58	30.0	10.3	13	55	78	26.9	8.73	16.0	54.0	67	29.2	9.07	15	45
Education level[d]	58	0.34	0.48	0	1	77	0.44	0.50	0.00	1.00	67	0.40	0.49	0	1
Wage[e]	56	10.0	0.55	7.86	11.0	78	9.44	1.03	5.30	10.7	67	9.64	0.86	7.44	11.2
Work hours per day	58	9.94	2.01	8	19	77	7.56	2.52	1.00	12.0	66	6.97	2.19	2	12
Job motivation	58	−0.17	0.39	−0.66	1.56	69	−0.04	0.90	−0.63	6.39	63	0.21	1.40	−0.66	6.39
Manager variables															
Expectation: Discipline & collaboration	58	0.44	0.33	0.02	0.96	80	−0.52	1.35	−3.19	0.71	67	0.24	0.50	−0.34	0.76
Gap: Initiative	58	−0.24	1.13	−4.00	2.00	80	0.33	1.56	−4.00	3.00	67	−0.58	1.21	−4.00	1.00

(continued)

Table 6.3 (continued)

Variable	Low-skill firm					Moderate-skill firm					High-skill firm				
	N	*M*	SD	Min	Max	*N*	*M*	SD	Min	Max	*N*	*M*	SD	Min	Max
Women stereotype	58	0.09	0.34	−0.19	0.86	80	−0.31	1.49	−4.18	0.82	67	0.30	0.35	−0.33	0.82
Firm variables															
OJT offerings	47	4.98	3.00	3	12	80	4.60	1.89	1.00	8.00	53	9.94	1.97	7	12
TVET collaboration	58	0.72	0.45	0	1	80	0.40	0.49	0.00	1.00	67	0.16	0.37	0	1
Firm size	58	2.36	0.64	1	3	80	1.65	0.86	1.00	3.00	67	1.51	0.50	1	2
Export firm	42	0.74	0.45	0	1	74	0.70	0.46	0.00	1.00	67	0.30	0.46	0	1

N observations, *M* mean, *SD* standard deviation, *TVET* technical and vocational education and training

[a] Aggregate of 11 rater-adjusted items standardized with a mean of 50 and an SD of 10, divided by 100

[b] Aggregate of predicted probabilities of correct response obtained from IRT of each item

[c] Constituted based on the formula of Big 5 scale

[d] Participant attained education level: 1 if equal to or above lower secondary level, 0 otherwise

[e] Log-transformed wage

Manager variables The second group of variables represented perceptions of a representative production manager from each firm. There were three variables included: "*Expectation: Discipline & Collaboration*", "*Gap: Initiative*", and "*Women stereotype.*" "*Expectation: Discipline & Collaboration*" was derived from the first component's factor score, estimated by a PCA of responses to 30 items in the production manager's questionnaire, which asked them what kinds of workplace behavior they want to see in their workers. The first component we obtained from this dataset suggested grouping 11 items. These items included behavioral skills, such as "To keep time and do not delay", "To follow the rules of the workplace and behave as expected", "To make sure that the work environment is safe", and "To be good at working in a team collaboratively," so we named this variable "Expectation: Discipline & Collaboration." This variable captured how much the production manager expects their workers to work carefully and tidily, be punctual, collaborate well with others, and follow workplace rules. Based on the descriptive analysis, managers of a low-skill firm expected their workers to possess these qualities most ($\bar{x}$ = 0.44). It was followed by managers of high-skill ($\bar{x}$ = 0.24) and middle-skill ($\bar{x}$ = −0.52) firms, respectively.

Another variable we focused on was "*Gap: Initiative,*" which referred to the gap in expectations between production managers and workers regarding the behavioral skills required for productive work. In the questionnaires for workers and production managers, we provided identical lists of skills and asked managers to rate the importance of each skill and workers to rate their self-efficacy for each skill. With this approach, our team had identified detailed and significant expectation mismatches among stakeholders in skills development ecosystems (see, for example, Chap. 4). This variable was calculated by subtracting the points managers assigned to a specific skill from the points workers assigned to that skill. Therefore, a higher score indicated a greater mismatch between employers and workers. We included "*Gap: Initiative* (To take initiative in the workplace)" as it was the only skill that demonstrated statistical significance. The average score for this variable ranged from the middle-skill ($\bar{x}$ = 0.33) to low-skill ($\bar{x}$ = −0.024) and high-skill ($\bar{x}$ = −0.58) firm groups.

The last variable we obtained from managers was "*Women stereotype.*" We computed this variable by estimating the first component's factor score from a PCA, applying a set of questions about stereotypes regarding women's employment (e.g., "A woman stays at home to support family and husband", "A woman receives pieces of work from SMEs and makes income", and "A woman is suitable for handicraft work"). Therefore, this variable represented the degree to which a manager believes that women should work part-time and do household work. A lower score indicated that managers hold fewer gender-role stereotypes. Based on the descriptive statistic, only the middle-skill firm group demonstrates a negative value ($\bar{x}$ = −0.31). Yet, its standard deviation was significantly larger (S.D. = 1.49) than those of the low-skill ($\bar{x}$ = 0.09; S.D. = 0.34) and high-skill firms ($\bar{x}$ = 0.30; S.D. = 0.35).

Firm variables The third set of variables was the business characteristics. These included "*OJT offerings*", "*TVET collaboration*", "*Firm size*", and "*Export firm.*" The "*OJT offerings*" referred to the total number of OJT types that the firm usually provides. The theoretical maximum number of OJT types is 12. The average number of high-skill firms ($\bar{x}$ = 9.94) was much higher than that of the middle-skill ($\bar{x}$ = 4.60) and low-skill ($\bar{x}$ = 4.98) groups. "*TVET collaboration*" was a dichotomous variable indicating whether the firm collaborates with technical and vocational education and training (TVET) institutions when hiring new workers. When '*yes*' was coded as 1, 72% of low-skill firms hired workers directly from TVET institutions, followed by 40% and 14% of middle-skill and high-skill firms, respectively. Moreover, another dichotomous variable, "*Export firm,*" indicated whether the firm exports the products (coded as 1) or sells only domestically (coded as 0). The low- and middle-skill firm groups showed similar proportions of 74% and 70%, respectively, while that of high-skill firms was only around 30%. The last firm variable was "*Firm size,*" a categorical variable grouped by the number of employees, according to the definition by the Small and Medium Enterprises Development Authority (SMEDA) of Pakistan in 2018 (Raza et al., 2018). Small size (up to 35 people) was coded as 1, medium size (36–250 people) was coded as 2, while large size (more than 251 people) was coded as 3. The mean of 2.36 for the low-skill firm group indicated that firms in this group were larger than those in the other two groups, which had mean values between 1.51 and 1.65.

6.4.2 Analysis and Results

The results of our models are presented in Fig. 6.2. Similar to the models presented in the first analysis, they were logistic regression models that used multiple imputation to handle missing data. Since it had more than two dependent variables, it was called ordered logistic regression instead of simple logistic regression. Otherwise, the way to read and interpret Fig. 6.2 is similar to Fig. 6.1. The markers accompanying each variable are the average marginal effects, which represent the percentage-point change in the probability of being in the outcome category when the respective independent variable changes by 1 unit.

To simplify the presentation, we decided to illustrate the coefficient values, placed next to markers, that were statistically significant, accompanied by asterisks. Similar to Fig. 6.1, the spikes extending from the makers illustrate the lower and upper confidence intervals of the respective coefficients. Differentiations of three groups of firms, namely high-, middle-, and low-skilled ones, are indicated by color and the shape of markers. The green circle markers and the solid lines, respectively, represent the coefficients and the confidence intervals of variables in the high-skill firm mode. The maroon square markers with dashed lines are those of the low-skill firm model. Lastly, gray diamond markers show the coefficient of each variable in the moderate-skill firm model.

6.4.3 Traits Thriving in Productivity

Because of the way we constituted the firm groups, naturally, the "*Practical skills*" variable indicated significance to two extreme directions for "highly-skilled" and "low-skilled" firms, with "medium-skilled" firms in the middle. In addition to the practical skills, contrasting results were observed in many variables across firm groups, particularly between low- and high-skill firms. We will begin by discussing the association between the firms' productivity and workers' skills, and then we will examine how it can be explained by variables related to workplace and employer conditions.

First, the high-skill firms tended to be workplaces that had more workers who are motivated to work by the opportunities to upskill and gain self-confidence (the variable "*Job motivation*" has a coefficient of 0.050 at $p < 0.01$), extravert ("*Extraversion*" with 0.047 at $p < 0.05$), and have a higher level of reading proficiency ("*Reading*" with 0.024 at $p < 0.01$). It was only reading proficiency among four cognitive skills (mathematics, integrated cognition, and vocational knowledge) which demonstrated a statistically significant contribution to the differences among three groups of firms. Still, together with some significant association of noncognitive skills represented by personality traits of extraversion and job motivation, we can say that the inter-firm differences in practical skills were matched with tendencies in other abilities of workers.

According to Fig. 6.2, we found that when one unit in the workers' job motivation grew, there was around 5% increase in the probability that their employer would be categorized as part of the high-skill firms. Based on the achievement goal theory, the precursor to mindset theory, individuals who are learning goal-oriented, or those motivated to commit to something by opportunities to improve themselves, believe that their qualities are malleable (Dweck, 2006; International Labour Office, 2018). They perceive efforts and failures as opportunities in the learning process, which lead to actions for consistent improvement, accompanied by the attitude of perseverance and a challenging spirit.

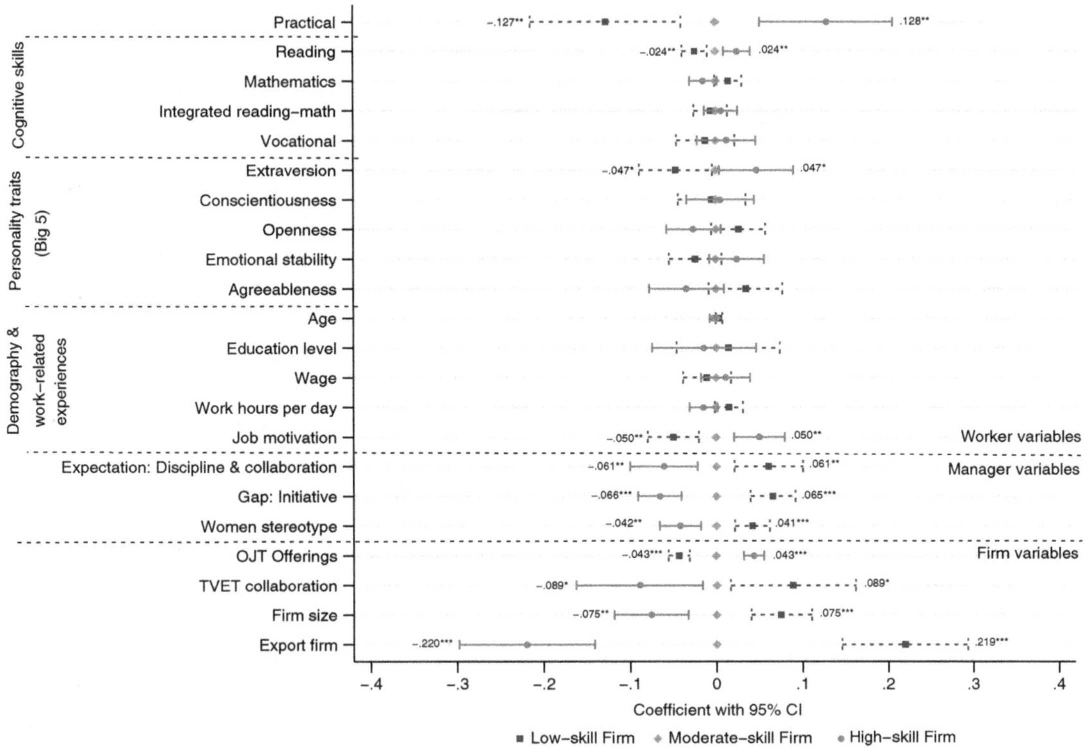

Fig. 6.2 The results of the ordered logistic regression of three categories of firms in Pakistan. The coefficient values are presented as average marginal effects (AME). The pooled Wald test of $F(22,210755.3) = 2.95$ (Prob > $F = 0.000$) indicated that predictors jointly improved model fit. $*p < 0.05$, $**p < 0.01$, $***p < 0.001$

Therefore, firms that provide more enabling environments would make female workers more committed and develop a desire to upskill themselves and gain more confidence, with greater motivation and perseverance to enhance their work-related practical skills. This, in turn, results in better productivity collectively (Ng, 2018; Rhew et al., 2018).

Next, as we discussed earlier, in terms of personality traits, a one-unit increase in workers' extraversion raised the probability that their companies would be part of the high-skill group by approximately 4.7%. In other words, workers who are sociable, talkative, assertive, and energetic tend to be in high-skill firms. A meta-analysis found that extraversion was positively associated with different types of job performance, including peer- and supervisor-rated performance (Wilmot et al., 2019). Similarly, in the South Asian apparel sector context, Dias and Jayasekara (2018) observed statistically significant positive correlations between extraversion and promotion in position and monthly salary. The extraversion personality trait has been empirically linked with behaviors that promote productivity. For instance, workers with high extraversion tended to pay close attention and speak up about workplace concerns, which affected efficiency and productivity (Tedone & Bruk-Lee, 2022). At the same time, a study using samples from an industrial sector in Pakistan found that, in conflicts, extraverted workers were more likely to negotiate with other parties to satisfy the goals of all involved, and this association moderated workers' efficiency and productivity (Alam et al., 2023). In addition, extraversion was strongly and positively correlated with workers' relational psychological contract, or the degree of workers' aspiration to work and loyalty toward the firm (Ranasinghe & Kottawatta, 2016). These empirical findings explain why the practical skills of workers in high-skill firms are more closely associated with their sociability and energy.

Lastly, let us discuss the association between reading abilities and practical skills. The likelihood that their company would be classified in the top-firm group increased by 2.4% for each one-unit increase in workers' reading test scores. This signified a considerable role of reading comprehension in enhancing firms' productivity. In garment factories, although workers are typically assigned to perform practical tasks, which readers may consider as not needing any reading abilities, understanding announcements and notes on the wall and bulletin boards requires literacy in a dominant language. Also, there are tasks, such as reviewing quality control guidelines, that require them to read. Therefore, workers who comprehend the language used in the firms well will become more effective with fewer mistakes, leading to better total productivity for the firm.

6.4.4 The Gender Paradox in Top Firms and Upskilling Opportunities

Now, we will turn our attention to another dimension in the firm's micro-ecology that would determine its workers' average practical skills and overall productivity, which is managers' perceptions and intra-firm conditions.

One of the most critical stakeholders we cannot ignore in the micro-ecology of skill formation is the perceptions and mindsets of managers, especially those who work closely with production. The results of our survey suggested the crucial impact of production managers' beliefs about women's work and social roles. The probability that a worker belongs to a high-skill firm decreased by 4.2% for every one-unit increase in their manager's negative perception of women's stereotypes. When managers hold onto social norms that women are suitable for home-based tasks rather than full-time formal employment, opportunities for women to be upskilled or promoted become fewer. For instance, if the managers believe that female employees do not typically stay as long as male workers due to their family responsibilities after marriage, they will prefer to invest in skill development among male workers. Existing studies have also discovered the relationship between gender stereotypes in the workplace and workers' negative mental constructs, such as anxiety, which in turn influenced their work-related performance (e.g., Kramer & Harris, 2016; Lavaysse & Probst, 2019). In cultural settings where intensive gender ideology is prevalent, managers' decisions and workplace arrangements based on such a social norm are likely to influence skill development for marginalized workers, particularly women.

Additionally, a greater mismatch between workers and their managers in appreciation of proactive behaviors at work ("*Gap: Initiative*" with 0.065 at $p < 0.001$) meant the firm tended to have workers with lower practical skills. For each one-unit rise in the disparity between how managers and workers value workers' initiative-taking, the probability of the firm being categorized as high-skill diminished by more than 6.6%. A prominent gap in the perception of proactive attitudes and behaviors between workers and employers could signal a malfunctioning communication within the firm, especially when supervisors undervalue the performance perceived to be good by their subordinates. This misalignment in expectations can demotivate workers from putting in their best efforts, committing to skill development, and collaborating with their peers. All of these are important building blocks of their productivity.

The last construct we derived from production managers' perspectives was "*Expectation: Discipline & collaboration.*" The results showed that the more tidiness, punctuality, discipline, and collaboration the supervisor expected from workers, the more likely the worker was to be associated with low-skill firms. For each unit increase in the expectation, the probability of the worker being classified into a high-skill firm decreased by 6.1% ("*Expectation: Discipline & collaboration,*" with −0.061 at $p < 0.01$ for high-skill firms). High expectations in discipline not only resulted in low worker autonomy but also meant that tasks may be highly controlled. In turn, a neuroscience experiment found that a less controlled environment was significantly associated with both greater self and team productivity (Johannsen & Zak, 2020). However, it could also be that, because productivity decreases, managers start to focus on these noncognitive skills. Given the limitations of this correlational study, the causal relationship between expectations and productivity cannot be confirmed.

For intra-firm conditions, firms in the high-skill group had a stronger tendency to provide diverse types of on-the-job training (OJT) (variable "*OJT offerings*" demonstrates a coefficient of 0.043 with $p < 0.001$). Meanwhile, it is the low-skill group, rather than the high-skill group, that collaborated more closely with TVET when seeking new employees ("*TVET collaboration*" shows 0.089 at $p < 0.05$ for low-skill firms). It is also noteworthy that the firm size and export-orientation were negatively correlated with the level of practical skills, suggesting that the more the number of employees and the more the firms were integrated into the global value chain, the lower the individual practical skills are ("*Firm size*" shows 0.075 and "*Export firm*" shows 0.219 both at $p < 0.001$ for low-skill firms). So far, the picture may look confusing. Then, let us get a clearer understanding of the determinants of the enabling skills development ecosystem at the firm level.

As expected, in the cultural contexts of Pakistan, when there was little intra-gender difference in the skills that female workers already possess, workplace conditions seem to play a vital role in shaping workers' productivity. Firstly, high-skill firms tended to offer a more diverse range of on-the-job training (OJT) options. Each additional type of training provided by the firm was associated with a 4.3% increase in the probability that the worker is employed in a high-skill firm. This result confirmed that the extent to which firms prioritize upskilling played a vital role in shaping female workers' skill formation. Our findings aligned with several prior studies observing a positive association between OJT and job performance (e.g., Andri & Mandataris, 2023; Toumahuw, 2022). The OJT is used as a tool for companies to upskill and reskill their employees throughout the course of their employment. It is often tailored to meet specific needs and provide practical experience in actual workplace contexts. Therefore, to enhance both workers' skills and firms' productivity, it is suggested that employers invest in on-the-job upskilling opportunities, not only in terms of frequency, but also in terms of training variety and quality.

In addition, with regard to firm profiles, the firm size and whether they are exporters were significantly associated with the likelihood of the classification into a low- or high-skill group. As the firm size decreased from large, medium, to small, the probability that the worker is in a high-skill firm increased by more than 7.5%. Similarly, belonging to a domestically oriented firm increased the probability of being a high-skilled firm by approximately 22%. These two factors were logically connected, given that smaller firms were less likely to export their products. In small firms, where they handle fewer orders, workers are likely to be involved in multiple tasks and different stages of production. For example, to make clothes, a worker needs to be able to perform a wide range of tasks, starting from reading patterns, cutting fabrics, stitching, and continuing through the final stages. Experiencing a variety of tasks tends to lead to greater practical skills. On the other hand, larger factories, focused on mass production for export, usually have organized production lines in which workers are assigned to specific tasks repeatedly. This circumstance could result in the mastery of a limited range of practical skills.

Since we could not identify significant variation in cognitive and noncognitive skills among workers in Pakistan, both in the formal and informal sectors, it was difficult to discuss how the econo-productive mechanism of the society affects their skills formation. In fact, it is not driven much by economic forces but more by the socio-cultural mechanism. Therefore, in this section, instead of finding the driver for skills development in the society at large, we came down to the firm level and tried to untangle the nexus of econo-productive and socio-cultural mechanisms with micro-ecology and see how that would contribute to making the firm an enabling environment for female workers' skills development. The provision of upskilling opportunities through OJT initiatives and encouraging workers to experience different types of tasks is positively linked with the workers' work-related skills. Therefore, workforce productivity development can be encouraged by consistent investment in a variety of practical training opportunities. Simultaneously, people in managerial roles are advised to reflect on their beliefs about women's aptitude and free themselves from a conventional value framework if they are serious about hiring more women. Managers' discriminatory attitude toward female workers, even if expressed unconsciously, could mean shutting down the opportunities and discouraging the efforts of women. Moreover, appreciation of proactive performance by supervisors is a potential driver of firm productivity. This highlights the importance of establishing clear criteria for performance evaluation to be shared among all parties, including frontline workers.

6.5 Conclusion

In this chapter, we have drawn upon cross-national data to discuss how the generative mechanisms explain the variation in competency formation among workers from the formal and informal sectors. The workforce in the informal segment dominates the garment and textile industry of both Ghana and Pakistan; however, the development and valuation of skills in each labor market differ significantly. Through the realist-constructivist lens, these divergent phenomena were explained by the function of generative mechanisms, particularly those concerning economic and socio-cultural aspects, surrounding the global ecology.

Initially, we hypothesized that there are significant differences in backgrounds, personality traits, and cognitive skills between informal and formal workers in both countries. This hypothesis was proved only in the context of Ghana. While informal and formal workers in Ghana differed in almost every demographic profile and skill, in the case of Pakistani participants, the variations found in Ghana were not found. The contrast observed between the two countries was explained by the nature of their garment industries, which are situated differently in the macroeconomic structure, and socio-cultural ideologies regarding women embedded in their respective societies.

In Ghana, a substantial space for informal entrepreneurship in the industry enables a greater heterogeneity of skill development in the labor market, making the skills and personal attributes differ between the informal and formal sector workers. With the intersection of this economic-productive mechanism and less restrictive gender norms, informal workers have more freedom in decision-making regarding where and how to work and advance their profession, according to their strengths and interests, regardless of their gender. Conversely, in Pakistan's export-oriented garment and textile industry, which is enmeshed within global value chains, establishing a business necessitates a significant investment of capital, which is beyond the means of vulnerable women. This limits the economic participation options in the informal sector, leaving female informal workers with temporary piece-rate jobs offered by firms. Such a limitation contributes to confirming a narrow conception of female competency, and female labor is treated in a similar manner across the boundaries of formal and informal sectors. Taken collectively, the observed trends reflect how generative mechanisms subtly shape women's labor market experiences. In Ghana, these factors encourage heterogeneity, whereas in Pakistan, they reinforce uniformity and limitation.

Nevertheless, the potentials and experience for upskilling and empowering female workers was found in the micro ecologies of firms and their managers in Pakistan. Firms' decisions on skill development opportunity provision are crucial for improving the capabilities of employees that are necessary for achieving overall productivity. At the same time, the perception of people in managerial positions on the necessity of certain personality traits and abilities plays a significant role in skill formation among female workers in this country. Taken together with the findings from the first half of the chapter, we have explained how the enabling micro-ecologies surrounding individual workers and their intersection of a few generative mechanisms determine the process of competency development in particular cultural contexts. They are micro-realities experienced by people in their daily practices but are linked within a larger framework even beyond that of a nation.

References

Abraham, A. Y., Ohemeng, F. N. A., & Ohemeng, W. (2017). Female labour force participation: Evidence from Ghana. *International Journal of Social Economics, 44*(11), 1489–1505. https://doi.org/10.1108/IJSE-06-2015-0159

Akhtar, S. (2020). *Home-based workers in Pakistan A statistical profile*. https://www.wiego.org/wp-content/uploads/2021/02/WIEGO_Statistical_Brief_N26_Pakistan_final.pdf

Alam, M. Z., Rafiq, M., Nasir, S., & Abdul Rehman, C. (2023). Problem-solving style as blessing in extraversion personality and corporate entrepreneurship: Evidence from automotive industry of Pakistan using Trait Activation Theory. *Kybernetes, 52*(11), 5427–5443. https://doi.org/10.1108/K-04-2022-0493

Amakye, S., Chimhutu, V., & Darkwah, E. (2022). Beyond the glass ceiling: An exploration of the experiences of female corporate organizational leaders in Ghana. *Journal of Human Behavior in the Social Environment, 32*(7), 858–875. https://doi.org/10.1080/10911359.2021.1970073

Amu, N. J. (2005). *The role of women in Ghana's economy*. Friedrich Ebert Foundation.

Andri, S., & Mandataris, M. (2023). The effect of job training, job supervision and employee commitment to job performance. *Jurnal Pamator: Jurnal Ilmiah Universitas Trunojoyo, 16*(2). https://doi.org/10.21107/pamator.v16i2.20017

Bray, J. H., & Maxwell, S. E. (1985). *Multivariate analysis of variance*. Sage.

Bruce-Amartey, E. J., Amissah, E. R. K., & Safo-Ankama, K. (2014). The decline of Ghana's textile industry: Its effects on textile education in Ghana. *Journal of Design History, 22*, 36–44.

Chemin, M. (2010). Entrepreneurship in Pakistan: Government policy on SMEs, environment for entrepreneurship, internationalisation of entrepreneurs and SMEs. *International Journal of Business and Globalisation, 5*(3), 238–247. https://doi.org/10.1504/IJBG.2010.035019

Dadheech, R., & Sharma, D. (2023). Home-based work or non-home-based work? Factors influencing work choices of women in the informal sector. *International Journal of Sociology and Social Policy, 43*(1/2), 89–106. https://doi.org/10.1108/IJSSP-08-2021-0200

Dias, S., & Jayasekara, P. (2018). The relationship between personality five factor theory and the career success of executive workers in apparel sector organizations in Sabaragamuwa province Sri Lanka. *Human Resource Management Journal, 5*(1), 19–34. https://doi.org/10.31357/hrmj.v5i1.3573

Dweck, C. S. (2006). *Mindset: The new psychology of success*. Random house.

Ellemers, N. (2018). Gender stereotypes. *Annual Review of Psychology, 69*(1), 275–298. https://doi.org/10.1146/annurev-psych-122216-011719

Fadliyanti, L., Hernanda, B. W. L., Husni, V. H., & Sutanto, H. (2023). Analysis of women labour force determinants in the formal and informal sectors. *Journal of Economics, Finance and Management Studies, 06*(07). https://doi.org/10.47191/jefms/v6-i7-19

Gudivada, V. N., Irfan, M. T., Fathi, E., & Rao, D. L. (2016). Cognitive analytics. In *Handbook of statistics* (pp. 169–205). Elsevier. https://doi.org/10.1016/bs.host.2016.07.010

Hadi, A. (2017). Patriarchy and gender-based violence in Pakistan. *European Journal of Social Sciences Education and Research, 10*(2), 297. https://doi.org/10.26417/ejser.v10i2.p297-304

Hughes, R. A., Heron, J., Sterne, J. A. C., & Tilling, K. (2019). Accounting for missing data in statistical analyses: Multiple imputation is not always the answer. *International Journal of Epidemiology, 48*(4), 1294–1304. https://doi.org/10.1093/ije/dyz032

Hunnicutt, G. (2009). Varieties of patriarchy and violence against women. *Violence Against Women, 15*(5), 553–573. https://doi.org/10.1177/1077801208331246

IFC. (2020). Textile (value addition) sector profile Pakistan. International Finance Cooperation (IFC). Accessed November 21, 2025, https://invest.gov.pk/sites/default/files/inline-files/Profile%20-%20Textile%20Sector_new.pdf?gtranslate=en

ILOSTAT database. (2020, September). Informal employment (% of total non-agricultural employment). International Labour Organization. Accessed November 20, 2025, https://genderdata.worldbank.org/en/indicator/sl-isv-ifrm-zs?gender=gender-gap

International Finance Cooperation (IFC). (2020). *Textile (value addition) sector profile Pakistan*. International Finance Cooperation (IFC). https://invest.gov.pk/sites/default/files/inline-files/Profile%20-%20Textile%20Sector_new.pdf?gtranslate=en

International Labour Office. (2018). *Women and men in the informal economy: A statistical picture*. Geneva. Accessed November 20, 2025, https://www.ilo.org/sites/default/files/2024-04/Women_men_informal_economy_statistical_picture.pdf

Johannsen, R., & Zak, P. J. (2020). Autonomy raises productivity: An experiment measuring neurophysiology. *Frontiers in Psychology, 11*. https://doi.org/10.3389/fpsyg.2020.00963

Judge, T. A., Scott, B. A., & Ilies, R. (2006). Hostility, job attitudes, and workplace deviance: Test of a multilevel model. *Journal of Applied Psychology, 91*(1), 126–138. https://doi.org/10.1037/0021-9010.91.1.126

Khan, S. U., Goldsmith, A. H., & Rajaguru, G. (2023). The dynamics of traditions and women's employment: Evidence from a developing country. *Economic Analysis Letters, 2*(4). https://doi.org/10.58567/eal02040006

Kramer, A. S., & Harris, A. B. (2016). Why women feel more stress at work. *Harvard Business Review Digital Articles.*

Lavaysse, L. M., & Probst, T. M. (2019). Stereotype threat: Impacts for women at work. In *Women, business and leadership*. Edward Elgar Publishing. https://doi.org/10.4337/9781786432711.00029

Mahapatro, S. (2019). Female employment in India: Determinants of choice of sector of activity. *Journal of Economic Studies, 46*(3), 748–759. https://doi.org/10.1108/JES-04-2017-0108

Maqsood, H., Che Sulaiman, N. F., Muhamad, S., Rohaizad, A. B., & N. A. (2024). Women's economic underdevelopment in Pakistan: The intersection of gender and female labour force participation. *Human Systems Management, 43*(6), 872–884. https://doi.org/10.3233/HSM-240002

Meyers, L. S., Gamst, G., & Guarino, A. J. (2016). *Applied multivariate research: Design and interpretation*. Sage.

Mullan, J., & Rolleston, C. (2020). Barriers to skills development in India's informal economy. *International Journal of Training Research, 18*(3), 211–230. https://doi.org/10.1080/14480220.2020.1864445

Nartey, P., Bahar, O. S., & Nabunya, P. (2023). A Review of the cultural gender norms contributing to gender inequality in Ghana: An ecological systems perspective. *Journal of international women's studies, 25*(7).

Ng, B. (2018). The neuroscience of growth mindset and intrinsic motivation. *Brain Sciences, 8*(2), 20. https://doi.org/10.3390/brainsci8020020

Nyeadi, J. D., Kamasa, K., & Kpinpuo, S. (2021). Female in top management and firm performance nexus: Empirical evidence from Ghana. *Cogent Economics & Finance, 9*(1). https://doi.org/10.1080/23322039.2021.1921323

Owusu, G., Quartey, P., & Bawakyillenuo, S. (2014, August). Are Ghana's women more entrepreneurial than its men? *Brookings*. Accessed November 20, 2025, https://www.brookings.edu/articles/are-ghanas-women-more-entrepreneurial-than-its-men/#ftnte1

Pierre, G., Sanchez Puerta, M. L., Valerio, A., & Rajadel, T. (2014). *STEP skills measurement surveys: Innovative tools for assessing skills* (Social Protection & Labor Discussion Paper No. 1421). World Bank.

Ranasinghe, V. R., & Kottawatta, K. H. H. (2016). The impact of employees' personality on their psychological contract in fabric manufacturing industry of Sri Lanka. *Human Resource Management Journal, 4*(1), 40–52.

Raza, S., Minai, M. S., Zain, A. Y. M., Tariq, T. A., & Khuwaja, F. M. (2018). Dissection of small businesses in Pakistan: Issues and directions. *International Journal of Entrepreneurship, 22*(4), 1–13.

Regel, I. J., & Pilz, M. (2019). Informal learning and skill formation within the Indian informal tailoring sector. *International Journal of Training Research, 17*(2), 140–156. https://doi.org/10.1080/14480220.2019.1624350

Reuters. (2024, July 31). Ghana parliament passes law to quicken women's empowerment. Accessed November 20, 2025, https://www.reuters.com/world/africa/ghana-parliament-passes-law-quicken-womens-empowerment-2024-07-30/

Rhew, E., Piro, J. S., Goolkasian, P., & Cosentino, P. (2018). The effects of a growth mindset on self-efficacy and motivation. *Cogent Education, 5*(1), 1492337. https://doi.org/10.1080/2331186X.2018.1492337

Ruwanpura, K. N., & Hughes, A. (2016). Empowered spaces? Management articulations of gendered spaces in apparel factories in Karachi, Pakistan. *Gender, Place & Culture, 23*(9), 1270–1285. https://doi.org/10.1080/0966369X.2015.1136815

Sandefur, J. (2010). *On the evolution of the firm size distribution in an African economy* (No. 2010).

Schofer, E., & Meyer, J. W. (2005). The worldwide expansion of higher education in the twentieth century. *American Sociological Review, 70*(6), 898–920. https://doi.org/10.1177/000312240507000602

Sowatey, E., Nyantakyi-Frimpong, H., Mkandawire, P., Arku, G., Hussey, L., & Amasaba, A. (2018). Spaces of resilience, ingenuity, and entrepreneurship in informal work in Ghana. *International Planning Studies, 23*(4), 327–339. https://doi.org/10.1080/13563475.2018.1480933

Takyi, B. K., & Gyimah, S. O. (2007). Matrilineal family ties and marital dissolution in Ghana. *Journal of Family Issues, 28*(5), 682–705. https://doi.org/10.1177/0192513X070280050401

Tay, L., Meade, A. W., & Cao, M. (2015). An overview and practical guide to IRT measurement equivalence analysis. *Organizational Research Methods, 18*(1), 3–46. https://doi.org/10.1177/1094428114553062

TDAP. (2024). *Pakistan's trade perspective: Annual trade review FY2022–23.*

Tedone, A. M., & Bruk-Lee, V. (2022). Speaking up at work: Personality's influence on employee voice behavior. *International Journal of Organizational Analysis, 30*(2), 289–304. https://doi.org/10.1108/IJOA-09-2020-2417

Toumahuw, N. Y. (2022). The influence of work motivation and job training on job satisfaction and employee performance (literature review of human resource management). *Dinasti International Journal of Education Management and Social Science, 4*(2).

Vyas, S., & Kumaranayake, L. (2006). Constructing socio-economic status indices: How to use principal components analysis. *Health Policy and Planning, 21*(6), 459–468. https://doi.org/10.1093/heapol/czl029

Wang, A., Bojanic, A. N., & Hamil, B. (2023). Women's labor participation in Ghana and effects on human development: A focus on entrepreneurship. *Journal of Student Research, 12*(3), 1–13.

Ware, J. K. (2019). Property value as a proxy of socioeconomic status in education. *Education and Urban Society, 51*(1), 99–119. https://doi.org/10.1177/0013124517714850

Williams, R. (2016). Understanding and interpreting generalized ordered logit models. *The Journal of Mathematical Sociology, 40*(1), 7–20. https://doi.org/10.1080/0022250X.2015.1112384

Wilmot, M. P., Wanberg, C. R., Kammeyer-Mueller, J. D., & Ones, D. S. (2019). Extraversion advantages at work: A quantitative review and synthesis of the meta-analytic evidence. *Journal of Applied Psychology, 104*(12), 1447–1470. https://doi.org/10.1037/apl0000415

World Economic Forum. (2023). *Global gender gap report 2023*. Geneva. Accessed November 21, 2025, http://reports.weforum.org/globalgender-gap-report-2023

Yamada, S. (2021). Traditional apprenticeship as an educational and life experience: Life stories of young auto repair apprentices in Kumasi, Ghana. In Y. Ofosu-Kusi & M. Matsuda (Eds.), *The challenge of African potentials: Conviviality, informality and futurity* (pp. 181–208). Langaa Publishing.

7 Game-Based Training of Noncognitive Abilities: Efficacy and Prospects

Emmanuel Estrellado, Pimmada Charoensilp, and Shoko Yamada

Abstract

This chapter examines the effects of the training program developed based on our competency assessment findings. Socio-emotional noncognitive abilities—consistently shown in our surveys to influence workers' productivity—are the focus of this intervention. To train these abilities effectively, our team created a board-game-based program grounded in behavior modeling theory, enabling trainees to learn through observation, simulation, and engaging game activities. The chapter analyzes the program's efficacy using data from 504 workers in Ethiopian garment-sector small and medium enterprises, applying a quasi-experimental design with pre- and post-intervention questionnaires. The training, centered on two board games and guided reflection, significantly improved participants' work-related soft skills, and the analysis further identifies factors associated with workers' levels of noncognitive abilities. To address the potential interests of training practitioners and policymakers in adopting the technique, the chapter outlines the steps to develop game-based training (GBT) for noncognitive abilities.

Keywords

Game-based training · Behavioral modeling · Noncognitive abilities · Development · Ethiopia · Garment industry · Board games

This chapter is based on and extends the analysis presented in an earlier publication by Estrellado et al. (2023).

E. Estrellado (✉)
Graduate School of International Development, Nagoya University, Nagoya, Japan
e-mail: eestrellado@nagoya-u.jp

P. Charoensilp
Center of Excellence on Migration and development, Institute of Asian Studies, Chulalongkorn University, Bangkok, Thailand

S. Yamada
Graduate School of International Development, Nagoya University, Nagoya, Japan

Graduate School of Asian and African Area Studies, Kyoto University, Kyoto, Japan
e-mail: syamada@nagoya-u.jp

7.1 Introduction

In a training center in the heart of Ethiopia's capital city of Addis Ababa, twenty garment factory workers gathered on what they initially assumed to be another routine skills training session. But today is not like any of the training programs they have had before. Today, the training room is humming with energy. Laughter can be heard across the tables, and workers are having animated conversations, while others cheer each other on.

S. Yamada (ed.), *Mitigating the "Skills Gaps"*, Sustainable Development Goals Series,
https://doi.org/10.1007/978-981-95-7968-6_7

The training facilitators are equally delighted to see enthusiasm from the participants as they have never experienced before. Before, they were used to conducting training sessions where participants were bored and unengaged. What's the secret behind this change? Nothing fancy. There were no flashy presentations with long-winded lectures, but something quite unexpected—board games. This one-day game-based training (GBT) program, designed by our team at the Skills and Knowledge for Youths (SKY) Project, transforms traditional training by mixing elements of learning and play. Through our original games, workers learn about noncognitive abilities necessary for their workplace in an intuitive manner. Skills such as occupational health and safety, tidiness, efficiency, quality control, and teamwork are seamlessly integrated into the game so that by the end of their play session, workers have internalized these skills.

By the end of the training program, workers leave the room transformed. Not just because they have gained new knowledge, but also because they have renewed their confidence and motivation to work and are eager to apply the skills they have learned on the factory floor. The trainers also left the training empowered, as they had witnessed a new form of training at its most powerful—enjoyable, easy to deploy, and leaving a lasting impression.

The scene described is from the experimental operation of the GBT conducted by the SKY project team in November 2022, which involved 504 participants from small and medium-sized enterprises (SMEs) in the vicinity of Addis Ababa, Ethiopia. The events described showcase the potential of game-based training using board games and how it can unlock abilities that traditional slide-based lectures struggle to provide. Becoming able to act on noncognitive abilities is fundamentally different from passively learning them as a concept, for which conventional slide-based lectures are not well-suited. The training program we developed engages participants in the process with enjoyment while helping them internalize how they can act effectively and productively at work. GBT programs help contextualize abstract concepts, making learning easier and more enjoyable, while transforming passive learners into active problem-solvers.

In this chapter, we will use the term 'noncognitive abilities' to refer to a set of socio-emotional noncognitive abilities necessary for performing tasks in the workplace. As discussed in Chap. 1, noncognitive abilities encompass a wide range of socio-emotional abilities and personality traits. Instead of trying to cover all of them, our GBT program was designed to focus on specific work-related socio-emotional noncognitive abilities, such as occupational health and safety, tidiness and cleanliness, efficiency, quality control, and teamwork. These skills will enable participants to act effectively, efficiently, and safely in a team while making informed judgments about workplace priorities.

In Ethiopia and similar economies, the development of the workforce's noncognitive abilities is a priority policy measure because it will improve manufacturing productivity and also enhance people's well-being by promoting skills-based decent employment, which in turn will contribute to reducing poverty and increasing job security (Yamada, 2023). The workers are the greatest assets any organization could have, and the performance of any organization is strongly dependent on the quality of the people it keeps. As we discussed in Chap. 1, there are various types of abilities. Among them, private sector employers are increasingly recognizing the importance of noncognitive abilities. It is because the adaptive ability to work in synergy with colleagues while following rules and expectations is considered to improve production. As Fig. 7.1 shows, online queries using the keyword 'soft skills' (another term to denote noncognitive abilities) have increased dramatically over time.[1] Despite recognition of their importance, many companies fail to provide training programs that lead to meaningful improvements in their employees' noncognitive abilities. This is where GBT comes in.

[1] The Google search interest is represented by a number between 0 and 100. A value of 100 represents the term's highest popularity. A value of 50 means that it is half as popular as the most popular term at that time. A value of zero indicates that there is insufficient information for the search term.

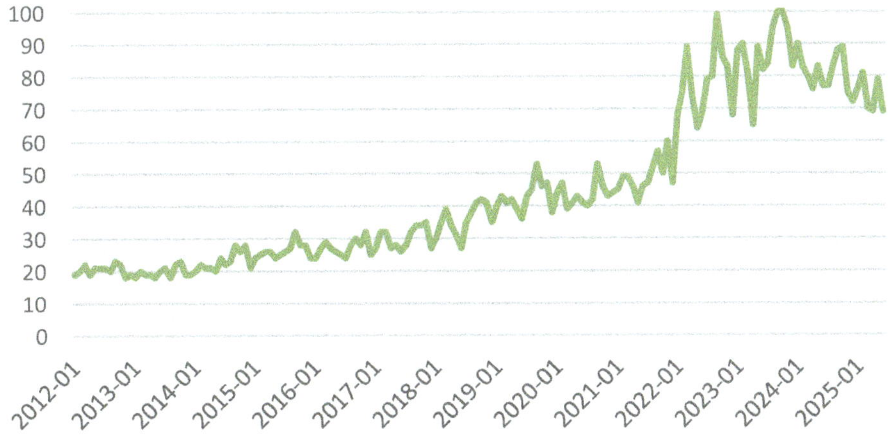

Fig. 7.1 Trends in interest in "soft skills", or noncognitive abilities, over time (Source: Google Trends, n.d.)

GBT flips the script in contrast to traditional lecture-based training. Instead of the participants passively listening to an avalanche of dull presentation slides, they become active participants responsible for their learning.

In this chapter, we will take you behind the scenes to explain how our team developed our unique GBT programs to foster workers' noncognitive abilities, firmly grounded in a theoretical foundation and supported by empirical evidence of GBT's efficacy from the outcomes of our quasi-experiment conducted in Ethiopia. We share our experience and procedure with readers because we believe that it will help many practitioners and policymakers revisit their current training programs and adopt this innovative approach. Throughout the development of the training program, our team learned and applied various game design principles, techniques, and elements to ensure that the original games we developed achieved their goals while being enjoyable. We also considered the balance in the game's level of difficulty so that factory workers with less than 9 years of formal education can participate. At the same time, we conducted it as an academic exercise, firmly grounded in a learning theory of social psychology, combined with expertise in manufacturing production management, cognitive development, and educational measurement. In summary, what we present in this chapter is the result of our unique effort, achieved by balancing two tiers: board game design and academic investigation for training innovation.

We begin the chapter by operationally defining GBT and why industries should adopt unconventional training methods like ours. Then, we will briefly examine some of the theories supporting GBT and how one theory, specifically the behavioral modeling theory, is considered and integrated into the design of the game and the training program. Since this chapter focuses more on practices than theories, which were discussed extensively in Chaps. 2 and 3, we encourage readers with theoretical interests to revisit these chapters. Afterward, we will discuss the experiment's outcome, supported by evidence of the effects of the GBT program we developed to enhance workers' socio-emotional and work-related noncognitive abilities, thereby increasing productivity. Finally, we will call attention to the opportunities that GBT programs offer for various populations and industries. We hope this chapter sparks fresh ideas for researchers and practitioners alike.

7.2 Game-Based Training and why It Works

The term 'game-based training' itself implies that it is a type of training that leverages the use of physical or digital games to deliver or teach skills, behaviors, or concepts. Just like any learning or training program, GBT has pre-defined learning outcomes. However, GBT goes beyond traditional lecture-based or slide-based training programs by incorporating standalone digital or physical games, creating a simulated interactive experience that engages participants to achieve the desired training objectives or outcomes.

Often, the term 'game-based training' is confused or used interchangeably with 'gamification.' Gamification is defined as the integration of game elements into the learning or work environment (Armstrong & Landers, 2018; Kapp, 2012). Gamification is primarily used to motivate people to engage in tasks or target specific behaviors (Kapp, 2012; Plass et al., 2015). This is facilitated by incorporating game design elements, such as point systems, achievements, and leaderboards, into activities to motivate participants to engage in the target behavior or skill. Imagine this: in a manufacturing company, a factory production process might be gamified by including a leaderboard that ranks the productivity of various production lines or by rewarding certain workers with achievements for meeting specific production targets. These elements do not create a standalone game but rather add game elements to the workers' existing tasks as a way to motivate them.

In contrast, game-based learning or training involves the use of actual physical or digital games that participants play to simulate situations that mirror their work environment. The games used in game-based learning are designed to provide participants with artificial conflicts or scenarios that allow them to practice the skills and behaviors necessary in the workplace (Estrellado et al., 2023; Plass et al., 2015). An example of GBT for the same factory production process involves repackaging the production process using game design in a digital or physical game format, which will simulate the work environment within the game. In this simulated setting, participants have an opportunity to rehearse or practice skills outside their regular practice, without real-world consequences, before they face similar challenges in the actual workplace (Estrellado et al., 2023).

Now that we have established what constitutes GBT, we would like to illustrate why and how it can be practically applied in teaching and enhancing participants' socio-emotional and noncognitive abilities. Some of the cited reasons for the effectiveness of using games for training are that they are enjoyable, motivating, engaging, and that they help simplify abstract concepts to participants (Merkuryev & Bikovska, 2012). To further explore why game-based training is effective, we categorize the various arguments that support the use of games in learning and training, which are presented in the following sub-sections.

7.2.1 Arguments on Motivation and Attitudes

One of the most commonly cited strengths of using games in training and learning is that games strongly affect the motivation and attitude of the participants (Krath et al., 2021). It is easy to see that games are inherently entertaining and engaging for training participants. Because games in general are fun and provide players with a sense of achievement, especially when they achieve their goals, participants are intrinsically motivated to play (Kapp, 2012).

One theory that may describe how games motivate participants is the self-determination theory (SDT) by Ryan and Deci (2000). According to SDT, humans have innate psychological needs that must be satisfied, which will result in enhanced self-motivation. These psychological needs are competence, autonomy, and relatedness (Ryan & Deci, 2000).

Competence is defined as the participant's need to feel capable and successful (Ryan et al., 2006). A concept related to competence is self-efficacy, which is defined by measures of one's personal capacity to perform tasks (Bandura, 1982). According to Ryan and Deci (2000), participants' perceived competence is enhanced when they are given optimal challenges, positive feedback, and are free from negative evaluation. This enhanced competence leads to better performance, persistence, and creativity when performing tasks, as well as improved well-being and self-efficacy (Ryan et al., 2006). Games facilitate this by providing players with tasks or challenges that are appropriate to their skill level. In the context of games, game objectives provide the player with specific and unambiguous goals and challenges that, when conquered, create a powerful sense of mastery and self-efficacy. Feedback in games is provided in various ways, such as points, coins, progress bars, and levels. Ultimately, the main metric for achieving the game's goal is winning. Games are also effective in providing players with feedback designed to evoke the correct behavior, thoughts, and actions. For example, in a board game like *Monopoly*, examining the game board provides players with visual cues regarding the game's objective, which is to buy, trade, and develop properties. As the game progresses, players receive visual feedback on their own progress and that of other players. For example, you see the amount of money, property, and development each player accumulates through their cash, land deeds, and structures built on the board. Depending on their performance, players gain insight into their competence based on how far they are from achieving the game's goal and how they compare to other players (Kapp, 2012).

Autonomy, in the context of SDT, is related to a person's sense of control over their own behavior and destiny. Autonomy is high when a person is given the freedom to choose and decide based on the information or feedback they receive (Ryan et al., 2006). In games, players are often given a variety of choices and options, which fosters a sense of autonomy. However, a single choice does not constitute a player's full sense of autonomy, but rather from the layered and interconnected web of decisions that they must constantly make in order to win. For example, in the classic game of *Settlers of Catan*, players take the role of settlers vying for dominance in the titular island of Catan. In the game, players are offered several paths to victory, including building cities and settlements, constructing the longest road, raising the largest army, and accumulating development cards that provide victory points. In the game, players are not told which path or strategy to take; instead, they must make their own independent decisions. As they progress through the game, players may switch strategies to adapt to the actions of other players. This level of freedom of choice afforded by games gives the players ownership of their strategy, which in turn increases their perceived autonomy.

The final psychological factor that helps enhance motivation is relatedness. Relatedness refers to the feeling of connection with others (Ryan et al., 2006). In the context of games, multiplayer or social games create a sense of collaboration, connection, and competition among the players. The video game *Animal Crossing: New Horizons*, for example, experienced a surge in popularity during the COVID-19 pandemic because it effectively satisfied people's psychological need for relatedness (Yee & Sng, 2022). Animal Crossing is a social simulation game where players develop and build their island. The social aspect of the game enabled people to interact with their friends and even strangers, particularly during a period when physical isolation restricted freedom of movement (Yee & Sng, 2022).

In cooperative board games like *Pandemic*, relatedness is not limited to being physically present to play the game; it also encompasses the shared experience of playing the game. The feelings of connection are woven into the social fabric of shared struggles, triumphs, and interactions between players. In *Pandemic*, players take on the roles of various specialists who must work together to combat a global pandemic. From the moment the game begins, a social dynamic is established among the players, and to overcome the challenge ahead, they must work cooperatively towards a common goal. Through interactions with other players and the game itself, the players' need for relatedness is satisfied, ultimately leading to enhanced motivation.

In the process of ensuring that these three psychological needs for motivation—competence, autonomy, and relatedness—are satisfied, we aim to foster intrinsically motivated participants who enjoy the training and learning program, ultimately leading to improved performance in the workplace and the enhancement of other noncognitive abilities. On the other hand, if the training programs provided activities that do not address or would diminish these needs, it would lead to reduced motivation, which in turn results in a decrease in performance.

Games, in general, are specifically designed to be engaging for players. One concept often associated with engagement in games is the flow state. Players are said to be in a state of flow when they are deeply immersed in a game or activity. Csikszentmihalyi (2008) describes in the flow theory that the flow state is the optimal experience achieved when there is a proper balance of difficulty or challenge and player skill. In the context of game-based training, providing participants with challenges that are perfectly balanced with their skill level will keep them engaged in the training for extended periods, turning training programs into an enjoyable and desirable activity. According to a study by Landers and Armstrong (2017), when the participants' attitudes towards the GBT program are high, it leads to increased perceived value of the training program, which they have linked to an increase in training outcomes.

7.2.2 Arguments on Behavior

For many training programs, the main objective is often to change a person's behavior. Traditional training methods (e.g., lectures and slide-based presentations) excel at delivering declarative or conceptual knowledge but struggle with procedural knowledge, which is the transfer or application of knowledge in the workplace. GBT programs directly address this "knowing-doing" gap through simulation and rehearsal, as well as the ability to make do-overs.

In GBT environments, games are designed to recreate experiences and scenarios in an abstract or realistic manner. Depending on the game, GBT can provide participants with a platform for practicing desired behavioral outcomes or skills, like how to navigate delicate social issues like bullying (Del Moral Pérez & Villalustre Martínez, 2018), how to manage a business (Beranič & Heričko, 2022; Ferreira et al., 2021; Ribeiro et al., 2012), or even how to conduct a surgery (Kowalewski et al., 2017; Sabri et al., 2010).

Traditional training or learning often stigmatizes failure or mistakes. However, in GBT, making mistakes is not only expected but is an integral part of the learning process. Games are designed to put participants in low-stakes situations, allowing them to experiment with their choices and strategies. Poor decisions in a business management game may lead to your in-game company going bankrupt, rather than incurring real-world financial loss. A wrong move in a game would allow participants to see the consequences of their actions without actually causing actual harm or damage. The concept of "learning from your mistakes" is crucial for achieving behavioral change. Games are designed to capitalize on these mistakes and utilize them as learning opportunities, providing participants with instant feedback based on their actions (Kapp, 2012). On the other hand, when participants make good and strategic choices, they are rewarded in-game with progression to the next level, points, or other beneficial effects. This reinforces good behavior or actions by the participants. In summary, by allowing participants to fail with minimal consequences, GBT encourages exploration, curiosity, and discovery learning.

The above examples are linked to the reinforcement theory, where stimuli in the form of behavior or actions are introduced to positive reinforcement, such as rewards and praise, to strengthen desired behavioral outcomes. On the other hand, negative reinforcement, such as punishments, is introduced to suppress undesired behavior (Kimble, 1956).

7.2.3 Arguments on Learning

The final argument regarding the effectiveness of games for learning and training is their impact on human learning. From the lens of cognitive psychology, GBT is effective because it aligns with how people learn and remember information. In a review by Krath et al. (2021), they identified that theories in support of GBT are primarily rooted in social learning theories and constructivism.

The central concept in social learning theories is that people mainly learn by observing other people in social situations (Bandura, 1977). In the context of GBT, this is facilitated by using in-game role models of the desired behavior or by observing other players. Social learning theories, particularly behavioral modeling, will be discussed in detail in the next section of this chapter.

Constructivist learning theories deal with the general process of knowledge construction through assimilation, accommodation, and equilibrium (Dagar & Yadav, 2016). GBT incorporates constructivist principles, such as active learning, experiential learning, participation, and reflection, to enhance learning outcomes. In traditional training programs, participants are often placed in passive roles, where they are expected to absorb knowledge like sponges. Games, by their nature, put participants in an active role, where they must make decisions, solve problems, and interact with the game or with other players. This active processing of information is crucial in transferring information from short-term to long-term memory (Dubinsky & Hamid, 2024).

Games utilize a multisensory approach to promote long-term retention of information. In the cognitive theory of multimedia learning, humans process information through both visual and verbal channels, where they must actively process information in order to commit it to long-term memory and ultimately be able to use it in new situations (Mayer, 2024). Games also aid in knowledge construction, as explained by the situated learning theory. The situated learning theory posits that knowledge is best acquired when it is relevant to the context in which it will be used (Lave & Wenger, 1991). GBT does this by simulating or recreating scenarios that are contextualized to the participants. For example, games used for military training utilize highly contextualized simulation games to help participants understand when and how to apply the content they have learned. In the abstracted and simulated environment of the game, participants learn firsthand the consequences of their actions, similar to what they will encounter in the real world. In contextualized learning, information is not abstract but is tied to specific situations relevant to the participants, making knowledge transfer easier for participants based on their specific context.

Another concept related to the social learning theories is Vygotsky's zone of proximal development (ZPD). ZPD is defined as the distance between a participant's current level of development and the next attainable level with the aid of a competent adult, peer, or learning tool (Cakir, 2008; Margolis, 2020). Under the ZPD concept, learning does not end with the cognitive acquisition of new knowledge. Instead, it continues to involve new and more complicated concepts (Margolis, 2020). To bridge the ZPD, the concept of scaffolding is introduced, which denotes the support provided through guidance or instruction to help participants reach the next development level that they cannot achieve on their own (Margolis, 2020). In traditional training, participants are often overwhelmed by information overload, as they are presented with excessive amounts of information all at once. In GBT, games are designed to be adaptive to the learners' ZPD by dividing the learning content into manageable levels, allowing them to scaffold and reach their next developmental level (Krath et al., 2021).

In summary, the arguments presented here demonstrate that GBT, as a training method, can transform participants' attitudes and motivation, bridge the 'knowing-doing' gap, and facilitate the formation and retention of knowledge. However, GBT is not a universal training solution. The success of GBT programs hinges on the successful application of the theories and arguments presented in this section in their design and implementation. When done successfully, GBT can usher in a paradigm shift in the way training and learning are implemented—from passive information consumption to a more active, experiential, and learner-centered approach.

As mentioned in Chap. 1, artificial intelligence (AI) is projected to replace many jobs, and skills are becoming increasingly specialized and more context-specific to the workplace. To quickly address the rapidly changing demands for the knowledge and skills of the workforce, while also considering industry- and locality-specific circumstances, we offer GBT as a method to meet these needs. GBT, as we have argued, can be tailored to the specific context of the industry in which the skills will be utilized. Carefully designed GBT programs can ensure engagement and lead to meaningful behavioral change in a short period, ultimately resulting in a more productive workforce.

In the next section, we will delve into Bandura's social learning theory of behavioral modeling and explore why and how it served as the pedagogical model guiding the design of our GBT program using board games.

7.3 Behavior Modeling Training in Designing Game-Based Training Programs

In the previous section, we gave arguments—frameworks and theories—that support the design and effectiveness of GBT as a training method. In this section, we will focus primarily on social learning theories, particularly behavioral modeling, as the primary pedagogical model to guide the design and development of our GBT program, which utilizes board games. We chose behavior modeling training (BMT) because it can explain how and why GBT can achieve desired motivational, attitudinal, behavioral, and learning effects in relation to other theories.

BMT is a training approach that is rooted in Bandura's (1977) social learning theory. According to social learning theory, we learn by observing others in a social context and model our behaviors based on those observations. Think, for example, of a time when you were young and tried to copy what you saw your parents doing, whether doing house chores or how they acted and behaved. You could also think of the first time you went to a fine restaurant and didn't know which cutlery to use. You observed the other patrons and attempted to imitate their actions. In both cases, you try to replicate what you perceive as good behavior by learning from an established model. Whether we are familiar with the concept or not, behavior modeling is a style of learning that we do for most of our lives. In the work context, behavior modeling can be observed in the form of apprenticeship, where apprentices learn by observing and mimicking the way skilled masters or artisans work, under their supervision. In many workplaces, new hires typically shadow senior workers for several days to become familiar with their tasks.

As mentioned in Chap. 1, there are four interrelated subprocesses followed in behavior modeling training: (1) attention, (2) retention, (3) reproduction, and (4) motivation (Bandura, 1977). BMT was developed to (1) guide people to know what should be learned, providing models of targeted behaviors (or skills), (2) get them to remember, (3) provide them with rehearsal opportunities in the setting that simulates their reality, and (4) motivate them to apply the targeted behaviors in real life after the training. BMT has been widely used in the fields of psychology and education. Several studies have found that participants who undergo BMT intervention retain the training content for longer periods, with a higher likelihood of applying it to their own contexts (Dawe, 2002; Shuman et al., 2005; Talavera & Perez-Gonzalez, 2007).

Building on the theories discussed in the earlier section, we will examine the relationship between BMT and its steps to the theories and concepts that support the argument for GBT in training applications. Fig. 7.2 illustrates the pedagogical framework of BMT and its relationship to some common theories cited in support of GBT. Theories are presented in color-coded bubbles depending on their target outcomes—motivation and attitudes, behavior, and learning. Solid arrows indicate that one theory/concept falls under another theory/concept, while broken lines indicate a close relationship between theories or concepts.

Attention The first step in the behavioral modeling process is attention. In attention, participants are guided toward critical features of the desired model or skills (Bandura, 1977). Attention to the learning points rather than just the models creates a clear path for participants to reach the target objective. According to a meta-analytic study by Taylor et al. (2005), presenting learning points in the form of rule codes significantly

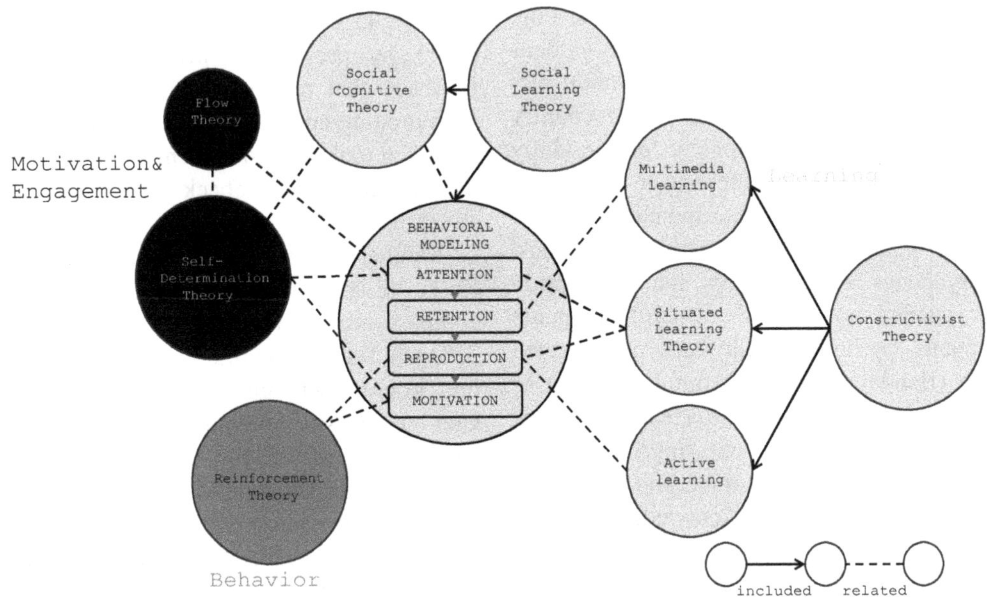

Fig. 7.2 Pedagogical framework of the behavioral modeling theory in relation to other theories

enhances the development of procedural knowledge. According to Decker (1980), rule codes describe the effect of the modeled behavior by presenting its benefits or consequences. In the context of GBT, rule codes are inherently embedded into the game in the form of cause and effect. Depending on the actions taken by the participant, the game's outcome may have either positive or negative effects. These cause-and-effect relationships are found in every aspect of the games and can be easily identified by the participants as they progress. These kinds of participant-identified or generated rule codes are found to significantly enhance skills transfer and retention (Decker, 1980).

Another aspect of the attentional process is ensuring that participants attend to the model presented. Simply presenting the models to them will not guarantee that they will attend to the models. To ensure that participants attend to the model, the models must be motivating, which can be ensured by satisfying the psychological needs for competence, autonomy, and relatedness according to the SDT. Attention is also related to the flow experiences, where participants are deeply immersed in the game. From a constructivist learning perspective, demonstrating and articulating the relevance of actions improves knowledge construction (Krath et al., 2021).

ZPD can also guide the attention process by introducing models that can be scaffolded with the participant's current skill level. Target models can be broken down into smaller components, making it easier for participants to understand and adopt the desired behavior.

Retention The second step in behavioral modeling is retention, which involves processes that will aid participants in remembering and recalling the modeled behaviors. As a social learning method that involves observational learning, the observed models are useless if the participant has no memory of them (Bandura, 1977). That is why it is essential to ensure that our participants will remember the models we presented. We achieve this by breaking down our rule codes into symbolic codes (visual and verbal), which facilitates observational learning and retention of the target skill. Visual codes are mental images formed through the perception of visual stimuli (e.g., images, illustrations, or videos) or observation of a model, while verbal codes are labels, names, and descriptions that are associated with the target skill (Bandura, 1977). Imagine this: I say the word "Japan," and mental images of Mt. Fuji, kimonos, ramen, temples, and tranquil gardens flood our minds. Likewise, I could present pictures of those things and ask which country comes to mind, and everyone would instantly answer "Japan." For this exercise, I don't even need to show pictures; the mental image is already in your mind, stored as memory codes. Memory codes are essentially the information that is retained in our brains, which helps guide participants on how to reproduce the targeted models (Bandura, 1977). Symbolic coding is directly related to the multimedia learning theory, which also involves the processing of information from different media formats and linking the learned models to prior knowledge (Mayer, 2005).

Another aspect of the retention process that can aid in retaining the modeled target skill is mental rehearsal. According to Bandura (1977), mental rehearsal of skill and behavioral patterns aids in the long-term retention of the target models. Sometimes it is easier to strengthen skills through mental rehearsal because opportunities to use these target skills are limited (e.g., due to social constraints or a lack of equipment). The process of mental rehearsal is associated with the constructivist concept of active learning, which involves the processing of mental models to construct new knowledge.

Reproduction The reproduction process is the third component of behavioral modeling. After being presented with a model of the target behavior or skill using symbolic coding, it is converted to memory codes, which will then be used to guide the overt behavioral reproduction or exhibit new patterns of behavior (Bandura, 1977). Reproduction, in a nutshell, is the practice or rehearsal of the target model. However, there may be constraints that limit the physical rehearsal of the target behavioral model, which may be due to limited resources or equipment. In these cases, games are effective because they provide simulations or abstractions of the target model to be rehearsed.

Bandura (1977) mentioned that one barrier to successful reproduction is the lack of feedback that will guide or correct the participant. This is where GBT excels more than regular BMT programs by providing participants with timely feedback that reinforces desired models while discouraging undesirable ones. This concept can be linked to the reinforcement theory, where positive and negative feedback guide participants to strengthen desired behavioral outcomes.

Another constraint in reproducing target models is the lack of prior skills required for more complex models (Bandura, 1977). Introducing ZPD and scaffolding into the design of the training program will ensure that participants will gain the necessary prerequisite skills or building blocks to perform the target model overtly. Games are very good at scaffolding, where models can be presented one by one or the game's difficulty can be adjusted to match the participant's current level of development.

Motivation The last step in the behavioral modeling process is reinforcement and motivational processes. It ties directly into how we keep participants engaged and encourage them to practice the targeted skill repeatedly. The participants may have acquired the necessary declarative and procedural knowledge to reproduce the target model, but if they lack motivation, the overt expression of the target model will not occur (Bandura, 1977). This stage of the behavioral modeling process is directly linked to SDT and reinforcement theory. According to SDT, intrinsically motivated learners exhibit improved work performance and long-term skill transfer (Ryan et al., 2006; Ryan & Deci, 2000). In the context of reinforcement theory, positive and negative reinforcement are used to help translate learned skills into overt action. Positive reinforcement, such as rewards and incentives, will make the desired skill more desirable, encouraging skill transfer in the actual workplace. Meanwhile, negative reinforcement involves consequences to discourage undesired behavior.

By incorporating feedback in the design of GBT programs, we enable players to feel driven to improve and succeed through intrinsic motivation. These, in turn, enhance the learning experience and facilitate the transfer of long-term skills.

7.4 Identifying the "Skills Gap" Through Workplace Analysis

Building on the rationale for GBT presented in Chap. 3 and armed with the pedagogical model of BMT discussed above, we proceeded to conceptualize the contents of the training program. Whether it is conventional or game-based, the training program should set a clear goal to be achieved. While the pedagogical framework of BMT addresses the "how" of learning, identifying the noncognitive abilities required is the "what." In our case, although we knew that the demand for work-related noncognitive abilities training was high, we had yet to specify the types and content of such noncognitive abilities that were to be developed. We need to move forward from general awareness of the need for noncognitive abilities to a specific inventory of the skills, behaviors, and attitudes necessary in the workplace. In other words, we needed to observe workplace situations and collect cases of both good and bad behaviors, which would then be incorporated as models in the game. This process of identifying the "skills gap" is a critical first step that ensures the GBT program being developed and the resulting training will be relevant, contextualized, and meaningful to the participants.

7.4.1 Limitations of Existing Training Programs and the SME Challenge

Between 2020 and 2021, our team reviewed the landscape of noncognitive abilities training programs in Ethiopia's garment industry. Our investigation revealed a commonality among the training programs provided. Most training programs offered by developmental agencies and civil society organizations are typically composed of lectures and group discussions, often held in meeting rooms. This approach creates a physical and mental disconnect with the participants, making it difficult for them to see the connection between the abstract concepts taught in the training program and the specific realities they face on the production line. When training is delivered using these traditional modalities, knowledge gained in the declarative form tends to fade easily as it fails to translate into the behavioral habits required for the job.

This problem is also felt by SMEs in developing countries. Most often, SMEs lack a dedicated human resources (HR) department with the necessary skills and resources to conduct vital skills assessments or needs assessments. As a result, the "skills gap" issue remains unaddressed, leaving workers ill-equipped to face daily work challenges and the company left to operate below its full potential. The gap in SMEs' internal capacity creates an opportunity for external specialists to provide this essential service.

As an academic team that provides this essential service, the SKY Project not only identifies the "skills gap" but also provides a diagnosis of the underlying problems faced by an organization. We do this by bringing an objective and scientific approach to a problem that the company feels but cannot easily identify. After identifying the "skills gap," a plan of action can be formulated to address the problem. Through our assessment module, we can identify whether there is a need for upskilling, behavioral noncognitive training, or both.

Addressing the problem requires a shift in understanding how noncognitive abilities function. We recognized that noncognitive abilities are not a checklist of skills to be blindly executed in the workplace but are a result of adaptive responses to a person's current reality. For example, the essence of a noncognitive ability like "tidiness" is not simply the action of cleaning itself. Its essence lies in understanding the reason for it—accident prevention, decreased time searching for tools, waste reduction, etc. Without understanding the reason behind it, the training will devolve into rote memorization of rules, which quickly fade from memory. Therefore, it is simply not enough to identify "what" the "skills gaps" are and the behaviors desired in the workplace; equally important is the "why" or the reasoning behind it. This understanding forced our team to reject a top-down, pre-defined list of skills. Instead, we opted to inductively discover the skills as they are contextualized in the specific cultural and industrial context of Ethiopia's garment sector.

7.4.2 Identifying the "Skills Gap"

To accurately capture the "skills gap," we employed a two-step approach. This will ensure that our needs assessment is both comprehensive and reliable. The following section outlines the methods employed in the current study to identify the "skills gap."

Expert Collaboration We consulted with experts in Ethiopia's garment manufacturing industry to discuss the characteristics and behaviors exhibited by effective workers. Experts include but are not limited to HR managers, production managers, engineers, and quality controllers. These people possess tacit and explicit knowledge of desired workplace behaviors relevant to the context of garment manufacturing in Ethiopia.

Workplace Observation Our team also collected photographs and videos provided by experts, which capture the various contexts in which the skills are applied at production sites. The photographs captured phenomena and situations that are typically observed in Ethiopia's garment firms. For example, there are several photos depicting what appears to be a disorganized tool rack, and then there are photos of the same tool rack, but in this one, the worker's tools are organized neatly. We asked the experts to explain why and how the phenomena or situations captured in the media we have collected are either desirable or undesirable in the workplace. This helped us identify the underlying principles and consequences that would help drive mastery. These cause-and-effect relationships would later form the basis for creating the rule codes that will ultimately guide the design and development of the board games used in the GBT program.

7.4.3 Framework for Work-Related Noncognitive Abilities

Thematic analysis of the observed behaviors and their respective explanation allowed our team to construct a framework for work-related noncognitive abilities. After careful deliberation among members, we identified a group of five core, measurable, work-related noncognitive ability domains, each comprising approximately six to seven subskills of behaviors. Both positive and negative models of behavior are included in our noncognitive abilities framework. In a meta-analytic review by Taylor et al. (2005), they compared the effects of BMT using positive-only models against mixed (positive and negative) models on changes in job behavior. They found that changes in job behavior are most significant when using mixed models.

The identified measurable domains of work-related noncognitive abilities are as follows: (1) occupational health and safety (OHS), (2) tidiness and cleanliness, (3) efficiency, (4) quality control, and (5) teamwork. We determined that teamwork, as an ability, cross-cuts the other four noncognitive abilities, as depicted in Fig. 7.3.

Occupational Health and Safety (OHS) was based on our team's observations of unsafe practices in the actual workplace, as well as expert explanations on the importance of preventing or minimizing injury and downtime. Behaviors that constitute OHS include reporting safety hazards and equipment malfunctions, using protective equipment, wearing proper attire, providing first aid, and taking regular breaks.

Tidiness and Cleanliness were primarily based on the visual lack of organization observed in the workplaces by our team. Employers and managers have emphasized the importance of keeping a clean and organized workstation. We define tidiness and cleanliness as the ability to minimize waste, clean up after a task, properly return, place, and organize tools and equipment, and clear the walkway.

Efficiency was identified when comparing workflows in the production lines. Efficiency highlights the ability of workers to meet production targets. Skills under efficiency include time

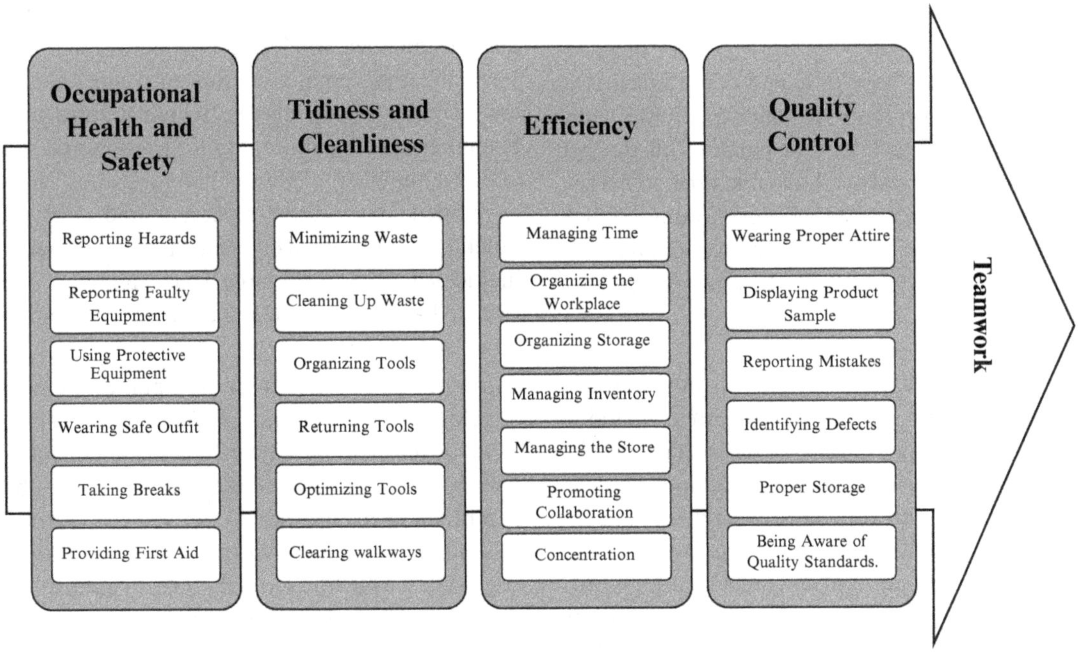

Fig. 7.3 Conceptual framework of the noncognitive abilities targeted by the developed game-based training program. (Reproduced from Estrellado et al., 2023)

management, workplace and storage organization, inventory management, warehouse management, the ability to promote collaboration, and the capacity for concentration.

Quality Control was born out of the need to prevent or minimize errors during production, thereby avoiding the high costs associated with rework or returned products that fail to meet quality standards. Identified subskills that exhibit quality control include wearing a proper outfit, understanding the value of having a reference model of the final product, identifying and reporting defects, proper inventory storage, and awareness of quality standards.

The last core ability, *Teamwork and Collaboration*, is observed in situations that require coordination among several workers and is an essential ability to complement the other four workplace-related noncognitive abilities, ensuring the smooth flow of the entire production line.

It can be noted that instead of confining each skill to a fixed definition, we describe or present them in the form of subskills or behaviors that are contextually familiar to workers in Ethiopia's garment industry. By doing so, we enable participants to observe these noncognitive abilities and construct their own definitions based on their specific realities.

To summarize this section, by applying ethnographic methods to understand the workplace within the context of Ethiopia's garment industry, our team identified the "skills gaps" that would comprise the target models for our GBT program. Through the methods we employed, we can ensure that the developed board games will address the real-world gap between actual and desired performance by understanding the current knowledge and skills of the workforce, while also considering industry- and locality-specific circumstances.

7.5 Game Design

We can now start developing our own GBT program after identifying the target skills to train or teach the participants. We begin by selecting the modality through which the training will be delivered. GBT can be either digital or physical. Both modalities have pros and cons, and it is up to the trainer or game designer to decide which modality will work best, depending on the purpose, audience, and available resources. This section will provide a brief description of both training modalities, with a greater emphasis on physical games (e.g., board games or tabletop games).

Digital Games Digital games are software designed to run on digital platforms, including computers, smartphones, tablets, and gaming consoles. Depending on the training's purpose, digital games can generate realistic settings and can be programmed to simulate real-world experiences in a virtual environment. Modeling is provided by digital avatars that can react to the participant's inputs and interact with a digitally recreated environment. Several studies have demonstrated that players experience a high sense of immersion and engagement while playing digital games (Cujzek & Vranic, 2017; Israel et al., 2016; Ryan et al., 2006; Yee & Sng, 2022). Though learning immersion and engagement are high on digital games, they also have their fair share of drawbacks. One such drawback is the high cost of development and implementation. Developing digital games for training requires specialized knowledge in various programming languages. Depending on the size, scope, and complexity of the game, development can become expensive and may take several months. Digital games also need to be constantly updated to ensure that they work with each hardware and firmware update. Another limitation of digital games is accessibility. Digital games require access to specialized hardware, including computers, smartphones, and game consoles, which may be difficult to come across in economies like Ethiopia.

Physical Games Physical games, like board games, can also be designed to simulate real-world experiences and settings through abstract and symbolic representations. Just like in digital games, physical games can be designed to reflect realistic settings, albeit in a more simplified or abstract manner. Modeling is done through both symbolic and verbal modeling of desired behaviors. Unlike digital games, which require huge resources (time and money) to develop and specialized knowledge, physical board games can be developed using fewer resources and deployed quickly. The downside of physical games includes finding a suitable space and the time required to set up and teach the game, depending on its complexity.

A helpful example is the board games we have developed for Ethiopian garment workers. We have developed two board games—*Garment-Go-Round* and *Garment Factory Fun*—that complement each other to deliver GBT that is grounded in the behavioral modeling training approach. The developed board games are shown in Fig. 7.4. *Garment-Go-Round* uses illustrated cards to model noncognitive abilities, boosting retention. *Garment Factory Fun* replicates factory challenges, enabling behavior rehearsal and skills transfer. We designed the game to symbolically represent different departments within the production process. Each player is given a department name with a specific function. The game elements, including the box and its internal components, were designed to resemble a factory's production floor.

After deciding on the training modality, several external factors must still be considered to ensure the delivery of an effective and engaging GBT experience to participants. These external factors are summarized in the following section.

7.5.1 External Factors to Consider

When designing a GBT program, external factors must be considered, as they can significantly influence the program's effectiveness. Many of these factors are usually beyond the control of game designers and must be taken into consideration when designing the training program. The following are some of the external factors we have identified as part of the training design process:

Fig. 7.4 The physical board games developed by SKY Project are grounded in behavioral modeling training

Training Population Before starting with the development of your training program, it is imperative to be familiar with the target demographic and their cultural background. Demographic factors that can affect the design of the GBT include the participants' age, education level, and digital literacy. Younger participants may be more open to games, while older participants may be more reluctant to try games for training. The game's theme can also be adjusted based on the target audience's age. Mature participants may opt for more grounded and serious themes, while younger participants might be more engaged with fantastical and creative themes. The participants' level of education is another important factor that must be considered while designing the game. For example, depending on their level of education, some participants may find it challenging to engage in games that require extensive reading and text comprehension. Including complex cognitive tasks, such as mathematical operations, may unnecessarily burden the participants, impeding their ability to truly enjoy the game. Lastly, GBT designers must also consider the training population's level of digital literacy, particularly in the use of devices such as computers, tablets, and smartphones. A digital GBT program could potentially perform poorly when used in a population that is not proficient in using and navigating electronic devices and software. In such cases, it might be more convenient to conduct the GBT using physical media such as board games.

The primary cultural factor that can affect your game design process is the language used by the target participants. Because of this, translating text-dependent elements is necessary to ensure that players will better understand the game. The translation of the text can be minimized or avoided entirely if symbols are used to convey commands, instructions, or effects in a game. For example, instead of writing the text "roll the dice" on a card, the game designer can simply opt to replace the text with an image or icon of a dice. For this reason, the games that we developed for Ethiopian garment workers were translated into the local Amharic language.

In the case of our GBT, the participants comprise both young and old garment factory workers in Ethiopia. To appeal to various age groups, we decided to use a more grounded theme while using cartoon visuals. The theme for the GBT is contextualized to the participants' working environment—a garment factory.

Ethiopia also has low basic literacy and numeracy levels, which raises concerns that many participants might have difficulty reading text-based materials. To curb this problem, the games are designed to be less text-dependent. Text-based elements, such as cards, also include matching illustrations that integrate well with the text. The illustrations also enhanced the textual content through the symbolic representation of abstract concepts, which can stimulate learners' higher-order thinking skills.

Another characteristic of the Ethiopian training population is the low access to digital devices. Digital penetration remains low in the country, particularly in rural areas, having only 4% access (Federal Democratic Republic of Ethiopia, 2018). Conducting training using digital games may prove challenging for participants who have little to no experience with digital devices, particularly when it comes to navigating and playing training software.

Lastly, the games that we developed for Ethiopian garment workers were translated into the local Amharic language. Although we aimed to reduce text dependence in the game elements, translating them into a language that is familiar and easy to understand for the participants ensures engagement and ease of interaction with the game itself.

Infrastructure The available infrastructure should also be considered when designing a GBT program. This would be particularly true when developing digital games that are highly dependent on the type of infrastructure available. For example, digital games may require a minimum hardware specification to run the software or program. As such, the availability of such hardware that meets the minimum requirements to run the game must be taken into account. Each participant may be required to have their own mobile device and internet connectivity if the GBT involves smartphones and is conducted online. Infrastructure considerations for GBT using board games include the availability of large playing tables that can accommodate the game elements and the number of players for each board game.

In Ethiopia, where there is a lack of infrastructure to support digital-based games, we made the conscious decision to use physical board games to deliver the training program. Doing so allows us to easily deploy the training in a variety of settings without depending on the availability of digital devices or internet access. This makes the training program more accessible than digital training programs by reducing overhead costs and infrastructure requirements.

Finally, in considering the characteristics of the training population and the available infrastructure, we can start designing a GBT program that is inclusive, accessible, and tailored to the specific needs and realities of our target training population. By following the guidelines we have outlined above, we ensure that we can provide an effective and powerful GBT program.

7.5.2 Game Mechanics for Effective Game-Based Training

The heart of any good game lies in the game mechanics that are utilized. For both physical and digital games, game mechanics refer to the rules that govern the actions players can perform during a game and how the game responds to those actions. Many games employ several mechanics that dictate the complexity of gameplay. The more mechanics your games have, the more difficult it is to teach the participants. Having too many mechanics could also cause frustration and confusion among the participants; whereas very simple games with only a few mechanics might be deemed too easy by participants, who would likely lose interest quickly, as they do not pose any significant challenge. Therefore, to craft a good game suited for training that is both immersive and memorable, game designers must strike a balance between complexity and ease of learning the game.

This section will present some of the broader game mechanics commonly used and how they may contribute to effective noncognitive abilities training.

7.5.2.1 Movement and Exploration

Many games involve the players taking control of characters or tokens that serve as symbolic representations of themselves. The implementation of movement depends on the game's format. For digital or video games, movement is commonly implemented by controlling the direction of your digital avatar in a two-dimensional or 3D space using a controller mechanism (keyboard and mouse, control pad, or touch gestures in the case of smartphones and tablets). Movement in these games involves actions such as running, jumping, climbing, and crawling to interact with and explore the world. Tabletop or physical games implement movement in other ways, which most often involve the physical manipulation of a token. One common movement mechanic is the *roll and move* that uses a die to determine the number of spaces a token can move across the board. Other movement mechanics in board games involve specific rules for each token, such as in chess, where each piece has a distinct set of rules governing its movement across the board.

Movement is important in board games as it gives players a sense of presence in the abstracted space that the game creates, which adds to the level of engagement in the game. Movement also allows the players to plan ahead. Seeing the path before them and the choices available, such as objectives, obstacles, and threats, players must be able to strategically think ahead and plan their next possible actions. This is best exemplified in games like chess. When movement is tied to a resource like stamina or points, players also need to consider how to spend those points in order to reach their desired goal or reward.

7.5.2.2 Physics and Interaction with the Environment

Many games utilize the environment and physical laws as game mechanics to solve problems, complete tasks, or improve a process. For example, digital games utilize physics concepts to simulate how objects in the world interact with the player's character. For example, the realistic simulation of physical laws on how objects interact is a core mechanic in racing games and shooters. There is also a proliferation of physics-based digital games, such as *Angry Birds*, *Cut the Rope*, *Bridge Constructor*, and *Kerbal Space Program*, among many others. There are also examples of tabletop games that utilize the physics and manipulation of the environment or space to solve puzzles and win, such as Jenga, Carrom, *Mouse Trap*, and *Twister*, to name a few. These games, especially the tabletop ones, employ an active learning approach that engages participants both physically and mentally, while simultaneously deepening their understanding.

7.5.2.3 Resource Management

Another broad category of mechanics that is common to many games is resource management. In resource management, players take control of resources that may be finite or earned. These resources are either collected, allocated, or used to meet objectives or gain advantages. Games that involve resource management can teach participants strategic planning, decision-making, and sometimes negotiation skills. The popular resource management game of *Settlers of Catan,* or simply *Catan*, pits players against each other to collect, use, or trade resources in a race to build settlements, cities, and roads. Other notable examples of resource management board games include *Everdell*, *Terraforming Mars*, and *Agricola*.

Another derivative of *resource management* is the *worker placement* mechanic. As the name suggests, you take control of a finite number of workers that would earn resources for you on limited slots on the board. Worker placement games often require players to plan ahead, make informed choices, and prioritize actions based on the game's needs and situation. Popular worker placement games include *Viticulture* and *Lords of Waterdeep*.

After selecting the appropriate mechanics and developing the game for training purposes, it is now crucial to ensure that the transfer of training occurs. In the next section, we will share our unique experience in developing our game-based training program to help provide game designers, researchers, and anyone interested with a framework to ensure the effective transfer of training by successfully linking the learned noncognitive abilities to the participants' work.

7.5.3 Transfer of Training: Linking Noncognitive Abilities and Work in Ethiopia's Garment Sector

To train garment workers in various domains of work-related noncognitive abilities, our team has developed a set of games based on the principles of BMT as our primary pedagogical tool. However, tools can only do so much—their effectiveness largely depends on how they are used, the user, and the context in which they are used. To ensure standardized and consistent results when using our developed games, our team has also developed a one-day training program, consistent with the principles of BMT, that complements the games—*Garment-Go-Round* and *Garment Factory Fun*. In doing so, our games are not stand-alone tools but are part of a broader pedagogical ecosystem aimed at developing workers' noncognitive abilities.

The training aims to enable participants to conceptualize noncognitive abilities and apply them to real-life workplace situations while enjoying the games we have developed in collaboration with colleagues.

The training comprises two main sessions, each focusing on one of the two developed board games. The sessions were designed following BMT principles, and the training program delivers the following activities: 1) Introduction session; 2) First game: *Garment-Go-Round*; 3) First game's reflection session; 4) Second game: *Garment Factory Fun*; 5) Second game's reflection session; 6) Wrap-up session.

The training day starts with an introduction session, during which the training's objectives and key learning points are explained to the participants. In one room, we can accommodate 25 ~ 30 participants who will be divided into groups of 4–5 people who play the same board game. Then, according to the BMT step of "attention" and "retention," the first game (*Garment-Go-Round*) is conducted. *Garment-Go-Round* is a roll-and-move game in which players assume the role of garment workers managing their inventory. Players move their game pieces forward depending on the outcome of their dice throw, which symbolizes their productivity at work. In this session, the game will present visual and verbal models of the five targeted domains of noncognitive abilities through illustrated playing cards. Although symbolic rehearsal involves short-term memory, it influences how much knowledge in the declarative form will be transformed into job behavior or procedural skills later (Driskell et al., 1994; Taylor et al., 2005).

Throughout the course of each game, players are constantly exposed to different rule codes on both positive and negative models. In the meta-analytic review by Taylor et al. (2005), the authors reported that exposure to both positive and negative models results in better transfer of training, with higher training effects. At this stage, the game is designed to enhance participants' mental practice through quizzes and open-ended questions.

Let's have an actual example of rule codes taken from the first game. The rule code presented is "practicing OHS helps improve productivity." Subskills under this OHS also have rule codes that support the noncognitive ability of OHS. One such rule code is "To wear protective equipment while operating machines to prevent serious injuries." This is represented through both visual and verbal codes. To further retention, learners are provided opportunities for mental rehearsal using simple memory recall and a quiz.

After the first game, the program enters a period of reflection. Participants are invited to consider the meanings of the different colors used for the cards, as the five colors correspond to the types of noncognitive abilities. This discussion aims to let participants recall work-related noncognitive abilities presented during the game and make sense of each skill category in their own way. The winner of each group receives a reward as an extrinsic reinforcement.

In the afternoon, the training continues with the second game—*Garment Factory Fun*. *Garment Factory Fun* is a cooperative role-playing board game where participants take on the roles of garment workers at different stages of the production line. Participants need to recall and reproduce the work-related noncognitive abilities learned in the morning session to overcome the challenges and achieve the team's objective for this game. The second game simulates actual work situations in a garment factory. Its design, rules, and setting enable participants to experience the problems they may encounter in real-world work, collaboration with colleagues, and decision-making as individuals and as a team.

The first game facilitated the mental rehearsal of the target model of noncognitive abilities, while the motor rehearsal or reproduction of the target skills is embedded in the second game, *Garment Factory Fun*. Several studies have shown that participants' skill reproduction is enhanced when behavioral rehearsal opportunities in work-related scenarios are given (Law et al., 2018; Taylor et al., 2005). In this game, participants must explore the possible outcomes resulting from their chosen behaviors, which impact the team's overall productivity. At the same time, this game requires participants to communicate constantly within the team to make shared decisions. Various game mechanics were used to help players practice and internalize the target skills. One such mechanic is the investment-and-event card mechanic, where players draw event cards, known as "hazard cards," in the game, which introduce random events that alter the game's state and may require immediate action. Depending on what the players have invested (or not), they will receive positive or negative feedback based on their choices.

From our earlier example, we are teaching the skill or behavior to "practice occupational health and safety." In reality, participants are not presented with real-life opportunities to practice this skill, for example, when someone gets in an accident, what should be done? We don't actually wait for someone to get hurt just so the learners can practice the target skill. However, using board games can present these scenarios in a simulated manner, giving the learners an opportunity to address them. For example, they can address this event by using a first aid kit or prevent it from happening in the first place by investing in protective equipment. In our game, we present the rewards and consequences of each choice to participants and let them internalize, on their own, what the best course of action is based on their own context.

In the reflection session after the game, participants are guided to reflect on their experience and discuss the individual and collective choices they made while playing. The reflection aims to have each participant scaffold how the skills observed in the first game are used in the simulated game and how these can be transferred to their real-world context. Finally, the facilitator will supervise participants to consider the abilities that would improve productivity.

During the implementation of our training program, we came to realize the value of reflection and wrap-up sessions in facilitating the effective transfer of training. The facilitators themselves are equally important as the games developed. Without proper guidance and supervision provided by well-trained facilitators, the quality of the GBT program will vary widely despite having carefully designed training materials and a facilitation program. Even the best training tools risk being underutilized in the hands of a novice facilitator. This is why our team has placed equal emphasis on training the facilitators who will deliver the GBT program. The facilitators are trained not only on how to play the game but also on techniques for handling GBT sessions to ensure the transfer of training occurs.

7.6 Pilot Study: GBT on Japanese TVET Students

Now that we have finished the development of the games and training program, it is time to determine the feasibility of the GBT intervention. Before fully operationalizing the developed board games for noncognitive abilities training in Ethiopia, the SKY Project team conducted a pilot study in Japan. A total of 37 second-year and third-year technical and vocational education and training (TVET) students enrolled in a vocational college specializing in fashion in central Japan participated in the pilot study. Most of the participants are aged between 19 to 21 years old. For this pilot study, data were collected from the questionnaire developed by the SKY Project team. The project-developed *Skills Development Survey Questionnaire for Participants* focuses on two sets of noncognitive abilities targeted in this study—workplace-related noncognitive abilities and personality traits. The first set of 15 questions targets workplace-related noncognitive abilities identified based on input from Ethiopian stakeholders: occupational health and safety, tidiness and cleanliness, workplace efficiency, ensuring product quality, and teamwork. The second set of 26 questions targets noncognitive abilities based on personality traits: extraversion, conscientiousness, openness, emotional stability, agreeableness, grit, decisiveness, and hostile bias. More information regarding the survey instruments can be found in Chap. 2. The characteristics of the participants prior to the intervention are summarized in Table 7.1. Dependent variables in the analysis were all linearly transformed into percentage of maximum possible (POMP) scores to easily facilitate the communication of findings from behavioral studies such as the one being conducted (Cohen et al., 1999).

Table 7.1 Information of pilot study participants in Japan before the intervention

	Total N = 37
Demographic characteristic	
Education level	
Second	17 (46%)
Third	20 (54%)
Female	33 (89%)
Age	19.62 (.64)
Work-related noncognitive abilities	
OHS	80.42 (12.02)
Tidiness	85.00 (12.69)
Efficiency	79.17 (12.23)
Quality control	87.29 (10.16)
Teamwork	87.50 (11.32)
Personality traits	
Extraversion	46.67 (20.22)
Conscientiousness	53.33 (19.23)
Openness	67.08 (19.97)
Emotional stability	47.29 (24.27)
Agreeableness	59.38 (17.42)
Grit	60.42 (24.07)
Decision making	67.81 (17.08)
Hostile bias	38.44 (21.26)

Note: Data are presented as mean (standard deviation) for continuous measures, and observations (%) for categorical measures. Work-related noncognitive abilities (OHS, Tidiness, Efficiency, Quality Control, Teamwork) and Personality traits (Extraversion, Conscientiousness, Openness, Emotional Stability, Agreeableness, Grit, Decision making, Hostile bias) are linearly transformed to POMP scores

The pilot study made use of a one-group pretest-posttest design with the principal unit of analysis being participant average scores for each noncognitive ability before and after the intervention. For the analysis, we estimated the following equation:

$$y_{it} = \beta_1 (GBT)_{it} + \ldots + \beta_n (\boldsymbol{X_n})_{it} + \alpha_i + u_{it} \#(1)$$

The primary covariate *GBT* is a dummy variable before (0) and after (1) receiving the intervention (game-based training). y_{it} is the outcome variable for student i at occasion t, where occasion $t = 0$ before, and $t = 1$ after the intervention. The model consists of the intercept α_i. The β are slope coefficients for the vector of covariates ($\boldsymbol{X_n}$) used in the model. The error term is denoted as u_{it}.

Despite the absence of a control group in the pilot study, at this stage, we aim to determine if the GBT intervention would cause a meaningful shift in the targeted work-related noncognitive abilities of a different population within the same industry. By analyzing shifts in their self-reported noncognitive abilities, behavior, and feedback, our team aims to establish an initial understanding of the effectiveness of a GBT approach. The subsequent implementation in Ethiopia's garment industry will address this limitation by incorporating a pretest-posttest non-equivalent group design to obtain a counterfactual, thereby determining the actual effects of the GBT intervention.

7.6.1 Results of the Pilot Study

7.6.1.1 On Personality-Related Noncognitive Abilities

The effects of the GBT on noncognitive abilities of personality traits are shown in Table 7.2. The results of the regression show a significant gain in the participants' degree of openness, emotional stability, and grit after participating in the

GBT. On average, participants' degree of *openness* is 6.08% points (p = 0.041) higher after the training program. There is also a significant change in participants' *emotional stability*, with an average increase of 10.81% points (p = 0.017). The *grit* or perseverance of participants also significantly rose by an average of 7.43% points (p = 0.004) after participating in the training program.

The largest shift was observed in the domain of *emotional stability* (10.81/45.50 = 23.76% change). This is followed by grit (7.43/60.36 = 12.31% change) and openness (6.08/66.44 = 9.15% change).

On the other hand, there are no significant changes in participants' traits of *conscientiousness, extraversion, agreeableness, decision making*, and *hostile bias*. The results align with the findings of Roberts et al. (2005) that investments in roles that align with the participants' future career can affect the shifting of personality traits. By creating an abstracted environment where the participants can simulate workplace situations that thematically match their prospective careers, the GBT helped the participants slide into roles in which they were able to invest on a personal level.

In order to compare the effects of the training with other BMT studies, we computed the effect size following the method used by Taylor et al. (2005). The computed effect sizes for openness, emotional stability, and grit are 0.53, 0.42, and 0.51, respectively. This is larger than the average reported effect size of 0.30 reported by Taylor et al. (2005) for BMT studies without control groups that target attitudes. The results tell us that not only was GBT grounded in BMT effective in improving the attitudes, but it also appears to be more effective than regular BMT training reported in previous studies.

7.6.1.2 On Workplace-Related Noncognitive Abilities

Table 7.3 shows a significant increase across all the participants' perceived importance of workplace-related noncognitive abilities. Participants perceived the importance of *occupational health and safety* significantly higher at an average of

Table 7.2 Game-based Training Effects on Noncognitive Abilities

	(1) Conscientiousness	(2) Extraversion	(3) Openness	(4) Emotional Stability	(5) Agreeableness	(6) Grit	(7) Decision making	(8) Hostile bias
GBT	1.126	.676	6.081*	10.811*	3.829	7.432**	1.52	5.068
	(2.584)	(2.353)	(2.865)	(4.324)	(2.072)	(2.407)	(2.817)	(3.324)
Constant	54.505***	45.495***	66.441***	45.495***	59.91***	60.36***	67.399***	38.851***
	(1.292)	(1.177)	(1.433)	(2.162)	(1.036)	(1.203)	(1.408)	(1.662)
N	74	74	74	74	74	74	74	74

Notes: Robust standard errors are in parentheses
GBT game-based training intervention,
* $p < .05$
** $p < .01$
*** $p < .001$

Table 7.3 Game-based Training Effects on Workplace-related Noncognitive abilities After Controlling for Noncognitive abilities

	(1) OHS	(2) Tidiness	(3) Efficiency	(4) Quality	(5) Teamwork
GBT	10.586*** (1.829)	9.685*** (2.044)	10.135*** (1.927)	7.207*** (1.46)	7.658*** (1.988)
Constant	80.18*** (.915)	84.91*** (1.022)	79.054*** (.964)	86.712*** (.73)	86.937*** (.994)
N	74	74	74	74	74

*** $p < .001$

10.59% points ($p = 0.00$) after the GBT approach. Perceived *tidiness* also considerably increased by 9.69% points ($p = 0.00$). Workplace noncognitive abilities in *efficiency, quality control management,* and *teamwork* significantly increased by 10.14 ($p = 0.00$), 7.21 ($p = 0.00$), and 7.66 ($p = 0.000$) percentage points consecutively. The results show that the participants could use the developed board games as a platform to model all the targeted workplace-related noncognitive abilities.

The largest gain was in the domain of occupational health and safety (OHS) at 13.20% (10.59/80.18) closely followed by efficiency at 12.82% (10.14/79.05) and tidiness at 11.41% (9.69/84.91). Effect sizes were also computed while removing the bias caused by the absence of a control group. In a paper by Carlson and Schmidt (1999), they suggested subtracting a control effects value of 0.154 from the effect size of behavioral measures in one-group pretest-posttest design studies.[2] The corrected effect sizes after correcting for the control effects are all above 0.50 ($d_{OHS} = 0.517; d_{Tidiness} = 0.524; d_{Efficiency} = 0.506; d_{Qlty\ Control} = 0.502;$ and $d_{Teamwork} = 0.508$) which are all way above the 0.27 average effect size for GBT targeting workplace-related noncognitive abilities in similar studies that didn't have a control group (Taylor et al., 2005).

The pilot study investigates the effectiveness of using a GBT approach in the soft-skills development of Japanese students in TVET schools. The GBT provided by the SKY Project team, grounded on Bandura's behavior-modeling theory, was the intervention used in the study. The initial findings from the pilot study reveal that GBT grounded in behavior-modeling theory effectively develops participants' noncognitive traits like openness, emotional stability, and grit. The results also showed a significant increase in participants' perceived importance of all the workplace-related noncognitive abilities targeted by the GBT. This provides us with a glimpse of the potential of the GBT approach using board games in fostering the noncognitive abilities (personality traits and workplace behavior) of participants.

7.7 Actual Implementation: GBT in Ethiopia's Garment Sector

This section will discuss the effects of the GBT program using board games on Ethiopia's garment workers. Detailed information about the participants, dataset, and survey instruments can be found in Chap. 2. Table 7.4 summarizes the baseline work-related noncognitive abilities, personality traits, and cognitive skills of the participants involved in the study.

In contrast to the one-group design implemented during the pilot study, the actual implementation of the GBT in Ethiopia will involve a quasi-experimental pretest-posttest design. Specifically, we will be employing difference-in-differences (DID) analysis to identify the causal effect of the GBT intervention on the noncognitive abilities of Ethiopian garment workers. DID as an analytical method is popularly used to examine the effect of enacted laws,

[2] Correcting for control effects for personality traits were not performed in the earlier section as Carlson and Schmidt (1999) found a near zero control group effect on attitudes.

Table 7.4 Baseline characteristics of intervention (GBT) and comparison groups

	Total	Comparison	GBT	p-value
	N = 504	N = 258	N = 246	
Demographic				
Female	82%	86%	78%	0.014
Age	26 (6)	25 (6)	26 (6)	0.029
Education	34.0%	29.2%	39.0%	0.020
Manager	10.3%	7.0%	13.8%	0.012
Factory size				0.017
Small	28.2%	22.9%	33.7%	
Medium	47.6%	49.6%	45.5%	
Large	24.2%	27.5%	20.7%	
Factory training	44.3%	47.7%	40.8%	0.12
Work-related noncognitive abilities				
OHS	72 (24)	73 (24)	72 (25)	0.94
Tidiness	80 (21)	79 (22)	81 (21)	0.28
Efficiency	63 (22)	62 (24)	65 (21)	0.077
Quality control	80 (20)	78 (22)	81 (18)	0.087
Teamwork	75 (22)	75 (23)	75 (21)	0.77
Personality traits				
Extraversion	49 (18)	48 (19)	50 (18)	0.38
Conscientiousness	76 (19)	75 (19)	77 (18)	0.19
Openness	71 (21)	69 (23)	72 (19)	0.13
Stability	45 (22)	46 (23)	44 (21)	0.30
Agreeableness	73 (21)	72 (23)	74 (19)	0.37
Grit	66 (24)	66 (25)	66 (23)	0.89
Decision	63 (21)	62 (23)	63 (20)	0.56
Hostile	38 (28)	40 (29)	36 (27)	0.080
Cognitive skills				
Reading	11 (3)	11 (3)	12 (3)	0.007
Math	12 (3)	12 (3)	12 (3)	<0.001
Integrated skills	7 (3)	7 (3)	8 (3)	0.043
Vocational skills	11 (4)	10 (4)	11 (4)	0.076

Note: Data are presented as mean (SD) for continuous measures, and % for categorical measures

policies, medical treatments, and educational interventions. The DID equation model, shown in Eq. (2), was used to estimate the effects of the intervention on garment workers' noncognitive abilities:

$$WRNA_{it} = \beta_0 + \beta_1 GBT_i + \beta_2 Post_t + \beta_3 \left(GBT \times Post\right)_{it} + \gamma \boldsymbol{Control}_{it} + \delta \boldsymbol{WRNA}_{i0} + \varepsilon \,\#(2)$$

WRNA is the outcome of interest, which refers to the various work-related noncognitive abilities explored in this study. *GBT* and *Post* are dummy variables that indicate the GBT and post-assessment status of the participants. The β_1 coefficient measures the baseline differences between the comparison and intervention groups. On the other hand, the β_2 coefficient captures the counterfactual, that is the impact of external factors outside the GBT program.

In DID regressions, the primary variable of interest is the interaction between the *GBT* status and *Post*. The coefficient β_3 measures the impact of the implemented GBT program using board games to Ethiopian garment workers by comparing the growth difference between the comparison and intervention groups.

Control is a vector of demographic variables incorporated in the model, such as age, gender, and education, among others. $WRNA_{i0}$ is a vector of the various baseline work-related noncognitive abilities targeted by the GBT program.

7.7.1 Game-Based Training Results

The following section presents our findings on the five domains of work-related noncognitive abilities between the intervention and comparison groups before and after the GBT. We find that the GBT significantly impacts the participants' noncognitive abilities development. This section will also discuss the factors that influence noncognitive ability development in Ethiopia's garment sector workers.

Fig. 7.5 shows the changes in each work-related noncognitive ability before and after the implementation of GBT for both trained and untrained workers. Before the training, the values of the various work-related noncognitive abilities and their average were comparable between the two groups. We can see that work-related noncognitive abilities for the trained group increased significantly after the training. In contrast, the work-related noncognitive abilities of the comparison group remained relatively the same. The results suggest that the GBT intervention had a positive impact on all five domains of work-related noncognitive abilities. The participants in the GBT intervention group demonstrated percentage point gains ranging from 6.43% to 11.9% compared to the untrained group.

Table 7.5 presents our findings on the impact of GBT on participants' work-related noncognitive abilities after controlling for other factors such as age, gender, education, wage, position, factory size, and on-the-job training (OJT). In all five domains of work-related noncognitive abili-

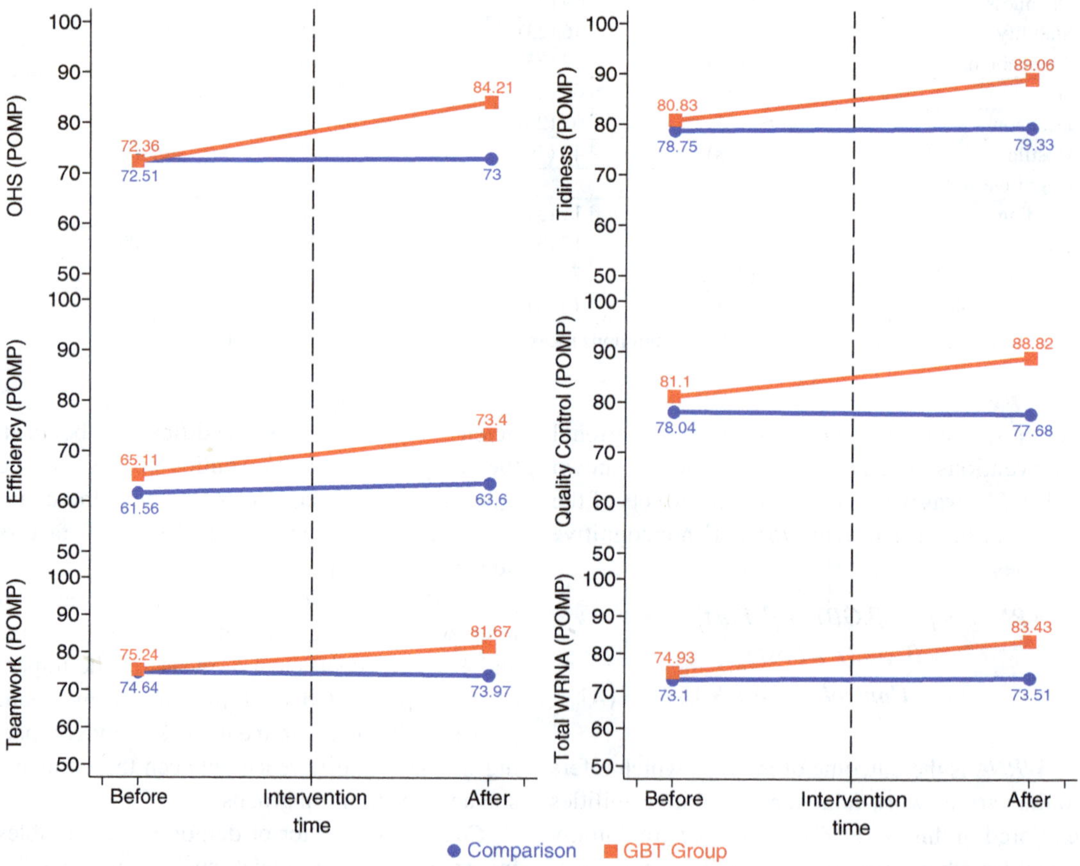

Fig. 7.5 Changes in the various work-related noncognitive abilities between the GBT group and the comparison group

Table 7.5 Effect of game-based BMT on work-related noncognitive abilities (Reproduced using data from Estrellado et al., 2023)

	(1) OHS	(2) Tidiness	(3) Efficiency	(4) Quality Control	(5) Teamwork	(6) Total WRNA
GBT	−.436 (.804)	.548 (.693)	1.297 (.842)	1.24 (.727)	.363 (.84)	.602 (.533)
Post	.357 (1.658)	.357 (1.455)	1.783 (1.744)	−.681 (1.552)	−.908 (1.786)	.182 (1.21)
GBT impact	11.548*** (2.359)	7.943*** (2.047)	6.637** (2.414)	8.266*** (1.999)	7.473** (2.352)	8.369*** (1.63)
Female	−.932 (1.125)	−.231 (1.089)	2.218 (1.341)	.372 (.854)	.645 (1.199)	.413 (.855)
Age	−.051 (.083)	−.035 (.06)	.059 (.078)	.022 (.059)	−.005 (.066)	−.002 (.051)
Education level	.013 (.903)	−.593 (.841)	.167 (.925)	.234 (.761)	−.469 (.929)	−.129 (.68)
Wage	−1.13 (1.11)	.004 (1.301)	−.006 (1.213)	−.173 (.887)	−1.216 (.862)	−.506 (.943)
Supervisor	1.446 (1.091)	.974 (.974)	3.249* (1.482)	.899 (1.04)	2.273* (.998)	1.77* (.818)
Firm size	−.236 (.652)	−.254 (.579)	−.372 (.619)	.234 (.544)	1.679** (.59)	.21 (.468)
OJT	1.099 (.907)	.028 (.776)	1.894* (.892)	.52 (.751)	−.576 (.871)	.595 (.644)
OHS Pre	.577*** (.029)	.019 (.024)	−.008 (.027)	.028 (.021)	.033 (.027)	.13*** (.02)
Tidiness Pre	.066* (.031)	.608*** (.026)	.028 (.031)	.03 (.024)	.077* (.031)	.162*** (.022)
Efficiency Pre	.012 (.025)	.005 (.023)	.558*** (.026)	−.007 (.021)	.016 (.024)	.117*** (.018)
Quality control Pre	.036 (.031)	.032 (.027)	.01 (.036)	.567*** (.028)	.006 (.03)	.13*** (.022)
Teamwork Pre	.029 (.026)	.003 (.022)	.046 (.028)	.029 (.021)	.538*** (.028)	.129*** (.018)
Constant	30.643** (9.56)	28.193* (10.976)	17.729 (10.472)	27.439*** (7.544)	30.497*** (7.357)	26.902*** (8.052)
N	1004	1004	1003	1004	1004	1004
R^2	.508	.501	.422	.47	.424	.534

Notes: Robust standard errors are in parentheses
OHS occupational health and safety, *WRNA* work-related noncognitive abilities, *GBT* game-based training intervention, *OJT* on-the-job training
* $p < .05$
** $p < .01$
*** $p < .001$

ties and the overall average, the GBT impact shows that the intervention had a significant effect on participants, with percentage point gains across all self-reported work-related noncognitive abilities scores ranging from 6.64 to 11.6 (Table 7.5, models 1 to 5). The percentage change in work-related noncognitive abilities is shown in Fig. 7.6. On average, the intervention effect is at 8.37% points, which equates to a 31.1% increase (8.37 / 26.9 = 31.1%) in workers' total work-related noncognitive abilities. All *GBT Impact* estimators are positive and statistically significant, at the 1% level or higher. Also, the effect size of our training program was significantly higher than those reported by earlier studies. For comparison, we computed the GBT effect size to be 0.51, whereas past BMT training targeting workplace behavior reported an average effect size of 0.25 (Taylor et al., 2005). A twofold increase!

The percentage increase in each domain of measurable work-related noncognitive abilities targeted in the study range from 24% to 38% as shown in Fig. 7.6. One of the domains of work-related noncognitive abilities for which the GBT had the biggest effects were *OHS* (11.5/30.6 = 37.7% change) and efficiency (6.64/17.3 = 37.4% change). These results indicate that before this training, participants had not been exposed to the concept of taking personal responsibility for their health, workplace safety, and performing assigned tasks efficiently. After participants were provided with behavior models and game-based rehearsal opportunities to consider these workplace issues, they retained their training. The noncognitive abilities of *quality control* (8.27/27.4 = 30.1% change) and *tidiness* (7.94/28.2 = 28.2% change) also benefited significantly from this training. Keeping workstations tidy and clean and ensuring the quality of production are frequently mentioned by employers as fundamental noncognitive abilities for newly employed workers. The study results suggest that organized GBT interventions like ours would enhance the development of these noncognitive abilities among workers. The fact that the variable OJT (1.92, $p = .027$) has a significant effect on the improvement of efficiency skills supports the interpretation that some support already exists within workplaces to improve these noncognitive abilities, albeit insufficiently, and that OJT enhances the efficacy of the provided GBT.

In some domains of noncognitive abilities, being in a managerial position affects the impact of GBT. Regarding *efficiency* and *teamwork*, managers outperformed others (3.26 at $p = .028$ and 2.30 at $p = .022$, respectively). This trend is also found in the overall average score of work-related noncognitive abilities (1.77 at $p = .031$).

7.7.2 Econo-Productive and Socio-Cultural Analysis of Work-Related Noncognitive Ability Gains

In the previous chapter, we explored how skills are developed due to the econo-productive and socio-cultural mechanisms in the garment industry of two countries—Ghana and Pakistan. In this section we will explore how skills are developed and acquired by Ethiopia's garment workers

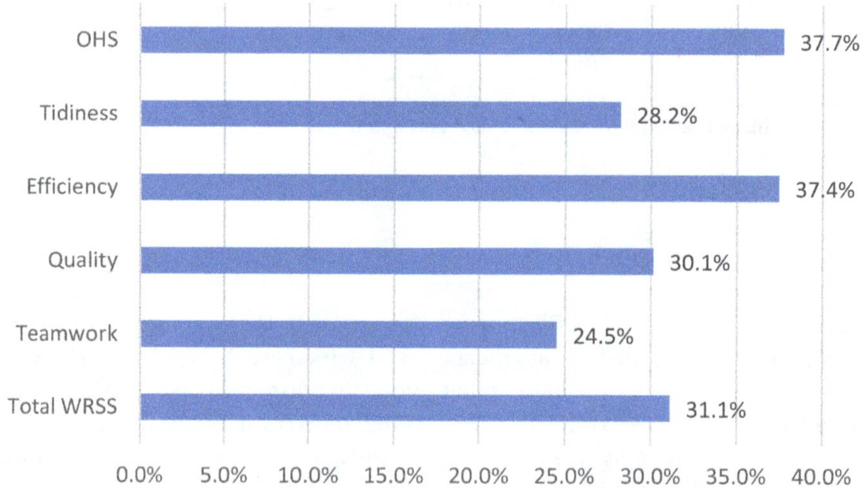

Fig. 7.6 Percentage change in work-related noncognitive abilities among Ethiopia's garment sector workers after receiving game-based behavior modeling training

(who underwent GBT using our developed board games) through the lens of the econo-productive and socio-cultural mechanism. To determine the effect of the GBT intervention, the training population was divided into subgroups based on gender, position, educational attainment, OJT status, and firm size, and then the intervention impact was estimated using Eq. (2).

7.7.2.1 Gender

The heterogeneous effects of GBT between male and female Ethiopian garment workers are summarized in Table 7.6. Results show that females gained the most in terms of appreciation for OHS principles compared to their male counterparts after the GBT. This could be due to the gender-based roles that women occupy in the garment production process. The majority of Ethiopia's garment factory workforce consists of women, who are often assigned to the production line as machine operators, where they are exposed to tasks that involve repetitive motion and poor posture for extended periods. On the other hand, most of the managerial and supervisory positions in the sector are held by men. Because women are more directly exposed to hazards than men, they may be more receptive to training that includes OHS models as they can relate the demonstrated models to the context of their work. Female workers may also see the value-added benefits of OHS not only for themselves at the workplace but also for their families, due to their additional roles as caregivers and homemakers.

Male garment workers, on the other hand, only exhibited shifts in the appreciation of *tidiness* and *quality control* in the workplace. This can be linked to both econo-productive and socio-cultural mechanisms. Both genders exhibited gains in terms of tidiness and quality control in the workplace; however, it is noteworthy that male workers showed a gain of more than 60% in both noncognitive abilities. Tidiness is one of the noncognitive abilities that managers often highlight as important. One possible reason for the huge shift in male participants' self-reported tidiness is the pre-existing societal norms and expectations between genders. Women are often perceived as prioritizing tidiness, again, because of their traditional roles in maintaining domestic cleanliness and order. As a result, the GBT may have had a less significant impact on women than on men, because women may view tidiness and maintaining quality as routine or expected of them. As a result, male workers may have a lower baseline appreciation of tidiness and quality control in the workplace before the training. Male workers are commonly assigned to more technical and quality-focused roles, such as fabric cutting and quality control, where these skills are highly relevant, especially for managers who are predominantly male. We observed that the provided GBT was able to produce a cognitive shift in male workers, enabling them to appreciate the value of tidiness and quality control following the training session.

Female garment workers demonstrated significant growth in their appreciation of efficiency and teamwork in the workplace. Econo-productive reasons include direct relevance to the nature of their job. Female workers are often assigned to line-based work where the effects of efficiency and teamwork can be strongly felt. The results of low efficiency and teamwork can be directly felt in line-based work, with pileups and delays in production. Providing female workers with GBT training that directly relates to their experiences leads to greater appreciation and recognition of the training's core message on these skills.

7.7.2.2 Managerial Position Status

The effect of the status of being in a managerial or supervisory role on the acquisition of work-related noncognitive abilities are summarized in Table 7.7. In summary, only non-managers benefited from the provided GBT. The econo-productive mechanism may explain that workers were able to directly relate the training to the context of their own work. The developed GBT was designed to simulate the worker's actual work setting, particularly that of production line workers. For example the second game, *Garment Factory Fun*, was designed to simulate line production with five departments working together to achieve production goals. The work-related

Table 7.6 Heterogeneous effects of GBT between male and female Ethiopian garment workers

	(1) OHS Male	(2) OHS Female	(3) Tidiness Male	(4) Tidiness Female	(5) Efficiency Male	(6) Efficiency Female	(7) Quality Control Male	(8) Quality Control Female	(9) Teamwork Male	(10) Teamwork Female
Post	3.241 (4.639)	−.113 (1.786)	−.463 (3.426)	.49 (1.606)	−3.009 (4.688)	2.564 (1.888)	−1.62 (2.822)	−.528 (1.751)	−5.556 (5.408)	−.151 (1.893)
GBT	−1.178 (2.248)	−.212 (.91)	−2.176 (2.005)	1.485* (.734)	−2.101 (2.042)	1.609 (.968)	.41 (1.516)	1.506 (.839)	1.233 (2.426)	−.091 (.938)
GBT impact	11.153 (5.893)	11.489*** (2.615)	13.493** (4.955)	6.212** (2.227)	10.585 (5.922)	6.166* (2.68)	9.499* (3.785)	7.935*** (2.287)	11.768 (6.31)	6.632* (2.581)
Constant	22.866 (16.798)	37.894*** (10.007)	21.197 (15.922)	38.736*** (8.706)	9.304 (14.764)	30.731** (10.013)	14.539 (8.699)	39.594*** (8.169)	25.572** (9.62)	44.863*** (8.763)
N	182	820	182	820	182	820	182	820	182	820
R^2	.523	.512	.536	.5	.417	.432	.628	.449	.424	.436

Notes: Robust standard errors are in parentheses

OHS occupational health and safety, *GBT* game-based training intervention

* $p < .05$

** $p < .01$

*** $p < .001$

Table 7.7 Heterogeneous effects of GBT between non-managers and managers in Ethiopia's garment workers

	(1) OHS Non-Manager	(2) OHS Manager	(3) Tidiness Non-Manager	(4) Tidiness Manager	(5) Efficiency Non-Manager	(6) Efficiency Manager	(7) Quality Control Non-Manager	(8) Quality Control Manager	(9) Teamwork Non-Manager	(10) Teamwork Manager
Post	.314 (1.743)	.926 (5.411)	.174 (1.523)	2.778 (5.129)	.453 (1.8)	19.444** (5.993)	−1.116 (1.603)	5.093 (6.485)	−1.046 (1.885)	.926 (5.317)
GBT	−.619 (.877)	1.776 (2.759)	.691 (.743)	1.725 (2.779)	1.059 (.887)	4.081 (3.385)	.527 (.778)	5.699 (3.121)	.345 (.905)	−1.437 (3.212)
GBT impact	12.226*** (2.558)	8.143 (6.488)	7.842*** (2.208)	6.046 (6.03)	8.475*** (2.555)	−13.807 (7.521)	9.727*** (2.14)	−4.357 (6.83)	7.435** (2.541)	5.692 (6.291)
Constant	29.314** (10.853)	43.286** (14.376)	24.883* (12.107)	43.103*** (10.443)	14.966 (11.486)	24.77 (20.611)	24.093** (8.145)	42.332** (15.16)	26.981** (8.2)	45.173*** (9.495)
N	898	104	898	104	898	104	898	104	898	104
R^2	.495	.666	.484	.695	.425	.52	.46	.601	.405	.669

Notes: Robust standard errors are in parentheses

OHS occupational health and safety, *GBT* game-based training intervention

* $p < .05$

** $p < .01$

*** $p < .001$

noncognitive abilities modeled in the first game and rehearsed in the second game are seen by non-managers to be essential to perform their work. Rule codes embedded in the fabric of the games resonated with the line workers, making the training highly effective for them. Managers on the other hand did not see the direct relationship of the simulated line-worker work on their actual tasks.

Another possible reason is that line workers started at a lower baseline level of appreciation of these noncognitive abilities, leaving more room for learning. Managers, on the other hand, may have already been familiar with and appreciative of the training's targeted noncognitive abilities, and may have started with a higher baseline appreciation of these skills compared to non-managers. The results, however, do not mean that managers should not participate in the training of their subordinates. In a meta-analysis by Taylor et al. (2005), they found that noncognitive abilities transfer is more effective when the training is conducted together with the participants' managers. This is because, during the GBT, managers can provide support during the training and discussion on how the modeled noncognitive abilities can be applied in the workplace (Taylor et al., 2005). Due to their managerial or supervisory roles, managers often distance themselves from training specifically designed for their subordinates. Their main goal for joining the training is not to learn but to manage participants who work with them.

The results highlight that training interventions are most effective when contextualized to the participants' experiences in the workplace. It can also be suggested from the findings that there is a need to develop GBT materials targeting managers to improve their work-related noncognitive abilities. Currently, the SKY Project is developing a GBT program tailored specifically for managers. The GBT for managers will utilize a new board game designed and contextualized specifically for managers, which will help them gain a fundamental understanding and appreciation of the noncognitive abilities necessary to enhance their team and business processes.

7.7.2.3 Education Status

Table 7.8 compares the GBT impact between those who received at least senior secondary[3] (grade 11 and above) level against those who did not. The results, at first glance, are almost similar to the heterogeneous effects of the managerial position status. In the previous section, only non-managers benefited from the intervention. Similarly, GBT benefits less educated workers by equipping them with the necessary work-related noncognitive abilities. On the other hand, educated participants (equal to or above senior secondary) showed gains only in the domain of *OHS*. It is reasonable to assume that those whose education is equal to or above senior secondary attended training (TVET) institutions, which provided them with pre-employment training on the necessary work-related noncognitive abilities, which may have attenuated the effect of the GBT intervention on the domains of *tidiness, efficiency, quality control*, and *teamwork*. On the other hand, the significant impact of GBT on educated participants' *OHS* may be interpreted from both an econo-productive and socio-cultural perspective. From the lens of the econo-productive mechanism, those who have higher levels of education tend to be assigned to semi-skilled or technical tasks on the garment production floor. These tasks often highlight the importance of safety during machine operation and adherence to safety protocols, which makes OHS relevant to their work contexts, thereby increasing their receptiveness to the OHS training content in the GBT materials.

7.7.2.4 On-the-Job Training Status

The results from the heterogeneous analysis of OJT status are presented in Table 7.9. The results obtained indicate that the training is more effective for participants who have received training from their current employer. Participants who had experienced OJT received significant gains

[3] In our data, we capped those with a lower education level as having achieved junior secondary education and below. This is because Ethiopia's general secondary TVET education track provides TVET level certificates 1–4 (UNESCO-UNEVOC, 2024).

Table 7.8 Heterogeneous effects of GBT by educational attainment, those who reached grade 11 and above or otherwise

	(1) OHS <Grade11	(2) OHS ≥Grade 11	(3) Tidiness <Grade11	(4) Tidiness ≥Grade 11	(5) Efficiency <Grade11	(6) Efficiency ≥Grade 11	(7) Quality Control <Grade11	(8) Quality Control ≥Grade 11	(9) Teamwork <Grade11	(10) Teamwork ≥Grade 11
Post	.608(2.392)	.069 (2.317)	.73 (2.135)	−.069 (1.983)	1.764 (2.547)	1.806 (2.397)	−2.129 (2.08)	.972 (2.357)	−1.703 (2.581)	0 (2.489)
GBT	−1.594 (1.32)	.235 (1.036)	−.914 (1.165)	1.663* (.825)	.046 (1.339)	2.276* (1.119)	−.197 (1.079)	2.803** (1.012)	−1.106 (1.411)	1.391 (1.049)
GBT impact	14.308*** (3.496)	9.264** (3.204)	10.755*** (3.024)	5.003 (2.755)	8.53* (3.525)	4.928 (3.333)	11.233*** (2.79)	5.028 (2.926)	9.686** (3.534)	4.933 (3.153)
Constant	52.028*** (10.992)	14.65 (11.049)	48.456*** (9.504)	16.32 (14.905)	43.616*** (12.907)	.437 (11.758)	35.13*** (9.762)	24.369* (9.879)	38.683*** (11.556)	29.042** (9.263)
N	512	490	512	490	512	490	512	490	512	490
R^2	.463	.566	.462	.555	.384	.478	.482	.472	.379	.488

Notes: Robust standard errors are in parentheses

OHS occupational health and safety, *GBT* game-based training intervention

* $p < .05$

** $p < .01$

*** $p < .001$

Table 7.9 Heterogeneous effects of GBT by OJT status

	(1) OHS No OJT	(2) OHS OJT	(3) Tidiness No OJT	(4) Tidiness OJT	(5) Efficiency No OJT	(6) Efficiency OJT	(7) Quality Control No OJT	(8) Quality Control OJT	(9) Teamwork No OJT	(10) Teamwork OJT
Post	−.309 (2.254)	1.093 (2.483)	1.049 (1.838)	−.41 (2.324)	1.42 (2.438)	2.186 (2.537)	−.741 (2.187)	−.615 (2.235)	1.296 (2.39)	−3.347 (2.701)
GBT	−1.267 (1.108)	.925 (1.276)	−.068 (.937)	1.738 (1.197)	1.396 (1.194)	1.852 (1.372)	.869 (1.055)	1.278 (1.121)	1.797 (1.196)	−1.921 (1.387)
GBT impact	14.892*** (3.24)	7.324* (3.421)	7.4** (2.713)	8.077** (3.094)	6.161 (3.341)	7.564* (3.523)	8.553** (2.806)	7.698** (2.866)	4.375 (3.169)	10.847** (3.524)
Constant	45.623*** (11.574)	20.25 (11.419)	47.887*** (10.44)	14.341 (12.875)	40.906*** (12.226)	7.835 (12.162)	36.495*** (8.908)	19.59* (9.447)	38.353*** (10.429)	23.337* (9.588)
N	558	444	558	444	558	444	558	444	558	444
R^2	.54	.462	.537	.464	.394	.472	.486	.455	.451	.419

Notes: Robust standard errors are in parentheses

OHS occupational health and safety, *GBT* game-based training intervention

* $p < .05$

** $p < .01$

*** $p < .001$

in all domains of work-related noncognitive abilities, with percentage gains ranging from 36.2% in *OHS* to as high as 96.5% in *efficiency*. Participants gained the most especially in the domains of *efficiency, tidiness,* and *teamwork*. In a report by Oya and Schaefer (2019), they noted that Chinese firms train their Ethiopian workers in noncognitive abilities predominantly in efficiency, work discipline, punctuality, and personal hygiene. What's interesting about the data presented in the table is that despite offering OJT, the training provided by firms is insufficient. The findings are consistent with those of Van Der Klink and Streumer (2002), who reported that OJT programs were only partially successful in realizing training goals. According to Johnson and Leach (2001), the effectiveness of OJT programs can vary widely due to their unstructured approach and the varying qualities of trainers. Due to this characteristic of OJT, we recommend augmenting existing OJT programs with contextualized training, such as our developed GBT program. The developed GBT program reinforces and deepens workers' noncognitive abilities, whereas those who did not receive OJT may have encountered some of the behavior models presented in the game for the first time, limiting the benefit they derive from the GBT program.

7.7.2.5 Firm Size

The disaggregated effect of the GBT program by the size of the firm is summarized in Table 7.10 and Table 7.11. In the analysis, we can see that only medium and large firms benefited from the GBT. Workers from medium-sized firms experienced noncognitive abilities gains from 16.6% (*tidiness*) to 27.5% (*quality control*). On the other hand, workers from large firms experienced larger work-related noncognitive ability gains from 36.6% (*teamwork*) to 67.0% (*OHS*). This may be linked to the provision of regular, formal training programs in medium- and large-sized firms. According to Oya and Schaefer (2019), about 80% of manufacturing firm workers report having received some form of training. This training is often facilitated by the parent firm/company to expedite the adoption of labor practices and standards in their manufacturing facilities in Ethiopia (Oya & Schaefer, 2019). Smaller firms, which primarily serve the domestic market and are not influenced by standards driven by foreign markets, may lack such training systems, as small firms typically offer fewer training sessions. Similar to the provision of OJT, the results suggest that workers from medium- and large-sized firms benefit more from the GBT program, as it provides avenues to reinforce and deepen their noncognitive abilities training through rehearsal, reproduction, and reflection in the developed GBT program.

7.7.2.6 Summary

Disaggregating the GBT effects by gender shows that female workers gained more from the training than their male counterparts. All WRNA significantly increased for female workers, whereas males only improved in terms of *OHS, tidiness, and quality control*. When analyzing the training impact by participants' position in the firm, only non-managers or line workers showed significant gains in their WRNA. Training effects by participants' level of education show that those without upper secondary education benefit the most from the game-based behavioral modeling training. The finding suggests that these subgroups do not possess the relevant work-related noncognitive abilities demanded by Ethiopia's garment and textile industry. Considering that the pool of human resources employed in the garment industry consists mainly of women (82%), non-managers (90%), and those with education below upper secondary (66%), Ethiopia's garment sector lacks a skilled workforce that is in demand by the industry.

Looking at whether or not participants received in-house training, participants who received OJT gained the most from the training, especially in the domains of efficiency and teamwork. The findings highlight that existing training provided by the firms is insufficient.

Analyzing the impact of the training by firm size reveals that medium and large firms stand to gain the most from the training intervention. The findings highlight that medium and large firms have a workforce that lacks the necessary work-related noncognitive abilities.

Table 7.10 Heterogeneous effects of GBT by firm size on OHS, Tidiness, and Efficiency

	(1) OHS Small	(2) OHS Medium	(3) OHS Large	(4) Tidiness Small	(5) Tidiness Medium	(6) Tidiness Large	(7) Efficiency Small	(8) Efficiency Medium	(9) Efficiency Large
Post	7.345 (4.113)	−.26 (2.298)	−4.405 (2.758)	5.932 (3.342)	−.26 (2.045)	−3.214 (2.632)	4.237 (3.623)	.26 (2.783)	2.5 (2.609)
GBT	.189 (1.909)	−.775 (1.213)	−.685 (1.426)	2.153 (1.558)	−.349 (1.152)	.291 (1.393)	.633 (1.742)	.796 (1.33)	1.293 (1.686)
GBT impact	2.411 (5.148)	9.194** (3.333)	26.954*** (4.346)	−2.07 (4.05)	7.468* (2.912)	20.208*** (4.416)	1.352 (4.626)	7.022 (3.619)	13.186** (4.962)
Constant	9.281 (14.771)	45.254*** (9.924)	40.235* (17.023)	1.442 (16.022)	45.014*** (8.717)	52.358** (19.394)	−22.556 (12.715)	40.879*** (10.538)	26.849 (22.328)
N	282	478	242	282	478	242	282	478	242
R^2	.462	.469	.685	.516	.429	.631	.49	.345	.537

Notes: Robust standard errors are in parentheses
OHS occupational health and safety, *GBT* game-based training intervention
* $p < .05$
** $p < .01$
*** $p < .001$

Table 7.11 Heterogeneous effects of GBT by firm size on quality control and teamwork

	(10) Quality Control Small	(11) Quality Control Medium	(12) Quality Control Large	(13) Teamwork Small	(14) Teamwork Medium	(15) Teamwork Large
Post	2.966 (2.719)	−1.172 (2.268)	−2.857 (3.286)	−1.13 (3.647)	−2.995 (2.668)	3.095 (3.274)
GBT	1.094 (1.209)	.82 (1.114)	.935 (1.65)	.319 (1.781)	−.22 (1.254)	.5 (1.79)
GBT impact	−.121 (3.529)	9.355** (2.845)	16.419*** (4.472)	3.975 (4.643)	8.25* (3.355)	11.611* (4.824)
Constant	12.546 (13.193)	33.962*** (7.481)	37.351* (17.497)	28.009** (10.697)	43.606*** (10.2)	31.754 (19.512)
N	282	478	242	282	478	242
R^2	.532	.437	.516	.467	.366	.522

Notes: Robust standard errors are in parentheses
GBT game-based training intervention
* $p < .05$
** $p < .01$
*** $p < .001$

Overall, the study provides empirical evidence that GBT grounded in behavioral modeling theory can effectively enhance work-related noncognitive abilities among garment sector workers. The results underscore the importance of incorporating contextually tailored training interventions and offering opportunities for rehearsal and skill transfer in the workplace.

These findings have significant implications for policy and practice in the garment sector and beyond. By recognizing the value of GBT and its impact on noncognitive ability development, policymakers and training providers can design and implement effective training programs that address the specific needs of workers in various industries. The study underscores the potential of GBT approaches in developing countries, where access to computers and the Internet may be limited.

7.8 Tips for Successful Game-Based Skills Training Programs

This chapter provides a framework for designing, developing, and implementing GBT. The findings, based on a quasi-experimental DID approach, also demonstrate that the GBT training program has a statistically significant effect on improving the work-related noncognitive abilities of Ethiopian garment workers. The computed effect size for our training is also larger than that of previous forms of BMT training. Therefore, this study provides statistical evidence of the efficacy of training in contextualized noncognitive abilities. Work-related skills training conducted in the workplace requires employers to commit time, space, and human resources needed for operations. However, we have demonstrated that by using board games to represent simplified workplace realities and combining them with a BMT approach, our one-day training program can minimize the resources required to effectively train noncognitive abilities and incorporate work-simulated rehearsal opportunities, thereby enhancing motivation, retention, and skills transfer that align with global standards.

In addition to the main results of our study, we identified subgroups that benefit the most from the GBT intervention. The study identified that inexperienced non-manager female workers with less formal education from medium and large firms benefit the most from our GBT program. The results suggest that BMT is well-suited for individuals who have difficulty processing abstract information but possess the capacity to do so when presented in a contextualized manner.

We would like to emphasize that the BMT approach, which utilizes physical games, is well-suited for developing countries like Ethiopia. BMT training has been proven effective by scholars; however, most studies have utilized web- or computer-based games, which can be expensive to implement and potentially exclude participation from underprivileged populations. Access to a computer or the internet remains relatively scarce in many developing countries, such as Ethiopia. Given these conditions, our game–based BMT using physical board games has great potential to support young industrial workers in Ethiopia and many other developing countries.

To maintain the quality of the GBT program, it is also important to invest in the quality of the trainers/facilitators who will deliver the GBT program. In our own experience, we have personally seen how proper training and engagement of facilitators help elevate the quality of training provided. The nexus of the training program lies in the reflection session, which reinforces the transfer of training or change in workplace behavior. Leading participants to reflect on how to apply the modeled behavior and skills in the workplace facilitates a better transfer of GBT, particularly when the facilitators are skilled in the art of questioning and guiding discussions grounded in the participants' work environment context. In sum, the success of the GBT program not only hinges on the mechanics, design, and quality of the training materials (i.e., physical board games in the case of our training program) but also on the pedagogical and interpersonal skills of the facilitators or trainers that deliver it. The training of trainers or facilitators is therefore an equally important aspect to maintain the quality and sustainability of training programs such as these.

This study presents a novel approach to noncognitive abilities training, utilizing a GBT method in conjunction with traditional rote-based lecture training. Our study also bridges the gap between the ongoing discussion on the importance of noncognitive abilities and the lack of effective training methods.

7.9 Pushing the Boundaries of Workplace Learning

In the SKY Project, we want to push the boundaries of workplace learning. Our collective activities of skills assessment and benchmarking, together with the provision of evidence-based reports to governments, industry associations, companies, and workers culminate in the development of our unique GBT program using board games that are grounded in the principles of BMT which we see as a way to address the supply and demand "skills gaps" prevalent in many industries in emerging economies. The developed games are more than just training tools—they serve as platforms for behavior rehearsal, which reinforce work-related noncognitive abilities through model observation, rehearsal, and reflection. Through our GBT initiatives, we hope to create a paradigm shift from the traditional top-down training to a more bottom-up, experiential, and active training approach.

Based on the results of our GBT activities in Ethiopia's garment sector, we suggest that policymakers and industry stakeholders consider the following policy actions to promote the development of work-related noncognitive abilities for production line workers in manufacturing sectors in emerging economies.

7.9.1 Promotion of Participatory Contextualized Training Programs

Prioritize training that is more participatory and takes place in settings that closely resemble the participants' actual workplace to enhance their noncognitive abilities. Even when workers received in-house training, those who underwent training still exhibited significant gains compared to their peers who did not receive any training. This highlights the limitations of traditional training methods, such as lecture-style presentations, which often lack hands-on learning components and are detached from the actual context of the participants' work. The following are suggestions to improve the noncognitive abilities training program in general:

1. Incorporate GBT grounded in behavioral modeling theory into existing noncognitive abilities training initiatives.
2. Encourage collaboration between training providers, industry associations, and garment firms to integrate game-based behavioral modeling training into existing on-the-job training.
3. Allocate resources for developing and distributing board games that simulate workplace environments for noncognitive abilities development in different industries.

7.9.2 Target Training for Women, the less Skilled and Inexperienced Population in SMEs

The study has demonstrated that population subgroups achieved significant gains when utilizing a game-based behavioral training approach. The following are suggestions for different population subgroups to develop a more motivated and skilled workforce:

1. *Women.* Developing targeted GBT programs for women in the garment sector will address the gender disparity in work-related noncognitive abilities.
2. *Non-managers.* Training programs tailored explicitly for non-managerial workers with low educational attainment will provide them with the necessary noncognitive abilities for professional growth and development.
3. *Workers from medium and large firms.* GBT is effective, particularly in medium- to large-sized firms. Focusing on this subgroup will ensure the development of the necessary noncognitive abilities across the industry.

7.9.3 Collaboration and Sharing Are the Keys to Noncognitive Abilities Improvement. Bridge the "Skills Gap!"

The game-based behavioral model training effectively develops the work-related noncognitive abilities of garment sector workers. This training method can also be used in different industrial contexts. We suggest the following measures in order to achieve this:

1. Create a platform for sharing best practices in GBT approaches and their application in different industrial contexts.
2. Establish industry-wide forums or networks to encourage knowledge exchange among firms, trainers, and policymakers.
3. Establish partnerships between training institutions, providers, industry associations, and firms to ensure alignment between training curricula and industry requirements.

By implementing these policy recommendations, stakeholders can enhance the work-related noncognitive abilities of garment sector workers in emerging economies, improve their employability, and contribute to the overall growth and productivity not only of the garment industry but also of other industries.

References

Armstrong, M. B., & Landers, R. N. (2018). Gamification of employee training and development. *International Journal of Training and Development, 22*(2), 162–169. https://doi.org/10.1111/IJTD.12124;WGROUP:STRING:PUBLICATION

Bandura, A. (1977). *Social learning theory*. Prentice Hall. Retrieved April 30, 2022.

Bandura, A. (1982). Self-efficacy mechanism in human agency. *American Psychologist, 37*(2), 122–147. https://doi.org/10.1037/0003-066X.37.2.122

Beranič, T., & Heričko, M. (2022). The impact of serious games in economic and business education: A case of ERP business simulation. *Sustainability (Switzerland), 14*(2), 683. https://doi.org/10.3390/su14020683

Cakir, M. (2008). Constructivist approaches to learning in science and their implications for science pedagogy: A literature review. *International Journal of Environmental & Science Education, 3*(4), 193–206. http://www.ijese.com/

Carlson, K. D., & Schmidt, F. L. (1999). Impact of experimental design on effect size: Findings from the research literature on training. *Journal of Applied Psychology, 84*(6), 851–862. https://doi.org/10.1037/0021-9010.84.6.851

Cohen, P., Cohen, J., Aiken, L. S., & West, S. G. (1999). The problem of units and the circumstance for POMP. *Multivariate Behavioral Research, 34*(3), 315–346. https://doi.org/10.1207/S15327906MBR3403_2

Csikszentmihalyi, M. (2008). *Flow: The psychology of optimal experience*. Harper Perennial Modern Classics.

Cujzek, M., & Vranic, A. (2017). Computerized tabletop games as a form of a video game training for old-old. *Aging, Neuropsychology, and Cognition, 24*(6), 631–648. https://doi.org/10.1080/13825585.2016.1246649

Dagar, V., & Yadav, A. (2016). Constructivism: A paradigm for teaching and learning. *Arts and Social Sciences Journal, 7*(4), 200. https://doi.org/10.4172/2151-6200.1000200

Dawe, S. (2002). *Focussing on generic skills in training packages*. NCVER.

Decker, P. J. (1980). Effects of symbolic coding and rehearsal in behavior-modeling training. *Journal of Applied Psychology, 65*(6), 627–634. https://doi.org/10.1037/0021-9010.65.6.627

Del Moral Pérez, M. E., & Villalustre Martínez, L. (2018). Analysis of serious games against anti-bullying: Playful resources to promote prosocial skills in schoolchildren. *Revista Complutense de Educacion, 29*(4), 1345. https://doi.org/10.5209/RCED.55419

Driskell, J. E., Copper, C., & Moran, A. (1994). Does mental practice enhance performance? *Journal of Applied Psychology, 79*(4), 481–492. https://doi.org/10.1037/0021-9010.79.4.481

Dubinsky, J. M., & Hamid, A. A. (2024). The neuroscience of active learning and direct instruction. *Neuroscience & Biobehavioral Reviews, 163*, 105737. https://doi.org/10.1016/J.NEUBIOREV.2024.105737

Estrellado, E., Charoensilp, P., & Yamada, S. (2023). The effects of game-based soft skills training: A quasi-experiment with Ethiopian garment workers. *International Journal of Educational Development, 101*, 102823. https://doi.org/10.1016/j.ijedudev.2023.102823

Federal Democratic Republic of Ethiopia. (2018). *Digital Ethiopia 2025-a strategy for Ethiopia inclusive prosperity*. Retrieved May 27, 2025, from https://www.lawethiopia.com/images/Policy_documents/Digital-Ethiopia-2025-Strategy-english.pdf

Ferreira, C. P., González-González, C. S., & Adamatti, D. F. (2021). Business simulation games analysis supported by human-computer interfaces: A systematic review. *Sensors, 21*, 4810. https://doi.org/10.3390/s21144810

Google Trends. (n.d.). *Soft skill—Explore—Google trends*. Retrieved June 12, 2025, from https://trends.google.com/trends/explore?date=2012-01-01%202025-06-11&q=soft%20skill&hl=en

Israel, M., Wang, S., & Marino, M. T. (2016). A multilevel analysis of diverse learners playing life science video games: Interactions between game content, learning disability status, reading proficiency, and gender. *Journal of Research in Science Teaching, 53*(2), 324–345. https://doi.org/10.1002/tea.21273

Johnson, S. D., & Leach, J. A. (2001). Using expert employees to train on the job. *Advances in Developing Human Resources, 3*(4), 425. https://doi.org/10.1177/15234220122238481

Kapp, K. M. (2012). *The gamification of learning and instruction: Game-based methods and strategies for training and education*. Pfeiffer.

Kimble, G. A. (1956). Reinforcement theory. *Journal of Counseling Psychology, 3*(2), 112. https://doi.org/10.1037/h0045475

Kowalewski, K. F., Hendrie, J. D., Schmidt, M. W., Proctor, T., Paul, S., Garrow, C. R., et al. (2017). Validation of the mobile serious game application touch surgeryTM for cognitive training and assessment of laparoscopic cholecystectomy. *Surgical Endoscopy, 31*(10), 4058. https://doi.org/10.1007/s00464-017-5452-x

Krath, J., Schürmann, L., & von Korflesch, H. F. O. (2021). Revealing the theoretical basis of gamification: A systematic review and analysis of theory in research on gamification, serious games and game-based learning. *Computers in Human Behavior, 125*, 106963. https://doi.org/10.1016/j.chb.2021.106963

Landers, R. N., & Armstrong, M. B. (2017). Enhancing instructional outcomes with gamification: An empirical test of the technology-enhanced training effectiveness model. *Computers in Human Behavior, 71*, 499–507. https://doi.org/10.1016/J.CHB.2015.07.031

Lave, J., & Wenger, E. (1991). *Situated learning*. Cambridge University Press. https://doi.org/10.1017/CBO9780511815355

Law, G. C., Neihart, M., & Dutt, A. (2018). The use of behavior modeling training in a mobile app parent training program to improve functional communication of young children with autism spectrum disorder. *Autism, 22*(4), 424–439. https://doi.org/10.1177/1362361316683887

Margolis, A. A. (2020). Zone of proximal development, scaffolding and teaching practice. *Cultural-Historical Psychology, 16*(3), 15. https://doi.org/10.17759/chp.2020160303

Mayer, R. E. (2005). Cognitive theory of multimedia learning. In *The Cambridge handbook of multimedia learning* (pp. 31–48). Cambridge University Press. https://doi.org/10.1017/CBO9780511816819.004

Mayer, R. E. (2024). The past, present, and future of the cognitive theory of multimedia learning. *Educational Psychology Review, 36*(1), 8. https://doi.org/10.1007/s10648-023-09842-1

Merkuryev, Y., & Bikovska, J. (2012). Business simulation game development for education and training in supply chain management. In *Proceedings—6th Asia international conference on mathematical modelling and computer simulation, AMS 2012* (pp. 179–184). https://doi.org/10.1109/AMS.2012.12

Oya, C., & Schaefer, F. (2019). *Chinese firms and employment dynamics in Africa: A comparative analysis synthesis report*. London. Retrieved June 14, 2025.

Plass, J. L., Homer, B. D., & Kinzer, C. K. (2015). Foundations of game-based learning. *Educational Psychologist, 50*(4), 258–283. https://doi.org/10.1080/00461520.2015.1122533

Ribeiro, C., Fernandes, J., Lourenço, A., Borbinha, J., & Pereira, J. (2012). Using serious games to teach business process modeling and simulation. *Proceedings*

of the International Conference on Modeling, Simulation and Visualization Methods (MSV).
Roberts, B. W., Wood, D., & Smith, J. L. (2005). Evaluating five factor theory and social investment perspectives on personality trait development. *Journal of Research in Personality, 39*(1), 166–184. https://doi.org/10.1016/J.JRP.2004.08.002
Ryan, R. M., & Deci, E. L. (2000). Self-determination theory and the facilitation of intrinsic motivation, social development, and well-being. *American Psychologist, 55*(1), 68–78. https://doi.org/10.1037/0003-066X.55.1.68
Ryan, R. M., Rigby, C. S., & Przybylski, A. (2006). The motivational pull of video games: A self-determination theory approach. *Motivation and Emotion, 30*(4), 344–360. https://doi.org/10.1007/s11031-006-9051-8
Sabri, H., Cowan, B., Kapralos, B., Porte, M., Backstein, D., & Dubrowskie, A. (2010). Serious games for knee replacement surgery procedure education and training. *Procedia—Social and Behavioral Sciences, 2*, 3483. https://doi.org/10.1016/j.sbspro.2010.03.539
Shuman, L. J., Besterfield-Sacre, M., & McGourty, J. (2005). The ABET "professional skills"—Can they be taught? Can they be assessed? *Journal of Engineering Education, 94*(1), 41–55. https://doi.org/10.1002/j.2168-9830.2005.tb00828.x
Talavera, E. R., & Perez-Gonzalez, J. C. (2007). Training in socio-emotional skills through on-site training. *European Journal of Vocational Training, 40*(1), 83–102. Retrieved December 11, 2025.
Taylor, P. J., Russ-Eft, D. F., & Chan, D. W. L. (2005). A meta-analytic review of behavior modeling training. *Journal of Applied Psychology, 90*(4), 692–709. https://doi.org/10.1037/0021-9010.90.4.692
UNESCO-UNEVOC. (2024, August). *TVET country profiles: Ethiopia.* Retrieved June 14, 2025, from https://unevoc.unesco.org/home/Dynamic+TVET+Country+Profiles/country=ETH
Van Der Klink, M. R., & Streumer, J. N. (2002). Effectiveness of on-the-job training. *Journal of European Industrial Training, 26*(2/3/4), 196. https://doi.org/10.1108/03090590210422076
Yamada, S. (2023). Constructivist analysis of cross-sectional data on varieties of skills: Contextualities and generalities of skills packages and rewards to them in Ghana and Ethiopia. *International Journal of Educational Development, 102*, 102851. https://doi.org/10.1016/j.ijedudev.2023.102851
Yee, A. Z. H., & Sng, J. R. H. (2022). Animal crossing and COVID-19: A qualitative study examining how video games satisfy basic psychological needs during the pandemic. *Frontiers in Psychology, 13*, 800683. https://doi.org/10.3389/FPSYG.2022.800683

8 Conclusion: Competencies at the Intersection of Subjectivity, Social Expectations, Economy, and Education

Shoko Yamada

Abstract

This chapter synthesizes the volume's examination of workforce competency development through a Realist-Constructivist lens, arguing that abilities emerge from the dynamic interplay of subjective perceptions, socio-cultural expectations, econo-productive demands, and structural-regulatory systems. Using comparative evidence from four countries in the Global South, the chapter demonstrates how fragmented schooling, informal production environments, gendered norms, and global value-chain pressures create diverse micro-ecologies of learning that challenge universal notions of "skills gaps." It further demonstrates how an abductive analytical approach of Realist-Constructivism bridges induction and deduction, enabling mechanism-based generalization without erasing contextual specificity. The chapter also reflects on the transition made by the authors from diagnosing competency patterns to cultivating them, highlighting the demonstrated effectiveness of a game-based intervention for strengthening noncognitive skills. Finally, it discusses the implications for government-led system reform in workforce competency development, arguing that policy must align with national ecologies and learner psychology rather than imposing externally derived models.

Keywords

Skills in the global south · Vocational school fallacy · Mechanisms of "skills gaps" · Psychology of "skills gaps" · Fallacy of competency-based training · Varieties of labor market

8.1 Ontological Realities of Workforce Competency Development

In less than a decade of our Skills and Knowledge for Youths (SKY) project, the macroecology of learning and knowledge for work has undergone fundamental reorientations. In the first part of Chap. 1, I discussed the evolution of technology, the accelerated pace of global economic exchanges, the altered mode of daily operation following the coronavirus pandemic, and the emergence of generative artificial intelligence (AI) as the causes of these changes. Most readers must have felt these changes directly and, accordingly, have adjusted their work methods,

S. Yamada (✉)
Graduate School of International Development, Nagoya University, Nagoya, Japan

Graduate School of Asian and African Area Studies, Kyoto University, Kyoto, Japan
e-mail: syamada@nagoya-u.jp

S. Yamada (ed.), *Mitigating the "Skills Gaps"*, Sustainable Development Goals Series,
https://doi.org/10.1007/978-981-95-7968-6_8

approaches to demonstrating performance to supervisors, and the content of knowledge and skills to learn in order to advance their abilities, either knowingly or unknowingly. Phenomena, such as technological advancements or pandemics, are ontological facts that all workers and job seekers in the global labor market encounter. As I wrote at the beginning, the ontological transition in macroecology has led to a fragmentation of demands for workforce abilities, which are not only diverse but also fluid, constantly transforming like a mirage. A type of ability that may have appeared essential for workers in an industry last year may become outdated or off-the-point this year. Buzzwords like twenty-first-century skills, core competencies, or employable skills all highlight the importance of adaptive capacities, which are evaluated by the results of "problem-solving" rather than specific techniques or knowledge.

Over the past few decades, we have been repeatedly told by influential scholars that the variations in workplace requirements have been reduced by the standardization of the production process in the global market. Many readers would recall that Hardt and Negri (2000) claim globalization creates a universal logic of labor, where workers everywhere are disciplined through similar criteria. The workforce becomes standardized because the *Empire*—a macroecology based on a common value framework—requires interchangeable, mobile, and governable labor (see also (Castells, 1996; Ritzer, 1993). The *World Culturalists* argued that economic globalization led to the diffusion of Western-originated norms, such as individual rights, which were accompanied by models of modern nation-states, rationalized organizations, and mass education, resulting in the isomorphism of institutions and practices worldwide (Boli & Thomas, 1999). Since the end of the Cold War, there has been a long period of scholarly imagination that assumed there would be no world culture to rival Western modernity, and the economic system of capitalism, under which variations tended to be reduced to mere local biases.

Today, we are witnessing two opposite forces shaping our ontological realities surrounding the workforce. On the one hand, the global market mechanism has further deepened the connectedness and integrated business entities and individuals into it. Particularly, the export-oriented producers and their employees are directly facing the requirements to fulfill the standards and specifications as part of global value chains. On the other hand, due to the emerging phenomena mentioned earlier, it is becoming increasingly difficult to discuss work-related abilities in a generic manner.

In fact, it is natural that our life experiences are influenced by forces from multiple directions, sometimes conflicting with one another. To grasp these influential factors to determine the experience of the individual workforce and try to develop their capacities to get better outcomes in the labor market, as a part of the Realist-Constructivist framework, I conceptualized three types of generative mechanisms—econo-productive, socio-cultural, and structural-regulatory ones, which affect the micro-ecologies of competency development. I also conceptualized that these mechanisms affect the micro-ecologies from different levels. Sometimes, the influence of the global mechanism directly affects the micro-ecologies, while at other times, national or industrial-level mechanisms determine the nature of micro-ecologies more clearly.

In the empirical analysis chapters from Chap. 4 to Chap. 6, we found that the global econo-productive mechanism affects the type of abilities required in the export-oriented firms, namely, technical skills to perform specified tasks accurately and noncognitive skills to be consistent and disciplined. At the same time, among the export-oriented firms, we also noticed that the influence of the socio-cultural mechanism varies according to the investors' countries of origin, with an outstanding characteristic of East Asian investors. Meanwhile, smaller domestic firms tend to appreciate workers who possess the technical capabilities to perform multiple tasks independently. Furthermore, we observed that the attitudes and personalities preferred in the workplace vary across countries, suggesting the role that socio-cultural mechanisms play in shaping employers' expectations of workers. For example, Pakistan's workplaces and their employees' abilities demonstrated peculiar patterns compared to the other three countries, which can largely be attributed to its cultural norms and female stereotypes, which condition not only women's self-evaluation and behavior but also employers' expectations of them.

Even with this highly simplified summary of the empirical findings, I believe we have demonstrated that generative mechanisms simultaneously affect the firm-level ecologies from different levels. For example, an export-oriented firm in a country would be under the influence of the global econo-productive mechanism, but whose organizational culture may be the extension of the socio-cultural mechanism of the investor's original society. Further, the characteristics of a firm-level ecology that determines the experience of individual workers cannot help but be conditioned by the national labor and product markets (econo-productive mechanism), people's beliefs and traditions (socio-cultural mechanism), and systems and regulations for business, employment, and skills development (structural-regulatory mechanism).

8.1.1 Why Focus on the Global South?

This volume focuses on the situations of less-experienced young workers in the garment production industry in four countries in the Global South: Ethiopia, Ghana, South Africa, and Pakistan. As a constructivist who pays close attention to the subjectivity and local meanings of the phenomenon, it has not always been my priority to claim that the cases I analyze are representative of the workforce of the Global South or the particular industry. However, in this volume, the reason why we propose the Realist-Constructivism rather than presenting our findings as another case study of mere constructivism was that we tried to overcome the limitations of relativism, in which, however much respective analyses provide rich contextual understanding, there is no common thread cross-cutting the cases to make them comparable. To make the findings reasonably generalizable, we developed the module to enable us to bridge the induction and deduction.

The cross-sectional analysis was mainly presented in Chap. 4, with a more thematically focused one in Chap. 6. Comparative evidence from garment industry workers in four countries suggests some commonalities that may be attributed to their being in the Global South, or, to put it in more accurate terms, in catch-up economies.

Across all study sites, formal schooling provides basic literacy and numeracy, but its contribution to labor market success is limited because many young workers enter the industry after experiencing under-resourced educational systems, inconsistent instructional quality, and limited exposure to applied or technical subjects. As a result, cognitive test scores vary widely; however, these variations do not reliably translate into differences in wages or advancement. Instead, workers with even modest schooling can catch up rapidly through work-based learning, which plays a disproportionately important role in labor markets of the Global South, where formal pathways into skilled work are scarce.

A central Global South characteristic is the dominance of informal or semi-structured production environments, especially where small and medium enterprises (SMEs) constitute the bulk of the industry. In these firms, standardized training systems are rare, and learning often occurs through observation, repetition, and peer support rather than planned instruction. Workers acquire competencies through coping with unpredictable production demands, multitasking across operations, and navigating resource constraints such as machine shortages or erratic electricity supply. These conditions cultivate practical adaptability and tacit knowledge—competencies that are essential for productivity in these contexts but poorly captured by formal assessments.

At the same time, as I mentioned earlier, in export-oriented clusters integrated into global value chains, foreign-invested firms introduce highly routinized, efficiency-driven work processes. These firms expect punctuality, discipline, and rapid learning, and they often emphasize behavioral traits, such as compliance and attentiveness, as much as technical skills. Workers who succeed in these environments typically demonstrate not only production-oriented competencies but also the ability to internalize global production norms despite having limited exposure to such norms in school or community settings. This tension between semi-structured domestic production and formalized global production systems is a distinctive feature of the Global South competency landscape.

Competency development is also shaped by socio-cultural norms that influence labor force participation and mobility. In many settings, young women with limited years of schooling often enter garment work as one of the few avenues for wage employment. Their performance often surpasses what their educational background would predict, because employers value reliability, patience, and fine manual work—attributes shaped partly by gendered expectations. However, these same expectations may restrict their access to supervisory tracks, limiting opportunities to develop more diverse competencies. Such gendered pathways reflect broader cultural norms that shape how skills are recognized and rewarded.

Survey evidence further shows that the alignment between workers' self-assessments and employers' expectations is influenced by local cultures of authority and communication. In contexts where young workers are discouraged from asserting their abilities, self-evaluations tend to be conservative, and modesty is interpreted positively by supervisors. Conversely, contexts where workers express confidence without corresponding observable performance may trigger supervisory skepticism, reinforcing wage penalties. These patterns underscore that competency development in the Global South is not just about what workers can do but about how they are expected to present themselves within culturally embedded hierarchies.

Finally, technical and vocational education and training (TVET) systems across these countries exhibit a characteristic disconnect from industry realities. What I am pointing out is not the cliché of the failure of partnership between the industry and educational institutions. Rather, the missing link emerges from the fact that regulations and systems for workforce preparation, typically those of TVET, are based on the premise that TVET graduates will be employed in the industry for which they are trained. Our findings suggest that students often enter TVET programs to extend their stay within the education system or to delay job search, rather than as preparation for industrial work. Particularly for the entry-level positions, employers tend not to expect the candidates to have previous industry-specific training. Thus, neither the supply nor the demand side has a strong motivation to align each other's expectations on workforce competencies. This is, of course, the situation of the garment sector, whose entry barrier is relatively lower for less skilled workers. The picture would be different for the types of work that require some advanced training, such as mechanics or electrical work. Still, it would be worth highlighting, as a Global South characteristic, the discrepancy between the national structural-regulatory mechanism of workforce competency development and the econo-productive mechanism, which is directly linked with the product market needs, either global or domestic.

One cause of such a disparity is that the prescription for government policies and programs often comes from elsewhere, with technical and financial support from the aid-providing agencies, rather than from within the country. Thus, we may even consider that the popular measures for promoting industrial human resources development, introduced in Chap. 2, contribute to inscribing in the mind of policymakers and other stakeholders the alien premise and expectations into the TVET system and creating the perceived "skills gaps". This is particularly true, as the aid providers, known for their promotion of TVET, are from countries where TVET has a history of successful partnership with the economic sector and has evolved in tandem with national growth, such as Germany, Switzerland, Japan, and South Korea.

In sum, the patterns that emerge from the four studied countries point to a constellation of conditions that characterize competency development in many parts of the Global South: uneven schooling systems, the predominance of informalized or semi-structured production environments, gendered socio-cultural norms, hierarchical workplace cultures, and fragmented institutional linkages between education and industry. These characteristics produce learning pathways that differ substantially from the assumptions embedded in policy models originating in OECD[1] contexts.

8.1.2 Lessons for the North?—Toward an Understanding of Interactive Processes

Throughout my academic career, I have often received comments from my Northern audience, whose primary geographic interest is not in the South: "Your research findings are interesting, but why did you do this about the societies that are too different from ours to draw any lessons?" Studies based on cases in the Global South are often treated as niche information on special regions for connoisseurs, and are rarely considered a source of inspiration or a frame of reference for reorienting the mindset. The Global South's image of low development and distinctive societal characteristics often prompts Northern readers to avert their eyes from extracting lessons or considering comparability, as if they can only learn from societies that are, in their imagination, either equally or more modernized than their own societies or similar in culture. In fact, such a mindset contributes to narrowing our range of options within the familiar institutionalist framework, which allows us only to make minor adjustments to the existing structural-regulatory mechanisms without fundamental reorientations.

I admit that the ontological phenomena of "skills gaps" in the Global North tend to differ largely due to the workforces' generally longer years of schooling and firms' greater integration into the structured global market framework. There would be more issues with the underutilization of people who are overly schooled than with upskilling the less-schooled workforce on the job. Also, it is reported that AI affects the landscape of employment and competency development unevenly between the Global North and South. In general, AI is anticipated to substitute white-collar routine work, pushing workers without independent analytical and problem-solving capacities to the verge of losing jobs. In the Global North, where we tend to see more over-educated white-collar job seekers, the call for "21st century skills" is made in this context of competition against AI. Meanwhile, in the Global South, rather than replacing workers, AI is more likely to coexist with or augment labor-intensive production, especially in sectors such as garments, agriculture, and services, where competitive advantage still relies on low labor costs and manual dexterity. The problem-solving capacities are as much valued in the Global South as we demonstrated in this volume, but their connotations are, in fact, not the same as in the North.

In this volume, we have argued that the ontological phenomena we observe are in constant flux, depending on the complex interactions among generative mechanisms and the epistemology of the stakeholders, such as employers, educators, policymakers, and job seekers, who try to make sense of the changes and successfully navigate through the dynamic environment. Thus, it is not only in the North and the South, but even within the same society the pace of change is increasing. In fact, the practice of drawing lines between categories of societies, such as the North vs. South, is, of itself, cognitive but not substantively fixed. The phenomena are the tips of icebergs that float on the surface. But what is more important for us to grasp the true nature of the "skills gaps" is to untangle the processes in which econo-productive, socio-cultural, and structural-regulatory mechanisms interact with the psychology of the stakeholders and their interpretations of the demands in the particular micro-ecology of the workforce competency development.

Based on this consideration, I hope that readers from both the North and the South will not be swayed solely by the specific phenomena described here. Certainly, they are important for

[1] Organisation for Economic Cooperation and Development.

practitioners to understand the challenges they face more clearly and to plan more effective solutions. We have made our best effort to ensure the accuracy of the evidence-based phenomenal descriptions, recognizing that it is a part of the responsibility of this volume to attend to such demands. At the same time, this volume is not intended to be a ready-made collection of reform recipes to be applied; rather, it proposes a perspective that continues to grasp the problem even as circumstances change.

8.2 Realist-Constructivism: Can We Overcome the Induction-Deduction Divide?

One of the central methodological aspirations of this volume was to bridge the long-standing divide between inductive and deductive approaches in social science research, using the case of workforce competency development. Constructivist scholarship has provided rich descriptions of how competencies are shaped by local meanings and social interactions; however, it has often struggled to identify common mechanisms that transcend specific cases. Conversely, deductive approaches grounded in standardized models of human capital or globalized competency frameworks have generated tidy conceptual schemas but frequently fail to capture the lived realities of workers whose experiences diverge from the assumptions embedded in those models. Our goal was neither to abandon contextual sensitivity nor to rely on abstract universals, but to construct an analytical approach that could move productively between the two.

The assessment module we developed for this purpose has the following characteristics. First, it attempts to capture the ontology and epistemology of workforce competencies by conducting performance assessments of workers (ontology), which will then be matched by questionnaires from different groups of stakeholders to untangle their expectations of the workers' abilities (epistemology), including self-evaluation by the workers themselves. Second, it is designed to disaggregate both actual performance and expectations according to the types of abilities—cognitive, noncognitive, and technical—so that we can grasp the unique packages of abilities demonstrated to be effective in particular contexts, without imposing a rigid yardstick of measurement on diverse micro-ecologies. Third, while avoiding rigidity, the module was standardized so that the data collected from different populations in four countries remain comparable on a common platform.

The data produced in this way enabled us to employ abductive reasoning in the analysis process, moving back and forth between inductive, constructivist analysis of people's psychology and contextually embedded behavior in competency development, and deductive observations of the impact of generative mechanisms at the macro, national, and industrial levels. This way, Realist-Constructivism provided the theoretical and methodological foundation for achieving a balance between ontology and epistemology, as well as between inductive and deductive reasoning.

The empirical chapters demonstrated how this iterative dialogue played out in practice. In Chap. 4, the cross-sectional comparative analysis revealed recurring patterns across Ethiopia, Ghana, South Africa, and Pakistan, which I have explained as features that can be generalized to the Global South safely. Chap. 5 closely untangled the interactions among actors and generative mechanisms to determine the nature of "skills gaps" in one national ecology: Ethiopia. In contrast to the macro cross-sectional analysis in Chap. 4 and meso-level analysis in Chap. 5, Chap. 6 provided a theme-based comparison between two national ecologies: Ghana and Pakistan. Using datasets from two countries, which allowed us to contrast workers in the informal sector with those in highly routinized formal firms, we illustrated the ways these distinct econo-productive environments characterize the capacity development of workers in both categories across two national settings. At the same time, we also recognized that the distinct socio-cultural mechanisms of the two countries affected the psychology of workers in developing their abilities, particularly noncognitive ones, and employers' expectations of them.

Altogether, we consider that we have successfully demonstrated the power of Realist-Constructivism, both theoretically and methodologically. Inductive patterns revealed through statistical analysis, surveys, and qualitative insights helped refine our deductive understanding of how generative mechanisms shape micro-ecologies. Conversely, deductively grasped mechanisms allowed us to interpret empirical variation as meaningful and comparable, rather than as isolated curiosities. The analytical modules we developed served precisely as bridges, encouraging us to look for cross-case regularities while still attending closely to the contextual roots of those regularities.

What this volume demonstrates is that generalization does not require uniformity. Instead, it requires identifying the latent causal processes that produce observable phenomena in different forms across different settings. Realist-Constructivism enabled us to generate such mechanism-based generalizations, grounded in data but not confined by it. In doing so, we were able to move beyond the limitations of both purely inductive case study work and purely deductive universal models.

8.3 From Assessment to Cultivation of Noncognitive Abilities: Bridging Evidence and Practice

Although in terms of page count, it is a small part of this volume, I shouldn't forget to mention an important transition we made during the team's decade-long practice. That is: we did not stop at identifying the mechanisms behind "skills gaps." Across all four countries, our analyses repeatedly showed that noncognitive abilities—such as reliability, attentiveness, emotional stability, and initiative—are decisive for workers' labor market outcomes, yet they are rarely cultivated through formal training programs, including schools. The recurrence of these findings, along with requests from policymakers and practitioners in the surveyed countries to conduct a program to mitigate the identified "skills gaps," led us to consider, in an inquiry into real-world issues, that analysis alone may not be sufficient. If competency development results from interactions of generative mechanisms and stakeholder interpretations, then interventions based on the findings that would facilitate the match between expectations on the supply and demand sides should also be possible.

The game-based training introduced in Chap. 7 represents the practical extension of this consideration. The positive impacts of the training were clear. Workers showed improvement in workplace-relevant behaviors, such as safety, tidiness, efficiency, and attention to quality, as well as in personality traits like openness and emotional stability. They also gained confidence and clearer self-awareness—factors shown earlier in the volume to shape labor market outcomes. Importantly, these improvements emerged through low-cost, culturally adaptable methods suited to the training realities of Global South workplaces.

By demonstrating that noncognitive skills can be strengthened through context-sensitive interventions, this volume shows that Realist-Constructivism is not only a framework for explaining how competencies develop but also a guide for cultivating them. This transition from diagnosis to practice underscores the broader contribution of the volume: that a mechanism-based understanding of workforce development can inform actionable strategies even in resource-constrained environments.

8.4 Lessons for Governmental Reform

Although deriving policy prescriptions is not the principal purpose of this volume, I notice that a certain number of readers would expect it. Therefore, in the final part of this chapter, I would like to synthesize some cross-cutting findings regarding the structural-regulatory mechanisms. As detailed in Chap. 2 and empirical chapters, Realist-Constructivism conceptualizes this category of generative mechanism as the national government-led arrangements of workforce competency development, which are commonly called, according to the terminology of the policy discourse, the "Skills Development System" or the "Competency-based Training System". For its national system to function effectively, the government typically adopts the Skills Development Act as the legal foundation, based on which the standard of evaluation for individual workforces' abilities (National Competency Framework), accreditation of educational institutions, and curriculum of TVET institutions are developed. Funds to financially support the system are earmarked from the revenue from corporate taxes. And typically, a coordinating body, independent of any specific ministries or business entities, is established. Such is the package of a structural-regulatory framework that we often find in countries of the Global South.

Throughout this volume, one of the recurring findings regarding the structural-regulatory mechanism was that TVET graduates often do not aspire to work in the sectors for which they are trained. Many enter TVET not because they seek industrial careers, but because it enables them to remain within the education system when the academic pathways are not available. In contrast to counterparts who are employed after completing basic education without attending TVET programs, they tend to come from better-off households whose parents are willing to support their children's education. This cross-nationally observed phenomenon appears to weaken the assumed pipeline from TVET to employment in the corresponding industry, deviating from its original design.

This leads to a broader problem: many skills-development reforms are shaped by externally promoted models of training systems—such as competency-based training or market-driven provision—whose underlying assumptions do not align with national socio-cultural, econo-productive, or micro-ecological realities. As I mentioned above, international aid-providing agencies known for promoting CBT[2]-type skills development reform refer to the experiences of Northern countries, whose structural and regulatory frameworks for skills development evolved alongside their industrial development, and have had a positive experience with productive partnerships between industry and education institutions. The chances that the premises developed based on the econo-productive and socio-cultural conditions of some historical periods of these "successful" countries also work well in the destinations to which they are transplanted may not be high. This fact highlights the importance of having a structural-regulatory framework that is derived from within the society in which it operates. At the same time, it is a common situation often found in countries in the Global South. While policymakers themselves buy into the model and its underlying assumptions, they rarely question its relevance.

Another dimension of the misfit of the structural-regulatory framework is with econo-productive mechanisms. Although the national skills development strategy is typically developed based on an analysis of the macroeconomic position of the national economy and the current capacities of human resources at the national aggregate level, it is often not grounded in close observations of the workplaces where citizens are employed. However, as this volume has demonstrated, the nature of skills demands is highly dependent on the work habits and expectations in a specific workplace. Even if policymakers may not need to delve as deeply into the individual firms, the analyses in this volume demonstrate contrasting expectations for the workforce in export-oriented invested firms, domestic SMEs, and the informal sector. Such differences among the categories of employers do not remain in their expectations of individual workers. They also result in differential attitudes to the TVET and the national skills development system.

Global firms integrated into value chains seldom demand TVET graduates because they prefer to shape workers' abilities to function well in their own tightly controlled production systems. SMEs, meanwhile, welcome TVET graduates but find that current training frameworks are not designed to meet their demands. As a result,

[2]Competency-based training.

TVET currently tends to be misaligned with both domestic and export-oriented formal-sector labor markets.

Yet this does not render TVET irrelevant altogether. Our analyses suggest that, if carefully reformed to meet the demands, TVET could play a crucial role in supporting domestic SMEs, which consistently lack the capacity to train workers in-house and require adaptable, multi-skilled employees. While TVET cannot fully replicate workplace practice, its broad and general preparation can complement the needs of small firms more than those of export-oriented global manufacturers. However, such potential can only be realized if policy recognizes the actual labor-market role of TVET, rather than the idealized one often assumed in reform blueprints.

The Ethiopian experience with *kaizen* inside TVET institutions, as discussed in Chap. 5, offers a more constructive insight. It shows that noncognitive skills—such as tidiness, discipline, safety awareness, and punctuality—are effectively developed not through curricula alone, but through sustained exposure to a coherent value framework. In this sense, TVET can serve as a site for cultivating socio-emotional readiness for work, precisely because these abilities are shaped through repeated interactions, norms, and institutional culture. This is an important lesson: noncognitive competencies require environments that socialize learners into the expectations of the workplace—something TVET can provide when its internal culture resonates with national or sectoral values.

Finally, any systemic reform must consider the psychology of learners and workers, as well as the structure of aspirations. As long as the overall education system is primarily designed for those who aim to continue their education, it is unrealistic to expect only those in TVET segments to smoothly transition into industrial employment. In this sense, drawing a clear line between school and work may not be an effective approach to continuously equip workforces with the necessary abilities throughout their career. More flexible methods, including non-school-based training, may be needed—that acknowledge the reality that not all learners thrive within formal educational trajectories, yet still possess the potential to develop valuable practical and adaptive capacities to solve problems in their respective real workplaces.

In sum, the policy implication of this volume is not to recommend the adoption or rejection of particular global models, but to emphasize that system reform must be rooted in a diagnosis of the actual national ecology of competency development. Effective reforms must align with the generative mechanisms that shape skills formation—socio-cultural norms, firm-level practices, learners' aspirations, and the diverse econo-productive pressures operating across industries. Imposing pre-set assumptions onto these realities is unlikely to close skills gaps. Working with the mechanisms already shaping micro-ecologies offers a more promising path.

References

Boli, J., & Thomas, G. M. (Eds.). (1999). *Constructing world culture*. Stanford University Press. https://doi.org/10.1515/9781503617681

Castells, M. (1996). *The rise of the network society*. Blackwell Publishers Ltd.

Hardt, M., & Negri, A. (2000). *Empire*. Harvard University Press.

Ritzer, G. (1993). *The McDonaldization of society: An investigation into the changing character of contemporary social life*. Pine Forge Press.

www.ingramcontent.com/pod-product-compliance
Lightning Source LLC
Chambersburg PA
CBHW051246140426
43115CB00005B/123
* 9 7 8 9 8 1 9 5 7 9 6 7 9 *